T0192239

Communications
in Computer and Information Science 1996

Rationale

The CCIS series is devoted to the publication of proceedings of computer science conferences. Its aim is to efficiently disseminate original research results in informatics in printed and electronic form. While the focus is on publication of peer-reviewed full papers presenting mature work, inclusion of reviewed short papers reporting on work in progress is welcome, too. Besides globally relevant meetings with internationally representative program committees guaranteeing a strict peer-reviewing and paper selection process, conferences run by societies or of high regional or national relevance are also considered for publication.

Topics

The topical scope of CCIS spans the entire spectrum of informatics ranging from foundational topics in the theory of computing to information and communications science and technology and a broad variety of interdisciplinary application fields.

Information for Volume Editors and Authors

Publication in CCIS is free of charge. No royalties are paid, however, we offer registered conference participants temporary free access to the online version of the conference proceedings on SpringerLink (http://link.springer.com) by means of an http referrer from the conference website and/or a number of complimentary printed copies, as specified in the official acceptance email of the event.

CCIS proceedings can be published in time for distribution at conferences or as post-proceedings, and delivered in the form of printed books and/or electronically as USBs and/or e-content licenses for accessing proceedings at SpringerLink. Furthermore, CCIS proceedings are included in the CCIS electronic book series hosted in the SpringerLink digital library at http://link.springer.com/bookseries/7899. Conferences publishing in CCIS are allowed to use Online Conference Service (OCS) for managing the whole proceedings lifecycle (from submission and reviewing to preparing for publication) free of charge.

Publication process

The language of publication is exclusively English. Authors publishing in CCIS have to sign the Springer CCIS copyright transfer form, however, they are free to use their material published in CCIS for substantially changed, more elaborate subsequent publications elsewhere. For the preparation of the camera-ready papers/files, authors have to strictly adhere to the Springer CCIS Authors' Instructions and are strongly encouraged to use the CCIS LaTeX style files or templates.

Abstracting/Indexing

CCIS is abstracted/indexed in DBLP, Google Scholar, EI-Compendex, Mathematical Reviews, SCImago, Scopus. CCIS volumes are also submitted for the inclusion in ISI Proceedings.

How to start

To start the evaluation of your proposal for inclusion in the CCIS series, please send an e-mail to ccis@springer.com.

Hugo Plácido da Silva · Pietro Cipresso
Editors

Computer-Human Interaction Research and Applications

7th International Conference, CHIRA 2023
Rome, Italy, November 16–17, 2023
Proceedings, Part I

 Springer

Editors
Hugo Plácido da Silva
IT - Institute of Telecommunications
Lisbon, Portugal

Instituto Superior Técnico
Lisbon, Portugal

Pietro Cipresso
University of Turin
Turin, Italy

ISSN 1865-0929   ISSN 1865-0937 (electronic)
Communications in Computer and Information Science
ISBN 978-3-031-49424-6   ISBN 978-3-031-49425-3 (eBook)
https://doi.org/10.1007/978-3-031-49425-3

This Springer imprint is published by the registered company Springer Nature Switzerland AG
The registered company address is: Gewerbestrasse 11, 6330 Cham, Switzerland

Paper in this product is recyclable.

Preface

This volume contains the proceedings of the 7th International Conference on Computer-Human Interaction Research and Applications (CHIRA 2023), which was held in Rome, Italy as a hybrid event, from 16 to 17 November.

CHIRA is sponsored by the Institute for Systems and Technologies of Information, Control and Communication (INSTICC), and is held in cooperation with the European Society for Socially Embedded Technologies (EUSSET).

The purpose of CHIRA is to bring together professionals, academics and students who are interested in the advancement of research and practical applications of human-technology & human-computer interaction. Different aspects of Computer-Human Interaction were covered in four parallel tracks: 1) Human Factors for Interactive Systems, Research, and Applications; 2) Interactive Devices; 3) Interaction Design; and 4) Adaptive and Intelligent Systems. Human-Computer Interaction is getting renewed interest as human-AI interaction due to the increasing success of artificial intelligence and its applications.

In addition to paper presentations, CHIRA's program included three invited talks delivered by internationally distinguished speakers: Antonio Camurri (Università degli Studi di Genova, Italy), "Aesthetically Resonant Multimodal Interactive Systems", Andrea Gaggioli (Università Cattolica del Sacro Cuore, Italy), "Designing Transformative Experiences: Exploring the Potential of Virtual Technologies for Personal Change", and Wendy E. Mackay (Inria, Paris-Saclay, and Université Paris-Saclay, France), "Creating Human-Computer Partnerships".

CHIRA received 69 paper submissions from 30 countries, of which 20% were accepted as full papers. The high quality of the papers received imposed difficult choices during the review process. To evaluate each submission, a double-blind paper review was performed by the Program Committee, whose members were highly qualified independent researchers in the CHIRA topic areas.

In addition, the Special Session on "Enhancing the Esports Experience (E3)", chaired by Sven Charleer and Laura Herrewijn, was held together with CHIRA 2023.

All accepted complete papers are published by Springer in these conference proceedings, under an ISBN reference. The proceedings are abstracted/indexed in DBLP, Google Scholar, EI-Compendex, INSPEC, Japanese Science and Technology Agency (JST), Norwegian Register for Scientific Journals and Series, Mathematical Reviews, SCImago, Scopus and zbMATH. CCIS volumes are also submitted for inclusion in ISI Proceedings.

We express our thanks to all participants. First to all the authors, whose quality work is the essence of this conference; secondly to all members of the Program Committee and auxiliary reviewers, who helped us with their expertise and valuable time. We also deeply thank the invited speakers for excellent contributions in sharing their knowledge and vision.

Finally, we acknowledge the professional support of the CHIRA 2023 team for all organizational processes, especially given the needs of a hybrid event, in order to make it possible for the CHIRA 2023 authors to present their work and share ideas with colleagues in spite of the logistic difficulties.

We hope you all had an inspiring conference. We hope to meet you again next year for the 8th edition of CHIRA, details of which will soon be available at http://www.chira.scitevents.org/.

November 2023

Hugo Plácido da Silva
Pietro Cipresso

Organization

Conference Chair

Pietro Cipresso   University of Turin, Italy

Program Chair

Hugo Plácido da Silva   IT - Instituto de Telecomunicações, Portugal

Program Committee

Iyad Abu Doush	American University of Kuwait, Kuwait
Christopher Anand	McMaster University, Canada
Martin Baumann	Ulm University, Germany
Samit Bhattacharya	Indian Institute of Technology Guwahati, India
Paolo Bottoni	Sapienza University of Rome, Italy
Chris Bowers	University of Worcester, UK
John Brooke	Independent Researcher, UK
Kursat Cagiltay	Sabanci University, Turkey
Valentín Cardeñoso Payo	Valentín Cardeñoso Payo, Spain
Eric Castelli	LIG Grenoble, France
Sven Charleer	AP University of Applied Sciences and Arts Antwerp, Belgium
Christine Chauvin	Université de Bretagne Sud, France
Isaac Cho	Utah State University, USA
Yang-Wai Chow	University of Wollongong, Australia
Cesar Collazos	Universidad del Cauca, Colombia
Arzu Coltekin	University of Applied Sciences and Arts Northwestern Switzerland, Switzerland
Lizette de Wet	University of the Free State, South Africa
Andrew Duchowski	Clemson University, USA
John Eklund	UX Research, Australia
Vania Estrela	Universidade Federal Fluminense, Brazil
Jesus Favela	Cicese, Mexico
Peter Forbrig	University of Rostock, Germany

Kaori Fujinami	Tokyo University of Agriculture and Technology, Japan
Gheorghita Ghinea	Brunel University London, UK
Thorsten Händler	Ferdinand Porsche Mobile University of Applied Sciences (FERNFH), Austria
Hiroshi Hashimoto	Advanced Institute of Industrial Technology, Japan
Christopher Healey	NCSU, USA
Martin Hitz	Alpen-Adria-Universität Klagenfurt, Austria
Mengjie Huang	Xi'an Jiaotong-Liverpool University, China
Junko Ichino	Tokyo City University, Japan
M.-Carmen Juan	Instituto Ai2, Universitat Politècnica de València, Spain
Adi Katz	Shamoon College of Engineering, Israel
Gerard Kim	Korea University, South Korea
Hai-Ning Liang	Xi'an Jiaotong-Liverpool University, China
Wen-Chieh Lin	National Chiao Tung University, Taiwan, Republic of China
Federico Manuri	Politecnico di Torino, Italy
Milosz Marek	Lublin University of Technology, Poland
Ecivaldo Matos	Universidade Federal da Bahia, Brazil
Daniel Mestre	Aix-Marseille University/CNRS, France
Giulio Mori	Institute of Information Science and Technologies, Italy
Max Mulder	TU Delft, The Netherlands
Max North	Kennesaw State University, USA
Stavroula Ntoa	Foundation for Research and Technology Hellas, Greece
Ian Oakley	Ulsan National Institute of Science and Technology, South Korea
Yoosoo Oh	Daegu University, South Korea
Malgorzata Plachawska-Wójcik	Lublin University of Technology, Poland
Charles Pontonnier	Normal Superior School of Rennes, France
Francisco Rebelo	ITI/LARSys and University of Lisbon, Portugal
Laura Ripamonti	University of Milan, Italy
Sandra Sanchez-Gordon	Escuela Politécnica Nacional, Ecuador
Antonio Sgorbissa	University of Genoa, Italy
Jungpil Shin	University of Aizu, Japan
Boštjan Šumak	University of Maribor, Slovenia
Markku Turunen	Tampere University, Finland
Frédéric Vanderhaegen	University of Valenciennes, France
Aleksandra Vuckovic	University of Glasgow, UK
Andreas Wendemuth	Otto von Guericke University, Germany

| Marcus Winter | University of Brighton, UK |
| Floriano Zini | Free University of Bozen-Bolzano, Italy |

Additional Reviewers

| Fu-Yin Cherng | National Chung Cheng University, Taiwan, Republic of China |
| Anand Deshpande | Angadi Institute of Technology and Management, India |

Invited Speakers

Andrea Gaggioli	Università Cattolica del Sacro Cuore, Italy
Wendy E. Mackay	Inria, Paris-Saclay, and Université Paris-Saclay, France
Antonio Camurri	Università degli Studi di Genova, Italy

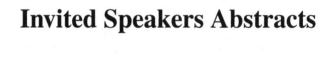

Invited Speakers Abstracts

Designing Transformative Experiences: Exploring the Potential of Virtual Technologies for Personal Change

Andrea Gaggioli

Università Cattolica del Sacro Cuore, Italy

Abstract: As the digital landscape rapidly evolves, virtual reality (VR) and augmented reality (AR) are poised to reshape the way we engage with experiences, particularly those aimed at personal growth and self-discovery. By enabling individuals to step into alternate realities and navigate simulated scenarios, these technologies have the potential to facilitate transformative experiences that lead to personal change, growth, and development. In this keynote, I will delve into the psychological mechanisms underpinning the efficacy of virtual transformative experiences, highlighting how these technologies can evoke emotional responses, challenge perspectives, and prompt introspection. Additionally, ethical considerations surrounding the design and implementation of such experiences will be addressed, ensuring that the potential of these technologies is harnessed responsibly and thoughtfully.

Aesthetically Resonant Multimodal Interactive Systems

Antonio Camurri

DIBRIS, Università degli Studi di Genova, Genova, Italy

Abstract: Art and science are often viewed as distant domains only loosely connected. In recent years we are now witnessing more interaction between the two. This has led to an increased awareness of how art and science are indeed two different but strongly coupled aspects of human creativity, both driving innovation as art influences science and technology, and as science and technology in turn inspire art. Recognizing this mutually beneficial relationship, the Casa Paganini research centre cultivates the intersection of scientific and technological research in human-centered computing where art and humanistic culture are a fundamental source of inspiration in a trans-disciplinary approach. In this seminar, I discuss concrete examples on how our collaboration with artists informed our work on the automated analysis of nonverbal expressive and social behavior and interactive sonification, including presentation of some of the scientific and technological results from the EU projects H2020 FET PROACTIVE EnTimeMent and EU Horizon Europe STARTS ICT ReSilence.

Contents – Part I

Invited Speaker

Creating Human-Computer Partnerships 3
    Wendy E. Mackay

Main Event

Empowering Production Workers to Program Robots: A No-Code,
Skill-Based Approach 21
    Charly Blanc, Lionel Boudry, Andreas Sonderegger, Julien Nembrini,
    and Sarah Dégallier-Rochat

Mobile Gaming EMG-Based Brain Computer Interface 40
    Abdulaziz Althekair, Mohanned Odeh, Mohammad AlBayaa,
    Marwa Sharawi, and Iyad Abu Doush

Towards Gesture Based Assistive Technology for Persons Experiencing
Involuntary Muscle Contractions 53
    Christine Pocock, Chris Porter, and May Agius

Towards a Methodology for Developing Human-AI Collaborative
Decision Support Systems 69
    Alexander Smirnov, Andrew Ponomarev, and Tatiana Levashova

Simplifying the Development of Conversational Speech Interfaces
by Non-Expert End-Users Through Dialogue Templates 89
    Maia Aguirre, Ariane Méndez, Manuel Torralbo, and Arantza del Pozo

Multiparty Dialogic Processes of Goal and Strategy Formation in Hybrid
Teams 110
    Andreas Wendemuth and Stefan Kopp

Adaptive Network Modelling of Informal Learning Within an Organization
by Asking for Help and Getting Help 121
    Debby Bouma and Jan Treur

Trust, Perspicuity, Efficiency: Important UX Aspects to Consider
for the Successful Adoption of Collaboration Tools in Organisations 143
    Anna-Lena Meiners, Andreas Hinderks, and Jörg Thomaschewski

Tracing Stress and Arousal in Virtual Reality Games Using Players' Motor
and Vocal Behaviour 163
   Susanna Brambilla, Giuseppe Boccignone, N. Alberto Borghese,
   Eleonora Chitti, Riccardo Lombardi, and Laura A. Ripamonti

Electro-oculographic Discrimination of Gazing Motion to a Smartphone
Notification Tone 187
   Masaki Omata and Shingo Ito

Why Career Orientation is Often Difficult and How Digital Platforms Can
Support Young People in This Process 201
   Jessica Brandenburger and Monique Janneck

3D Reconstruction Using a Mirror-Mounted Drone: Development
and Evaluation of Actual Equipment 216
   Ayumi Noda, Kimi Ueda, Hirotake Ishii, and Hiroshi Shimoda

Do Users Tolerate Errors? Effects of Observed Failures on the Subjective
Evaluation of a Gesture-Based Virtual Reality Application 232
   Lisa Graichen and Matthias Graichen

A Bi-national Investigation of the Needs of Visually Disabled People
from Mexico and Japan 244
   Alexandro del Valle, Zilu Liang, and Ian Piumarta

A Three Level Design Study Approach to Develop a Student-Centered
Learner Dashboard 262
   Gilbert Drzyzga and Thorleif Harder

Why are You Blinking at Me? Exploring Users' Understanding of Robotic
Status Indicators 282
   E. Liberman-Pincu, S. Honig, and T. Oron-Gilad

Immediate-After Effect of Enhancement Push-Off at a Terminal Stance
Phase of Gait Using Heating of Insole Tip for the Development of Smart
Insole 295
   Kazushige Oshita

An Intuitive Interface for Technical Documentation Based on Semantic
Knowledge Graphs 307
   Frieder Loch and Markus Stolze

Augmenting the Human in Industry 4.0 to Add Value: A Taxonomy
of Human Augmentation Approach 318
   Jacqueline Humphries, Pepijn Van de Ven, and Alan Ryan

Gesture Me: A Machine Learning Tool for Designers to Train Gesture
Classifiers 336
    Marcus Winter, Phil Jackson, and Sanaz Fallahkhair

A Case Study on Netychords: Crafting Accessible Digital Musical
Instrument Interaction for a Special Needs Scenario 353
    Nicola Davanzo, Federico Avanzini, Luca A. Ludovico,
    Davys Moreno, António Moreira, Oksana Tymoshchuk, Júlia Azevedo,
    and Carlos Marques

Author Index 373

Contents – Part II

Main Event

I Am in Love with the Shape of You: The Effect of Mass Customization
on the Human-Robot Relationship 3
E. Liberman-Pincu, A. Bulgaro, and T. Oron-Gilad

Eco-Design of a Smart Module to Provide Customizable and Effective
Interaction for the Elderly 13
*Simona D'Attanasio, Tanguy Dalléas, Dorian Le Boulc'h,
and Marie Verel*

Technology Enhanced Mulsemedia Learning: Insights of an Evaluation 24
*M. Mohana, Aleph Campos da Silveira, P. Subashini,
Celso Alberto Saibel Santos, and Gheorghita Ghinea*

Accessible Applications to Improve the Tourist Experience 43
Irene De Paoli, Alessia M. Di Campi, and Flaminia L. Luccio

An Augmented Reality Environment for Testing Cockpit Display Systems 66
Caner Potur and Gökhan İnce

Human-Centred Digital Sovereignty: Explorative Conceptual Model
and Ways Forward 84
Dennis Lawo, Thomas Neifer, Margarita Esau, and Gunnar Stevens

MAS4Games: A Reinforced Learning-Based Multi-agent System
to Improve Player Retention in Virtual Reality Video Games 104
Natalia Maury-Castañeda, Sergio Villarruel-Vasquez, and Willy Ugarte

Human-Centered AI Goals for Speech Therapy Tools 121
*Chinmoy Deka, Abhishek Shrivastava, Saurabh Nautiyal,
and Praveen Chauhan*

Designing a WhatsApp Inspired Healthcare Application for Older Adults:
A Focus on Ease of Use 137
Saurabh Nautiyal and Abhishek Shrivastava

Understanding Adoption of Last Mile Electric Micromobility in Rural
Areas: A Structural Equation Modeling Approach 160
    Thomas Neifer, Ariane Stöbitsch, Kalvin Kroth, Caroline Baja,
    Dennis Lawo, Lukas Böhm, Paul Bossauer, and Alexander Boden

Participative Development of a Learning Dashboard for Online Students
Using Traditional Design Concepts 176
    Gilbert Drzyzga, Thorleif Harder, and Monique Janneck

Easy Induction: A Serious Game Using Participatory Design 192
    Yuwen Li, Yue Li, Jiachen Liang, and Hai-Ning Liang

Creating StoryLines: Participatory Design with Power Grid Operators 212
    Wissal Sahel, Wendy E. Mackay, and Antoine Marot

Visual Representations for Data Analytics: User Study 231
    Ladislav Peska, Ivana Sixtova, David Hoksza, David Bernhauer,
    and Tomas Skopal

A Web Platform to Investigate the Relationship Between Sounds, Colors
and Emotions 244
    Silvia Dini, Luca A. Ludovico, Alessandro Rizzi, Beatrice Sarti,
    and María Joaquina Valero Gisbert

Continuous Time Elicitation Through Virtual Reality to Model Affect
Dynamics 258
    Francesca Borghesi, Vittorio Murtas, Valentina Mancuso,
    and Alice Chirico

Who Pays Attention to the User Experience Content Embedded in Mobile
APP Reviews 277
    Silas Formunyuy Verkijika

Special Session on E3: Enhancing the Esports Experience

Gamers' Eden: The Functioning and Role of Gaming Houses Inside
the Esports Ecosystem 299
    alessandro franzó and Attila Bruni

The Communication Effectiveness of AI Win Prediction Applied
in Esports Live Streaming: A Pilot Study 315
    Minglei Wang

Using Audience Avatars to Increase Sense of Presence in Live-Streams 326
    Tomáš Pagáč and Simone Kriglstein

Initial Developments of Teamwork and Mental Health Focused Minigames
for the Purpose of Esports Training 338
    Danielle K. Langlois and Simone Kriglstein

Power to the Spectator: Towards an Enhanced Video Game Stream
Discovery Experience 349
    Laura Herrewijn and Sven Charleer

Author Index 361

Invited Speaker

Creating Human-Computer Partnerships

Wendy E. Mackay[✉]

Université Paris-Saclay, CNRS, Inria Saclay, Gif-sur-Yvette, France
`wendy.mackay@inria.fr`

Abstract. How can we can design "human-computer partnerships" that take optimal advantage of human skills and system capabilities? Artificial Intelligence research is usually measured in terms of the effectiveness of an algorithm, whereas Human-Computer Interaction research focuses on enhancing human abilities. I argue that better AI algorithms are neither necessary nor sufficient for creating more effective intelligent systems. Instead, we need to focus on the details of interaction and how to successfully balance the simplicity of the user's interaction with the expressive power of the system. After describing our approach to "generative theories of interaction", I illustrate how to create interactive intelligent systems where users can discover relevant functionality, express individual differences and appropriate the system for their own personal use.

Keywords: Generative theories of interaction · Human-centered artificial intelligence · Human-computer partnerships · Participatory design · Upskilling

1 Introduction

My research in the field of Human-Computer Interaction (HCI) focuses on *human-centered AI*, i.e. how to create intelligent interactive systems with a measurably positive impact on human users. We seek to design *"human-computer partnerships"* that combine human skills and system capabilities so that humans and intelligent agents perform better together than either individually. This requires not only taking advantage of the best characteristics of each, but also considering how to improve human capabilities over time, thus "upskilling" rather than deskilling or replacing the users of these systems [24].

Unfortunately, most current AI research is measured in terms of improving the algorithm, not its effect on human users. Systems such as ChatGPT are rightly hailed as major technical breakthroughs, but carry many embedded assumptions about how to interact with them. Asking people to converse with a simulated person appeals to our very human tendency to anthropomorphize the objects and animals we interact with. However, this can lead to severe problems when the intelligent agent is wrong or "hallucinates" [12].

© The Author(s), under exclusive license to Springer Nature Switzerland AG 2023
H. P. da Silva and P. Cipresso (Eds.): CHIRA 2023, CCIS 1996, pp. 3–17, 2023.
https://doi.org/10.1007/978-3-031-49425-3_1

1.1   The Cost of System-Induced Errors

Consider the recent fiasco surrounding Meta's *Galactica* whose language-based AI model was trained on a large body of scientific literature to support writing scientific papers. Unfortunately, *Galactica* was prone to generating dangerous pseudo-science. The journalist Tristan Green got it to generate *"well-written research papers on the benefits of committing suicide, practicing antisemitism, and eating crushed glass."* [10]. *Galactica* was shut down after only three days, not because of the algorithm per se, but rather because the designers had not sufficiently considered how humans might interact with it. Legitimate science takes expertise, discipline and time, but *Galactica* allowed non-scientists to produce fake science with a highly authoritative voice. Although designed to save time, it was equally ripe for misuse.

Of course, not all intelligent systems exhibit such dramatic failures. We are all confronted daily with more a more innocuous version of this problem: the smartphone's "auto-correct" feature. Here, the designer's assumption is that the user made an error — which may or may not be true — and that the correction is actually correct, which also may or may not be true. The designer may also assume that any errors that are produced by the system are innocuous and that the benefits of using the system outweigh the cost of introducing new errors.

Another more subtle effect is the transformation of the user's role from "author" to "error corrector". Although a touch typist can simultaneously type and read text on a laptop screen, phone typing requires continually shifting attention between the soft keyboard, the suggested words and the text output window. Producing error-free text requires constant monitoring to ensure that the system has not introduced errors, a notoriously poor use of human skills [9].

Worse, incorrect words require immediate action from the user. I usually catch errors only after I press "send", if I notice them at all. I must then decide whether or not to shift the topic of conversation to a discussion of the perils of auto-correct. This may be amusing when chatting with friends and family, but is less acceptable for work-related texts.

Finally, people and intelligent agents produce very different kinds of mistakes. If a person misspells a word, other people are very good at inferring the correct one. By contrast, some auto-corrected errors are impossible to guess. For example, my phone always transforms the verb "is" into "OSS". I cannot inform the system that this is incorrect and must either remember to slow down my typing and explicitly choose "is" from the suggestion window or else waste time explaining my phone's odd quirk to the message recipient. A good human speller may question the advantage of using "auto-correct" if the act of correcting the corrections wastes more time than simply typing in the first place.

1.2   Shaping the User's Behavior

Not only do humans *adapt* their behavior to accommodate the system, but the system also *shapes* [25] the user's actions. For example, auto-correct clearly affects how we type over time. Instead of fully typing each word, we may just type the beginning of a long word and wait for the system to propose the complete word. Some people take this even further, typing the fewest possible letters and waiting for the system to produce a good-enough suggestion. This can be efficient and save keystrokes but risks producing only pat, stereotypical phrases.

We also might choose to accept a proposed word even if it was not quite what we wanted to say. For example, if I type an informal "congrats", the system might replace it with the more formal "congratulations" or a highly informal champagne emoji. Now I must not only decide the "right" level of formality but also whether or not to take time correcting it.

Human conversations operate differently from chats with intelligent agents. Conversation partners establish what Clark [7] calls "common ground" and rely on mutual knowledge, beliefs and assumptions to communicate efficiently. Intelligent agents and people have access to different, overlapping sets of data but only humans can share beliefs and assumptions. Humans react to each others' conversation styles and shape each other's behavior during the conversation. However, humans also tend to treat intelligent agents as if they were human.

I witnessed an early example of this in the mid 1980s when I worked on Digital Equipment Corporation's *IVIS*, the first commercial interactive video system. My research group developed an intelligent tutor, "Dwayne", an animated claymation character who spoke with *DECtalk* as he explained how to fix a printer. We found that field service technicians typed much simpler, requests when Dwayne spoke with a child's rather than an adult's voice. The presentation and interaction mode shaped users' behavior, encouraging them to limit their word choices as if they were talking to a child, which made it much easier for us to interpret them.

1.3   Presentation Details Matter

Sometimes, showing additional information reduces human skills. For example, my studies of air traffic controllers [17] led to a system called *Caméléon* [19] that augmented controller's interactions with paper flight strips. They greatly appreciated being able to tap on a flight strip to visually locate that aircraft on the RADAR screen. Yet they objected to another feature that calculated and displayed the aircraft's expected trajectory, since it would interfere with developing and maintaining their mental model of the air traffic.

A related example involves an intelligent system designed to help ship captains plot an acceptable course when entering a harbor[1]. The first version presented the AI's suggestion *before* the captain plotted their own course. The captains rejected this version because they feared it would reduce their expertise while still holding them responsible if it made an error. However, they accepted the same system with a reversed presentation order: the captain first plotted a course and only then saw suggestions that they could choose to adopt. Here, the same algorithm with a different interface produced very different results: the first risked deskilling users whereas the second helped improve their skills.

---

[1] Personal communication.

Users may have difficulty determining the effectiveness of their interactions with intelligent agents. A recent study of 54 cybersecurity experts at Stanford University found that programmers who used an intelligent code assistant (*Github*'s *Co-Pilot*) wrote significantly less secure code but believed they wrote better code [23]. Another study of 49 students in a Behavioral Economics class at the HEC Business school showed that students who wrote their own analytical essays performed 28% better than those who corrected an essay written by ChatGPT [11].

1.4   Interacting with AI

Traditional characterizations of intelligent systems treat users as just another component of the system, either as a useful source of data or an unwanted source of error. Rafner et al. [24] distinguish among *"Human-In-The-Loop"* (HITL) systems that plan, execute or evaluate data acquisition tasks [21]; *"Human-On-The-Loop"* (HOTL) systems that require a human to check the results [22]; and *"Human-Out-Of-The-Loop"* (HOOTL) systems that do not include human users at all [26].

Note that each frames the user's role in terms of the system's requirements, not the user's needs. These characterizations also raise important questions: For example, if humans are "out of the loop" does that save them time and free them for more interesting cognitive tasks or will it replace them altogether? If the system takes over the repetitive and "boring" elements of a task, will this enhance the user's job satisfaction or reduce their ability to learn and enhance their expertise over time? A concert pianist does not become a virtuoso by performing only the most interesting elements of a piece — practicing scales is also necessary for honing motor skills and developing one's ear. The assumption that intelligent systems will provide users with more interesting cognitive tasks is just that: an assumption. It simply will not happen unless intelligent system designers adopt the goal of enhancing the user's experience, which requires focusing on the interaction.

Humans and intelligent systems also fail in different ways, each with associated risks. For example, under normal conditions, the French national energy grid's automated systems balance loads somewhat better than human experts. However, when the COVID-19 pandemic caused radical shifts in energy requirements, the automated systems made strange, costly errors and the human experts performed significantly better.[2] Consider too what will happen with almost-autonomous vehicles where drivers need not pay attention until the car suddenly faces a crisis that the system cannot handle. Such systems will both deskill drivers and blame them when they lack the expertise necessary to immediately avert disaster.

We also need to consider interaction at multiple levels of scale. Designers of intelligent systems must consider the back-and-forth interaction between the user and the system, not only when everything works well but also when the system makes errors. Does the system limit the user's power of expression to make their

---

[2] Personal communication from staff.

inputs easier to interpret? Does the system transform the user from an author into a system monitor who detects and corrects errors? What are the longer term effects on the user's behavior? Do users learn and enhance their skills when using the system? Or does removing "easy" tasks and suggesting answers reduce their ability to develop and maintain expertise, effectively deskilling them?

This paper describes our approach to creating human-computer partnerships. I begin with a brief overview of our approach to "generative theory", which offers a principled approach for designing effective interaction. I then present a series of examples that illustrate how we can significantly improve human-computer interaction with intelligent systems by shifting the focus from the *algorithm* to the *interaction*.

2   Generative Theories of Interaction

I argue that we need to re-frame how we think about artificial intelligence research. Rather than treating human users as mere "input" to a computer algorithm and measuring success in terms of the algorithm's performance, we must explicitly design intelligent systems so that they increase *human* capabilities.

My research group, ExSitu, explores how to design *human-computer partnerships*, where humans share agency with intelligent, interactive technologies, while explicitly retaining control. Our research is deeply influenced by what we call *Generative Theories of Interaction* [5]. The key insight is that *interaction* can be studied as a phenomenon in its own right [6], with short- and long-term impacts that can be characterized, measured and evaluated. When we apply this approach to the design of intelligent systems, we see that an excellent algorithm can perform poorly if embedded in an inappropriate interface while a simpler, more sustainable algorithm can perform better if embedded in an effective interface.

Generative Theories of interaction (see Fig. 1) begin with concepts drawn from established theories from the natural and social sciences. We then decompose each concept into one or more actionable principles that can be applied to the study and design of interactive systems. We can examine existing interactive systems with an analytical lens, to see if the principles apply and with a critical lens, to see if the system can be improved by applying those principles. Finally, we can explore how to improve existing systems or create new ones by applying a constructive lens that applies the principles in innovative ways.

Much of our work builds on the concept of *co-adaptation* [17] inspired by evolutionary biology, where humans both *adapt to* or learn how to interact with the technology as well as *adapt* or appropriate the system for their own purposes. Darwin's classic text *The Origin of Species* [8] describes *co-evolution*, where species are both affected by and affect the environments in which they live as well as *co-adaptation*, which describes the interactions among individual organisms affect each other: "*Co-adaptation* emphasizes this on-going, potentially asymmetrical process of mutual influence between organisms and the environment, where *survival of the fittest* is not simply a matter of an organism adapting to a changing environment, but also of it physically changing that environment to

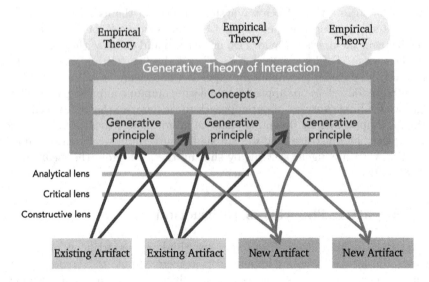

Fig. 1. Generative theories of interaction generate actionable design principles drawn from the natural and social sciences.

ensure its survival." We can examine the phenomenon of co-adaptation with respect to human users and intelligent agents. If we take the user's perspective, we see that users establish an ongoing dual relationship with the technology, where they discover how it works but also modify it for new purposes. If we switch to an intelligent system's perspective, the dual relationship is similar, although not identical, since some systems adapt to the user while others seek to change the user's behavior [5,17]. We call this set of inter-related interactions *reciprocal co-adaptation*, where both users and intelligent systems *adapt to* or learn from each other, as well as *adapt* or shape each other's behavior.

Of course, human users and intelligent agents access, interpret and present information differently. Intelligent systems, especially those based on statistical models such as machine learning and neural networks, are essentially impossible for human users to understand. The examples in the next section illustrate how we have employed generative theories of interaction to address the challenge of building effective interactive intelligent systems.

3   Creating Effective Human-Computer Partnerships

How can we design effective "human-computer partnerships" that make the most of human skills and system capabilities? The first examples explore how to increase a smartphone user's power of expression while maintaining simplicity of execution [18]. This involves creating intelligent co-adaptive systems that are discoverable — easy to learn and adapt to — as well as expressive and appropriable — easy to personalize and adapt. The next examples illustrate how human users can successfully share agency with intelligent agents. The final examples explore how we can exploit principles from behavioral psychology [25] where humans and agents shape each others' behavior.

3.1 Discoverability

Even though today's smartphones are extremely powerful, the interaction is extremely limited and takes little advantage of the expressive power of our fingers. Users press buttons, select from menus, fill out forms and enter text with tapping, swiping or pinching gestures. The advantage of this approach is the very low barrier to entry — almost anyone can use the system with little training. The disadvantage is that users have very little power of expression. They can only react to the buttons and controls displayed on the screen, rather than generating commands directly.

What if we could express commands by drawing gestures, for example, drawing a "pigtail" gesture to delete a phrase? The phone is certainly capable of identifying such gestures, so why is this not an option? This is a problem of discovery: users must be aware that such gesture-commands exist as well as recall the mappings between gestures and commands. The design challenge is how to provide in-context help for novice users when they need it, without slowing down experts.

We introduced the concept of "dynamic guides" [4] which combines on-screen feedforward and feedback to help users learn, execute and remember gesture sets. We take advantage of the fact that users who are unsure tend to pause, whereas experts simply draw the gesture. Figure 2 shows what happens when the user starts to draw but hesitates: a visual guide appears around the cursor or their finger, with different paths for each gesture-command combination. The classification model updates dynamically as the user follows the desired template, providing feedback as to what the user has already drawn and feedforward as other alternatives diminish or disappear. Novices can learn these gesture commands over time and smoothly transition into experts. If they forget a gesture, they can always pause to display the guide.

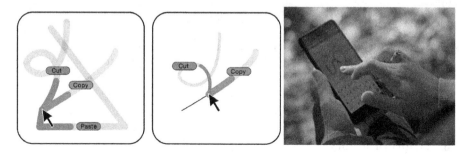

Fig. 2. *Octopocus* displays a dynamic, in-context guide that shows how to draw different command gestures. Continuously updated feedforward and feedback appear as the user draws.

3.2 Expressivity

A fully co-adaptive system does not simply help users adapt to the existing system, but also lets them adapt it to meet their individual needs. For example, human-produced handwriting is highly personal. We can recognize who wrote what and make educated guesses about the conditions under which it was written, such as in a rush or slowly and carefully. By contrast, text messages all look the same.

How can we offer users the expressive power of handwriting, but on a phone? Zhai and Kristensson [27] introduced "gesture typing", where users glide their fingers between letters, lifting only between words, and showed that it is 40% faster than tapping on a soft keyboard. Today's smartphones all offer this feature, with extremely proficient algorithms that identify the correct word and discard all extraneous human variation as unwanted "noise".

By contrast, we were interested in the details of this human variation and how to transform it into expressive output, such as color and font. Figure 3 shows the *Expressive Keyboard* [2], which maps the variation in how users glide between letters into different colors or fonts. For example, we can create the full RGB color space by mapping "curviness" to red, size to "green" and speed variation to "blue". Users can then consciously control both the content and the color of gesture-typed words. We thus "recycle" otherwise ignored gesture variation to create rich output without sacrificing accuracy. We also created the *CommandBoard* [1], which offers a full range of custom-designed fonts and the *MojiBoard* [3], which transforms gesture-typed words into emojis with a single stroke.

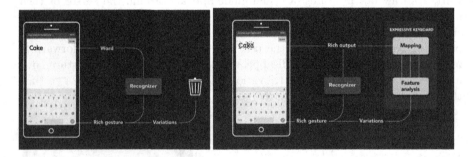

Fig. 3. Standard gesture typing recognizers discard user variation as "noise". The *Expressive Keyboard* transforms individual variation into rich output, such as color or font style, without sacrificing accuracy.

3.3 Appropriability

In addition to creating expressive output, users also want to personalize their input by choosing their own gestures and mappings to their preferred commands.

Here, the challenge is to balance the needs of the human user, who wants to create gestures that are easy to recall and the system, which needs to reliably recognize and distinguish each gesture within the set of gesture-commands.

We developed the *Fieldward* [20] dynamic guide as an interactive colored heat map that visualizes the "negative space" of unused gestures and verifies whether or not the current gesture is unique (see Fig. 4). The user simply enters a command to define and begins to draw the desired gesture.

Fig. 4. *Fieldward* displays a dynamic heat map that shows if the user's preferred gesture will be recognized (gesture stops in a blue zone) or not (gesture stops in a red zone). (Color figure online)

As the user draws, the display changes color: Ending the gesture in a red zone indicates that gesture already exists. Ending it in a purple zone means that the gesture is ambiguous and it is safer to either continue or try another option. Ending it in a blue zone means that the current gesture can be recognized reliably and is suitable as a new gesture-command.

Users enjoyed exploring different gesture possibilities, such as drawing a heart to phone a user's boyfriend. Another user not only designed individual gesture-commands but also created his own personal gesture syntax. He associated certain gestures with commands, e.g., "call" or "text" and others with people, e.g. "Mom" and "Bob". He could then create fluid gesture combinations to create compound commands, such as "Call Mom".

3.4 Sharing Agency

One of the major challenges in creating human-computer partnerships is how to share agency between human users and intelligent agents, broadly defined as exerting control over the outcome. We worked closely with designers to create *Semantic Collage*, a digital mood board creation tool that attaches semantic labels to images [14]. Designers propose images that *Semantic Collage* translates into semantic labels, which designers can then adjust to improve the search. This back-and-forth approach allows designers to share agency with the algorithm, where each proposes possibilities and provides specific feedback to the other.

A subsequent project, *ImageSense* [13] (see Fig. 5) combined individual and shared work spaces as well as collaboration with multiple forms of intelligent

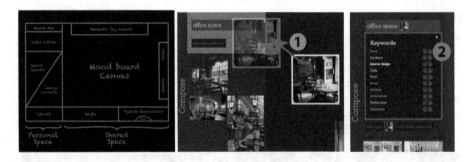

Fig. 5. *ImageSense* lets designers vary their level of agency with an intelligent mood board (left). *Image Cascade* supports full user control, *Semantic Collage* supports shared user-agent control and *Select-o-matic* offers primarily agent control.

agents. *ImageSense* allows users to transition smoothly between different levels of agency, from user-directed selection of curated images (*ImageCascade*), to alternating between user-initiated and system-initiated search (*Semantic Collage*) to responding to system-driven recommendations (*Select-o-matic*). Designers can tweak the agent's behavior, e.g. by specifying "fewer images like this" and modify the types of generated semantic labels, color palettes or tag clouds and adjust their level of importance.

Intelligent systems such as those described above are intended to facilitate the interaction. But what if we instead ask an intelligent agent to challenge the user in order to gain efficiency?

We created *BIGNav* [15], a multi-scale navigation technique based on Bayesian Experimental Design. The goal is to maximize the information-theoretic concept of mutual information, also known as "information gain" (see Fig. 6.) Rather than simply executing user navigation commands, *BIGNav* interprets the user's input to update its knowledge about the user's intended target. It then produces a new view that maximizes the expected information gain i.e. that

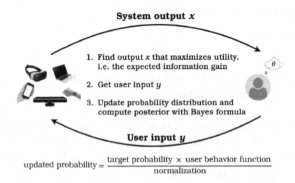

Fig. 6. *BIGNav* presents the user with choices selected to maximize the information gained from each user response and then updates the probability distribution accordingly.

should provide the most information from the user's next input. *BIGFile* [16] uses a similar approach for file navigation. The split interface combines standard file system navigation with an adaptive area that includes shortcuts calculated with *BIG*. Both *BIGNav* and *BIGFile* were 40% faster than the standard interface, but each increases the user's cognitive load. This type of human-computer partnership highlights the trade-off that can arise between increasing human efficiency and creating a satisfying user experience. A remaining challenge is how to let users choose an appropriate level of difficulty based on their needs in the moment.

3.5   Shaping Human and Agent Behavior

We also explored how humans and intelligent agents can shape each other's behavior using full-body interaction. In the context of an art-science collaboration sponsored by *Curiositas* and *La Diagonale* at the Université Paris-Saclay, we collaborated with the *N+1 Theater Group* to produce a wall-sized interactive Christmas display, first for a month in a shopping center and then at an art-science fair (see Fig. 7).

The goal was to create an entertaining interactive experience where users share control with the system. The theater company created a mechanical interactive Santa-making factory that would operate only if a user had successfully engaged with an animated Santa Claus character. Our job was to teach passersby to perform a specific movement, without explaining the movement or even that they were supposed to learn a movement. We designed the interaction so that the user thought they controlled the animated character but the character

Fig. 7. Users interact with the Santa Claus figure. After first mirroring the user's movements, Santa starts to act independently. Users are rewarded for successive approximations to the final behavior: If the user performs an appropriate movement, Santa moves up another step. If the user performs the final movement, Santa pulls a level and launches the mechanical "Santa-making factory".

also "controlled" them. We used the concept of "reinforcement" from behavioral psychology, where the reinforcer (or reward) is Santa's attention.

When the user first arrives, Santa mirrors her movements, which keeps her engaged, but only for the first 30 s or so. Next, Santa starts to act independently and waits until she starts to copy Santa's movements according to the behavioral phenomenon of "extinction". This begins the shaping process: a stair with three steps appears and Santa moves up each step as the user makes successive approximations to the correct movement. If the movement is too far from desired movement, Santa looks bored and taps his foot. If she does not respond appropriately, the stairs disappear and Santa drops through the floor. If she successfully discovers the correct movements through trial and error, Santa climbs to the top step and jumps up to grab a virtual lever. This in turn operates a mechanical lever that launches the machine.

The system was a great success and a number of people returned over successive days to play with Santa. Although it was created primarily as a source of entertainment for the public, it also helped us to better understand how an intelligent agent can both respond to the user and also guide (or control) them.

4   Conclusion

In a 1984 interview, Steve Jobs famously observed that, even though he could not, as a human, outrun many animals, if you gave him a bicycle, he could beat them all. He viewed computers as tools for augmenting human capabilities and argued that computers should act as "bicycles for the mind". In the intervening decades, computers have touched every aspect of our lives, including commerce, entertainment and education. After multiple highs and lows, recent advances in artificial intelligence offer exciting new possibilities for significantly improving our lives, but remain controversial, with conflicting views as to their risks and benefits.

I argue that, in order to truly benefit from AI, we need to reconsider how we conduct AI research and build intelligent systems. We need to shift from measuring the efficiency of the *algorithm* to measuring the effectiveness of the *interaction* over time. We need to create successful "human-computer-partnerships" that augment rather than deskill or replace human users such that the combination of human and AI capabilities together are better than either alone.

We must view human users, not as a source of errors or as cogs in the machine, but rather as the system's *raison d'être*. Designers of intelligent interactive systems should ask themselves whether or not their users are forced to:

- Monitor the system over long periods of time?
- Remove interesting tasks and replace them with boring, repetitive ones?
- Jump into action to solve a crisis that the system cannot solve, after passively letting the system do everything else?
- Feed data into the system in the system's terms rather than the user's?
- Generate yes/no answers to complex questions?
- Behave in prescribed ways to achieve a particular goal?

Clearly, AI researchers must continue developing new algorithms. However, we also need extensive research into how those algorithms are embedded into intelligent interactive systems. We need to carefully design the way information is presented and how users control their interaction with these systems. We must recognize that the same algorithm embedded in a different interface may affect users in extremely different ways. At the same time, we can choose among different algorithms to produce a particular interaction style and develop more "sustainable" AI that achieves the same effect with less data or computing power. Focusing on developing effective human-computer partnerships instead of more powerful algorithms will improve not only how we approach AI research but also AI policy, ethics and law.

Acknowledgments. My thanks to Michel Beaudouin-Lafon, Janin Koch and members of the ExSitu research lab for numerous productive discussions about these ideas. This work was supported by the European Union Horizon 2020 research and innovation program under grant agreement No 952091 (*ALMA: Human-Centric Algebraic Machine Learnning*) and grant agreement No 952026 (*HumanE-AI Network*), as well as the *ERC European Research Council* grant No 321135 (*CREATIV: Creating Co-Adaptive Human-Computer Partnerships*).

References

1. Alvina, J., Griggio, C.F., Bi, X., Mackay, W.E.: Commandboard: creating a general-purpose command gesture input space for soft keyboard. In: Proceedings of the 30th Annual ACM Symposium on User Interface Software and Technology (UIST 2017), pp. 17–28. Association for Computing Machinery, New York (2017). https://doi.org/10.1145/3126594.3126639
2. Alvina, J., Malloch, J., Mackay, W.: Expressive keyboards: enriching gesture-typing on mobile devices. In: Proceedings of the 29th ACM Symposium on User Interface Software and Technology (UIST 2016), pp. 583–593. ACM, Tokyo (2016). https://doi.org/10.1145/2984511.2984560
3. Alvina, J., Qu, C., Mcgrenere, J., Mackay, W.: Mojiboard: generating parametric emojis with gesture keyboards. In: CHI 2019 Extended Abstracts (CHI EA 2019), Glasgow (2019). https://doi.org/10.1145/3290607.3312771
4. Bau, O., Mackay, W.E.: Octopocus: a dynamic guide for learning gesture-based command sets. In: Proceedings of the 21st Annual ACM Symposium on User Interface Software and Technology (UIST 2008), pp. 37–46. Association for Computing Machinery, New York (2008). https://doi.org/10.1145/1449715.1449724
5. Beaudouin-Lafon, M., Bødker, S., Mackay, W.E.: Generative theories of interaction. ACM Trans. Comput. Hum. Interact. **28**(6), 1–54 (2021)
6. Beaudouin-Lafon, M., Mackay, W.E.: Rethinking interaction: from instrumental interaction to human-computer partnerships. In: Extended Abstracts of the 2018 CHI Conference on Human Factors in Computing Systems, pp. 1–5 (2018)
7. Clark, H.H.: Using Language. Cambridge University Press, Cambridge (1996)
8. Darwin, C. (ed.): On the Origin of Species by Means of Natural Selection, or the Preservation of Favoured Races in the Struggle for Life. John Murray, London (1859)

9. Fitts, P.M., et al.: Human engineering for an effective air navigation and traffic-control system. Tech. rep., Defense Technical Information Center (1951)

10. Green, T.: Meta takes new AI system offline because twitter users are mean. In: TNW (2022). https://thenextweb.com/news/meta-takes-new-ai-system-offline-because-twitter-users-mean

11. Hill, B.: Taking the help or going alone: Chatgpt and class assignments. In: HEC Research Paper (2023). https://doi.org/10.2139/ssrn.4465833

12. Klein, N.: AI machines aren't 'hallucinating' but their makers are. The Gardian (2023)

13. Koch, J., Taffin, N., Beaudouin-Lafon, M., Laine, M., Lucero, A., Mackay, W.E.: Imagesense: an intelligent collaborative ideation tool to support diverse human-computer partnerships. Proc. ACM Hum. Comput. Interact. **4**(CSCW1), 1–27 (2020)

14. Koch, J., Taffin, N., Lucero, A., Mackay, W.E.: Semanticcollage: enriching digital mood board design with semantic labels. In: Proceedings of the 2020 ACM Designing Interactive Systems Conference, pp. 407–418 (2020)

15. Liu, W., D'Oliveira, R.L., Beaudouin-Lafon, M., Rioul, O.: Bignav: Bayesian information gain for guiding multiscale navigation. In: Proceedings of the 2017 CHI Conference on Human Factors in Computing Systems (CHI 2017), pp. 5869–5880. Association for Computing Machinery, New York (2017). https://doi.org/10.1145/3025453.3025524

16. Liu, W., Rioul, O., McGrenere, J., Mackay, W.E., Beaudouin-Lafon, M.: Bigfile: Bayesian information gain for fast file retrieval. In: Proceedings of the 2018 CHI Conference on Human Factors in Computing Systems (CHI 2018), pp. 1–13. Association for Computing Machinery, New York (2018). https://doi.org/10.1145/3173574.3173959

17. Mackay, W.: Responding to cognitive overload?: co-adaptation between users and technology. Intellectica **30**(1), 177–193 (2000). https://doi.org/10.3406/intel.2000.1597

18. Mackay, W.E.: Réimaginer nos interactions avec le monde numérique. Leçons inaugurales du Collège de France, Collège de France — Fayard (2022)

19. Mackay, W.E., Fayard, A.L., Frobert, L., Médini, L.: Reinventing the familiar: exploring an augmented reality design space for air traffic control. In: Proceedings of the SIGCHI Conference on Human Factors in Computing Systems (CHI 1998), pp. 558–565. ACM Press/Addison-Wesley Publishing Co. (1998). https://doi.org/10.1145/274644.274719

20. Malloch, J., Griggio, C.F., McGrenere, J., Mackay, W.E.: Fieldward and pathward: dynamic guides for defining your own gestures. In: Proceedings of the 2017 CHI Conference on Human Factors in Computing Systems (CHI 2017), pp. 4266–4277. Association for Computing Machinery, New York (2017). https://doi.org/10.1145/3025453.3025764

21. Monarch, R.M.: Human-in-the-Loop Machine Learning: Active Learning and Annotation for Human-Centered AI. Manning, New York (2021)

22. Nahavandi, S.: Trusted autonomy between humans and robots: Toward human-on-the-loop in robotics and autonomous systems. IEEE Syst. Man. Cybernet. Magaz. **3**(1), 10–17 (2017). https://doi.org/10.1109/MSMC.2016.2623867

23. Perry, N., Srivastava, M., Kumar, D., Boneh, D.: Do users write more insecure code with AI assistants? (2022)

24. Rafner, J., et al.: Deskilling, upskilling, and reskilling: a case for hybrid intelligence. Moral. Mach. **1**, 24–39 (2021). https://doi.org/10.5771/2747-5174-2021-2-24

25. Reynolds, G.S.: A Primer of Operant Conditioning. Scott Foresman, Glenview (1968)

26. Steelberg, C.: The path to an AI-connected government. Tech. rep., Data Center Dynamics (2019). https://www.datacenterdynamics.com/en/opinions/path-ai-connected-government

27. Zhai, S., Kristensson, P.O.: The word-gesture keyboard: reimagining keyboard interaction. Commun. ACM **55**(9), 91–101 (2012). https://doi.org/10.1145/2330667.2330689

Main Event

Empowering Production Workers to Program Robots: A No-Code, Skill-Based Approach

Charly Blanc[1,2]([✉])(iD), Lionel Boudry[3], Andreas Sonderegger[3](iD), Julien Nembrini[2](iD), and Sarah Dégallier-Rochat[1](iD)

[1] HuCE Institute, Bern University of Applied Sciences, Quellgasse 21, Bienne 2502, Switzerland
[2] Human-IST Institute, University of Fribourg, Boulevard de Pérolles 90, Fribourg 1700, Switzerland
charly.blanc@bfh.ch
[3] Institute for New Work, Bern University of Applied Sciences, Bern, Switzerland

Abstract. The current market requires automated production systems to be reprogrammed by the shop floor workers to meet dynamic production needs. This requires new interfaces allowing the workers to acquire the needed skills for efficient and safe programming. In this article, an intuitive interface is introduced to foster both upskilling and empowerment through guided tutorials. A no-code approach to programming based on the notion of robotic skills enables interactions that are based on the worker's competencies. A preliminary study with students (N = 58) using between-group testing was performed to evaluate the usability of the interface and skill acquisition through the tutorials. The effect of a basic understanding of robots' behavior on users' performance was evaluated: a demonstration with a real robot was presented to half of the participants before the study. Our results indicate that the proposed approach enabled most novice users to achieve simple programming tasks. The demonstration with the robot had a positive impact on performance suggesting the need for real robot interaction to improve learning. In summary, the combination of a no-code, skill-based approach with problem-based tutorials and demonstrations with real robots can help non-expert users develop the competencies and confidence to autonomously program a robot. Further tests with intended target users are planned in the future.

Keywords: Robotics · Human computer interaction · Programming learning · Upskilling · Empowerment

1 Introduction

Traditionally, most assembly processes are either fully automated or manual. Automation solutions have been optimized for decades to become ever more precise, rapid, and robust. Such solutions are ideal for repetitive tasks in a structured environment, but not feasible for tasks requiring fine manipulation, problem-solving capabilities and adaptability, where manual work is still required [10]. Recently, a new paradigm for automation as emerged with collaborative robots (cobots). These robots fulfill safety

© The Author(s), under exclusive license to Springer Nature Switzerland AG 2023
H. P. da Silva and P. Cipresso (Eds.): CHIRA 2023, CCIS 1996, pp. 21–39, 2023.
https://doi.org/10.1007/978-3-031-49425-3_2

requirements that allow them to share the workspace with humans, contrarily to traditional industrial robots that work in a closed, separated environment [4]. This possibility of sharing a common workspace enables a new form of automation, called partial automation, where the human and the robot can work simultaneously together on the same task, leading to new, narrower forms of human-robot collaborations [38].

If full automation has been the main focus in the industry until recently, the ever growing versatility of the market, the constant acceleration of technology development, the growing demand for customized products and the tendency for shorter product life duration has lead to a growing interest in partial automation [30,35]. Indeed, while machines are faster, more precise and have a greater repeatability, humans are much more flexible and can rapidly adapt to new tasks [37]. The aim of partial automation is thus to combine the flexibility of human work with the efficiency of automation [41]. In particular, it should be possible to use the same robot for different tasks and to easily and rapidly reprogram the robot according to the market demands, bringing the needed agility for the company to cope with market versatility [14].

However, companies that could benefit from partial automation are typically small to medium companies that cannot afford automation experts. Outsourcing the re-programming takes time and is expensive and thus strongly reduces the advantages of partial automation. In order to fully leverage its potential, it is thus required for the workers on the shop floor to be able to reprogram the process by themselves [32]. The goal is indeed that an expert in the process, instead of an expert in the technology, shall be the one to program the robot. A new approach to worker-machine interaction is therefore required for partial automation to work [7], similar to what window-based graphical user interfaces did for personal computers 40 years ago: rather than expert systems, intuitive solutions that can leverage the worker's task expertise are needed. This also represents an opportunity to make production work more attractive: the robot takes over the dull, tedious or dangerous tasks, while the worker focuses on the advanced tasks requiring human capabilities [29]. For the worker, it could also mean a greater autonomy and opportunities for self-development [15].

Giving the possibility to the worker to reprogram the machines represents a big paradigm shift, sometimes refer to as Operator 4.0 [30], in the context of Industry 4.0, or augmented worker [25]: traditionally, automation solutions are expert systems designed to reduce as much as possible the intervention of non experts to minimize the risk of errors [23]. For partial automation to work, the power relationship between the worker and the machine needs to be changed, with the worker taking control over the system. This requires not only the worker to acquire the needed competencies to interact safely and efficiently with the machine, *i.e. upskilling*, but also to develop a feeling of ownership over the system, *i.e. empowerment* [6]. To better understand how to foster the transition from passive user to active programmer, a socio-technological perspective is needed to guide the design of the human-machine interaction.

In this article, we propose a first step in this direction. An interface for robotic programming was implemented based on the tried and tested block-based approach to learning programming [26,39]. This approach doesn't require the user to learn any programming syntax (compared to text based approach) making it easier to use. A set of step-by-step tutorials were developed to help the user to progressively acquire the needed competencies and gain a feeling of control over the system. Combining a block-based approach with robotic specific language was already tested [39] and shows that user could successfully implement robot programs with high score of usability, learnability and overall satisfaction. But since our goal is to empower workers to autonomously control the robot, the feeling of control is an important aspect that, to our knowledge, have not been yet investigated. We believe that a feeling of control on the machine can be achieve by providing a good understanding of how does this one work, combined with an effective and satisfactory interaction with the machine enabling the user to reach their goal efficiently. Improving the feeling of control over the machine will be therefore the main focus of this article. The research question tackled is the then the following: How does providing workers with a deep understanding of how a robot works, along with an effective and satisfactory interaction with the machine, impact their perceived feeling of control over the robot and their ability to autonomously control it for efficient task completion? A study focusing on upskilling was conducted with students to evaluate the relevance of our approach. A 2-group experiment was performed to assess the effect of basic knowledge about robotics on programming performance. The usability of the interface was also evaluated.

We start by presenting the relevant literature in the next section. Section 3 presents the interface and the tutorials that were developed for this study. The study is presented and discussed in Sect. 4. A discussion is proposed in Sect. 6, including future work. Finally, a conclusion is presented in Sect. 8.

2 Related Work

In the past decade, there has been a large movement to democratize the usage of robotics, sometimes referred as the no-code revolution [28]. Cobots have opened the path to this democratization: since they allow for physical interactions with the device, ad hoc solutions can be developed by non-expert users by directly interacting with the robot, without having to code. Most cobots are now endowed with intuitive programming interfaces allowing to easily concatenate pre-defined, parametrizable behaviors. However, these systems are typically design to be as intuitive to use as possible, which results in a lack of flexibility that limits the usage of the cobots to simple, repetitive tasks in controlled environments [38], which can explain the relative low adoption of plug-and-play cobotic systems in the industry. To fully leverage the potential of partial automation systems for non-expert users, an interface is required that is not only easy to use, but also easy to learn.

In our framework, we propose a block-based interface, similar to the well-known Blockly [40] or Scratch [26], build on top of a skill-based architecture [32]. Robot skills are associated to predefined behaviours combining sensory and motor information. Previous work successfully combined Blockly with industrial robots [40], enabling the programming of a pick-and-place task of a virtual robot by adult novices. Other studies investigated robot programming teaching for adult novices [39] using Blockly with a framework called CoBlox, compared to two widely used industrial programming approaches. The results demonstrate that participants successfully completed the robot programming tasks while receiving higher scores for usability, learnability, and general satisfaction. The participants were specifically instructed to focus on a limited range of functionality, such as implementing a *pick and place* task. However, important programming concepts like loops and conditions were not introduced, despite their necessity when working on more extensive programming tasks in real case scenario.

In fact, the concept of loops in programming is central but was shown to be difficult to understand by novices [12]. Another study [13] showed that students usually lack familiarity with variables and have misunderstandings regarding their usage. Other difficulties come from the visual representation of the program itself, and were explored by the Blockly team [9] who describe a non-exhaustive list of problems faced by novice programmers while learning programming with Blockly. To tackle these problems, a collection of user-centered tutorials were developed (Blockly games) to teach how to use the interface as well as the difficult programming functionalities. The combination of a block-based interface with tutorials has shown good results in terms of breaking learning barriers [9]. We will therefore use a similar approach for our framework and adapt it our target group, the production workers.

Another critical step while programming is the creation of functions (or skills in the context of robotics). In fact, functions provide a better organization of a code and enable to reuse of this last one in an efficient way. In the context of block-based programming, Blockly [9] and Scratch [20] gives the possibility to create functions, by passing arguments to the body of the function, similarly to text based programming. This approach is based on a top-down approach (the user needs to know first what the function needs to do), requiring a fairly good level of expertise of the user. In Sect. 3.1, we will present a new, bottom-up approach, enabling the user to more easily create functions/skills from the body of a function.

More generally, our focus lies on providing interfaces that are not only *easy to use*, but also *easy to learn*. It has been observed that if the introduction of cobots in manufacturing environments can improve the quality of activities and enhance the significance of workers' role, reskilling is needed [16]. In this context, our work aims to bridge the gap between intuitiveness and empowerment by exploring user-centered methods to enable greater customization and autonomy in robot programming, ultimately fostering a more adaptable and efficient human-robot collaboration.

3   An Intuitive Robotic Interface

We believe that the desired empowerment of the production workers can be achieved by designing an interface that enables them to develop a better understanding of the system and, consequently, a feeling of control over the machine. In order to achieve this, an interface is needed that is easy to take in hand, but that also fosters the learning to acquire the needed competencies to fully leverage the flexibility of the system. Indeed, an interface emphasizing intuitiveness may typically trade-off flexibility to increase the worker's autonomy, while an interface offering too many possibilities will be difficult to handle for beginners. To overcome this trade-off, we propose an adaptive interface that takes in account the users' skills and needs, but also tutorials to allow them to gain the skills needed to use the more advanced functionalities.

Our adaptive interface is based on a block-based approach, where blocks can be combined to create complex behaviors. Different levels of blocks are defined that correspond to different types of users (normal, intermediary, advanced), which allow us to easily adapt the interface to the user needs. The high-level blocks are based on natural language and provide a very intuitive interface, while the lower level blocks reflect the robot commands and thus provide a flexibility similar to typed languages, but without the burden of the syntax. An intermediate layer, based on the concept of skills, allow for the smooth transition between the high and the low-level layers.

In addition, a collection of tutorial was developed to foster learning-by-doing and upskilling of the users and to teach them progressively the different functionalities of the interface, as well as some programming concepts.

In the following subsections, the concept and the implementation of the interface and the tutorials are explained in more details.

3.1   A New Block-Based Programming Interface: PrograBlock

One of the main problems faced by computer programming learners is the syntax of the programming language. To simplify the programming approach and remove the complexity of syntax, tools like Blockly [40] and Scratch [26] have been developed, both of which use block-based programming interfaces. Deeply inspired by this programming paradigm, we have developed a new block-based interface named *PrograBlock* tailored to the specific needs of robot programming in industrial settings. The user can choose a block from a library, drag and drop it in the programming area, and by connecting the different blocks together, can create a variety of programs. The different parameters can be changed directly within the block itself. Loops and if-else conditions are implemented the same way Blockly or Scratch does by wrapping blocks to be repeated, providing control over the program flow (see Fig. 1).

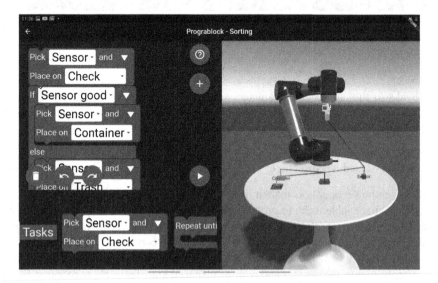

Fig. 1. Prograblock interface including a programming area (top left) and a library of blocks (bottom left), with the 3D simulation (right).

The biggest difference with other block-based programming interface (Blockly, Scratch, etc.) is the simplification of the creation of new blocks: when a new functionality is created through a program (Fig. 2a), the user has the possibility to create a block out of it. Parameters specifying the program functionality can then be chosen by the user (Fig. 2b) to appear as block parameters, in such a way that less important parameters are hidden within the newly created block (Fig. 2c). The creation of new blocks is also possible in the framework Blockly, but the user has to use variables to achieve the passing of arguments, which was shown to be difficult for novices [13].

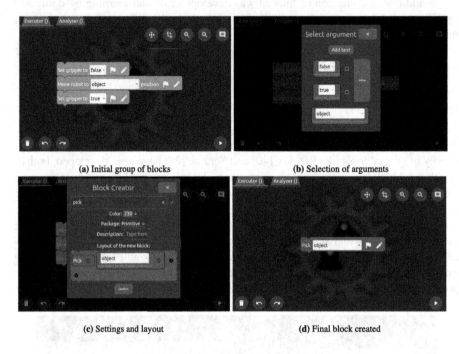

(a) Initial group of blocks   (b) Selection of arguments

(c) Settings and layout   (d) Final block created

Fig. 2. Simplified block creator.

Thanks to this approach, parameters such as the objects to interact with can be parameterized, enabling the implementation of more abstract blocks that can be easily used by non-expert users.

3.2   A Skill-Based Architecture

In order to empower operators in their interaction with robots, a three-layer, block-based architecture that enable users to progressively gain control over the system was developed. There are three levels of blocks: tasks, skills and device primitives [24], examples of each level of blocks are illustrated on Fig. 3. Tasks correspond to the natural language that an operator would use with a colleague, while device primitives correspond to the capabilities of the devices and require advanced knowledge about robotics. Skills are object-oriented and serve as a communication bridge: they offer an intermediate language that can be used to describe the process steps in relation to the object being handled [32]. For example, the skill *Pick object* describes a strategy allowing the grasping of a specific object, being the parameter of the skill. New tasks can then be created by simply parameterizing and combining skills. All blocks can be parameterized and thus easily adapted to new situations.

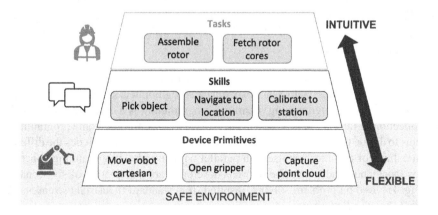

Fig. 3. Abstraction Layers.

By offering different levels of abstraction, such structure efficiently overcome the traditional flexibility-usability trade-off [32]. On one hand, it allows novices to easily adopt the high level functionalities, such as tasks and skills, to quickly create functioning programs, therefore lowering programming barriers [1]. On the other hand, experts keep the full control on the hardware capabilities thanks to the device primitives, enabling them to develop complex functionalities.

Another advantage of this architecture is the possibility to easily navigate between the different abstraction layers. It allows the user to progressively learn more complex functionalities according to their needs. In order to support this learning process, tutorials were developed that allow for the users to progressively learn new functionalities.

3.3 Virtual Environment

Complementary to the programming interface, a virtual environment (based on the game engine Unity) was developed to provide visual feedback to the user. The final application was deployed on a tablet, where the user could visualize the workspace with the robot, the camera and different objects available in the workspace. We took advantage of the virtual environment to show additional information about the state of the system, to improve the shared ground between the user and the machine and therefore the interaction. The user was able to rotate the view around the robot to show potentially hidden objects or to better visualize estimated trajectories (see Fig. 1, right).

A preview of the robot trajectory, represented by a blue line in the Fig. 1, was implemented to help the user to debug its program, and represent the trajectory of the tool center point of the robot. The difference of color along the trajectory indicate the different position over time: dark blue indicates the beginning of the trajectory and slowly

turn to light blue until reaching the end of the program. A collision detection functionality was as well developed to warn the user and allow her/him to correct the program. It
was indicated by a red cross at the location of the potential collision between the robot
and an object. By using a virtual environment, we intended to reduce the fear of the user
of breaking or being hurt by the robot and therefore to improve the learning conditions.
This hypothesis will be further tested in a future experiment.

3.4   Tutorials

Our skill-based architecture and block-based visual programming interface simplifies
the programming of the system, but inexperienced programmers still have to understand
the fundamentals of programming. Learning programming is a complex process [27],
so a collection of tutorials was developed to progressively introduce some programming
concepts to divide the intrinsic cognitive load [34] of the learner. It includes the different
functionalities of the interface itself, in parallel with complex programming concepts,
such as loops and conditions. The tutorials developed are a collection of six scenarios
(see Fig. 4) based on problem-solving, inspired from standard industrial use cases, like
Pick and Place or *Palletizing*.

The tutorials consist of four guided scenarios (see Fig. 4a, 4b, 4c and 4d) that teach
participants about the different functionalities of the interface, as well as some programming concepts, such as loops and conditions, that are important for the automation of
repetitive tasks. The four guided scenarios can be described as follows:

- **Pick and Place:** Teach how to create a simple program and how to parameterize it.
  In this scenario, the goal is to pick the cube, and place it on the green square.
- **Palletizing:** Teach the concept of loops.
  Here the goal is to pick and place cubes on the pallet until this last one is full.
- **Sorting**: Teach the concept of conditions.
  The goal here is to pick a cube, check the color of this last one and then place it on
  one of the corresponding square.
- **Pick Navigate and Place:** Teach the concept of task modification.
  If the user program this task the same way he did in the first tutorial 4a, a collision
  will occur with the obstacle (indicated with a red cross). To avoid the collision, the
  user has to modify the *Pick and Place* block and add a way-point between the *Pick*
  and the *Place* blocks. By doing so, the robot can successfully bring the cube on the
  green square.

In order for the user to test his/her progress and see how much was learned, two
more scenario are implemented where the user is not guided anymore and has to solve
the task by her/himself. The two unguided scenarios are the following:

- **Palletizing and Sorting:** Very similar to the tutorials and mainly tests the acquisition of the programming concept.
  Here the goal is to pick all the cubes, check their colors and place them on the corresponding pallet.
- **Palletizing and Sorting with Obstacle:** Same as Palletizing and sorting with an
  additional complexity due to the addition of an obstacle between the mirror and the
  cubes, forcing to re-program trajectories to avoid collisions.

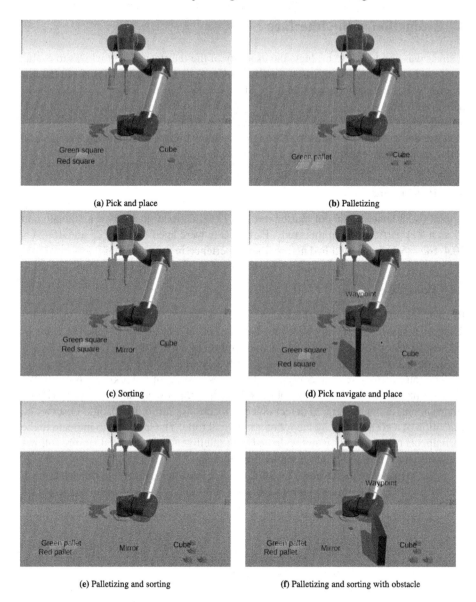

(a) Pick and place

(b) Palletizing

(c) Sorting

(d) Pick navigate and place

(e) Palletizing and sorting

(f) Palletizing and sorting with obstacle

Fig. 4. Tutorials.

The goal is the same than the previous exercise 4e: pick all the cubes, check their colors and place them on the corresponding pallet.

In order to test the relevance of our approach, the interface was tested with students in a between-group study. The details of the experiment are explained in the next section.

4   Evaluation of the Interface

A study was conducted to evaluate the usability of the interface. The goal was to evaluate if the four first guided tutorials were sufficient to enable the users to perform the last two test scenarios without external help. Since most of our users had never seen a real industrial robot before, we also tested if a small demonstration of a robot performing an industrial task would have an influence on the performance and the affective state (valence and arousal) of the users. During the demonstration, the challenges associated with robotics were explained, such as vision or picking.

4.1   Participants

A total of 58 business school master students (21 identified themselves as female and 37 as male) participated in this study. Participants were aged between 23 and 46 (M = 30.4, SD = 5.1) years, and had no previous experience in programming.

4.2   Procedure

Participants were randomly attributed in two experimental groups. In one group (introductory session), participants were introduced to a real robotic cell in function while in the second group (control group) no demonstration of the robot was offered and participants started the programming tutorial directly (see Fig. 5).

The introductory session consisted of the presentation of a working robot cell that was composed of a collaborative robot and a gripper, allowing an interaction with its environment, and a camera, to detect objects' locations. Participants could observe the execution of a sorting task by the robot arm in real time. The idea was to indicate to the participants that the robot is not endowed with intelligence, but instead simply follows the instructions previously programmed by a human.

Participants were then teamed in groups of two to enhance knowledge sharing. Each pair of participants completed a tutorial and a subsequent test session interacting (see Fig. 6).

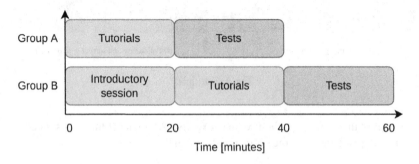

Fig. 5. Groups procedure.

4.3 Measures

The following indicators of performances were automatically logged by the system for each phase of the task: the **time** needed to successfully finish a task, the **number of modifications** (i.e., program changes) such as connecting or disconnecting blocks (increased number of modifications indicates reduced performance), the **number of trials** (i.e., executions of the program) before successfully finishing an exercise (large number of trials can be interpreted as low performance, but also as an exploratory behavior). In addition, the following subjective measures were assessed (for each participant individually):

System Usability Scale (SUS) [5] measures the usability of the interface allowing us to compare it with existing systems and future version of the interface. Over the years, the System Usability Scale has become an increasingly popular tool for measuring the usability of a wide range of products and systems. The SUS score is quick and easy to administer, making it a popular choice for evaluating usability in a variety of contexts. In the field of Human-Robot Interaction (HRI), some study [42] highlight the need and relevance of the usability assessment of robotic system interfaces.

Affective States Using Animated Visualization (AniSAM) [33] for the evaluation of valence and arousal of the user through the use of animated visualization. It is based on the circumplex model of affect described in [31] over time to give us information of the evolution of the user's emotions and detect potential design issues encountered during the use of the interface. The affective state was evaluated four times along the different tutorials (see Fig. 6).

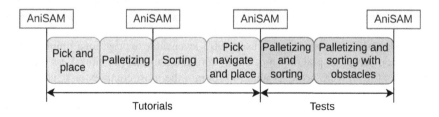

Fig. 6. Affective states evaluation procedure.

4.4 Data Analysis

To test the hypotheses regarding the behavioural data, two-sided t-test were calculated. For the analysis of affective states (AniSAM), repeated measures ANOVA (GLM) were calculated, with the first measure (baseline measure) entered as covariate.

5 Results

Analysis of **behavioural data** revealed that no differences were observed between the two groups in the guided tutorial phase regarding time spent on the tutorial, total number of trials and total number of modifications (see Table 1 for descriptive and inferential statistics). During the test session, no differences were observed between the two experimental groups for the first, simpler task. However, for the second, more complex task, significant differences were observed (see Test 2 in Table 1, completion time with p = 0.044 and modifications with p = 0.046), with participants who received an introductory session completing the task faster and making a lower number of modifications compared to the group not receiving the introductory session.

Table 1. Descriptive and inferential statistics.

	Without introduction M (SD)	With introduction M (SD)	Test statistics t(N), p, 95% CI
Tutorials			
Completion time	563 (166)	639 (258)	t(22)=0.86, p=0.40 [-260, 107]
Number of trials	6.1 (3.2)	8.1 (4.23)	t(22)=1.31, p=0.21 [-5.18, 1.18]
Modifications	55.67 (23.46)	60.67 (36.69)	t(22)=0.40, p=0.70 [-31.07, 21.07]
Test 1			
Completion time	359 (238)	386 (307)	t(23)=0.25, p=0.80 [-254, 199]
Number of trials	4 (3.51)	4.5 (4.38)	t(23)=-0.32, p=0.76 [-3.77, 2.77]
Modifications	43.85 (30.3)	46.83 (40.39)	t(23)=-0.21, p=0.84 [-32.73, 26.40]
Test 2			
Completion time	378 (129)	238 (37)	**t(9)=2.34, p=0.044 [4.46, 276.18]**
Number of trials	4.17 (3.76)	2.40 (1.34)	t(9)=0.99, p=0.35 [-2.27, 5.80]
Modifications	51 (28.23)	20.6 (4.29)	**t(5.27)=2.60, p=0.046 [0.48, 59.97]**

Regarding skill acquisition, most users (90%) were able to program a simple robotic tasks by themselves despite the short duration of the tutorials (20 min). Less than half of the users (38%) were however able to program the most complex task, potentially because of the time limitation.

The **usability** assessment of the system resulted in a SUS-score [5] of 71.5 (SD=12.3) which can be considered to be between good and excellent in terms of adjective ratings [2]. Statistical analysis comparing the two experimental groups indicates very small mean-differences with no effect of significance ($t(40) = 0.31$, $p = 0.76$, $d = 0.1$).

Analysis of participants' affective state over the different phases of the experimental study revealed higher levels of **arousal** for participants in the introductory session group compared to participants not receiving an introduction ($F(1, 20) = 4.76$, $p = 0.041$, $\eta^2 = 0.19$; see Fig. 7a). The evolution of the valence over time ($F(2, 40) = 2.82$, $p = 0.072$, $\eta^2 = 0.12$) and the interaction (introductory session x time) did not reach significance level ($F < 1$).

With regard to **valence**, data analysis revealed that the effect of the experimental manipulation was not significant ($F(1, 20) = 2.42$, $p = 0.14$, $\eta^2 = 0.11$; see Fig. 7b) while the effect of time was significant ($F(2, 40) = 5.74$, $p = 0.006$, $\eta^2 = 0.22$). Sidak-corrected pairwise comparisons (statistical procedure for comparing multiple groups, considering the issue of multiple comparisons) however indicated no significant differences between the three measurement points. Furthermore, the interaction (introductory session x time) did not reach significance level ($F(2, 40)=1.05$, $p=0.36$, $\eta^2=0.05$).

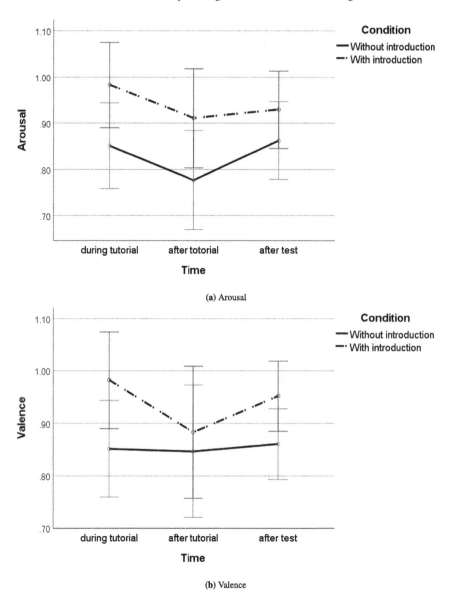

(a) Arousal

(b) Valence

Fig. 7. Evolution of affective states over time and experimental conditions.

6   Discussion

The findings indicate that the majority of participants (90%) effectively programmed the simple task (Fig. 4e), demonstrating the interface's user-friendliness and the successful acquisition of necessary programming skills through the tutorials by the users.

An important findings from this study relate to the effect of the experimental manipulation on the performance data in the test tasks (Fig. 4e and 4f). While no effect of the introductory session on the (easier) first task was observed, participants performed better in the (difficult) second task if they participated in the introductory session. In the first test task, the goal of the exercise was to palletize several cubes on different pallets. In the second test task, an obstacle had to be avoided by the robot arm while palletizing cubes. Most participants successfully programmed the robot to avoid the added obstacle between pick-up and placement areas using a waypoint. However, a significant amount of them had difficulties realizing that this avoidance procedure was also needed on the way back of the robot arm to the pick-up area because of the repetition of the pick-up and placement behavior inherent to the palletizing task. The percentage of participant who had the time to finish this second test task being relatively low (38%), exploring the performances without time restriction could bring even more information about this finding.

The observation that the group who followed the introductory session displayed better performance in this test may be a consequence of a better understanding of the way how robots work. Being machines, robots follow 'blindly' a list of actions defined (programmed) by a human and are not able to 'understand' contextual information. If one considers the robot endowed with information contextualization capacity, one would expect the robot to avoid the obstacle on both ways; while a clearer understanding that the robot blindly follows a list of instructions leads to correctly solving the task. This indicates that following the introductory session influences the mental model [17] of participants, which allows to predict or explain a system's behavior. In other words, the results suggest that the user's mental model of the robot plays an important role in the learning performance of robot programming.

Participants receiving the introductory session showed a higher level of arousal compared to the control group. Although the origin of this effect can only be speculated, it is possible that experiencing a real robot arm in action is related to this increased arousal, which might be linked with an increased level of experienced stress. It could be that possible negative consequences of this stressful experience were compensated by the positive effects of better understanding of the way how robots work. Further research is needed to replicate this result and determine its origin.

In a similar vein, it is difficult to interpret the change in the valence measurement because of the non-significant post-hoc comparisons. Further studies with more power are needed here to allow for clearer statements regarding the affective consequences of such introductory sessions.

Limitations of this study include the rather small sample size and the programming being conducted in groups of two. Although group evaluations are a sometimes used method in the field of interface development [3,8], group effects may influence the results in this study. A replication of these results in a single study with more power is therefore planned.

A current limitation of the study is its focus on assessing the system interface's immediate intuitiveness and the effect of user training on efficient utilization. Indeed, this study involves novices recruited from a master's program, while the target demographic for an end-user product based on this system is likely to be made up of blue-collar workers who are heavily invested in using the system efficiently while at work for an extended period of time. These employees will likely take the time to become used to the technology and are mostly focused on workflow issues unique to their production activities. They place more focus on the system's medium to long term integration into the production cycle than on how intuitive or simple it is to use right now. However, the assessment of the usability of the system is still relevant to promote the acceptance of the technology, since a user-friendly and well-designed system reduces the learning curve, minimizes user errors, and ultimately enhances user confidence, which are all key factors that contribute to the successful adoption and utilization of the technology. A future experiment including our target users in industrial settings is already planned and will be the subject of a future publication.

In summary, this study showed interesting results indicating a positive impact of our newly developed interface on robotic learning. An initiation with real robots seems to enhance learning outcomes by fostering a deeper comprehension of the situation, including mental models and situation awareness. However, it is important to note that this immersive approach could also lead to increase arousal levels, potentially indicating an increase of stress. As predicted when developing the virtual environment of the robotic system (see Sect. 3.3), being exposed to the real robot can be associated with an increase in arousal and stress. It seems that the positive effect of increased situational understanding was able to compensate for the possible negative consequences of experiencing additional stress due to exposure to real robots. The question arises whether it is possible to facilitate the positive effects of the presentation of the robot without additional stress experience - a question that should be addressed in future studies.

Altogether, this study show encouraging results on our journey to make robotics programming more accessible for novices, although test with our target users are still needed.

7   Future Work

Using a virtual environment to learn robot programming has been favoured for better learning performances, especially allowing to bypass the fear of breaking the system or being hurt by the robotic arm [18], more especially with the close interaction allowed with cobots. The results presented here suggest that working with the real functional robot may instead bring more tangibility during the interaction and making programming easier to learn. Future studies are planned to verify this hypothesis.

It is important to highlight that the current focus of the tutorials is on comprehending programming concepts. However, based on our findings, it is evident that additional tutorials will be necessary to help users develop a more comprehensive understanding of how the robot functions. Developing effective programming interfaces requires a deep understanding of the factors that influence learning and performance, particularly in relation to novice programmers who often face barriers known as the Gulf of Execution and Evaluation (GEE) [22]. In programming the GEE can be seen as the challenge of converting intentions into code and interpreting input from the programming environment [1]. But utilizing robots as a learning tool appears to be an effective approach for beginners to grasp fundamental programming concepts [19]. Overcoming the

GEE is a common struggle for inexperienced programmers. Therefore, the construction of mental models becomes essential in surmounting these barriers, as learners' internal representations of programming concepts and environments can significantly assist them in bridging the GEE more effectively and honing their programming skills [17].

At the time of the study, the interface was still a prototype and we decided to test it first with students to gain insights on its potential and limitations before testing it with our target users. We are now working with a company to integrate our system to their shop floor and we will start testing it with the employees in the coming months. The goal of the project is to incrementally improve the interface based on their feedback.

8   Conclusion

Our results indicate that integrating a no-code, block-based interface with problem-oriented tutorials and practical demonstrations involving actual robots can empower inexperienced users to independently program a robot while enhancing their abilities.

We understand empowerment not only as skill acquisition, but also as the development of a feeling of control over the machine. This shift of paradigm led us to the development of a new block-based language integrated with robotic skills, enhanced with a collection of problem-based tutorials enabling the empowerment the user. While the results of the study are promising, further research is needed to better understand the key factors of worker empowerment. Indeed, if clear methodologies are available for usability and user experience, tools for designing empowering interfaces are still missing [11].

We believe that designing interfaces that will improve worker independence will be key in the future. Indeed, there is a common agreement in the literature that humans will remain central to manufacturing in the next decades [21]. Contrarily to the common vision of future workers, referred to as *Operators 4.0*, who are empowered by technologies like artificial intelligence, augmented reality, and robotics to enhance their performance and efficiency, leading to the concept of a *Super Operator* [29], our focus in this work is on identifying the key factors necessary to enable workers to become active programmers, as coined in Taylor's work [36] as *Makers 1.0*. The goal is to give back the control of the production means to the workers so that they can fully leverage their knowledge of the customer needs, the processes and the tools to implement innovative automation solutions [36].

Acknowledgements. This study was financed by the Swiss National Science Foundation (SNSF) as part of the National Research Program NRP77 Digital Transformation, project no. 187298.

References

1. Andrew, J.K., Myers, B.A., Aung, H.H.: Six learning barriers in end-user programming systems. In: 2004 IEEE Symposium on Visual Languages - Human Centric Computing, pp. 199–206 (2004). https://doi.org/10.1109/VLHCC.2004.47
2. Bangor, A., Kortum, P., Miller, J.: Determining what individual SUS scores mean: Adding an adjective rating scale (2009). https://slsp-bfh.primo.exlibrisgroup.com

3. Battarbee, K.: Defining co-experience. In: Proceedings of the 2003 international conference on Designing pleasurable products and interfaces, pp. 109–113. DPPI 2003, Association for Computing Machinery, New York, NY, USA (2003). https://doi.org/10.1145/782896.782923

4. Bogue, R.: Europe continues to lead the way in the collaborative robot business. Ind. Robot Int. J. **43**(1), 6–11 (2016). https://doi.org/10.1108/IR-10-2015-0195

5. Brooke, J.: SUS: A 'Quick and Dirty' Usability Scale, pp. 207-212. CRC Press (1996). https://doi.org/10.1201/9781498710411-35, https://www.taylorfrancis.com/

6. Digmayer, C., Jakobs, E.M.: Employee empowerment in the context of domain-specific risks in Industry 4.0. In: 2018 IEEE International Professional Communication Conference (Pro-Comm), pp. 125–133 (2018). https://doi.org/10.1109/ProComm.2018.00034, iSSN: 2158-1002

7. Fantini, P., Pinzone, M., Taisch, M.: Placing the operator at the centre of Industry 4.0 design: modelling and assessing human activities within cyber-physical systems. Comput. Ind. Eng, **139**, 105058 (2020). https://doi.org/10.1016/j.cie.2018.01.025, https://www.sciencedirect.com/science/article/pii/S0360835218300329

8. Forlizzi, J., Battarbee, K.: Understanding experience in interactive systems. In: Proceedings of the 5th Conference on Designing Interactive Systems: Processes, Practices, Methods, and Techniques, pp. 261–268. DIS 2004. Association for Computing Machinery, New York, NY, USA (2004). https://doi.org/10.1145/1013115.1013152

9. Fraser, N.: Ten things we've learned from Blockly. In: 2015 IEEE Blocks and Beyond Workshop (Blocks and Beyond), pp. 49–50 (2015). https://doi.org/10.1109/BLOCKS.2015.7369000

10. Frohm, J., Lindström, V., Winroth, M., Stahre, J.: The industry's view on automation in manufacturing. IFAC Proc. Vol. **39**(4), 453–458 (2006). https://doi.org/10.3182/20060522-3-FR-2904.00073, https://www.sciencedirect.com/science/article/pii/S1474667015330925

11. Gallula, D., Ronen, H., Shichel, I., Katz, A.: User empowering design: expanding the users' hierarchy of needs. In: Proceedings of the 6th International Conference on Computer-Human Interaction Research and Applications, pp. 201–208. SCITEPRESS - Science and Technology Publications, Valletta, Malta (2022). https://doi.org/10.5220/0011552500003323, https://www.scitepress.org/DigitalLibrary/Link.aspx?doi=10.5220/0011552500003323

12. Ginat, D.: On novice loop boundaries and range conceptions. Comput. Sci. Educ. **14**(3), 165–181 (2004). https://doi.org/10.1080/0899340042000302709

13. Grover, S., Basu, S.: Measuring student learning in introductory block-based programming: examining misconceptions of loops, variables, and boolean logic. In: Proceedings of the 2017 ACM SIGCSE Technical Symposium on Computer Science Education, pp. 267–272. SIGCSE 2017. Association for Computing Machinery, New York, NY, USA (2017). https://doi.org/10.1145/3017680.3017723

14. Jain, A., Jain, P., Chan, F.T., Singh, S.: A review on manufacturing flexibility. Int. J. Prod. Res. **51**(19), 5946–5970 (2013). https://doi.org/10.1080/00207543.2013.824627

15. Kaasinen, E., et al.: Empowering and engaging industrial workers with Operator 4.0 solutions. Comput. Ind. Eng. **139**, 105678 (2020). https://doi.org/10.1016/j.cie.2019.01.052, https://www.sciencedirect.com/science/article/pii/S036083521930066X

16. Kadir, B.A., Broberg, O.: Human well-being and system performance in the transition to industry 4.0. Int. J. Ind. Ergon. **76**, 102936 (2020)

17. Kieras, D.E., Bovair, S.: The role of a mental model in learning to operate a device. Cogn. Sci. **8**(3), 255–273 (1984). https://doi.org/10.1016/S0364-0213(84)80003-8, https://www.sciencedirect.com/science/article/pii/S0364021384800038

18. Kulić, D., Croft, E.: Pre-collision safety strategies for human-robot interaction. Auton. Robot. **22**(2), 149–164 (2007). https://doi.org/10.1007/s10514-006-9009-4

19. Major, L., Kyriacou, T., Brereton, O.P.: Systematic literature review: teaching novices programming using robots. IET Softw. **6**(6), 502–513 (2012). https://doi.org/10.1049/iet-sen.2011.0125, https://digital-library.theiet.org/content/journals/10.1049/iet-sen.2011.0125
20. Maloney, J., Burd, L., Kafai, Y., Rusk, N., Silverman, B., Resnick, M.: Scratch: a sneak preview [education]. In: Proceedings. Second International Conference on Creating, Connecting and Collaborating through Computing, 2004, pp. 104–109 (2004). https://doi.org/10.1109/C5.2004.1314376
21. Nelles, J., Kuz, S., Mertens, A., Schlick, C.M.: Human-centered design of assistance systems for production planning and control: the role of the human in Industry 4.0. In: 2016 IEEE International Conference on Industrial Technology (ICIT), pp. 2099–2104 (2016). https://doi.org/10.1109/ICIT.2016.7475093
22. Norman, D.A.: The Design of Everyday Things. Basic Books, New York, revised and expanded edition edn (2013)
23. Noroozi, A., Khakzad, N., Khan, F., MacKinnon, S., Abbassi, R.: The role of human error in risk analysis: application to pre- and post-maintenance procedures of process facilities. Reliab. Eng. Syst. Safety **119**, 251–258 (2013). https://doi.org/10.1016/j.ress.2013.06.038, https://www.sciencedirect.com/science/article/pii/S0951832013002032
24. Pedersen, M.R., et al.: Robot skills for manufacturing: From concept to industrial deployment. Robot. Comput. Integrated Manuf. **37**, 282–291 (2016). https://doi.org/10.1016/j.rcim.2015.04.002, https://www.sciencedirect.com/science/article/pii/S0736584515000575
25. Ras, E., Wild, F., Stahl, C., Baudet, A.: Bridging the skills gap of workers in Industry 4.0 by human performance augmentation tools: challenges and roadmap. In: Proceedings of the 10th International Conference on PErvasive Technologies Related to Assistive Environments, pp. 428–432. PETRA 2017. Association for Computing Machinery, New York, NY, USA (2017). https://doi.org/10.1145/3056540.3076192, https://dl.acm.org/doi/10.1145/3056540.3076192
26. Resnick, M., et al.: Scratch: programming for all. Commun. ACM **52**(11), 60–67 (2009). https://doi.org/10.1145/1592761.1592779
27. Robins, A., Rountree, J., Rountree, N.: Learning and teaching programming: a review and discussion. Comp. Sci. Educ. **13**(2), 137–172 (2003). https://doi.org/10.1076/csed.13.2.137.14200
28. Rokis, K., Kirikova, M.: Challenges of low-code/no-code software development: a literature review. In: Nazaruka, E., Sandkuhl, K., Seigerroth, U. (eds.) Perspectives in Business Informatics Research. LNBIP, pp. 3–17. Springer, Cham (2022). https://doi.org/10.1007/978-3-031-16947-2_1
29. Romero, D., Bernus, P., Noran, O., Stahre, J., Fast-Berglund, A.: The Operator 4.0: human cyber-physical systems & adaptive automation towards human-automation symbiosis work systems. In: Nääs, I., Vendrametto, O., Mendes Reis, J., Gonçalves, R.F., Silva, M.T., von Cieminski, G., Kiritsis, D. (eds.) Advances in Production Management Systems. Initiatives for a Sustainable World. IFIP Advances in Information and Communication Technology, pp. 677–686. Springer, Cham (2016). https://doi.org/10.1007/978-3-319-51133-7_80
30. Romero, D., Stahre, J., Taisch, M.: The Operator 4.0: towards socially sustainable factories of the future. Comp. Ind. Eng. **139**, 106128 (2020). https://doi.org/10.1016/j.cie.2019.106128, https://www.sciencedirect.com/science/article/pii/S0360835219305972
31. Russell, J.A.: A circumplex model of affect. J. Pers. Soc. Psychol. **39**(6), 1161–1178 (1980). https://doi.org/10.1037/h0077714. place: US Publisher: American Psychological Association
32. Schou, C., Andersen, R.S., Chrysostomou, D., Bøgh, S., Madsen, O.: Skill-based instruction of collaborative robots in industrial settings. Robot. Comp. Integrated Manuf. **53**, 72–80 (2018). https://doi.org/10.1016/j.rcim.2018.03.008, https://linkinghub.elsevier.com/retrieve/pii/S0736584516301910

33. Sonderegger, A., Heyden, K., Chavaillaz, A., Sauer, J.: AniSAM & AniAvatar: animated visualizations of affective states. In: Proceedings of the 2016 CHI Conference on Human Factors in Computing Systems, p. 4837 (2016). https://doi.org/10.1145/2858036.2858365

34. Sweller, J.: Element interactivity and intrinsic, extraneous, and germane cognitive load. Educ. Psychol. Rev. **22**(2), 123–138 (2010). https://doi.org/10.1007/s10648-010-9128-5

35. Tan, Q., Tong, Y., Wu, S., Li, D.: Anthropocentric approach for smart assembly: integration and collaboration. J. Robot. **2019**, e3146782 (2019). https://doi.org/10.1155/2019/3146782, https://www.hindawi.com/journals/jr/2019/3146782/

36. Taylor, M.P., Boxall, P., Chen, J.J.J., Xu, X., Liew, A., Adeniji, A.: Operator 4.0 or Maker 1.0? Exploring the implications of Industrie 4.0 for innovation, safety and quality of work in small economies and enterprises. Comp. Ind. Eng **139**, 105486 (2020). https://doi.org/10.1016/j.cie.2018.10.047, https://www.sciencedirect.com/science/article/pii/S0360835218305278

37. Terveen, L.G.: Overview of human-computer collaboration. Knowl. Based Syst. **8**(2), 67–81 (1995). https://doi.org/10.1016/0950-7051(95)98369-H, https://www.sciencedirect.com/science/article/pii/095070519598369H

38. Villani, V., Pini, F., Leali, F., Secchi, C.: Survey on human-robot collaboration in industrial settings: safety, intuitive interfaces and applications. Mechatronics **55**, 248–266 (2018). https://doi.org/10.1016/j.mechatronics.2018.02.009, https://linkinghub.elsevier.com/retrieve/pii/S0957415818300321

39. Weintrop, D., Afzal, A., Salac, J., Francis, P., Li, B., Shepherd, D.C., Franklin, D.: Evaluating CoBlox: a comparative study of robotics programming environments for adult novices. In: Proceedings of the 2018 CHI Conference on Human Factors in Computing Systems, pp. 1–12. CHI 2018. Association for Computing Machinery, New York, NY, USA (2018). https://doi.org/10.1145/3173574.3173940

40. Weintrop, D., Shepherd, D.C., Francis, P., Franklin, D.: Blockly goes to work: Block-based programming for industrial robots. In: 2017 IEEE Blocks and Beyond Workshop (B&B), pp. 29–36 (2017). https://doi.org/10.1109/BLOCKS.2017.8120406

41. Wilson, H.J., Daugherty, P.R.: Collaborative Intelligence: Humans and AI Are Joining Forces. Harvard Business Review (2018)

42. Yanco, H.A., Drury, J.L., Scholtz, J.: Beyond usability evaluation: analysis of human-robot interaction at a major robotics competition. Hum.-Comp. Interact. **19**(1–2), 117–149 (2004). https://doi.org/10.1080/07370024.2004.9667342, https://www.tandfonline.com/doi/abs/10.1080/07370024.2004.9667342

Mobile Gaming EMG-Based Brain Computer Interface

Abdulaziz Althekair, Mohanned Odeh, Mohammad AlBayaa, Marwa Sharawi$^{(\boxtimes)}$ ⓘ,
and Iyad Abu Doush ⓘ

College of Engineering and Applied Sciences, American University of Kuwait, Salmiyah,
Kuwait
{S00032563,S00045606,S00050746,mamostafa,idoush}@auk.edu.kw

Abstract. Brain Computer Interface (BCI) has demonstrated significant effectiveness in optimizing the usability of mobile applications, particularly in the realm of mobile gaming. With the increasing popularity of video games, they offer an opportune platform for exploring novel control interfaces for mobile devices. This paper introduces the Mobile Gaming Electromyography (EMG)-Based Brain Computer Interface (MGaming EMG-BCI), which aims to enhance the user experience and address challenges related to input methods, gestures, accessibility, and inclusivity associated with conventional mobile device usage in mobile gaming. The system improves device usability by offering a new input method and gestures that players can utilize to interact with the game without the requirement of maintaining a fixed posture alleviating neck stiffness commonly associated with GUI-based mobile gaming. This expands the accessibility of games for different groups of players. Furthermore, it opens up opportunities for game developers to innovate and explore new possibilities in game design. The proposed interface integrates a BCI system with a game using EMG signaling, enabling real-time communication between the BCI and the game through a database. This integration allows users to interact with the game in a handsfree manner, alleviating the need for physical touch input. The results of this study indicate that the proposed BCI Mobile Gaming Interface has the potential to serve as a universal control scheme that can be seamlessly applied to a diverse range of games.

Keywords: Brain Computer Interface (BCI) · User interface · Electromyography (EMG) · Mobile gaming

1 Introduction

Brain Computer Interface (BCI) utilizes electromyography (EMG) as an input method to effectively control electronic devices in a mobile setting [1]. The objective is to optimize the performance of the classical graphical user interfaces (GUI) while addressing the neck strain issues caused by the mobile phone usage postures and gestures [5]. This work eliminates the constant need for physically holding the mobile device while using it. Moreover, it offers users an exciting and immersive gaming experience by introducing a new control scheme. The BCI technology and EMG are employed to translate EMG activity signals into control actions for mobile devices. It tests and evaluates the

ⓒ The Author(s), under exclusive license to Springer Nature Switzerland AG 2023
H. P. da Silva and P. Cipresso (Eds.): CHIRA 2023, CCIS 1996, pp. 40–52, 2023.
https://doi.org/10.1007/978-3-031-49425-3_3

usage of tap-style games for a mobile device by using OpenBCI headset equipped with a Cyton board and handled through Firebase Realtime database to control the game actions.

2   Related Work

This section presents some related literatures for BCI systems developments for mobile devices, and BCI systems developments for gaming.

2.1   Brain Computer Interface for Mobile Device

Many researchers have addressed the utilization of Brain Computer Interface (BCI) technology in the context of mobile devices. However, most of the existing research are mainly focus on diverse application domains rather than exploring BCI utilization for mobile gaming. Martínez-Cagigal, 2018 introduces the application of BCI technology in mobile devices. The solution controls a mobile phone utilizing the OpenBCI unit. The researchers narrowed down their scope to Twitter and Telegram applications, wherein the BCI headset was utilized to manipulate specific functionalities of these social media platforms, such as retweeting and liking tweets. To ensure the effectiveness of this approach, the researchers conducted a comprehensive evaluation of the proposed application involving multiple participants. The test cases were designed to validate the functionality of the application using brainwave data from more than one individual. The evaluation tasks were divided into three distinct parts, including toggling between the two apps, retweeting a tweet, and composing a new tweet. Additional applications leveraging the Brain Computer Interface (BCI) system have been developed for mobile phones. A notable example is an application that enables users to accept or reject incoming calls through the act of winking. This functionality is achieved using a comparable EMG detection method, which aligns with the primary focus of the current research [2]. While most BCI-based applications for mobile phones have centered around basic service tasks, our study aims to push the boundaries by investigating the potential of BCI technology in the context of tap-style mobile gaming. By exploring this novel avenue, we seek to expand the scope of BCI technology and its application possibilities.

2.2   Brain Computer Interface for Gaming

The Brain-Computer Interface system is greatly related to the game application. Scholars have been using it as an application to test, validate, and adjust the user adaptation with the BCI. It has been utilized for various applications, ranging from medical tests to entertainment [4]. BCI games have also undergone testing with different enhancements and modifications to facilitate gameplaying. A notable example is the use of AI to assist users in controlling the BCI system while playing Mahjong, which has shown successful results [6]. One group focused on employing BCI technology to control a Tetris game (Piers et al., 2011) and explored its potential benefits for assisting children with ADHD. However, BCI is not solely intended for individuals who are neurologically atypical. Studies have been conducted to determine the most effective utilization of BCI systems in gaming, ensuring that a broader audience can appreciate its merits and have an enjoyable experience [8]. Research has also been carried out to validate the use of BCI in healthy users, enhancing their gaming experience and treating the use of BCI as comparable to other procedural skills [9]. Furthermore, studies have indicated that while the gaming experience with BCI may not be as proficient as using a keyboard, the control provided by BCI is considered interesting, and many participants find the experience less monotonous [10]. BCI also offers advantages in the realm of virtual reality (VR). Since VR already requires the use of a headset, it aligns well with BCI technology. Efforts have been made to develop a VR racing game that combines VR and BCI [11]. Another example of BCI in gaming involves playing a virtual Rubik's Cube using hand gestures and a combination of EMG and accelerometer readings [12]. Finally, it is worth noting that BCI is not limited to single-player games. A study was conducted to assess the effectiveness of BCI systems in multiplayer games, revealing that users can collaborate and synchronize their mental activities to achieve goals or compete against each other. The study employed a football game, and participants noted improved performance when playing together or against each other [13].

3   Methodology

The goal of our solution is to enrich the user experience, allowing for new possibilities in gaming and to ease the strain of the user on their body from being seated in improper positions during gaming sessions. We developed a use of the BCI system in where a tap-style game would be playable with a simple action of blinking or winking. The application itself was developed in Unity, the control scheme runs off a python script and uses the OpenBCI GUI, paired with a Firebase Realtime Database to oversee the variables and process the commands onto the phone. This project enhances the user experience, providing new possibilities in gaming while improving the physical strain placed on users due to improper seating positions during gaming sessions. Our approach adapts the Brain Computer Interface (BCI) system to enable the playability of a tap-style game through a simple action like blinking or winking.

3.1   Mobile Gaming BCI Development

OpenBCI Interface. The Brain Computer Interface (BCI) headset utilized in this study for capturing EMG signals from the brain provided by OpenBCI. For the game application, any headset capable of reading eyeblink EMG with two channels will suffice. Therefore, both the Ultracortex and headband options can be used for our mobile application, providing flexibility in terms of user budget.

OpenBCI GUI is employed in this research, an open-source software, to facilitate data reading. This software not only enables us to access the acquired data but also allows for seamless streaming of the data using the Laboratory Streaming Layer (LSL) into our Python script. This Python script will handle all aspects of the control scheme execution for the game.

Python Script. The Python script receives the data stream transmitted by the LSL stream of the OpenBCI GUI. Once the stream is obtained, the script proceeds to calculate the EMG thresholds derived from the stream. The threshold calculation is fundamental for detecting EMG spikes originating from the electrode placed near the user's eye. To avoid double inputs in the game, the script ensures that enough time has elapsed since the previous blink or wink. This precautionary measure is implemented to ensure that the user's experience remains unaffected by any unintended negative impacts caused by erroneous input signals.

Firebase Database. The Firebase Database acts as an integral part of the system as it serves as a link to the Python script running on the PC and the mobile device. This connection is established by the Python script receiving the data stream and processing the EMG spikes and time elapsed thresholds. When the user indicates their intention to tap on the screen through an eye blink, the Python script updates a Realtime database hosted by Firebase with a new variable. Throughout the execution of the game, it continuously listens for these updates. This seamless integration with the Firebase Realtime database ensures efficient communication and synchronization between the Python script and the mobile device, facilitating smooth gameplay.

Game Development. The developed game is a tap-style game, where the player's avatar performs a jump upon executing a tap. However, in the context of our BCI system, the jump action is triggered when the player blinks or winks. This unique control scheme adds an innovative twist to the gameplay mechanics. The objective of the game is to achieve a high score, as there is no specific end goal. The score is calculated each time the player's avatar successfully jumps over an obstacle. The game offers a continuous challenge for players to strive for higher scores, fostering a sense of competition and improvement.

3.2   Participants

A total of five participants were involved in the evaluation of the proposed system. These participants were young adults residing in Kuwait, with educational backgrounds ranging from high school to university level. It is noteworthy that all participants possessed fluency in either English or Arabic. Furthermore, it is important to highlight that all participants were neurotypical, indicating that they did not have any neurological conditions or disorders that could potentially impact their cognitive or motor functions.

3.3   Evaluation Procedure

Tasks. For the testing trials, users will be requested to engage in playing a mobile game. This game incorporates a movable object that is expected to be controlled through deliberate actions, such as eye blinks. The rules entail intermittently executing unintentional actions, such as adjusting the seated position. Meanwhile, participants will be instructed to simultaneously perform intentional actions. The goal is to manipulate the object solely through intentional actions, maintaining a consistent streak of successful attempts for a specific number of consecutive times. The precise number of attempts required will be determined after analyzing user behavior. Initially, our objective revolves around successfully navigating through three obstacles in a game inspired by Flappy Bird." The initial phase of evaluating our system involves establishing a set of standardized tasks that will be uniformly followed by all participants. The following tasks we utilized to assess the performance of the proposed system:

Task 1: The user is instructed to execute a normal jump action without any obstacles. This task ensures that the system is properly accepting and registering the user's input.

Task 2: The user is then requested to play the game with the objective of achieving a score of 3 or higher. If the user fails to reach this score within 10 attempts, they will proceed to the subsequent survey phase. These predefined tasks provide a consistent framework for evaluating the system's functionality and the user's performance. They allow for a systematic assessment of the system's responsiveness and the user's ability to interact with the game effectively.

Evaluation Process. The evaluation process begins with providing each participant a comprehensive demonstration of the system to ensure their familiarity with its operation. Following this, a verbal description of the project will be presented, including a disclosure regarding the potential discomfort associated with wearing the headset. Participants instructed to be seated, and the headset will be carefully positioned on the tester's head. Subsequently, they asked to perform a blink action to verify the correct placement of the headset and the successful capture of EMG data. Once it is confirmed that the EMG data is being accurately read and is usable, the game is launched for the tester. The objective for the tester is to achieve a score of 3 or higher within the game. Subsequently, participants are provided with a survey to gather their feedback. In cases where the tester fails to reach a score of 3 or higher after 10 attempts, they will also be directed to complete the survey.

4   Results

The outcomes will be assessed through a survey designed to gather user feedback regarding their perception of the system and the BCI device. Additionally, we will employ a metric to quantify the number of attempts needed to achieve a score of 3 or higher. Successfully attaining the target within a reasonable timeframe or experiencing difficulty in doing so will aid in assessing the user-friendliness of the system. This section encompasses a detailed discussion of the results obtained and concludes with the evaluation's conclusion.

4.1   MGaming EMG-BCI Version01

SUS Results. The SUS questionnaire is used to evaluate the system usability. The following table shows the 11 SUS questions used for the evaluation:

Six of the questions on the survey has a possible score using a five-level scale. The results are demonstrated in Fig. 1 below. Based on the results, 80% of the participants

Table 1. Survey Questionnaire.

No.	SUS Questions	Relevance to System Usability and future
Q1	I see myself using such device in the future	Measures the systems future viability
Q2	I was able to control the game easily	Tests the ease of use of the system
Q3	The device was easy to use	Tests the ease of use of the system
Q4	I was able to learn to use the device quickly	Tests the participant's receptiveness to learning the device
Q5	Have you ever used a device that lets you control devices through EMG before?	Tests the participant's familiarity with the device prior to experiment
Q6	Do you think this device could be used in our daily lives? If no, why?	Questioning the future possibilities of the system and device
Q7	I would purchase such a device in the future	Testing the economic feasibility of the system
Q8	I play video games regularly	Checking the participant's familiarity with usages for the system
Q9	What type of video game genre do you enjoy most?	Checking possible future genres to explore
Q10	What would you like to use the device for?	Measures the participant's future wants of the system
Q11	What could be improved?	Checking what the user wishes to make sure they enjoy the system

expressed their willingness to utilize such a device in the future. Among the respondents, 60% reported that the game was easily controllable, while 40% maintained a neutral stance on the matter. Regarding the ease of device use, 60% of the participants were neutral, citing concerns about its responsiveness to muscle movement and the sensitivity of blink detection. However, 80% of the participants found that the device could be quickly learned with some practice, while the remaining 20% remained neutral. These metrics indicate that most participants found both the game and the device easy to learn and adapt to, which is a positive outcome for the adoption of new technologies. Additionally, 60% of the participants expressed their willingness to purchase such a device in the future, contingent upon the price. Notably, all the participants in the study were regular video game players.

Regarding the responses to the open-ended questions, it was found that none of the participants had prior experience with this type of device before the initial survey. The majority of participants expressed their hesitation to incorporate the device into their daily lives at present, primarily citing a lack of available mobile applications or concerns about unintended muscle triggers activating the device. Participants had diverse preferences when it came to their usual choice of games, with no significant correlation observed between specific game genres and interest in the device.

The participants expressed a desire to see the device evolve for broader usage in daily life and expand its game library. One participant even suggested exploring its application in smart homes to facilitate household control. In terms of improvements, most participants highlighted the need to address device sensitivity and game speed. Adjustments to the threshold were recommended to ensure a smoother gaming experience for participants.

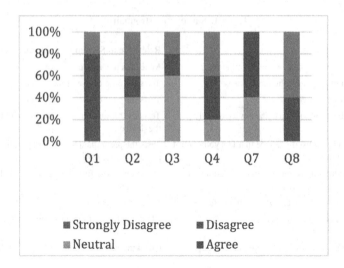

Fig. 1. MGaming EMG-BCI Version01-SUS Result.

Game Scoring. The concluding phase of our evaluation involved assessing the number of attempts required by each participant to achieve a score of three or higher. This metric was chosen as it provides a reliable measure to evaluate the system's consistency. Figure 2 illustrates the system first testing trial. This will be repeated up to 10 times to reach score 3.

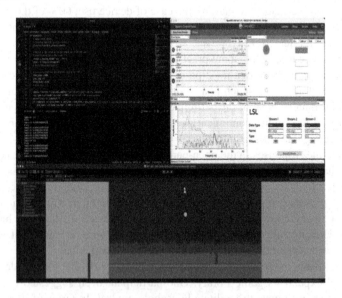

Fig. 2. MGaming EMG-BCI Version01 Testing.

To evaluate the participants' performance, it was necessary for them to achieve a score of three within a single play session. Testers closely monitored the participants to ensure their ability to reach this target score. In case the participants were unable to reach the score, the test was repeated for a maximum of 10 times. Notably, all participants successfully achieved the desired score within the 10-play limit. The number of attempts each participant needed can be found in Table 2 below.

Table 2. MGaming EMG-BCI Version01-Attempts needed for a score of three.

Participant	Attempts needed
1	2
2	3
3	1
4	2
5	2

The participants were able to reach the target score within a relatively short duration of time. This outcome reflects positively on the testing process, highlighting the user-friendly nature of the system and its ease of use. Figure 3 illustrates a successful scoring trial. Figure 4 shows that although participants could reach the required score after few trials, they still failed to go for further scoring.

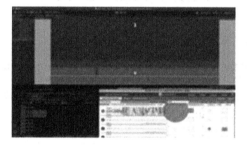

Fig. 3. MGaming EMG-BCI Version01 Scoring.

Fig. 4. MGaming EMG-BCI Version01 Game Over.

User Recommendations. Following the testing phase, participants provided their valuable feedback, which, when combined with the survey results, enabled us to identify key areas for improvement in order to enhance the user enjoyment. The majority of suggestions primarily revolved around improving the system's responsiveness. Based on the testers' recommendations, the following improvements were suggested: Firstly, increasing the speed of the game, as participants felt it was somewhat sluggish. Secondly, reducing the spacing between jumps in the game. Lastly, enhancing the responsiveness of the blink detection mechanism. Additionally, it was noted that most participants expressed a desire for the system to have broader applications beyond just gaming, indicating a potential for diversifying its functionality. These valuable insights provided by the participants and testers will guide us in refining and optimizing the system to address their concerns and create a more satisfying user experience.

4.2 MGaming EMG-BCI Version02

After analyzing the feedback provided by participants in the initial round of testing, certain adjustments were implemented to enhance the system. Specifically, changes were made to the thresholds of the system as well as the game speed. To improve overall player enjoyment, the game was made slightly faster, allowing participants to experience a more engaging gameplay. Moreover, the blink threshold was increased, resulting in a reduced sensitivity to detect blinks. This modification aimed to enhance the participants' perception of the game's responsiveness. Additionally, the time threshold utilized for spacing out jumps was lowered, enabling users to execute jumps more rapidly, particularly in the event of mistimed jumps. These modifications were implemented based on the participants' feedback to ensure an improved user experience and address their concerns effectively.

SUS Results. Using the SUS questionnaire applied in the initial testing (Table 1) and following the same procedure mentioned before we gathered the responses presented in Fig. 5, the system usability will be evaluated. The following table shows the 11 SUS questions used for the evaluation:

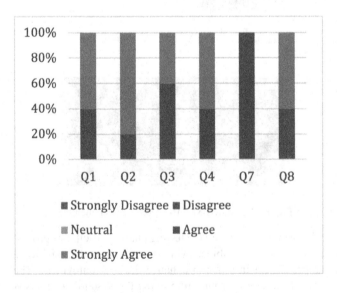

Fig. 5. MGaming EMG-BCI Version02-SUS Result.

Following the implementation of improvements, a notable shift was observed in participants' outlook towards the device in comparison to the initial version. All participants expressed a willingness to utilize the device in the future. This positive response highlighted the effectiveness of the enhancements made. The controls of both the system and the game were fine-tuned, resulting in participants finding it significantly easier to navigate and manipulate them compared to their experience with the initial version. This improved control was positively acknowledged by the participants.

While there was not a significant change in participants' intention to purchase the device, those who initially remained neutral exhibited greater receptiveness towards the idea of purchasing it after the additional testing. This demonstrated that further refinements and adjustments positively impacted their perception.

Overall, the participants' perception and enjoyment of the system increased following the implementation of these changes. The improvements made to the device and game controls contributed to a more favorable experience, indicating a positive trajectory for the system's development.

Game Scoring. In the second round of testing, all users exhibited a notable improvement in their adaptation to both the system and the game, successfully reaching the score goal in their initial attempt. This positive outcome can be attributed to several factors, including a better understanding and familiarity with the system, increased comfort with the game mechanics, and the refined tuning of the game controls (Table 3).

Table 3. Attempts needed for a score of three after second test.

Participant	Attempts needed
1	1
2	1
3	1
4	1
5	1

Participants' enhanced performance can be attributed to their growing familiarity with the system, suggesting a learning effect and improved proficiency in utilizing the device. Additionally, the fine-tuning of the game controls played a crucial role in facilitating smoother gameplay, enabling participants to navigate and interact with the game more effectively. This overall progress and successful achievement of the score goal in the first attempt signify the participants' improved adaptability and mastery of the system and game, highlighting the positive impact of familiarity and optimized game control adjustments. Figure 6 shows that participants could successfully reach score 9 with the proposed modifications.

User Recommendations. For the second version of the system, users provided suggestions for further enhancements. These recommendations included implementing

Fig. 6. MGaming EMG-BCI Version02 Game Over.

improved feedback mechanisms to provide a clearer indication when a score was achieved. Users also suggested increasing the spacing between obstacles to avoid instances where they were positioned too closely together after each spawn. Participants expressed their appreciation for the smoother and more user-friendly controls in the second iteration. The fine-tuning of the controls resulted in a significantly improved gameplay experience, leading to heightened enjoyment of the game. These suggestions from the users highlighted the importance of incorporating better feedback mechanisms and adjusting the spacing between obstacles to optimize the gameplay experience. Additionally, the positive feedback regarding the smoother and easier-to-use controls affirmed the impact of fine-tuning in enhancing user satisfaction and engagement with the game.

5   Discussion

The results indicate that the time required to achieve the target score improved significantly after implementing the threshold enhancements. It is worth noting that further enhancements and fine-tuning options remain viable, specifically tailored to individual users in future iterations. Based on our findings, we can outline the following recommendations for progressing with a Brain-Computer Interface (BCI) system for video games: User Satisfaction: Participants expressed satisfaction with the control scheme of the game and demonstrated a rapid ability to adapt to it. This indicates that controlling the game through eye blinks was straightforward and easily comprehensible for users. Customizable Thresholds: Participants expressed a desire for varied thresholds to control the game, encompassing factors such as game speed, sensitivity of blink detection, and the timing between blinks. Incorporating a mechanism that allows users to modify these thresholds during startup would enhance the overall user experience. Universal Control Scheme: Implementing a universal control scheme proved advantageous. Although currently limited to a single game, the control scheme can be easily adapted to other tap-style games. This flexibility enables users to select games of their preference, expanding their gaming options across various genres using the headband as the control unit. By addressing these recommendations, we can enhance the user experience and optimize the effectiveness of the BCI system for video games. As is apparent in the results, the time to reach the goal score was met quicker after the improvements to the threshold. Further improvements and fine tuning are possible and can be tuned to specific users in the future.

6   Conclusion and Future Work

This paper presents a new Brain-Computer Interface (BCI) approach that enables users to play tap-style games utilizing Electromyography (EMG). The initial version of the developed solution was evaluated through a SUS questionnaire, considering the number of attempts required by users to achieve a target score of three. Feedback on the initial system prompted suggestions for adjusting the system's threshold to enhance usability. Additionally, the game's speed was reduced to allow users more time and flexibility in executing commands. The suggestions were incorporated into the second version of the system. Increasing the blink detection threshold resulted in improved user experience, as it made command execution easier and reduced system sensitivity. Moreover, the game speed was slightly increased, while the time threshold between blinks was decreased. This adjustment allowed for more frequent triggering of jumps, providing users with greater maneuverability and the ability to recover from early jumps. In future research, the BCI system can be expanded to explore alternative control methods beyond EMG. For instance, incorporating Electroencephalography (EEG) readings could enable control through imagined movement thoughts, potentially elevating the user experience by allowing game control through cognitive processes rather than muscle movements via blinks. This expanded scope demonstrates the potential of BCI not only for game control but also as a novel means of phone control. The versatility of the control scheme options represents a significant advantage for the system. Overall, BCI holds promising prospects as a transformative approach for phone control, extending beyond gaming applications. The ability to explore diverse control methods opens up exciting possibilities for the future of this technology.

References

1. Martínez-Cagigal, V., Santamaría-Vázquez, E., Hornero, R.: Controlling a smartphone with brain-computer interfaces: a preliminary study. In: Perales, F.J., Kittler, J. (eds.) AMDO 2018. LNCS, vol. 10945, pp. 34–43. Springer, Cham (2018). https://doi.org/10.1007/978-3-319-94544-6_4
2. Valeriani, D., Matran-Fernandez, A.: Towards a wearable device for controlling a smartphone with eye winks. In: 2015 7th Computer Science and Electronic Engineering Conference (CEEC), pp. 41–46. IEEE (2015)
3. Hack the Brain UK - Control Your Smartphone by Winking. OpenBCI. https://openbci.com/community/hack-the-brain-uk-control-your-smartphone-by-winking/. Posted 28 Apr 2015 by D. V. —. (28 Apr 2015). Accessed 27 Dec 2022
4. Thomasson, N.: An introduction to BCI and its use in video games: a review. J. Stud. Res. **12**, 1 (2023)
5. Lee, S., Kang, H., Shin, G.: Head flexion angle while using a smartphone. Ergonomics **58**(2), 220–226 (2015)
6. Wu, X., et al.: A brain-controlled Mahjong game with artificial intelligence augmentation. In: Fang, L., Povey, D., Zhai, G., Mei, T., Wang, R. (eds.) CICAI 2022. LNCS, vol. 13606, pp. 548–553. Springer, Cham (2022). https://doi.org/10.1007/978-3-031-20503-3_47

7. Pires, G., et al.: Playing tetris with non-invasive BCI. In: 2011 IEEE 1st International Conference on Serious Games and Applications for Health (SEGAH), pp. 1–6. IEEE (2011)
8. Bos, D.P.-O., et al.: Human-computer interaction for BCI games: usability and user experience. In: 2010 International Conference on Cyberworlds, pp. 277–281. IEEE (2010)
9. Allison, B., Graimann, B., Gräser, A.: Why use a BCI if you are healthy. In: ACE Workshop-Brain-Computer Interfaces and Games, pp. 7–11 (2007)
10. Bos, D.O., Reuderink, B.: Brainbasher: a BCI game. In: Extended Abstracts of the International Conference on Fun and Games, pp. 36–39. Eind-hoven University of Technology Eindhoven (2008)
11. Subramanian, R.R., Varma, K.K., Balaji, K., Reddy, M.D., Akash, A., Reddy, K.N.: Multiplayer online car racing with BCI in VR. In: 2021 5th International Conference on Intelligent Computing and Control Systems (ICICCS), pp. 1835–1839. IEEE (2021)
12. Zhang, X., Chen, X., Wang, W.-H., Yang, J.-H., Lantz, V., Wang, K.-G.: Hand gesture recognition and virtual game control based on 3D accelerometer and EMG sensors. In: Proceedings of the 14th International Conference on Intelligent User Interfaces, pp. 401–406 (2009)
13. Bonnet, L., Lotte, F., Lécuyer, A.: Two brains, one game: design and evaluation of a multiuser BCI video game based on motor imagery. IEEE Trans. Computat. Intell. AI Games 5(2), 185–198 (2013)

Towards Gesture Based Assistive Technology for Persons Experiencing Involuntary Muscle Contractions

Christine Pocock[1] , Chris Porter[1]([✉]) , and May Agius[2]

[1] Department of Computer Information Systems, University of Malta, Msida, Malta
{christine.pocock.15,chris.porter}@um.edu.mt
[2] Department of Communication Therapy, University of Malta, Msida, Malta
may.agius@um.edu.mt

Abstract. This research investigates the viability of leveraging Machine Learning (ML) algorithms to develop gesture recognition systems that may benefit people who experience involuntary muscle contractions. This presents distinct challenges, such as the reduced ability to perform gestures accurately and repeatedly (flawed gestures) as well as the ability to provide sufficient data to pre-train models. This investigation revolves around three shortlisted gesture recognition algorithms which were evaluated in a controlled lab environment. The primary objective was to observe specific characteristics such as robustness under different simulated conditions, training requirements, as well as classification latency and accuracy. Results show distinct properties for each shortlisted algorithm. k-Nearest Neighbour (KNN) with Dynamic Time Warping (DTW), or KNN-DTW, is well suited where accurate gesture training is challenging due to frequent involuntary movements. Although this approach works well with one sample, the classification response time is significantly longer than KNN and Support Vector Machine (SVM). However, timing may not always be a priority, depending on the context of use. On the other hand, when real-time responses are necessary, KNN and SVM both offer a good level of performance. These, however, rely on training data to produce accurate classifications, in which case the user must be able to perform gestures in a reasonably repeatable manner. This work also presents a dataset of 1600 samples for four gesture classes, including a corresponding set of flawed gesture samples for each class.

Keywords: Human-Computer Interaction (HCI) · Assistive Technology (AT) · Involuntary gestures

1 Introduction

The term Assistive Technology (AT) refers to a wide variety of systems, devices and equipment that can be used to support individuals with disabilities in performing tasks with greater ease and independence [41]. Several specialised assistive devices exist, ranging from simple facilities like handrails to advanced equipment, such as digital hearing aids and electric wheelchairs [11]. Moreover, a vital component of AT is

© The Author(s), under exclusive license to Springer Nature Switzerland AG 2023
H. P. da Silva and P. Cipresso (Eds.): CHIRA 2023, CCIS 1996, pp. 53–68, 2023.
https://doi.org/10.1007/978-3-031-49425-3_4

Augmentative and Alternative Communication (AAC), which incorporates a variety of strategies that can be used to reduce communication barriers [9].

For certain groups of people, ATs are limited in their applicability and remain underserved by research and practice [31,42]. This is particularly true for people with rarer conditions, such as dystonia. This work aims to contribute insights that can be applied in developing ATs for non-verbal individuals with severe motor impairments characterised by involuntary muscle contractions. Existing ATs present two major challenges for this group of people; independence and interaction efficiency [17,24,42]. Relying on position-dependent equipment, such as switches, may pose several challenges for people who experience involuntary muscle contractions. This is mainly because such events may inadvertently shift their sitting position, and re-aligning themselves back with their physical switch or Eye Trackers (ETs) may be challenging without direct and constant support from caregivers. It is hypothesised that wearable input devices may mitigate some of the limitations posed by commercially available position-based AT. Furthermore, gesture-based interaction presents a plausible solution for individuals who do not have complete limb paralysis but lack the fine motor skills required to control traditional input devices [31]. While several gesture-based systems exist, these are typically unsuitable for people who may perform gestures in an inconsistent manner [38].

This paper contributes evidence-based insights about three shortlisted Machine Learning (ML) algorithms with particular emphasis on three central characteristics: (a) classification performance (accuracy, specificity and sensitivity), (b) training requirements (training set sizes and inclusion of gesture variations) and (c) classification efficiency (recognition time). A raw labelled gesture dataset[1] is also published to afford replicability of these results as well as further related research.

This paper is based on the primary author's postgraduate research at the HCI Lab within the Faculty of ICT, University of Malta [35]. This research is in conformity with the University of Malta's Research Code of Practice and Research Ethics Review Procedures.

The rest of the paper is organised as follows. We first provide an overview of related work, followed by the research methodology adopted for this study. We then present study execution details along with the results obtained. These results are then contextualised within a persona-centric discussion, outlining how the measured characteristics can inform the design and development of Gesture Recognition Systems (GRSs) as ATs in different usage scenarios.

2   Related Work

2.1   Gesture Classification Algorithms

Researchers have investigated various techniques to interpret human gestures recorded from wearable technology [30], and these can be largely subdivided into two categories; template-based and model-based methods [48]. Template matching is a technique for comparing time series using a single or a few templates to represent each gesture class [48]. These predefined templates are then used to recognise undetermined

---

[1] Available from: https://osf.io/6sm89.

patterns, such that the template with the highest similarity is identified as the most probable occurrence [32,47]. Many Template Matching Methods (TMMs) have been used in academic literature, including Euclidean distance [29], linear time warping [7], and longest common subsequence [32]. However, DTW is one of the most popular algorithms as it is simple to implement, only requires a single training sample to initiate [48], and can achieve very high accuracy [23,43,47].

The second approach involves the use of ML-based methods to classify gestures. This approach attains higher accuracy than TMMs but has higher computational complexity and requires a larger quantity of training samples. Various classifiers have been explored in related literature. For instance, Wu et al. [44] used the SVM classifier to build a wearable system to recognise gestures in American Sign Language (ASL). The experimental results show that the system achieved an average classification accuracy of 96% [44]. More recently, Bashir et al. [5] developed a wearable system for media player control that supports 12 gestures. The gestures were classified using three different ML algorithms; Random Forest (RF), Naive Bayes (NB) and KNN; however, the KNN classifier achieved the highest accuracy [5]. Some researchers have also investigated the use of ML-based approaches in combination with TMMs. For instance, Kim et al. [14] built an efficient Hand Gesture Recognition (HGR) system that can cope with time-dependent data and support real-time learning. Their system achieved an accuracy of 98% using the Artificial Neural Network (ANN) classifier and the DTW algorithm. However, the DTW algorithm in combination with KNN is known to be an excellent method for time-series classification and has been found difficult to outperform [6,21,27,45].

2.2 Gesture-Based Assistive Technology

Despite their potential, and to the best of our knowledge, there is little work on the adoption of wearable gesture-based systems for people with severe motor impairments characterised by involuntary muscle contractions. Also, the majority of studies in this area focus on wearable sensors for activities such as rehabilitation and diagnostics rather than on their use as an alternative input modality. Lemmens et al. [20] adopted devices with built-in accelerometers, gyroscopes and magnetometers to assess arm-hand performance objectively to evaluate therapies for neurological patients. Lipovsky et al. [22] present HandTherapist, a hand rehabilitation system aimed at patients recovering from strokes. On the other hand, Singh et al. [39] adopted an accelerometer-based GRS to detect involuntary gestures for Cerebral Palsy (CP) diagnosis in high-risk infants. Patel et al. [34], also adopted accelerometer readings to evaluate the severity of symptoms in patients with Parkinson's Disease (PD).

On the other hand, Kundu et al. [19] present research for a hand-gesture driven wheelchair using an Inertial Measurement Unit (IMU)-based GRS. The authors obtained 90% accuracy using an SVM classifier. A more wide-reaching GRS was proposed by Nelson et al. [31], who adopted an Electrooculography (EOG) headband along with a data glove equipped with an accelerometer and flex sensors. This setup allowed the team to capture eye movements and hand gestures to interpret interaction intents. Although more complex to set up and operate away from the lab, this approach offers more flexibility and could be adapted for a wider variety of people, depending on their limitations and the severity of their condition.

3   Research Methodology

This section will present the methodology adopted to address the objectives set out for this study. This research was centred around a lab-based study aimed at building an in-depth understanding of shortlisted algorithms and their characteristics, including training requirements and classification latency in a controlled environment. For this reason, it was consciously decided to control for variances related to motor abilities. The three shortlisted Gesture Recognition (GR) algorithms; KNN, SVM and KNN-DTW, were selected based on their predominance in related work [2,5,6,26,44,45].

3.1   Subject Recruitment

A convenience sampling approach [36] was adopted to recruit 10 participants with no known motor impairments. This was a conscious decision taken primarily to control for gesture variances that may arise from different motor neuron conditions and physical ranges of motion, isolating and highlighting GR algorithm performance within known and well-defined parameters and experimental conditions, as explained below.

3.2   Data Collection

Recruited participants were requested to wear an IMU sensor on their dominant hand and perform several repetitions of a set of basic gestures (see Fig. 1), which were informed through discussions with occupational therapists as well as in-situ observations and conversations with individuals living with dystonia, including their caregivers. It was clear that gestures needed to be simple (in shape) and short (in performance time). One individual used a two-switch system to interact with a computer, so the tap-left/right gestures were naturally considered. The swipe right gesture was considered for its simplicity, which could also generalise to other swipe directions. In contrast, the circle gesture was selected since it was deemed hard to perform accurately and repeatedly by these individuals. The shortlisted gesture classes were primarily selected to cover varying difficulty levels and are not meant to be a representative set.

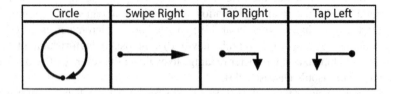

Fig. 1. The four selected gesture classes used in this study.

During the study, participants, sitting in an upright position, were initially asked to perform their gestures as consistently as possible in terms of speed and size. However, at a later stage, they were instructed to carry out significant variations to the gestures assigned, such as increasing and decreasing the speed of execution of the specified gestures as well as pausing briefly during their execution. These variations are referred to as flawed gestures and were carried out to assess the degree to which flawed templates affect each algorithm's performance. This was inspired by the method outlined in Kluge et al.'s work [15]. Achieving satisfactory results when gestures are varied is a particularly noteworthy property for people with motor impairments, some of whom may lack enough motor control to perform gestures consistently.

A Graphical User Interface (GUI) was developed for this study (see Fig. 2) to indicate when participants should start and stop their gestures and which gesture to perform, along with additional instructions. Participants were given three seconds to perform each gesture, and following completion of the gesture, they were asked to hold their hand still.

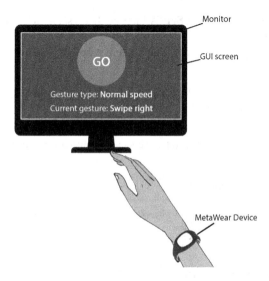

Fig. 2. Experimental setup, including MetaWear's MetaMotion sensor worn on the dominant hand.

3.3   Data Preprocessing

During data collection, participants often finished the gestures before the specified time interval. Hence, following the experiment, the collected data was manually trimmed to exclude the readings where the participants held their hands still following gesture completion. Following this step, the raw data was transformed into features via the methods described in Sect. 4.1 (see *Feature Extraction* and *Feature Selection and Dimensionality Reduction*).

3.4   Data Analysis

An approach similar to the one adopted by Kluge et al. [15] was used to assess the degree to which flawed templates affect each algorithm's performance. Flawed templates are gestures performed in a way that deviate significantly from the labelled template. It is important to note that the goal of this study was not to replicate gestures as performed by people from the target user group but to understand how these techniques fare with flawed gesture data in either or both the training and test sets. This, in turn, helps in shaping a better understanding of which techniques apply best when, for instance, repetitive movements are not always possible or when muscle tone fluctuations occur unpredictably, making obligatory training steps before system use counterproductive.

For this reason, the following sub-experiments were planned and executed:

1. **No Flawed Templates:** Flawed templates are excluded from both training and test sets.
2. **Flawed Templates in the Training Set:** Flawed templates are added to the training set only.
3. **Flawed Templates in the Test Set:** A more realistic scenario in which flawed templates are only in the test set.
4. **Flawed Templates in Both Sets:** Flawed templates are added to both the training and test sets.

For each sub-experiment, the metrics outlined in Table 1 were calculated to analyse each algorithm's performance.

Table 1. Metrics used to assess the shortlisted algorithms.

Assessment Criteria	Metric	Description
Performance	Accuracy	Correct predictions divided by the test set size
	AUC/ROC	A measure of the specificity and sensitivity of a model
Amount of training data required	Accuracy (per training set size)	The accuracy achieved with various training set sizes
Efficiency	Recognition time	The time taken to classify a single gesture in milliseconds

4   Study Execution and Results

The three shortlisted GR algorithms, KNN, SVM and KNN-DTW, were evaluated against several criteria, including Cross-Validation (CV) accuracy, Area Under the Curve (AUC)/Receiver Operator Characteristic (ROC) score, accuracy with various training set sizes, and the time taken to classify a gesture. These insights would, in turn, inform design decisions when applied in different contexts of use and with different people with varying motor abilities (e.g., which algorithms would fare best for people who are more likely to perform gestures irregularly some or most of the time?). For this reason, it was consciously decided to control for variances related to motor abilities and recruit able-bodied individuals who were asked to perform a series of guided gestures, including flawed gestures.

4.1   Experimental Study

During the experimental study, participants were asked to perform 40 repetitions of a set of gestures; circle, swipe right, tap right, and tap left (see Fig. 1). For each gesture class, participants were asked to perform 12 repetitions (30%) with significant variances from the original gesture (i.e., following the method outlined in [15]), as shown below:

- 28 gestures performed at a consistent speed as shown in Fig. 1 (normal)
- 4 gestures performed with a brief pause at any point during the execution (flawed)
- 4 gestures performed very quickly (flawed)
- 4 gestures performed very slowly (flawed)

Participants were also given short breaks between repetitions to control for fatigue. Each participant's data collection session took approximately 120 min. A total of 1600 gestures (4 gestures × 40 repetitions × 10 participants) were collected, of which 480 were labelled as flawed.

Sensor Technology Selection. For the scope of this study, which emphasises the need to provide target users with more independence, the most sought-after feature in a sensor is position independence, which does not require the precise positioning and calibration of equipment. This is a noteworthy advantage of IMU devices over other sensors, such as eye trackers. MbientLab MetaWear sensors were used as they offer good levels of precision [4,5] when compared to other commercial IMUs at a relatively low price point.

Data Collection Interface. A data collection tool was implemented using Python to collect and save sensor data as participants performed gestures on a Windows 10 machine with an Intel Core i7-8565U CPU and 16 GB of RAM. The data collection tool uses the MetaWear Application Programming Interface (API) to stream real-time accelerometer and gyroscope signals over a Bluetooth Low Energy (BLE) connection with a sampling frequency of 100 Hz. An external TP-Link UB400 Bluetooth 4.0 USB adapter was used. The GUI was implemented using the *PySimpleGUI* package to guide participants through the experiment using both visual and auditory cues. Data streaming was automatically initiated once the start screen was displayed, and participants were given three seconds to perform each gesture, following the instructions provided on the screen. Following data collection, the data were manually trimmed to exclude records where the participants held their hands still.

Data Analysis Tool. Automation of the data analysis process was achieved by implementing a data analysis tool that processes the collected data and evaluates the shortlisted algorithms against selected performance metrics (see Table 1) for each of the four sub-experiments outlined in the previous section. Furthermore, to ensure fairness, the total number of samples used in each sub-experiment was limited to 112 samples per participant to maintain an equal number of samples in all sub-experiments. This is because sub-experiment 1 does not include the 48 flawed samples collected from each participant. The implementation details of the data analysis tool are discussed in more depth in the following sections.

Gesture Detection. Gesture detection relies on the identification of the start and end points of gestures from a continuous input signal. Typically, threshold-based methods are employed for IMU sensors and involve the computation of features such as the average energy from raw accelerometer signals [50]. However, Park et al. [33] argue that gyroscope-based gesture detection, as a threshold-based method, proves more reliable than accelerometer-based methods. Gyroscope-based approaches rely on angular velocity (degrees per second), while accelerometer-based methods rely on acceleration (G's). Accelerometer-based approaches introduce a problem known as gesture splitting, which is particularly problematic if gestures take time to complete or have multi-step movement patterns. Park et al. [33] mitigated this problem by introducing temporal thresholds to 'wait' before a gesture is deemed as completed (e.g., 375 ms). Based on this, it was decided to opt for a gyroscope-based threshold method for gesture segmentation. Similarly to Park et al. [33], the magnitude of the signal is calculated using Eq. 1, and is compared to a threshold value to detect the start and end of the gesture, such that when the magnitude exceeds a predefined threshold t the start of a gesture is detected, whereas if it falls below the threshold, the gesture is assumed to have ended.

$$|gyro| = \sqrt{gyro\_x^2 + gyro\_y^2 + gyro\_z^2} \tag{1}$$

Feature Extraction. In the field of signal analysis, the main feature sets are comprised of time-domain and frequency-domain features. However, for KNN and SVM, time-domain features were used since the reviewed literature indicates that time-domain features are more efficient and better suited for real-time GRSs [3,12,37,44]. A total of 96 time-series features per gesture were extracted (16 features × 3 accelerometer × 3 gyroscope) using the TSFEL package. For KNN-DTW, rather than extracting features from data, raw data was compressed using a moving average filter and adopted directly as features [8,16]. This process included post-padding raw data with zeros to address the length inequality of time-series data [25] before applying a moving average filter with a window size of 50 ms, and a 30 ms overlap [23,28]. A list of hyperparameters chosen for the different algorithms is outlined in Table 2.

Table 2. Chosen hyperparameters for the shortlisted approaches.

Algorithm	Hyperparameter	Value	Description
KNN	K	1	The number of neighbours
SVM	C	0.01	Controls the margin size of the classifier
	Gamma	Scale	The influence a training sample exerts
	Kernel	Linear	The kernel function used
KNN-DTW	K	1	The number of neighbours
	Radius	1	Additional cells on each side of the projected warp path

Feature Selection and Dimensionality Reduction. In the context of ML, it is essential to select a reduced and meaningful subset of the extracted features. In this study, backward elimination was employed to select the best subset of features since, according to Wah et al. [40], wrapper methods were found to be more effective at selecting significant features in comparison to filter methods. The authors also suggest that backward elimination is often preferred over forward selection since the latter cannot remove features that become insignificant after adding other features [40]. Principal Component Analysis (PCA) was also used to further improve efficiency through the Scikit-learn package [1,26,46]. PCA is a widely used statistical method that projects features into a low-dimensional space by computing new uncorrelated variables, referred to as principal components, that successively minimise variance [13].

Gesture Classification. For each shortlisted algorithm, the classifier implementation offered by the Scikit-learn package was adopted. For the KNN-DTW implementation, we adopted the KNN classifier from Scikit-learn in combination with the Fast-DTW implementation, which provides an expedited implementation of the DTW algorithm [10,18,49]. Additionally, the algorithms' hyperparameters were tuned using Grid Search cross-validation.

4.2 Results

In this section, the results obtained from the experimental study for each sub-experiment are presented.

Sub-Experiment 1: No Flawed Templates. All three GR algorithms attained very high accuracy when no flawed templates were present in the dataset (see Table 3); however, KNN-DTW achieved the highest CV accuracy and AUC/ROC scores. KNN-DTW also achieved the highest accuracy across all training sizes and obtained a 97.4% accuracy with only a single sample per gesture type, henceforth referred to as class (see Table 4). In contrast, SVM consistently achieved the lowest accuracy and attained an accuracy of 85.5% with a single training sample per class. Results indicate that larger training sets had less impact on recognition time for KNN and SVM, as opposed to KNN-DTW.

Table 3. Sub-experiment 1: 5-fold cross-validation results.

	Accuracy (%)	AUC/ROC (%)	Recognition Time (ms)
KNN	99.4 (σ=1.26)	99.6 (σ=0.84)	19.841
KNN-DTW	99.8 (σ=0.28)	99.9 (σ=0.18)	521.743
SVM	99.3 (σ=1.16)	99.5 (σ=0.77)	19.421

Table 4. Sub-experiment 1: Classification accuracy and classification recognition time per training set size.

Training Samples	Flawed Sample Count		KNN		KNN-DTW		SVM	
	Training Set	Test Set	Accuracy (%)	Time (ms)	Accuracy (%)	Time (ms)	Accuracy (%)	Time (ms)
4	0	0	93.9 (σ=6.82)	19.695	97.4 (σ=3.29)	37.932	85.5 (σ=10.74)	19.673
12	0	0	97.9 (σ=2.33)	19.163	99.1 (σ=1.60)	85.182	97.0 (σ=3.53)	19.806
20	0	0	98.3 (σ=1.86)	19.029	99.2 (σ=1.36)	137.709	96.8 (σ=3.14)	19.741
40	0	0	98.8 (σ=2.12)	21.109	99.9 (σ=0.59)	248.106	99.4 (σ=0.97)	20.933
60	0	0	99.4 (σ=1.30)	20.117	99.8 (σ=0.61)	351.063	99.4 (σ=1.30)	19.577

Sub-Experiment 2: Flawed Templates in The Training Set. In the second sub-experiment, all algorithms still attained very high CV accuracy and AUC/ROC scores (see Table 5), and similarly, KNN-DTW also achieved the highest CV accuracy and accuracy with a single training sample per class (see Table 6). Furthermore, following the addition of flawed templates in the training set, SVM required a larger amount of training data to achieve results that matched those obtained in sub-experiment 1 and as a result, SVM's classification accuracy in this sub-experiment (see Table 6) is consistently lower than that achieved in sub-experiment 1 (see Table 4). Also, results indicate that larger training sets had less impact on recognition time for KNN and SVM, as opposed to KNN-DTW.

Table 5. Sub-experiment 2: 5-fold cross-validation results.

	Accuracy (%)	AUC/ROC (%)	Recognition Time (ms)
KNN	99.7 (σ=0.67)	99.8 (σ=0.45)	20.991
KNN-DTW	99.8 (σ=0.37)	99.9 (σ=0.24)	543.420
SVM	99.6 (σ=0.70)	99.7 (σ=0.47)	20.593

Table 6. Sub-experiment 2: Classification accuracy and classification recognition time per training set size.

Training Samples	Flawed Sample Count		KNN		KNN-DTW		SVM	
	Training Set	Test Set	Accuracy (%)	Time (ms)	Accuracy (%)	Time (ms)	Accuracy (%)	Time (ms)
4	4	0	60.4 (σ=11.67)	21.640	78.2 (σ=17.76)	35.976	54.3 (σ=18.12)	23.831
12	4	0	98.9 (σ=1.20)	21.537	98.7 (σ=1.95)	89.968	93.3 (σ=6.55)	22.854
20	8	0	99.0 (σ=2.37)	21.576	99.2 (σ=1.15)	139.747	89.0 (σ=9.98)	23.035
40	12	0	99.7 (σ=0.59)	22.771	99.9 (σ=0.44)	249.617	95.6 (σ=8.01)	25.211
60	20	0	99.4 (σ=0.93)	22.045	99.8 (σ=0.61)	352.762	99.4 (σ=1.30)	22.434

Sub-Experiment 3: Flawed Templates in the Test Set. In sub-experiment 3, all algorithms suffered a slight degradation in overall accuracy and AUC/ROC scores (see Table 7). This is because the test set differs significantly from the samples on which the classifier was trained. However, the results shown in Table 8 indicate that KNN-DTW lends itself well to scenarios where gesture performance may vary, and it comfortably outperforms the other algorithms. With respect to classification time, results are comparable to previous sub-experiments where larger training sets had less impact on recognition time for KNN and SVM, as opposed to KNN-DTW.

Table 7. Sub-experiment 3: 5-fold cross-validation results.

	Accuracy (%)	AUC/ROC (%)	Recognition Time (ms)
KNN	97.2 (σ=2.25)	98.1 (σ=1.50)	20.024
KNN-DTW	98.2 (σ=1.81)	98.8 (σ=1.21)	526.098
SVM	96.7 (σ=0.61)	97.8 (σ=0.53)	18.970

Sub-Experiment 4: Flawed Templates in both Sets. The results presented in Table 9 showed that all algorithms achieved higher CV accuracy and AUC/ROC scores than in sub-experiment 3, indicating that the addition of flawed templates in the training set improved gesture prediction in scenarios when the test set contained samples with significant variations. In fact, the CV results achieved in this sub-experiment are comparable to those of the best-case scenario presented in sub-experiment 1 (see Table 3). Furthermore, similar to previous sub-experiments, KNN-DTW also achieved the highest accuracy across all training set sizes (see Table 10), but also showed the slowest recognition time. Conversely, SVM and KNN require less time to classify gestures, making them more advantageous for real-time systems.

Table 8. Sub-experiment 3: Classification accuracy and classification recognition time per training set size.

Training Samples	Flawed Sample Count		KNN		KNN-DTW		SVM	
	Training Set	Test Set	Accuracy (%)	Time (ms)	Accuracy (%)	Time (ms)	Accuracy (%)	Time (ms)
4	0	16	83.9 (σ=10.41)	20.198	90.1 (σ=5.31)	39.616	85.5 (σ=6.25)	23.337
12	0	16	89.8 (σ=7.02)	22.593	92.9 (σ=4.09)	87.089	85.6 (σ=7.11)	21.617
20	0	16	90.0 (σ=5.49)	20.954	93.8 (σ=4.44)	131.620	85.5 (σ=6.66)	21.433
40	0	16	87.5 (σ=9.28)	20.324	91.9 (σ=5.43)	243.913	88.8 (σ=7.76)	22.755
60	0	16	85.6 (σ=13.36)	20.037	90.8 (σ=6.33)	347.030	83.9 (σ=12.27)	21.747

Table 9. Sub-experiment 4: 5-fold cross-validation results.

	Accuracy (%)	AUC/ROC (%)	Recognition Time (ms)
KNN	99.4 (σ=0.84)	99.6 (σ=0.56)	20.461
KNN-DTW	99.8 (σ=0.37)	99.9 (σ=0.24)	561.423
SVM	99.2 (σ=1.03)	99.5 (σ=0.69)	18.279

Table 10. Sub-experiment 4: Classification accuracy and classification recognition time per training set size.

Training Samples	Flawed Sample Count		KNN		KNN-DTW		SVM	
	Training Set	Test Set	Accuracy (%)	Time (ms)	Accuracy (%)	Time (ms)	Accuracy (%)	Time (ms)
4	4	16	66.5 (σ=12.24)	20.441	75.5 (σ=13.07)	33.933	64.8 (σ=14.76)	19.156
12	4	16	92.7 (σ=5.77)	21.032	94.4 (σ=2.72)	87.003	85.0 (σ=5.46)	19.621
20	8	16	93.0 (σ=4.11)	20.624	96.6 (σ=2.32)	142.044	87.6 (σ=9.96)	20.818
40	12	16	94.7 (σ=4.38)	21.091	98.1 (σ=2.64)	261.626	92.2 (σ=7.18)	21.186
60	20	16	97.7 (σ=3.60)	20.229	99.0 (σ=1.87)	346.080	97.1 (σ=3.42)	19.661

5   Persona-Centric Discussion

Personas are used to shed light on each GR algorithm's applicability from a target user's point of view based on the evaluation criteria considered in the experimental study;

CV accuracy, AUC/ROC score, accuracy with various training set sizes, and recognition time. These personas were developed through discussions with domain experts and occupational therapists as well as in-situ observations with persons living with dystonia.

5.1   Persona 1: Martha

Martha is a non-verbal 11-year-old girl living with focal dystonia affecting her arms. Martha uses an eye-tracker (ET) for communication, configured with a dwell time of 1.2 s. This means she needs to hold her gaze for 1.2 s before selecting on-screen targets. Martha can make coarse movements with her arms, but due to her condition, she also frequently experiences involuntary movements where her arms are extended. Martha has been using her ET for a long time and can use it efficiently. However, she finds her ET tiring, and it becomes progressively more difficult for her to fixate on desired targets after using her ET for long periods of time. Introducing a gesture-based switch to act as a second input modality presents itself as a plausible solution to eliminate dwell time and, in turn, minimise fatigue. Nevertheless, Martha's frequent involuntary movements may also trigger unintentional selections. A potential solution is to collect samples of these unintentional movements so that they may be identified and disregarded, leaving other movements as potential target activation gestures. However, it is challenging for Martha to provide significant training data. In such a scenario, despite having the slowest recognition time overall, KNN-DTW would still be the best option. This is because KNN-DTW consistently achieved the highest accuracy with minimal training samples, and recording one or two of these movements could suffice. Also, the gesture recognition times for KNN-DTW presented in this paper are still well below the typical dwell times used for eye-tracking interaction, therefore speeding up on-screen trigger selection.

5.2   Persona 2: Matthew

Matthew is a non-verbal 16-year-old living with generalised dystonia. He can, however, make repeatable movements with his right hand, through which he can operate a two-switch scanning system to control his PC and also communicate. Matthew has been using his AT from a very young age, and when he is optimally positioned in relation to the physical switches, he can carry out advanced tasks efficiently, including word processing and photo manipulation. However, when Matthew inadvertently shifts positions due to involuntary muscle contractions, he would require assistance from his caregivers to regain access to the switches. Matthew also feels frustrated when he uses his AT with a long scan delay because even a seemingly insignificant increase in scan delay can substantially impact how efficiently he is able to communicate and carry out tasks. Replacing Matthew's physical switches with a wearable sensor would eliminate the need for his switches to be precisely positioned. Nevertheless, it is crucial for Matthew that the GR algorithm selected affords quasi-real-time gesture classification since this will contribute to minimising the necessary scan delay. In this scenario, and given that Matthew can repeat certain gestures with a reasonable degree of consistency, both KNN and SVM are good candidates for any wearable AT built for him, given that they satisfy both the performance and accuracy requirements.

6   Conclusion

This work is meant to provide further insights towards the design and development of gesture-driven systems within the context of assistive technologies, specifically in scenarios where motor abilities and requirements vary. Results show distinct properties for each shortlisted algorithm, along with potential benefits in different contexts of use. For instance, KNN-DTW is well suited where accurate gesture training is not possible due to frequent involuntary movements. Instead, the algorithm could be used to build a model for these movements (e.g., tremors or contractions), which could, in turn, be discarded. Although this approach works well with one sample, the classification response time is significantly longer compared to KNN and SVM. However, timing is not always a priority, depending on the context. On the other hand, when real-time responses are necessary (e.g., when using scanning-based ATs with short scan delays), KNN and SVM both offer good performance; however, these typically rely on some training data to produce accurate classifications (see Sect. 4.2). In this case, the user should be able to perform gestures in a reasonably consistent manner.

Acknowledgements. We would like to thank Sharon Borg for her expert insights as an occupational therapist with the Access to Communication & Technology Unit (ACTU). We would also like to thank Dr Colin Layfield from the Department of Computer Information Systems at the University of Malta for his insights on aspects related to machine learning.

References

1. Alavi, S., Arsenault, D., Whitehead, A.: Quaternion-based gesture recognition using wireless wearable motion capture sensors. Sensors **16**(5), 605 (2016)
2. Hamdy Ali, A., Atia, A., Sami, M.: A comparative study of user dependent and independent accelerometer-based gesture recognition algorithms. In: Streitz, N., Markopoulos, P. (eds.) DAPI 2014. LNCS, vol. 8530, pp. 119–129. Springer, Cham (2014). https://doi.org/10.1007/978-3-319-07788-8_12
3. Altın, C., Er, O.: Comparison of different time and frequency domain feature extraction methods on elbow gesture's emg. Europ. J. Interdisc. Stud. **2**(3), 35–44 (2016)
4. Anderez, D.O., Dos Santos, L.P., Lotfi, A., Yahaya, S.W.: Accelerometer-based hand gesture recognition for human-robot interaction. In: 2019 IEEE Symposium Series on Computational Intelligence (SSCI), pp. 1402–1406. IEEE (2019)
5. Bashir, A., Malik, F., Haider, F., Ehatisham-ul Haq, M., Raheel, A., Arsalan, A.: A smart sensor-based gesture recognition system for media player control. In: 2020 3rd International Conference on Computing, Mathematics and Engineering Technologies (iCoMET), pp. 1–6. IEEE (2020)
6. Benalcázar, M.E., et al.: Real-time hand gesture recognition using the myo armband and muscle activity detection. In: 2017 IEEE Second Ecuador Technical Chapters Meeting (ETCM), pp. 1–6. IEEE (2017)
7. Gabayan, K., Lansel, S.: Programming-by-example gesture recognition. Report CS229, Department of Statistics, Stanford University (2006)
8. Gama, J., et al.: IoT Streams for Data-Driven Predictive Maintenance. Springer International Publishing (2020). https://doi.org/10.1007/978-3-030-66770-2
9. Griffiths, T., Bloch, S., Price, K., Clarke, M.: Alternative and augmentative communication. In: Handbook of Electronic Assistive Technology, pp. 181–213. Elsevier (2019)

10. Gupta, A.: Using unlabeled 3D motion examples for human activity understanding. Ph.D. thesis, University of British Columbia (2016)
11. Hurst, A., Tobias, J.: Empowering individuals with do-it-yourself assistive technology. In: The Proceedings of the 13th International ACM SIGACCESS Conference on Computers and Accessibility, pp. 11–18 (2011)
12. Jiang, S., et al.: Feasibility of wrist-worn, real-time hand, and surface gesture recognition via semg and imu sensing. IEEE Trans. Industr. Inf. **14**(8), 3376–3385 (2017)
13. Jolliffe, I.T., Cadima, J.: Principal component analysis: a review and recent developments. Philosoph. Trans. Royal Society A: Math., Phys. Eng. Sci. **374**(2065), 20150202 (2016)
14. Kim, M., Cho, J., Lee, S., Jung, Y.: Imu sensor-based hand gesture recognition for human-machine interfaces. Sensors **19**(18), 3827 (2019)
15. Kluge, R.: Online Accelerometer Gesture Recognition using Dynamic Time Warping and K-Nearest Neighbors Clustering with Flawed Templates. Bachelor's thesis, Radboud University Nijmegen (2017)
16. Ko, M.H., West, G., Venkatesh, S., Kumar, M.: Online context recognition in multisensor systems using dynamic time warping. In: 2005 International Conference on Intelligent Sensors, Sensor Networks and Information Processing, pp. 283–288. IEEE (2005)
17. Koch Fager, S., Fried-Oken, M., Jakobs, T., Beukelman, D.R.: New and emerging access technologies for adults with complex communication needs and severe motor impairments: State of the science. Augment. Altern. Commun. **35**(1), 13–25 (2019)
18. Kühnel, C., Westermann, T., Hemmert, F., Kratz, S., Müller, A., Möller, S.: I'm home: defining and evaluating a gesture set for smart-home control. Int. J. Hum Comput Stud. **69**(11), 693–704 (2011)
19. Kundu, A.S., Mazumder, O., Lenka, P.K., Bhaumik, S.: Hand gesture recognition based omnidirectional wheelchair control using imu and emg sensors. J. Intell. Robot. Syst. **91**(3–4), 529–541 (2018)
20. Lemmens, R.J.M., Janssen-Potten, Y.J.M., Timmermans, A.A.A., Smeets, R.J.E.M., Seelen, H.A.M.: Recognizing complex upper extremity activities using body worn sensors. PLoS ONE **10**(3), 1–20 (2015). https://doi.org/10.1371/journal.pone.0118642
21. Li, H., Yang, W., Wang, J., Xu, Y., Huang, L.: Wifinger: Talk to your smart devices with finger-grained gesture. In: Proceedings of the 2016 ACM International Joint Conference on Pervasive and Ubiquitous Computing, pp. 250–261 (2016)
22. Lipovský, R., Ferreira, H.A.: Hand therapist: a rehabilitation approach based on wearable technology and video gaming. In: 2015 IEEE 4th Portuguese Meeting on Bioengineering (ENBENG), pp. 1–2. IEEE (2015)
23. Liu, J., Zhong, L., Wickramasuriya, J., Vasudevan, V.: uwave: accelerometer-based personalized gesture recognition and its applications. Pervasive Mob. Comput. **5**(6), 657–675 (2009)
24. Ljubić, S., Arbula, D., Smrekar, K.: An adaptable scan-based text entry for mobile devices: Design, predictive modeling, and empirical evaluation. Eng. Rev. **37**(1), 38–49 (2017)
25. Mahato, V., O'Reilly, M., Cunningham, P.: A comparison of k-nn methods for time series classification and regression. In: AICS, pp. 102–113 (2018)
26. Marqués, G., Basterretxea, K.: Efficient algorithms for accelerometer-based wearable hand gesture recognition systems. In: 2015 IEEE 13th International Conference on Embedded and Ubiquitous Computing, pp. 132–139. IEEE (2015)
27. Melgarejo, P., Zhang, X., Ramanathan, P., Chu, D.: Leveraging directional antenna capabilities for fine-grained gesture recognition. In: Proceedings of the 2014 ACM International Joint Conference on Pervasive and Ubiquitous Computing, pp. 541–551 (2014)
28. MerlinLivingston, L., Deepika, P., Benisha, M.: An inertial pen with dynamic time warping recognizer for handwriting and gesture recognition. Int. J. Eng. Trends Technolo. (IJETT)-Volume **35** (2016)

29. Mezari, A., Maglogiannis, I.: An easily customized gesture recognizer for assisted living using commodity mobile devices. J. Healthcare Eng. (2018)
30. Murthy, G., Jadon, R.: A review of vision based hand gestures recognition. Int. J. Inform. Technol. Knowl. Manage. **2**(2), 405–410 (2009)
31. Nelson, A., et al.: Wearable multi-sensor gesture recognition for paralysis patients. In: SENSORS, 2013 IEEE, pp. 1–4. IEEE (2013)
32. Nguyen-Dinh, L.V., Roggen, D., Calatroni, A., Tröster, G.: Improving online gesture recognition with template matching methods in accelerometer data. In: 2012 12th International Conference on Intelligent Systems Design and Applications (ISDA), pp. 831–836. IEEE (2012)
33. Park, T., Lee, J., Hwang, I., Yoo, C., Nachman, L., Song, J.: E-gesture: a collaborative architecture for energy-efficient gesture recognition with hand-worn sensor and mobile devices. In: Proceedings of the 9th ACM Conference on Embedded Networked Sensor Systems, pp. 260–273 (2011)
34. Patel, S., et al.: Monitoring motor fluctuations in patients with Parkinson's disease using wearable sensors. IEEE Trans. Inf. Technol. Biomed. **13**(6), 864–873 (2009)
35. Pocock, C.: Wearable Gesture-based Assistive Technology for People with Motor Impairments. Master's thesis, Department of Computer Information Systems, Faculty of ICT (2021)
36. Sedgwick, P.: Convenience sampling. BMJ 347 (2013). https://doi.org/10.1136/bmj.f6304, https://www.bmj.com/content/347/bmj.f6304
37. Siddiqui, N., Chan, R.H.: Multimodal hand gesture recognition using single imu and acoustic measurements at wrist. PLoS ONE **15**(1), e0227039 (2020)
38. Singh, G., Nelson, A., Robucci, R., Patel, C., Banerjee, N.: Inviz: low-power personalized gesture recognition using wearable textile capacitive sensor arrays. In: 2015 IEEE International Conference on Pervasive Computing and Communications (PerCom), pp. 198–206. IEEE (2015)
39. Singh, M., Patterson, D.J.: Involuntary gesture recognition for predicting cerebral palsy in high-risk infants. In: International Symposium on Wearable Computers (ISWC) 2010, pp. 1–8. IEEE (2010)
40. Wah, Y.B., Ibrahim, N., Hamid, H.A., Abdul-Rahman, S., Fong, S.: Feature selection methods: Case of filter and wrapper approaches for maximising classification accuracy. Pertanika J. Sci. Technol. **26**(1) (2018)
41. WHO: Assistive technology. https://www.who.int/news-room/fact-sheets/detail/assistive-technology (2018) Accessed 06 May 2021
42. Wiegand, K., Patel, R.: Impact of motor impairment on full-screen touch interaction. J. Technol. Persons Disab. **3**(22), 58–76 (2015)
43. Wu, J., Pan, G., Zhang, D., Qi, G., Li, S.: Gesture recognition with a 3-d accelerometer. In: Zhang, D., Portmann, M., Tan, A.-H., Indulska, J. (eds.) UIC 2009. LNCS, vol. 5585, pp. 25–38. Springer, Heidelberg (2009). https://doi.org/10.1007/978-3-642-02830-4_4
44. Wu, J., Sun, L., Jafari, R.: A wearable system for recognizing American sign language in real-time using imu and surface emg sensors. IEEE J. Biomed. Health Inform. **20**(5), 1281–1290 (2016)
45. Xi, X., Keogh, E., Shelton, C., Wei, L., Ratanamahatana, C.A.: Fast time series classification using numerosity reduction. In: Proceedings of the 23rd International Conference on Machine Learning, pp. 1033–1040 (2006)
46. Xu, C., Pathak, P.H., Mohapatra, P.: Finger-writing with smartwatch: a case for finger and hand gesture recognition using smartwatch. In: Proceedings of the 16th International Workshop on Mobile Computing Systems and Applications, pp. 9–14 (2015)
47. Xu, C., He, J., Zhang, X., Wang, C., Duan, S.: Detection of freezing of gait using template-matching-based approaches. J. Sensors 2017 (2017)

48. Yin, L., Dong, M., Duan, Y., Deng, W., Zhao, K., Guo, J.: A high-performance training-free approach for hand gesture recognition with accelerometer. Multimed. Tools Appl. **72**(1), 843–864 (2014)
49. Zhang, H., Fu, M., Luo, H., Zhou, W.: Robust human action recognition using dynamic movement features. In: Huang, Y.A., Wu, H., Liu, H., Yin, Z. (eds.) ICIRA 2017. LNCS (LNAI), vol. 10462, pp. 474–484. Springer, Cham (2017). https://doi.org/10.1007/978-3-319-65289-4_45
50. Zhou, Y., Cheng, Z., Jing, L.: Threshold selection and adjustment for online segmentation of one-stroke finger gestures using single tri-axial accelerometer. Multimed. Tools Appl. **74**(21), 9387–9406 (2015)

Towards a Methodology for Developing Human-AI Collaborative Decision Support Systems

Alexander Smirnov, Andrew Ponomarev, and Tatiana Levashova[✉]

St. Petersburg Federal Research Center of the Russian Academy of Sciences, 14th Line, 39, St. Petersburg 199178, Russia

{Smir,Ponomarev,tatiana.levashova}@iias.spb.su

Abstract. Decision-making is a complex activity, often demanding collaboration, sometimes even in the form of dynamic (ad hoc) teams of loosely coupled participants collected to deal with a particular problem. At the same time, recent developments in the AI have shown that AI plays an important role in decision-making, and AI-agents may become full-fledged participants of collaborative decision support systems. However, integration of AI-agents into collaborative processes requires solving a number of tasks concerning human-AI interaction, interpretability, mutual learning, etc. This paper is a step towards a methodology to create decision support systems based on human-AI collaboration. An analysis of typical requirements to the collaborative decision support systems and typical scenarios that such systems have to implement sustains the introduced methodology. Based on this analysis, foundational problems needed settlements to develop human-AI collaborative decision support systems have been identified, and their possible solutions are offered. In the proposed methodology, ontologies play an important role, providing interoperability among heterogeneous participants. The methodology implies a technological backing in the form of a collaborative computational environment, helping to develop decision support systems for particular domains.

Keywords: Decision support · Collaborative systems · Human-AI collaboration · Ontology-based systems

1 Introduction

Decision-making in many large-scale dynamic domains (e.g., complex production systems, municipal/state management, etc.) often requires collaborative effort, when the organization forms *ad hoc* problem-specific teams either from its own employees, or even from external expert pools. Recent developments in the artificial intelligence (AI) have shown that the AI-technologies enable tighter and more effective human-AI collaboration. AI opens the opportunity for a new generation of collaborative decision support, provided by teams of diverse participants (including experts and software agents acting on the basis of AI).

© The Author(s), under exclusive license to Springer Nature Switzerland AG 2023
H. P. da Silva and P. Cipresso (Eds.): CHIRA 2023, CCIS 1996, pp. 69–88, 2023.
https://doi.org/10.1007/978-3-031-49425-3_5

Human-AI collaboration recently have attracted the attention of researchers, due to multiple issues associated with it: mutual understanding and explanation, semantic and syntactic interoperability, accountability, and many others.

The paper attempts to summarize specific features of collaborative decision support systems (DSSs) discussed in various research works and propose a methodology for the developing DSSs organized through the collaboration of human experts and AI agents. This methodology, on the one hand, is based on recent software development methodologies, on the other hand, is adapted (and specialized) to take into account the specific requirements that arise in collaborative systems and, in particular, in human-AI collaborative DSSs.

Typically, any methodology has some technological support. The proposed methodology is based on a collaborative environment [1, 2] that provides certain mechanisms and methods for implementing the methodology steps.

The structure of the paper is following. Section 2 introduces requirements to human-AI collaborative DSSs, extracted from the literature review. Section 3 describes foundational challenges in the development of collaborative DSSs and their possible solutions. Section 4 introduces the proposed methodology. Discussion and Conclusion describe the methodology features with their relation to the requirements to human-AI collaborative DSSs, present the methodology limitations, outline directions of the future research, and summarize the major results.

2   Requirements to Human-AI Collaborative DSSs

The requirements to human-AI collaborative DSSs are specified based on a semi-systematic review [3] of research on the complex topic "human-AI collaboration for decision support". This review is purposed to investigate types of collaborations and interactions occurring between AIs and humans [4–10], overview matured approaches and challenges to the development of collaborative DSSs [9–15], and study real-world scenarios of human-AI collaboration in DSSs [10–12, 16–22]. Keywords related to the research topic constitute a set of search terms. They include "human", "AI", "collaboration", "human-machine teamwork", "decision support". The google search engine and the databases of Springer and Elsevier are used to search for materials providing a contribution to the review. Reports, articles, papers, book chapters, theses, and application websites are included in the consideration. Research published in a language other than English, studies that focus only on collaboration of AI agents, and works aiming at the evaluation of collaborative systems through interviewing are excluded from the analysis. For the present paper, publications explicitly postulated requirements to human-AI collaboration are selected out of the whole set of the reviewed works. These publications provide a set of requirements described below.

The set of the requirements comprises requirements to a DSS (SR) and requirements to participants of the collaboration (PR) that are AIs and human.

Requirements to a DSS:

- SR1. Partnerships between human and AI in collaborative DSSs should be in preference to automation. There are at least two reasons for this. First, the ability of the computer-based components to interact with human overcomes many of the difficulties, such as the representation and validation of knowledge. Second, although human and computer capabilities are in many respects complementary, human is vulnerable to emotional influences that are an intrinsic part of the human nature and therefore largely beyond the control [11];

- SR2. Time for human-AI collaboration should be consumed efficiently. Human time needs to be kept to a minimum. AI should not disturb humans in their daily work [9];
- SR3. Human must be involved in decision making. Any attempt to automate the decision making process to the exclusion of the human element is not only likely to be counterproductive, but dangerous as well. Human should be given the opportunity to interfere with the AI activity, bring other knowledge to bear on the situation and thereby influence the final determination since it is human who is responsible for the final decision [9, 11];
- SR4. Human and AI should both collect and analyze information in a decentralized way. Human and AI serve equally well as collectors and generators of information, as they do as recipients of information. The decentralization of the data analysis process is particularly valuable in terms of distributing the communication traffic and validating the results of the analysis at the collection source [11];
- SR5. Information within a DSS should be represented in a form that is, if not equivalent to, at least compatible with human cognition [11], possibly with multiple coordinated views implemented on different visualization modalities [12];
- SR6. The interests of AI and human need to be well aligned, such that the AI does not act opportunistically or contrary to the human's interest [13].

Requirements to a collaborative DSS put forward a set of requirements to the participants of the collaboration. These requirements are grouped into three categories: 1) requirements to both humans and AIs, 2) requirements to human experts, and 3) requirements to AI agents.

1) Requirements to Humans and AIs:
- PR1. Human and AI should meet the requirements of mutual observability, predictability, and directability, that is [10]:
- observability implies that each participant should be aware of the status of all participants, the team as a whole, the goal, and the environment;
- predictability means that actions of the participants are – to some extent – predictable, so that they can anticipate to them;
- directability refers to the property that the participants are able to take over and delegate tasks among each other, both reactively and pro-actively;
- PR2. Human and AI should maintain common ground, which includes the pertinent knowledge, beliefs, and assumptions that the participants share. Common ground enables the participants to comprehend the messages and signals that help coordinate their joint actions and prevent potential failures to achieve the goal [10, 14];
- PR3. Human and AI should be able to recognize misunderstandings and misalignments which can occur while collaboration, both kinds of participants need to be able to diagnose the cause of these, and to generate an explanation that gets the DSS as whole back on track [10];

- PR4. Human and AI should be able to mutual learning. Such learning includes human feedback that can be used to improve the AI's decision quality over time by providing it with verified instances that contribute to its learning process the most, and also the AI teaching human, e.g., by highlighting relevant information humans might not have been aware of, or providing explanations how the AI arrived at its decisions [9]. Collaboration of human and AI in diverse domains and situations requires from them an ability to learn from demonstration, explanation and experience [15];
- PR5. Human and AI should have complementary skills and knowledge, and complement and expand each other's strengths as well they need to recognize that complementarities between two participants exist and that the tasks should be performed by the better-suited participant, the most important ability here is to estimate one's own ability [9, 22];
- PR6. AI and human especially need to be sufficiently skilled, knowledgeable, and competent to make a good decision or effectively execute a task [13].
2) Requirements to AI Agents:
- PR7-A. AI needs to be 'human aware'. This includes awareness of human tendencies in general (e.g., proneness to bias), but also of characteristics of specific human participants (e.g., current work load; preferences, prior knowledge; emotional state; competencies; history of making biased judgments; etc.) [9, 10];
- PR8-A. AI needs to be capable to recognize a social situation and adopt the appropriate social role to interact to human. Much of everyday human interaction is guided by social norms that provide protocols for interaction. Socially collaborative AIs require abilities to communicate, sense and express emotions and to interact socially with humans using speech, gesture, vision and natural language [15];
- PR9-A. AI should have knowledge of the context within which decisions have to be made and should be able to explain the understanding of the situation and the expected development of it [10, 15];
- PR10-A. AI should be aware of its role within the decision support process and its authority [10, 15];
- PR11-A. AI requires the capabilities to initiate human interactions, and to exchange information freely without requests from humans or other AIs [11];
- PR12-A. AI should not be dependent solely on human, it should assist human in solving tasks and making decisions [11];
- PR13-A. AI requires the capability to explain its recommendations to human [9, 12].
3) Requirements to Human Experts:
- PR14-H. Human should complement AI through interpersonal tasks (show empathy, consider boundary conditions and external factors and classify these in a holistic cross-domain picture) [9];
- PR15-H. Human should understand the AI's language and state their needs in a form or language that the AI can understand [10];
- PR16-H. Humans should be 'AI-aware'. Human should develop, and eventually have, a proper understanding of the contributions that the AI-partner can deliver, and which not [10].

The identified requirements are organized into several groups. They are team formation – PR5, PR6, PR7-A; distribution of the responsibilities and activities of the end-user and team participants – SR2, SR3, SR4, PR1; interoperability of the team participants –SR5, PR2, PR3, PR4, PR9-A, PR13-A, PR15-H; explainable AI – PR9-A, PR13-A; smart human-AI partnership – SR1, SR2, SR4, PR12-A, PR14-H; conflict resolutions – SR6; multimodal communications – PR8-A. The requirements to AI awareness of its authority and role (PR10-A), AI capabilities to initiate interactions and push information (PR11-A), and the human awareness of AI (PR16-H) are implicitly contained in the requirements SR3 and SR4 of the group dealing with the responsibilities and activities of the team participants.

3   Foundational Problems Behind the Development of Human-AI Collaborative DSS

In this Section, foundational problems are discussed that underlie human-AI collaboration and possible solutions for these problems are proposed.

A generic human-AI collaborative decision support scenario is considered to identify the problems in question. The scenario is derived from existing human-AI systems [11, 12, 16–23] and decision-making methodologies [24–26]. With relation to the purpose of the present research, it is supposed that an *ad hoc* team of human experts and AI agents provide decision support (without any pre-defined workflow that would specify the team activities). The decision-maker (end user) initiates the scenario by formulating the problem in a natural language. An *ad hoc* team organized specifically to address this problem receives the problem description as the user presented it. The team solves the problem introduced by the end-user as decision support problem. Team activities comprise identifying possible alternatives, evaluating them, refining evaluations, etc. The result of these activities is presented to the end user who can make an informed decision. The fact, that the participants of the collaborative team can be both humans and AI agents (i.e., some software entities), causes a number of principal (or foundational) problems. These problems are discussed below.

Information Exchange between the Participants of the Collaborative DSS. The problem arises in situations where it is necessary to organize information exchange between the heterogeneous team participants. They can exchange information directly with each other or indirectly through a (smart) space where the shared information is published. A possible solution for this problem requires a model for a shared information representation, a means of information exchange, and information access modes. A solution for such a shared information representation is challenging because the information must be understandable to both humans and AI agents, which can be based on various techniques.

Reformulation of the Problem Introduced by the Decision Maker According to the Machine-Understandable Symbolic Representation. Initially the problem is formulated in a natural language and, therefore, is understandable by human participants and hybrid teams, but AI agents face difficulties in understanding it (e.g., each team agent has to be capable to solve a natural language processing task). However, if the problem definition is augmented by a structured machine-readable representation, it could be interpretable by much simpler agents. For instance, decision support problem includes problem of choice between the alternatives. If a structural representation of the *Choice*

Problem proposes concepts of *Alternative* and *Alternative Evaluation Criterion*, with further structuring *Alternative* as *Tourist Attraction* and *Alternative Evaluation Criterion* as *Location*, the problem could be interpretable by any agent that just aware of the proposed abstract concepts and tourist attractions. In this example, the italicized words need to be interpreted unambiguously by both humans and AI agents, therefore, a machine-readable representation should include some domain vocabulary providing sharable term semantics.

Explanation of AI Decisions and Actions by Means of Some Symbolic Representation. The issue is aimed at providing explanations of the decisions made by AI in a form that enables human to understand and interpret these explanations. The form of these explanations should be aligned with human worldview (e.g., should use familiar for human terms) and should be compatible with the shared structured representation (see above). Obtaining a symbolic explanation of AI decisions can be a challenge. In a simplest way, when an AI agent is knowledge-based, symbolic explanation is just a set of observations, complemented with a set of inference steps resulting in the output decision. However, symbolic explanation (to some extent) can be possible even for neural AI agents, but it requires establishing connections between concepts and sub-symbolic representations [27, 28]. Also, specialized provenance models [29] can help with some explainability aspects.

Planning Decision Support Process. The issue is purposed to the development of a sequence of actions of the participants to achieve the collaboration goal, which here is support of the end-user with the decision. Depending on how activities among the participants are divided, the plan can be developed in a centralized or decentralized fashion. The centralized method assumes the role of planner, which fulfills a participant responsible for planning activities. The decentralized method solves the planning problem through negotiations between the participants (as they exchange information on the collaboration goal, each other's intentions, individual goals, tasks, and plans for actions).

Team Formation. The purpose of team formation problem is organizing an efficient team. This issue involves the necessity of a choice or the development of a mechanism that allows organizing such a team. The quantity of participants, the division of activities among them, the participant workloads, the qualifications and competencies of the participants, and other factors can influence on team efficiency. A set of efficiency criteria has to underlie the chosen or developed mechanism for the collaborators selection.

Learning AI Through Human Feedback. The issue is determined by a human reaction to the AI's actions. Usually, this problem arises when the AI model requires some refinement (for instance, human sees that the AI infers wrong conclusions). To provide AI learning, it is required to choose or develop a learning model, human interface feedback, and learning interface. At that, the concrete learning method may vary depending on the implementation of the AI agent. For instance, knowledge-based agents (and some neuro-symbolic agents) may allow explicit transfer of decision rules from humans. Applied to some other implementations, it may be an implicit transfer, where an agent receives only human decision and adjusts its logics to take into account this decision. The agent can use inductive logical programming or machine learning techniques for the logics adjustment.

Human Learning Through AI Explanations. As a consequence of receiving an *explanation of AI-actions by means of some symbolic representation*, humans learn something new for themselves and acquire new knowledge or experience, which means that AI has taught humans something. It should be noted that another consequence of receiving explanations from AI is related to the evidence that human realizes that AI works correctly (incorrectly); this consequence does not lead to the acquisition of new knowledge by humans.

4   Methodology

The proposed methodology is based on the identified requirements to human-AI collaborative DSSs (Sect. 2) and embeds prospective solutions to the foundational problems (Sect. 3). The core of the methodology is a set of principles, postulating certain view on the structure and functions of human-AI collaborative DSSs. These principles "codify" some ways of addressing the foundational problems and meeting the requirements to collaborative DSSs. Besides that, the methodology proposes a set of activities (a process) guiding the DSS development procedure.

4.1   Principles of the Methodology

The principles of the methodology are intended, on the one hand, to more accurately specify the scope of the considered collaborative systems through listing and expressing the main assumptions regarding the tasks, participants, and nature of the team's activities. On the other hand, these principles are aimed at fixing fundamental conceptual decisions that are important from the point of the methodology view. The set of the principles is as follows.

1. A *team* consisting of human experts and intelligent agents (software entities acting on the basis of AI, AI agents) carries out the decision support process. The team is organized to deal with a specific decision support problem, after solving which it is disbanded. A pool of potential participants provides access to a collection of possible collaborators, which can be employees of an enterprise, members of a professional community, etc. (complemented by AI agents). In decision support tasks, team members are often not interchangeable and have unique abilities, so it is important to select out participants with sufficient and complementary skills and knowledge to they effectively work on the given problem. This principle meets the requirements of the team formation group (PR5, PR6, PR7-A).
2. The end user (human decision maker), who formulates the problem and initiates the organization of the team (SR3), is responsible for the final decision. The team provides decision support through a set of actions aimed at identifying criteria and alternatives, evaluating the alternatives, and determining the criteria importance. The implementation of these actions may lead to the tasks of collecting and processing information about the formulated problem, as well as the need to evaluate hypothetical

decision support scenarios (SR4). The principle meets the requirements of the group related to the distribution of the responsibilities and activities.

3. The team is involved in the processes of two classes: work on the problem formulated by the end-user (so-called 'taskwork') and collaboration activities (so-called 'teamwork') (SR4, PR1). The principle meets the requirements of the group related to the distribution of the responsibilities and activities.

4. Ontology represents knowledge about the problem and the collaboration activities (teamwork) (SR5, PR2, PR9-A). As it is noted in Sect. 3, communication in a mixed human-AI group is much simpler if it is based on some structured machine-readable representation that provides unambiguous terms. Ontologies suggest a convenient way to build such representations. Since their introduction to the IT industry during the Semantic Web initiative the ontologies have proven themselves both quite efficient for solving the interoperability problems and quite unpretentious for non-expert users. Still, we argue that for mixed human-machine teams, the ontologies provide a kind of *lingua franca*, acceptable by both human and software agents, and enable interoperability of heterogeneous team participants. However, as the direct usage of an ontology language may require certain proficiency in logics and knowledge engineering, the use of ontologies may remain "under the hood", being complemented by some intuitive end-user interface (PR15-H). Structured representation can always be translated into a text via relatively simple procedure, but reverse process is much more complex. For example, the procedure of augmenting a problem description by a structured ontological representation can be done interactively by analyzing the text definition of the problem, asking the end user what exactly he/she means, and offering to the user possible ontology structures for the problem representation. This procedure implies existence of an ontology that provides some structure for the domain knowledge based on which the possible problem structures are determined. Obviously, building a new ontology for each decision support process is infeasible, but the main ontology needed to represent the required knowledge is a domain ontology, defining concepts of the problem domain and relationships between them. The presence of a domain ontology is a pre-requisite for the proposed methodology. Plenty of high-quality ontologies have been developed in the last decades for many domains and collaborative DSSs can reuse them. It should be noted that a variety of decision support processes in the same domain could leverage the same domain ontology. The principle meets the requirements of the participants interoperability group.

5. Multi-aspect ontology supports multiple views on information that appears in the decision support process. An information piece (fact, statement) can play several roles in the teamwork (PR2). This, in particular, follows from the complex structure of the team and necessitates the use of multi-aspect ontologies that provide a consistent representation of information from the perspectives of various problem aspects and team participant views [30]. A multi-aspect ontology comprises three levels: local, aspect, and global. Each aspect can be represented by a specific formalism. The local level represents concepts and relationships observed only from one view. The aspect level represents concepts and relationships from the local level that are shared by two or more aspects. It defines the formalism of the multi-aspect ontology. The global level is the common part for the aspects of the multi-aspect ontology represented using the multi-aspect ontology formalism. The concepts represented at this level are

related to those of the aspect level. The methodology adopts the model of the decision support aspect that the multi-aspect ontology for decision support based on human-machine collective intelligence [30] represents. The principle meets the requirements of the participants interoperability group.

6. Participant interactions are based on an ontology-based knowledge representation. The key processes of interaction between the participants are explanation of the results obtained by AI agents to human (PR9-A, PR13-A), and learning, i.e. transfer of the knowledge from a human expert to an AI agent (PR4). Both of these processes are based on an ontological representation of the information and suggest the existence of ontology-oriented methods for explaining and using ontologies as a priori knowledge. If a task (some part of the whole decision support problem) solved by an AI agent can be expressed as ontological inference, then this inference (optionally, reformulated in a natural language) is a valid explanation. It is a powerful method and recent publications show that sometimes it can be used even with neural agents (see, e.g. [27]). However, other methods may also be used. For instance, ontology concepts can be just linked to features or feature combinations, making traditional explanation techniques of machine learning models more understandable (e.g., [31]). The principle meets the requirements of the groups of the participants interoperability and explainable AI.

7. Conflict situations that may arise in the course of collaborative activities are recognized and resolved (SR2, SR6, PR3). This concerns various difficulties and errors in understanding the current situation, intentions and goals of the participants, conflicts of interests, etc. The principle meets the requirements of the groups of the participants interoperability and conflict resolutions.

8. A smart human-AI partnership is ensured (SR4) through:
   (a) reasonable autonomy of AI (can initiate actions of AI and human, make decisions, solve problems (especially those that are difficult for a person to solve), support a human expert in understanding information (present information in a human-readable form, explain the process of its reasoning) (PR12-A);
   (b) involvement of human in the collaboration with minimal effort, human support by AI agents, and suggesting to human activities that only human is able to carry out and manifest (feelings, recognition of unknown objects, the ability to explain, systematize, interpersonal interaction, etc.) (SR1, SR2, PR14-H).

   The principle meets the requirements of the group of the smart human-AI partnership.

9. A human-AI collaborative environment [1, 2] provides the technological basis for the system development activities.

4.2 Processes

A set of activities on the development of a human-AI collaborative DSS aims at performing two sorts of concretizing processes. They are concretizing the description of the decision support problem and concretizing interactions between the team participants (Fig. 1). There is a certain set of typical mechanisms and models that ensure the operating of a wide class of collaborative systems (for example, user profile model, mechanism for recording feedback on the results of solving a problem to modify performance parameters, etc.) These typical constructions are supposed be implemented in the general-purpose collaborative environment [1, 2]. In this environment, only general assumptions about the organization of the DSS are made. In fact, it is the organization, which follows the methodology principles. For example, the environment introduces a user profile [32] to model the team participants by a set of model parameters. For a particular DSS, this set can be modified, but specific algorithms for this modification are not "hard-coded" – they have to be defined down the line. The collaborative environment reduces the space of design solutions and, at the same time, embodies established practices in the domain of communication & collaboration, facilitates the organization of collaborative DSSs, and provides technological support for the proposed methodology.

The problem concretization process follows two steps (Fig. 2).

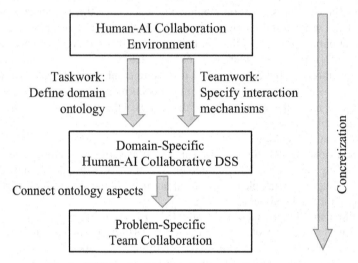

Fig. 1. DSS development through concretization process.

The first step is adaptation, which is carried out along two "dimensions" (according to principle 3): concretization of the "problem" content (taskwork) and concretization of the "process" content (teamwork). The activities on choosing a domain ontology, which provides the domain concepts and relationships between them, sustain the process of the problem content concretization. The concretization of the process content supposes a choice/setting of mechanisms for the collaboration. The result of the first step is a collaborative human-AI DSS for the specific domain and the given method (scenario) of application (corporate, open, mixed, etc.) The first step suggests a set of activities that forms the core of the methodology. They are discussed below in this Section where the methodology is introduced.

The second step of the problem concretization is the specification of a multi-aspect representation for the decision support problem. This step is dictated, in particular, by the methodology for the multi-aspect ontology development [30]. The outcome of this step is the specification of a multi-aspect ontology that supports the interactions between the team participants in the decision support process. In particular, the definition of mappings between the aspects allows the AI agents to interpret correctly the information

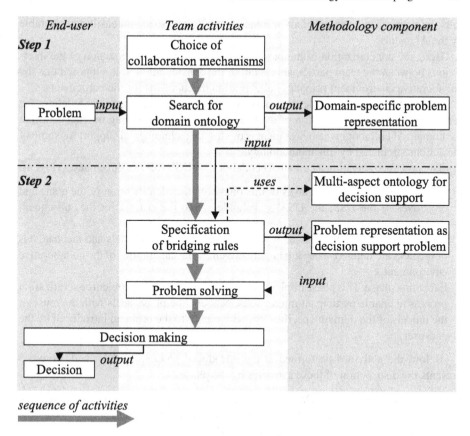

Fig. 2. Problem concretization.

related to the problem. According to the methodology [30], a multi-aspect ontology is constructed at local, aspect, and global levels, linked via bridging rules. At the step under consideration, the problem-specific bridging rules are established. An example of such rules is a bridging rule relating a specific domain concept of the local level and the concept *"Alternative"* of the decision support aspect. This rule allows the AI agents to think of the specific concept as an alternative solution.

The difference between the two steps of the problem concretization process can be explained by the following example. Suppose, the collaborative environment that back-ups the methodology, is domain-agnostic and cannot be used directly for decision support. However, it allows one to specify a domain ontology and select a number of interaction mechanisms. By providing an ontology of infomobility in smart city, which represents concepts like *"Attraction"*, *"Route"*, *"Point of interest"*, etc. and the corresponding relationships, one can create a collaborative DSS for the infomobility domain. A possible problem in this domain can be the trip route planning. This problem among other supposes the selection of attractions to visit. Relating the concepts *"Attraction"* of the domain ontology and *"Alternative"* of the decision support aspect by the bridging rule, the decision support problem becomes formally specified and easily interpretable by the AI agents.

Here, the concretization of the process content that is a concretization of the interactions between the team participants is out of the consideration. It is supposed that the collaborative environment provides collaboration mechanisms for the participants.

The methodology for the development of a human-AI collaborative DSS defines the activities for the implementation of the specified above steps, taking into account that the human-AI collaborative environment provides the technological support for some of the actions stipulated by this methodology.

The process of creating a human-AI collaborative DSS follows three phases (Fig. 3):

- Inception phase. The main tasks of this phase are the identification of the goals and objectives of the DSS, the DSS' stakeholders, and the criteria for the subsequent system evaluation.
- Development phase. It is the main phase. At it, the specific models and mechanisms of the DSS are defined. They are largely driven by the capabilities of the collaborative environment.
- Execution phase. This phase implements the second step of the problem concretization process to enable participant interactions. Namely, the phase deals with the reuse of the models of the domain-specific DSS with regard to the problem introduced by the end-user.

Below, the activities performed at the introduced phases are described. Figure 3 presents the distribution of these activities by the phases.

1. The identification of the DSS goals. The obvious goal is to ensure the quality of decision support. However, the DSS can pursue some additional goals also, e.g., the development of participants' competencies (for an intra-corporate DSS).
2. The determination of the measurable quality indicators covering the identified goals. Various techniques and tools propose quality indicators and provide support in measuring. For instance, the decision quality framework [33] can be used to measure quality of the decisions, the framework for measuring the effectiveness of DSS [34] offer methods and measuring factors to measure the effectiveness of decision support, the general diagnostic framework [35] provides assessment concepts to measure and evaluate competence, etc.
3. Building the participant models (profiling). The determination of the essential participants' characteristics that affect the effectiveness of the team comprising these participants (e.g., participants' competencies, their accessibility, etc.).
4. Building the team model (profiling). The determination of the essential characteristics of the team. Depending on the task the team will engage in, the degree of coordination, the team formation procedure, and the team size [36], a choice between various team models is possible. For instance, the team model of the Katzenbach and Smith model [37] suits for teams of small size that come together for a specific time to solve a specific problem, the LaFasto and Larson model [38] can be used when characteristics of individual participants (traits, skills, abilities, etc.) make the basis of the team formation activity, the Robbins and Judge model [39] is useful to align four dimension of team productivity (context, composition, work design, process).

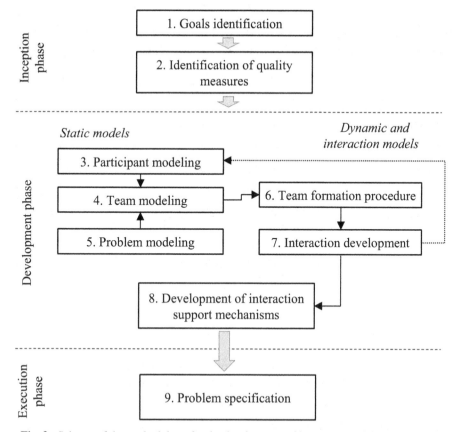

Fig. 3. Scheme of the methodology for the development of human-AI collaborative DSSs.

5. Building the problem model. The development/adaptation of ontology-based models for i) problem specification as ontology-based representation of the domain knowledge, ii) problem specification as ontology-based multi-aspect representation of the decision support problem, and iii) ontology-based representation for the structure of the discussion as a sequence of the interactions.
6. The development of a team formation procedure, taking into account the goals, quality indicators, and essential characteristics of the participants.
7. The development of ways of interactions between the team participants (e.g., role-based interactions, peer-to-peer interactions, etc.).
8. The development of interaction support mechanisms. The interaction model imposes such mechanisms.
9. The problem specification. The development or reuse of the multi-aspect ontology [30] with regard to the problem introduced by the end-user.

As it is said above, the *Development* phase is the main one. The activities at this phase can be divided into two groups: the development of static (information) models for the key entities of the collaborative DSS (participant, team, and problem) and the development of the dynamic models (processes) that ensure achievement of the DSS goals. The phase is considered completed when a set of consistent models has been obtained and (optionally) mechanisms have been defined to support the team interaction.

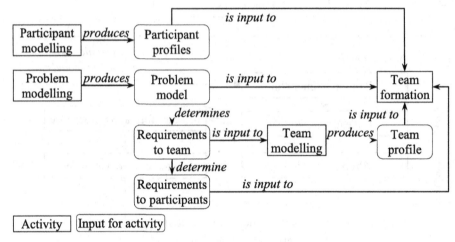

Fig. 4. Dependencies between the activities of the *Development* phase.

Dependencies between the activities determine their sequence (Fig. 4). The DSS goals and the problem determine requirements to the team. In turn, these requirements

Table 1. Compliance of the methodology with the requirements to human-AI collaborative DSSs.

Group	Requirement	Methodology address
Team formation	PR5	Participant profiling
	PR6	
	PR7-A	
Distribution of responsibilities and activities of the end-user and team participants	SR3, PR10-A, PR16-H	Involvement of the end-user and human team participants in decision-making
	SR4, PR11-A	Collecting and processing information about the problem by team participants, including information from each other
	PR1	Usage of collaboration mechanisms in the teamwork, which support mutual observability, predictability, and directability of participants

(continued)

Table 1. (*continued*)

Group	Requirement	Methodology address
	SR2	Usage of team efficiency criteria for team formation, which, e.g., may be minimization of human workload, minimization of the number of AI requests to human, etc
Interoperability of team participants	SR5	Ontology-based representation of the problem and collaboration activities
	PR2	Usage of the multi-aspect otology, which support multiple views on the problem
	PR3	Resolving conflict situations
	PR4	Learning AI through human feedback, human learning due to explanation of the results obtained by AI
	PR9-A	Ontology-based problem representation, explainable AI
	PR13-A	Explainable AI
	PR15-H	Ontology-based problem representation, intuitive interface
Explainable AI	PR9-A	Ontology-based problem representation
	PR13-A	Explanation of the results obtained by AI to human
Smart human-AI partnership	SR1	Involvement of human in the collaboration with minimal effort, human support by AI agents, and suggesting to human activities that only human is able to carry out and manifest
	SR2	Usage of team efficiency criteria for team formation
	SR4	Collecting and processing information about the problem by team participants, including information from each other

(*continued*)

Table 1. (*continued*)

Group	Requirement	Methodology address
	PR12-A	Reasonable autonomy of AI
	PR14-H	Involvement of human in the collaboration with minimal effort
Conflict resolutions	SR6	Resolving conflict situations
Multimodal communications	PR8-A	Out of the consideration

determine the requirements to the participants from which the team is formed. Therefore, initially the problem modelling is performed and then the team model is built. Independently on these two kinds of activities, the participant models can be created. The problem model, team model, participant models, and requirements to the participants make the inputs to the team formation activity. The specification of the dynamic models often requires some refining of the static ones (e.g., if the implementation of a particular mechanism requires the presence of some characteristics for the corresponding entities). Figure 3 displays this fact with the dotted arrow linking activities 7 and 3.

The *Execution* phase is associated with a problem instance specifying the problem introduced by the end-user as decision support problem.

5   Discussion and Conclusion

The paper proposes a methodology to create decision support systems based on human-AI collaboration. Researches considering collaboration levels between AI agents and between AI agents and humans, approaches to the development of collaborative DSSs, and scenarios of human-AI collaboration in such DSSs have been analyzed in order to formulate the methodology. Based on the analysis, typical requirements to the collaborative decision support systems are specified, foundational problems needed settlements to develop such systems are found out, and their possible solutions are proposed. In accordance with the requirements to the collaborative DSSs, a set of the methodology principles is put forward. Relying on these principles, the methodology prescribes a set of the system development activities. Table 1 presents the compliance of the methodology with the specified requirements to human-AI collaborative DSSs.

Although the methodology supposes two-dimensional processes, i.e., the human-AI collaboration towards solving the problem formulated by the end-user and the organization of a collaborative team, so far the detailed description of the methodology is limited to building a shared problem model that a collaborative human-AI team can process as decision support problem. The current methodology version does not provide recommendations for choosing a team model, communication protocol, collaboration mechanism, team efficiency criteria, etc. In addition, the methodology presumes some strategy for resolution of possible conflicts between the team participants, but the present version does not specify kinds of the conflicts and techniques of their resolutions. The methodology does not pay attention to the issues of AI obsolescence and multimodal communications. While for the former issue the methodology can provide for mechanisms that found out this fact, the latter issue is not supposed to be a focus of the present research. Nevertheless, mechanisms proposed by a study on multimodal human-computer interactions [40] can contribute to this issue.

Most of the limitations predefine directions of the future research. The most important of them is the technological support of the proposed methodology. The collaborative environment for human-AI teams [1, 2] is planned to be refined towards supplementing it with the mechanisms and models that would support the proposed methodology and assist in the activities prescribed by it. While, strictly speaking, the proposed methodology can be used itself, without the environment (or even supported by third-party tools); this pilot implementation will simplify putting the environment into practice.

Another direction of the future work is a refinement of the system development activities by preparing recommendations that would help to select appropriate models and procedures to better satisfy the goals of the DSS.

Finally, the methodology is planned to be validated through real-world scenarios from the domains of configuring complex systems and infomobility support in smart space.

Summing up, the paper proposes a prime version of the methodology for building decision support systems based on human-AI collaboration. The core of the methodology is an ontology-based problem representation that enables a human-AI team to solve the problem formulated by the end-user as decision support one, provides interoperability of the heterogeneous collaborators, and offers the model to produce AI explanations. A collaborative environment provides the technological foundation for the decision support system developed. The resorting to the collaborative environment technology simplifies the development of collaborative human-AI DSSs for variety of complex domains (emergency and natural disaster response, government and business scenarios).

Acknowledgement. The presented research is due to the grant no. 22–11-00214 from Russian Science Foundation.

References

1. Smirnov, A., Ponomarev, A.: Supporting collective intelligence of human-machine teams in decision-making scenarios. In: Russo, D., Ahram, T., Karwowski, W., Di Bucchianico, G., Taiar, R. (eds.) IHSI 2021. AISC, vol. 1322, pp. 773–778. Springer, Cham (2021). https://doi.org/10.1007/978-3-030-68017-6_115

2. Smirnov, A., Ponomarev, A., Levashova, T., Shilov, N.: Conceptual framework of a human-machine collective intelligence environment for decision support. Proc. Bulg. Acad. Sci. **75**, 102–109 (2022). https://doi.org/10.7546/CRABS.2022.01.12

3. Snyder, H.: Literature review as a research methodology: an overview and guidelines. J. Bus. Res. **104**, 333–339 (2019). https://doi.org/10.1016/j.jbusres.2019.07.039

4. Demartini, G., Mizzaro, S., Spina, D.: Human-in-the-loop artificial intelligence for fighting online misinformation: challenges and opportunities. Bull. Tech. Comm. Data Eng. **43**, 65–74 (2020)

5. Nakahashi, R., Yamada, S.: Balancing performance and human autonomy with implicit guidance agent. Front. Artif. Intell. **4**, 736321 (2021). https://doi.org/10.3389/frai.2021.736321

6. Neef, M.: A taxonomy of human - agent team collaborations. In: Proceedings of the 18th BeNeLux Conference on Artificial Intelligence (BNAIC 2006), pp. 245–250 (2006)

7. Umbrico, A., Orlandini, A., Cesta, A.: An ontology for human-robot collaboration. Procedia CIRP. **93**, 1097–1102 (2020). https://doi.org/10.1016/j.procir.2020.04.045

8. Wilson, H.J., Daugherty, P.R.: Collaborative Intelligence: Humans and AI are Joining Forces (2018). https://hbr.org/2018/07/collaborative-intelligence-humans-and-ai-are-joining-forces. Accessed 21 Aug 2023

9. Hemmer, P., Schemmer, M., Riefle, L., Rosellen, N., Vössing, M., Kühl, N.: Factors that influence the adoption of human-AI collaboration in clinical decision-making (2022). http://arxiv.org/abs/2204.09082

10. van den Bosch, K., Bronkhorst, A.: Human-AI cooperation to benefit military decision making. In: Proceedings of Specialist Meeting Big Data & Artificial Intelligence for Military Decision Making, pp. S3–1–1-S3–1–13 (2018). https://doi.org/10.14339/STO-MP-IST-160

11. Pohl, J.: Collaborative decision-support and the human-machine relationship. In: A Decision-Making Tools Workshop, pp. 21–46. Collaborative Agent Design Research Center, San Luis (2019)

12. Kase, S.E., Hung, C.P., Krayzman, T., Hare, J.Z., Rinderspacher, B.C., Su, S.M.: The future of collaborative human-artificial intelligence decision-making for mission planning. Front. Psychol. **13**, 850628 (2022). https://doi.org/10.3389/fpsyg.2022.850628

13. Candrian, C., Scherer, A.: Rise of the machines: Delegating decisions to autonomous AI. Comput. Human Behav. **134**, 107308 (2022). https://doi.org/10.1016/j.chb.2022.107308

14. Klein, G., Woods, D.D., Bradshaw, J.M., Hoffman, R.R., Feltovich, P.J.: Ten challenges for making automation a "Team Player" in joint human-agent activity. IEEE Intell. Syst. **19**, 91–95 (2004). https://doi.org/10.1109/MIS.2004.74

15. Crowley, J.L., et al.: A hierarchical framework for collaborative artificial intelligence. IEEE Pervasive Comput. **22**(1), 1–10 (2022). https://doi.org/10.1109/MPRV.2022.3208321

16. Chen, J., Lim, C.P., Tan, K.H., Govindan, K., Kumar, A.: Artificial intelligence-based human-centric decision support framework: an application to predictive maintenance in asset management under pandemic environments. Ann. Oper. Res. **11**, 1–24 (2021). https://doi.org/10.1007/s10479-021-04373-w

17. Bouabdallaoui, Y., Lafhaj, Z., Yim, P., Ducoulombier, L., Bennadji, B.: Predictive maintenance in building facilities: a machine learning-based approach. Sensors **21**, 1044 (2021). https://doi.org/10.3390/s21041044

18. Lee, M.H., Siewiorek, D.P.P., Smailagic, A., Bernardino, A., Bermúdez i Badia, S.B.: A human-AI collaborative approach for clinical decision making on rehabilitation assessment. In: Proceedings of the 2021 CHI Conference on Human Factors in Computing Systems, pp. 1–14. ACM, New York, NY, USA (2021). https://doi.org/10.1145/3411764.3445472

19. Puranam, P.: Human–AI collaborative decision-making as an organization design problem. J. Organ. Des. **10**, 75–80 (2021). https://doi.org/10.1007/s41469-021-00095-2

20. Lai, V., Carton, S., Bhatnagar, R., Liao, Q.V., Zhang, Y., Tan, C.: Human-AI collaboration via conditional delegation: a case study of content moderation. In: CHI Conference on Human Factors in Computing Systems, pp. 1–18. ACM, New York, NY, USA (2022). https://doi.org/10.1145/3491102.3501999

21. Cortes, C., DeSalvo, G., Mohri, M.: Learning with rejection. In: Ortner, R., Simon, H.U., Zilles, S. (eds.) ALT 2016. LNCS (LNAI), vol. 9925, pp. 67–82. Springer, Cham (2016). https://doi.org/10.1007/978-3-319-46379-7_5

22. Fuegener, A., Grahl, J., Gupta, A., Ketter, W.: Cognitive challenges in human-AI collaboration: Investigating the path towards productive delegation. Inf. Syst. Res. **33**, 678–696 (2022)
23. Bosch, K. van den, Bronkhorst, A.: Human-AI cooperation to benefit military decision making. In: Proceedings of Specialist Meeting Big Data & Artificial Intelligence for Military Decision Making, pp. S3–1–1–S3–1–13. S&T Organization (2018). https://doi.org/10.14339/STO-MP-IST-160
24. Simon, H.: Rational decision making in business organizations. Am. Econ. Assoc. **69**, 493–513 (1979)
25. Mann, L., Harmoni, R., Power, C.: The GOFER course in decision making. In: Baron, J., Brown, R.V. (eds.) Teaching decision making to adolescents, pp. 61–78. Lawrence Erlbaum Associates, Hillsdale (1991)
26. Guo, K.L.: DECIDE: a decision-making model for more effective decision making by health care managers. Health Care Manag. (Frederick) **27**, 118–127 (2008). https://doi.org/10.1097/01.HCM.0000285046.27290.90
27. de Sousa Ribeiro, M., Leite, J.: Aligning artificial neural networks and ontologies towards explainable AI. In: Proceedings of the AAAI Conference on Artificial Intelligence, vol. 35, no. 6, pp. 4932–4940. AAAI Press (2021)
28. Bourgeais, V., Zehraoui, F., Ben Hamdoune, M., Hanczar, B.: Deep GONet: self-explainable deep neural network based on Gene Ontology for phenotype prediction from gene expression data. BMC Bioinform. **22**, 1–24 (2021). https://doi.org/10.1186/s12859-021-04370-7
29. Moreau, L., Groth, P.: The prov Ontology. In: Moreau, L., Groth, P. (eds.) Provenance: An Introduction to PROV, pp. 21–38. Springer International Publishing, Cham (2013). https://doi.org/10.1007/978-3-031-79450-6_3
30. Smirnov, A., Levashova, T., Ponomarev, A., Shilov, N.: Methodology for multi-aspect ontology development: ontology for decision support based on human-machine collective intelligence. IEEE Access. **9**, 135167–135185 (2021). https://doi.org/10.1109/ACCESS.2021.3116870
31. Seeliger, A., Pfaff, M., Krcmar, H.: Semantic web technologies for explainable machine learning models: a literature review. CEUR Workshop Proc. **2465**, 30–45 (2019)
32. Smirnov, A., Levashova, T.: Context-aware personalized decision support based on user digital life model. In: Proceedings of the 6th International Conference on Computer-Human Interaction Research and Applications, pp. 129–136. SCITEPRESS - Science and Technology Publications (2022). https://doi.org/10.5220/0011526900003323
33. Spetzler, C., Winter, H., Meyer, J.: Decision Quality: Value Creation from Better Business Decisions. Wiley (2016)
34. Fayoumi, A.G.: Evaluating the effectiveness of decision support system: findings and comparison. Int. J. Adv. Comput. Sci. Appl. **9**, 195–200 (2018). https://doi.org/10.14569/IJACSA.2018.091023
35. Straka, G.A.: Measurement and evaluation of competence. Cedefop Reference series, no. 58, pp. 263–311. Luxembourg, Office for Official Publications of the European Communities (2004).
36. Is Your Team Too Big? Too Small? What's the Right Number?, https://knowledge.wharton.upenn.edu/podcast/knowledge-at-wharton-podcast/is-your-team-too-big-too-small-whats-the-right-number-2/. Accessed 21 Aug 2023
37. Katzenbach, J.R., Smith, D.K.: The Wisdom of Teams: Creating the High-Performance Organization. Harvard Business Review Press, Harvard (2015)
38. LaFasto, F., Larson, C.: When Teams Work Best: 6,000 Team Members and Leaders Tell What it Takes to Succeed. 1st edn. SAGE Publications, Inc (2001)

39. Robbins, S.P., Judge, T.A.: Organizational Behavior. Prentice Hall, Upper Saddle River (2006)
40. Karpov, A.A., Lale, A., Ronzhin, A.L.: Multimodal assistive systems for a smart living environment. SPIIRAS Proc. **4**(19), 48–64 (2014). https://doi.org/10.15622/sp.19.3

Simplifying the Development of Conversational Speech Interfaces by Non-Expert End-Users Through Dialogue Templates

Maia Aguirre[1,2(✉)], Ariane Méndez[1], Manuel Torralbo[1], and Arantza del Pozo[1]

[1] Vicomtech Foundation, Basque Research and Technology Alliance (BRTA), Parque Científico y Tecnológico de Gipuzkoa, Paseo Mikeletegi 57, Donostia/San Sebastián, Spain
{magirre,amendez,mtorralbo,adelpozo}@vicomtech.org
[2] UPV/EHU, Department of Electrical and Electronics, Faculty of Science and Technology, Campus de Leioa, 48940 Leioa, Bizkaia, Spain

Abstract. Conversational speech interface development, maintenance and evolution is challenging for non-experts as it requires linguistic knowledge and proficiency in chatbot design and implementation. To address this issue, this work proposes the use of Dialogue Templates, compact conversational interfaces intended to cater specific interaction capabilities which can be easily adapted to a particular use case by non-expert end-users, just with knowledge of the application domain. Our implementation of Dialogue Templates is presented and detailed for three relevant conversational spoken interaction use cases in the industrial environment: navigating maintenance management systems, recording manufacturing plant activity data and registering warehouse inventory. In addition, a comparative analysis is also conducted to assess the effort required to develop sample conversational assistants in such scenarios using our conventional development platform versus Dialogue Templates. Results show that Dialogue Templates significantly simplify the development of conversational speech interfaces, without demanding linguistic expertise.

Keywords: Conversational speech interfaces · Task-oriented dialogue systems · Dialogue templates

1 Introduction

The undeniable technological progress that society is experiencing has brought changes in the way we communicate. Telecommunications are part of our everyday life and we increasingly consume digital channels such as web messaging platforms (e.g. Skype, Hangouts, Slack, Microsoft Teams, Discord, etc.). This digital revolution has brought new ways of interaction, in an immediate, personalized and friction-less way. Technological advances have also been reflected in the Artificial Intelligence (AI) field, where speech recognition, speech synthesis, natural language processing and reasoning, among others, have opened novel communication paradigms [1].

M. Aguirre and A. Méndez—These authors contributed equally to this work.

H. P. da Silva and P. Cipresso (Eds.): CHIRA 2023, CCIS 1996, pp. 89–109, 2023.
https://doi.org/10.1007/978-3-031-49425-3_6

Within this context, conversational interfaces (also known as chatbots, voice assistants and/or smart speakers) are being increasingly demanded by companies and administrations, as they allow task automation through natural language communication [1]. Conversational assistants are particularly useful to communicate with knowledge and data platforms in settings where users are involved in manual operations, because they enable hands-free, natural and flexible interaction. Industrial environments are one of those settings, where conversational speech interfaces are specially relevant solutions that can be applied to optimize tasks such as navigating through maintenance management systems, recording manufacturing plant activity data or registering warehouse inventory, alongside other examples [2].

However, building conversational spoken interfaces that fit the necessities of each task is not easy. Expert knowledge is needed to identify linguistic information relevant to the interaction use case, design dialogue flows and adjust speech recognition, natural language understanding and dialogue management components so they can process task-specific information appropriately. Once a conversational interface is deployed, expert linguistic knowledge is also required to further adjust components to user interactions [3]. Since most industrial companies lack such professional profiles, they usually outsource the development of conversational interfaces. Unfortunately, this makes it difficult for end-user companies to develop spoken interfaces as well as to maintain and evolve them according to updated domain knowledge, hindering their practical use.

With the aim of fostering the application of conversational speech interfaces in industrial scenarios, this work proposes a new methodology for developing conversational assistants that simplifies their development, maintenance and evolution over time by non-experts. Our proposal builds on defining specific dialogue capabilities relevant to an interaction use case and introduces a template-based approach to instantiate them, allowing personalized conversational interfaces to be built easily.

The present article is structured as follows: Sect. 2 provides some background on dialogue systems and reviews the main characteristics of the conversational assistant development platforms in the market. In Sect. 3, three relevant application use cases of conversational speech interaction in the industrial environment are presented. Section 4 then describes our own conversational assistant development platform and presents our proposal to simplify the development of conversational speech interfaces by non-expert users using Dialogue Templates. The design and implementation of three Dialogue Templates, corresponding to each of the presented industrial use case scenarios, is also described in detail. In Sect. 5, the cost of implementing a conversational assistant using our conventional platform and Dialogue Templates is compared for the considered three use cases. Finally, Sect. 6 highlights the main contributions of this work and proposes tentative lines to develop in the future.

2   Background and Related Work

Conversational interfaces are complex programs designed to handle conversations with human users and perform certain actions based on such interactions. In order to understand user utterances and automate responses, conversational assistants are comprised of multiple interconnected AI and natural language processing components.

The first step to build a custom conversational interface for a specific use case is to define the interaction flow, that is, the sequence of utterances that the user can say to interact with the assistant and their corresponding responses, which act upon a request or guide the conversation. To understand these utterances, the most common strategy is to employ an intent/entity annotation schema, where intents categorize the communicative purpose, and entities gather the variable and significant information related to each intent. For example, in the utterance "I want to fly to Madrid tomorrow", the intent behind the user's request is to book a flight with the value *Madrid* as the destination entity and *tomorrow* as the date entity. With the information extracted from the user, the state of the conversation is determined and the dialogue strategy to follow is defined in order to form the according response. This can also involve the use of external resources that act upon a given request, provide conversation logic or access the necessary information to generate responses.

Due to their increasing popularity, there are many tools available for the development of conversational agents. Google offers a platform for the design and integration of conversational assistants called Dialogflow. It comes in two different versions: Dialogflow ES [4], which is oriented to small and simple agents; and Dialogflow CX [5], which supports more complex interaction models. To that end, Dialogflow CX includes the concepts of *flows* and *pages*. Flows separate complex dialogues in multiple conversation topics. Each flow is represented as a state machine where the states are called pages. At any given point of the conversation there is a single active flow and page. After each user utterance the page can remain the same or transition to another one, which could lead to a different flow, or ultimately, to the end of the conversation.

Amazon has an analogous development platform, LEX [6], and allows third-party developers to build conversational interfaces known as Skills [7], on top of its smart home assistant Alexa. Microsoft offers its own conversational assistant development platform Power Virtual Agents [8] and a natural language understanding service called LUIS [9] to identify intents and entities in user words and phrases. As an open source alternative, Rasa [10] is a popular conversational interface development framework that runs in the local premises. Editing specially formatted configuration files to define the desired behaviour, Rasa can automatically train and deploy the resulting assistant.

All mentioned conversational interface development tools rely on the concepts of intents and entities to understand human interaction. Granted, each tool uses its own user interface or configuration file format, but they follow the same development pattern: enter the intents that provide the functionality, assign each intent its respective entities, and annotate a set of sample utterances to train the AI models that detect the intent and fill the relevant entities [11] from the user's actual utterances.

Although it also shares the same underlying schema, IBM Watson Assistant [12] takes a slightly different approach and provides an additional level of abstraction with *actions* and *steps*. Similar to intents, actions represent the set of outcomes that the assistant can perform in response to a user's request. However, an action comprises not only the invocation, but also the dialogue until the particular request has been fulfilled. Therefore, actions consist of one or more steps or conversation turns that follow the initial trigger input. Steps may be direct answers to user inquiries, follow up questions asking for additional information, or effects that act upon the requests. Steps are processed in a given order and, if necessary, only when certain conditions are met.

Most conversational assistant development tools are rule based and handle conversations that always follow the same script, the reason being that usually there are not enough saved past conversations of each particular use case to consider other data-driven AI approaches [13]. The Rasa framework, however, allows using sample dialogue outlines to train models able to generalize to unseen conversation paths. These representations of exchanges between user and assistant are called *stories* [14, 15].

Regarding the generation of the response, some platforms enable the use of static responses, template responses that append run-time parameters such as entities, and calls to external resources. Dialogflow, Microsoft Power Virtual Agents, Rasa and IBM Watson Assistant include these features. Contrarily, with Amazon LEX, Alexa Skills and Microsoft LUIS the response has to be constructed programmatically handling the information extracted from the user utterances as a separate service.

The described assistant implementation alternatives are convenient to develop chatbots that consider a single use case. Nonetheless, there is an increasing demand for conversational interfaces that are able to handle multiple user goals in different domains. A common approach to deal with the growth in complexity is to unify and orchestrate multiple assistants using a main process that routes each user to the corresponding agent based on their request. This increased modularity also allows multiple teams or members to be responsible of individual assistants, which avoids possible conflicts. Furthermore, since each sub-agent can be delimited to a certain set of capabilities to deal with a specific purpose, this opens the opportunity for a simpler and more user friendly development process.

When it comes to the orchestration of multiple conversational assistants, Dialogflow ES has *mega agents* [16] that combine *sub-agents*. When a mega agent performs an intent classification, it considers the intents of all of its sub-agents and delegates the generation of the response to the most fitting one. Likewise, Amazon LEX provides a unified experience across multiple assistants with *networks of bots* [17] that expose a single interface to the end-user and route each request to the appropriate agent based on user input. Alexa can extend its capabilities with skills, which intrinsically are also conversational assistants that the user can access saying *invocation names* [18]. Nevertheless, creating and maintaining sub-agents in these platforms still requires expert linguistic knowledge since, by themselves, they are still treated as regular conversational interfaces in their respective environments.

The aforementioned conversational interface development platforms use state-of-the-art AI models and strategies to create task-oriented assistants that can be deployed in production settings. Nevertheless, the surge in popularity of Large Language Models (LLM), given their superior performance across many NLP tasks, has also recently seen the emergence of models trained with humans in the loop that are very good at following user instructions in a conversational way [19, 20]. Such LLM are trained on immense amounts of open-domain data, and consequently, they are not intended for use in specific domain use cases. Research is currently being conducted on how to leverage the capabilities of LLM for task-oriented dialogue system development. In this line, the Rasa framework already allows the use of LLM at various stages of the conversational interface development process: for intent classification, to select the most suitable fallback response and/or to rephrase responses with context [21]. In addition, end-to-end approaches are also being considered, where LLM are used sequentially for domain detection, slot filling and response generation. LLM in these end-to-end settings can be fine-tuned [22] or prompted using in-context learning [23], but results still fall behind those achieved by traditional task-oriented dialogue system architectures.

3 Conversational Speech Interfaces in Industrial Environments

Industrial environments in which users are involved in manual operations can greatly benefit from conversational spoken interfaces enabling hands-free, natural and flexible interaction with knowledge and data sources. This section describes three use cases identified as prevalent within the Basque industrial sector [24], on which we have tested the template-based methodology proposed to facilitate the development, maintenance and evolution of conversational spoken assistants.

Navigating Maintenance Management Systems: the first use case applies to the scenario of navigating Computerized Maintenance Management Systems (CMMS). CMMS are software packages that include a computer database containing information pertaining to an organization's maintenance operations. These systems contain large amounts of information grouped in tree format, often nested down to very low levels. This means that navigating to the desired level can sometimes be slow and requires some knowledge of where a particular drill-down is located. Operators often need to interact with CMMS while performing maintenance services in industrial plants, stopping manual upkeep tasks in order to browse the graphical user interface of CMMS applications. Voice-based interaction can be used in this case to allow hands-free operation and enable faster and more agile navigation of maintenance management systems. The features of Sisteplant's Prisma[1] CMMS system can be checked for further information as an example.

Recording Manufacturing Plant Activity Data: the second use case scenario involves the interaction of operators with Manufacturing Execution Systems (MES). This software applications are designed to record plant activity data, enabling manufacturing decision-makers to gain insights into how current conditions on the plant floor can be optimized to enhance production output. MES operate as real-time monitoring systems, tracking interdependent fields and their associated dependencies. Facility operators must record inputs, outputs, operation orders, machine preparations, parts produced, material consumed, etc. through the MES graphical user interface on a computer often located far from their workplace in the manufacturing plant. Operators can use spoken interfaces in this scenario to entry data into the MES through a series of questionnaires that model the dependencies between fields, while continuing with manual work in the

---

[1] https://www.youtube.com/watch?v=7DG1xXd795I.

corresponding workstations. The features of Zucchetti's[2] MES system can be checked for further information as an example.

Registering Warehouse Inventory: the third use case relates to inventorying product information in a Warehouse Management System (WMS). The main objective of a WMS is to maintain the stock values, main features and positions of the articles in the warehouse correctly, together with the information related to their movements. Operators register inventory information by freely filling in independent fields of the WMS graphical user interface in any desired order, providing both the name of the field and its corresponding value. Allowing to fill in information independently makes data collection more flexible and agile. However, operators still need to stop manual work in order to register inventory data. Once again, voice data entry can enable operators in this scenario to keep their hands free in order to carry on with their manual warehouse work. The features of Micolet's[3] WMS system can be checked for further information as an example.

4   Proposed Approach

4.1   Adilib: Our Conversational Assistant Development Platform

Adilib[4] is a user-friendly platform that enables the creation of versatile conversational assistants. Comparable to most conversational interface development platforms, Adilib allows understanding information expressed by users in natural language, contextualizing user input based on previous interactions and/or external information, and generating diverse types of responses, whether static or dynamic in nature. Unlike other platforms, Adilib employs the concept of attributes [25] to store the dialogue state and manage the rules that govern the dialogue. In order to define the actual state of the dialogue, an Adilib assistant can have as many attributes as desired, whose values are assigned using memory rules. On the other hand, interaction rules are defined based on the attribute values, as well as on the user's and the system's last turns. On top of those technological components, Adilib also includes training, deployment and monitoring functionalities, streamlining both the development of conversational assistants and their consumption. Adilib also supports several languages, allowing the development of multilingual conversational assistants, capable of identifying and adapting to the detected language at all times.

Figure 1 shows the architecture of the Adilib platform. It is divided into the following components:

- **Adilib User Interface:** web graphical user interface that allows the development of conversational assistants.
- **Adilib Core:** component responsible for the training and inference of the following technological modules:
  - Language Identifier (LangID): module that identifies the input language.

---

[2] https://www.youtube.com/watch?v=7ZJ-67NCA1E.

[3] https://vicomtech.box.com/v/micoletusecase.

[4] https://www.vicomtech.org/upload/download/librerias/sdk_adilib_QLX05.pdf.

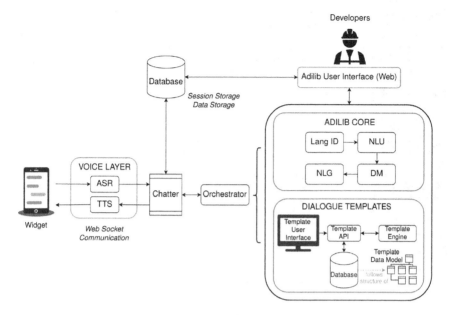

Fig. 1. The architecture of Adilib.

- Natural Language Understanding (NLU): module in charge of user comprehension.
- Dialogue Manager (DM): module that oversees decision making, actively tracks the progress of the dialogue and retains memory of the past interactions within a conversation.
- Natural Language Generation (NLG): module that generates responses based on the information received from the DM.
– **Chatter:** component in charge of maintaining dialogues with users across different channels, by communicating with Adilib Core.
– **Database:** persistence of logs and interaction data in a database for visualization and/or analysis purposes.
– **Voice Layer:** component that enables spoken interaction of Adilib Core with the users. It is composed of the following modules:
  - Automatic Speech Recognition (ASR): module that transcribes the spoken utterances of the users.
  - Text to Speech (TTS): module that synthesizes the textual responses generated by the NLG module into audio.
– **Widget:** web graphical user interface that users can employ to interact with the conversational assistants developed using Adilib.
– **Dialogue Templates:** components that endow Adilib conversational assistants with specific capabilities and correspond to the main contribution of this work. They are further described in Sect. 4.2.
– **Orchestrator:** component that directs user inputs to the appropriate Dialogue Template or main conversational assistant. See Sect. 4.3 for further details.

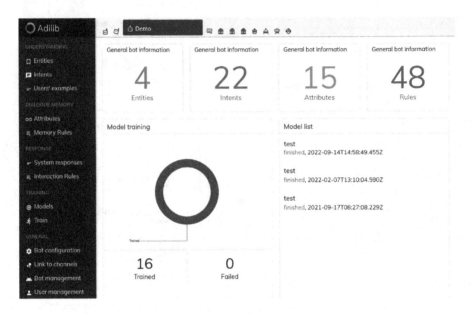

Fig. 2. Adilib User Interface.

The Adilib User Interface can be seen in Fig. 2. The navigation menu on the left displays the sections that must be completed in order to develop a conversational assistant:

– The first section concerns **Understanding**. Inside, *Intents* and *Entities* that encode natural language into semantic representations can be defined. Within the *Users' examples* subsection, variations of sentences labeled with the defined intents and entities can be introduced.
– The second section can be used to define the **Dialogue Memory**. On the one hand, the *Attributes* that will serve as memory for the dialog can be defined. On the other, the *Memory Rules* that will activate, deactivate or change the attribute values can be added, taking into account events such as the user's or system's last turn.
– In the **Response** section the *System responses* can be defined. Besides, the *Interaction Rules* that activate each of the defined answers can also be set, considering the user's input, the active attributes and the system's response in the last turn.
– In the **Training** section the NLU and DM *Models* can be *Trained* and the desired version of the models can be activated.
– Finally, the **General** area can be used to configure different settings of the conversational assistant such as the supported languages, websocket channels, external services and/or user management, among others.

With the described approach, implementing a conversational assistant for each of the use cases described in Sect. 3 is not simple. To begin with, it is necessary to conceptualize and design the conversational assistant to be implemented. This task involves theoretical work to establish the capabilities of the assistant and define the interaction model to be handled by the system. The interaction model is the basis for developing the assistant and requires determining the intents, entities, and attributes that the

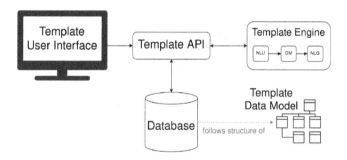

Fig. 3. Adilib Dialogue Template components.

conversational assistant will support. This process calls for a certain level of linguistic knowledge. Then, user examples need to be provided for each intent and entity using the Adilib User Interface, as well as defining attributes, memory and interaction rules and writing system responses. Despite the Adilib User Interface being designed to make this process highly intuitive, it can still be long and laborious. In addition, implementations cannot be reused across conversational assistants. If a use case remains the same but the domain changes, it would be necessary to re-implement the assistant from scratch in Adilib. In order to simplify the process of creating conversational assistants for non-expert users and leverage the knowledge of certain closed logics, we have incorporated Dialogue Templates into Adilib.

4.2   Adilib Dialogue Templates

Adilib Dialogue Templates are components that endow a conversational assistant with specific capabilities. These Templates can be interpreted as compact assistants, given that each of them is formed by its own NLU, DM and NLG modules. Adilib Dialogue Templates need to be linked to a main Adilib conversational assistant. The content and complexity of this main assistant do not impact the performance of the Dialogue Template, meaning that if only the closed capability of the Dialogue Template is desired, the main assistant can be left empty. However, the fact that a Dialogue Template has to be associated with a main conversational assistant opens up interesting possibilities, such as the combination of personalized intents, entities and rules with a Dialogue Template or even endowing a single assistant with capabilities of several Dialogue Templates. Having the ability to build a conversational assistant where several Templates co-exist means that a mechanism to determine which Dialogue Template, if any, should manage each user input is needed. For that purpose, along with the Dialogue Templates, an Orchestrator module which is described in Sect. 4.3 has also been integrated in Adilib.

Our implementation of Dialogue Templates is divided in two main stages: (i) the design of the Dialogue Template and its **Template Data Model**, and (ii) the implementation of the core Dialogue Template components, which are shown in Fig. 3 and described as follows:

– **Template User Interface:** a web graphical user interface that allows defining the possible values of the data structures to be managed by the Dialogue Template.

The information collected through the Template User Interfaces will always follow the data model defined for the Dialogue Template.

- **Template API** (Application Programming Interface): allows the storage of and access to the information added via the Template User Interfaces. It also allows additional functionalities such as search, candidate matching, modification and deletion of said information.
- **Template Engine:** in charge of understanding the user input, applying a set of rules and generating the corresponding output.

The main advantage of Adilib Dialogue Templates is that their implementation is handled by the Adilib development team, so Dialogue Template end-users do not need to face the challenge of implementing their own logic and rules in order for the conversational assistant to behave as they desire. Instead, end-users can employ the developed Template User Interfaces to feed the Dialogue Templates with information related to their particular use case or domain. Template User Interfaces let users define the information they want a Dialogue Template to manage without having to define intents, entities, attributes or rules, which makes it accessible for people who are not trained on conversational speech interface design or development. Additionally, information can be input through Template User Interfaces as many times as desired, enabling the development of conversational assistants for different use cases and domains without having to re-implement dialog flows each time. Once a user saves the desired data in a Template User Interface, the introduced information is instantly accessible through the conversational assistant and the corresponding Dialogue Template Engine is capable of managing related dialogues without having to re-train the assistant nor any of its modules.

The following subsections detail the implementation of three Dialogue Templates aimed at satisfying the conversational spoken interaction needs of the use cases of the industrial environment described in Sect. 3: a **Navigation Dialogue Template** to simplify the development of spoken interfaces to navigate maintenance management systems; a **Questionnaire Dialogue Template** to simplify the development of voice-based interaction interfaces to record manufacturing plant activity data; and a **Slot-Filling Dialogue Template** to simplify the development of conversational speech interfaces to register warehouse inventory. Nevertheless, the implemented Dialogue Templates could also be used as is to navigate other types of tree-structures, answer other types of questionnaires or fill in other information-slot pairs in alternative domains such as technical support services or the social health environment.

Navigation Dialogue Template. For cases where users need to navigate extensive menus in their software systems or information tracking programs, the Navigation Dialogue Template is proposed. The logic behind this Dialogue Template is designed to, given all options of a menu and their dependencies, provide an easy navigation, both step by step or directly jumping to the final level. The Navigation Dialogue Template is thought up to suit users with different levels of expertise. For instance, senior profiles are more likely to know all the options of the menu in their software by heart and may find navigating step by step tiring. In such cases, the Navigation Dialogue Template allows jumping directly to the desired node in the menu, saving time and reducing the

Create New Navigation Menu

Fig. 4. Navigation Template User Interface.

toll of repetitive work. On the other hand, for junior profiles not yet familiar with the software, the Navigation Dialogue Template offers guidance at each stage by indicating which options are available in the next step. Additionally, there may be options within a menu that belong to different branches but share the same name. On such occasions, the logic behind the Navigation Dialogue Template is capable of identifying the ambiguity point, asking users to choose between different options only when necessary.

The *Navigation Template Data Model* includes the title and language of the navigation menu, the navigation levels and their possible options. The *Navigation Template User Interface* is illustrated in Fig. 4. In the example, the layout of an editing menu is instantiated so that end-users can navigate through it. As can be seen, the proposed navigation menu offers two main options to choose from: "Edit" or "View". If the "Edit" path is chosen, two new options are made available: "Open File" and "Save File". On the contrary, if "View" is picked in the first step, "Syntax" is automatically selected, because there are no more available options in that level, and three new choices are presented to end the navigation: "Plain Text", "Python" or "JSON". The *Navigation Template API* allows saving information entered through said interface in a database and reading or deleting it, based on the title and/or identifier of each element in the navigation menu. Then, the *Navigation Template Engine* internally builds a graph based on the dependencies of each level and the options in the menu, allowing their navigation in as many steps as the user desires. The engine has been implemented to understand 12 intents and 6 entities, relies on 8 attributes to define the dialogue state in each turn, includes 29 memory and 25 interaction rules and can provide up to 26 different responses depending on the user input.

Questionnaire Dialogue Template. The Questionnaire Dialogue Template is designed to define questionnaires and collect the answers provided by users in dialogue form. This Dialogue Template is highly flexible and adaptable to multiple scenarios. Users have the freedom to determine the number of questions per questionnaire, define the questions, specify the type of answer for each question, and determine whether to skip or navigate to different questions based on the previous answers. In addition, questions can be set as mandatory or optional and different ways of asking the same question can also be listed.

The *Questionnaire Template Data Model* includes the title and language of the questionnaire, the list of questions, the response type for each of them, whether the question is mandatory and, if applicable, the list of possible answers to choose from, the range among which the answer can be found, and what question to jump to depending on the given answer. Figure 5 shows a questionnaire directed to plant operators being created using the *Questionnaire Template User Interface*. In the depicted example, the number of manufactured pieces is asked, the response type is set to be free text and it is established that answering the question is compulsory. The information entered is saved in a database via the *Questionnaire Template API*, which allows consulting all questionnaires stored in the database, deleting them and/or identifying questionnaires by their name or identifier. To enable interaction, the *Questionnaire Template Engine* can understand 9 user intents and 6 entities, uses 7 attributes to track the dialogue state, includes 29 memory and 19 interaction rules and can provide 16 different responses depending on the user input.

Slot Filling Dialogue Template. The purpose of the Slot Filling Dialogue Template is to help users log data into a database in the order they prefer and without having to follow a specific dialogue flow. This is optimal for environments where the amount of data that needs to be registered every day is important, such as inventory facilities or warehouses. In these scenarios, operators are expected to go through considerable quantities of products and register their features, e.g. type, color, size, price, or whether they are faulty. Using the Slot Filling Dialogue Template users can fill in data forms by indicating slot and value pairs (e.g."color blue") in each turn. If the slot exists in the form and the value is given in the correct format, the system will give a sound alert so that the user knows the information has been correctly saved. While users keep giving slot and value pairs in the appropriate format, they will not be interrupted unless

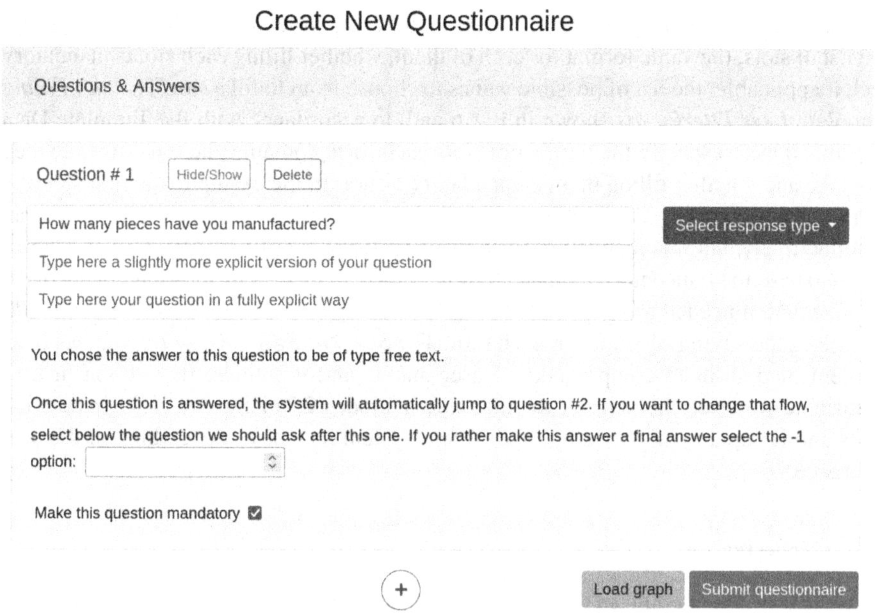

Create New Questionnaire

Questions & Answers

Question # 1   Hide/Show   Delete

How many pieces have you manufactured?   Select response type ▾

Type here a slightly more explicit version of your question

Type here your question in a fully explicit way

You chose the answer to this question to be of type free text.

Once this question is answered, the system will automatically jump to question #2. If you want to change that flow,
select below the question we should ask after this one. If you rather make this answer a final answer select the -1
option: [⇕]

Make this question mandatory ☑

(+)   Load graph   Submit questionnaire

Fig. 5. Questionnaire Template User Interface.

explicitly asked. At any stage of the interaction users can request the list of remaining
slots to be filled or can rewrite previously stored values, in which case the system will
give the corresponding information to the users.

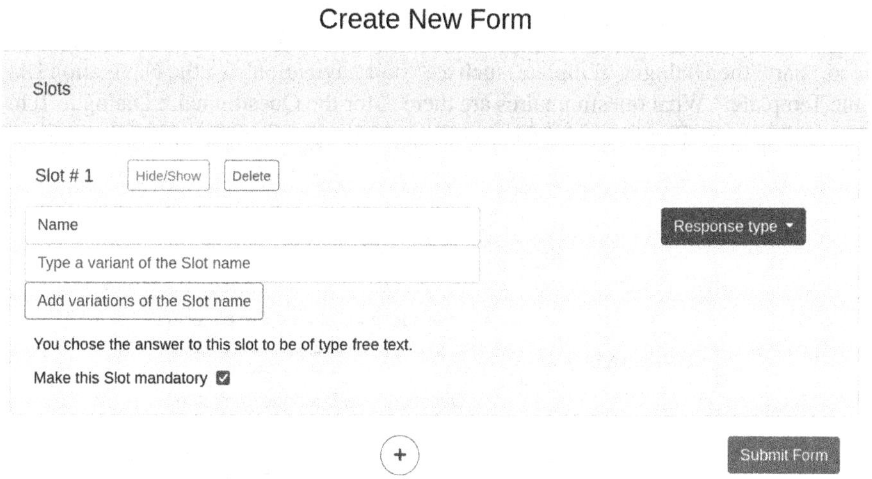

Create New Form

Slots

Slot # 1   Hide/Show   Delete

Name   Response type ▾

Type a variant of the Slot name

Add variations of the Slot name

You chose the answer to this slot to be of type free text.

Make this Slot mandatory ☑

(+)   Submit Form

Fig. 6. Slot Filling Template User Interface.

The *Slot Filling Template Data Model* includes the title and language of the form, the list of slots, the value format for each of them, whether filling each slot is mandatory and, if applicable, the list of possible values to choose from to fill a slot. The *Slot Filling Template User Interface* is shown in Fig. 6 and, in accordance with the Template Data Model, allows to specify the number of slots each form contains, the type of value they can take and whether filling them is mandatory or not. In the example, the first slot of a form is being defined. This slot is intended to store the name of the product and it can be filled freely, but it is mandatory to complete it. The *Slot Filling Template API* stores in a database the data entered via the Template User Interface. In addition, the retrieval of information needed to verify valid slot and value pairs is also performed via the API, as well as the saving of values in each turn. The *Slot Filling Template Engine* has been implemented so as to comprehend 14 user intents and 9 entities. In addition, it uses 7 attributes to track the state of the dialogue, includes 25 memory and 49 interaction rules and is capable of providing 33 different system responses depending on the user utterance.

4.3 Orchestrator

The Orchestrator module in Adilib is a text classifier based on BERT [26] that is in charge of deciding whether each user utterance has to be processed by the main conversational assistant or by a Dialogue Template. Considering the Dialogue Templates presented in this paper, if we were to work with a conversational assistant that contained the three of them, the Orchestrator would be the one shown in Fig. 7.

The Orchestrator is trained with a set of sentences from the main conversational assistant, i.e. user utterance examples of the intents defined in the main assistant, and activation sentences for each of the Dialogue Templates. All these sentences are labeled according to the assistant or Dialogue Template they correspond to, so the Orchestrator can learn the type of sentences each of them can manage.

Activation sentences for Dialogue Templates are examples of utterances one would use to "start" the Dialogue Template, such as "Start navigation" for the Navigation Dialogue Template, "What questionnaires are there?" for the Questionnaire Dialogue Template or "I want to fill a form" for the Slot Filling Dialogue Template. The Orchestrator

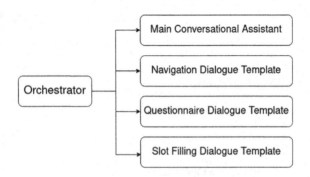

Fig. 7. Orchestrator module for a conversational assistant with the Navigation, Questionnaire and Slot Filling Dialogue Templates.

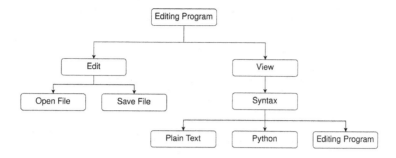

Fig. 8. Navigation menu.

is designed so that, once one of these sentences is detected and a Dialogue Template is activated, the dialogue is handled by said Dialogue Template until it is exited – be it because the end-user requests it explicitly or because the flow inside the Dialogue Template reaches its end. In other words, once a Dialogue Template is activated, the Orchestrator is kept inactive until the Dialogue Template is exited.

5 Evaluation

In order to assess the effort required to develop a conversational speech interface for each use case described in Sect. 3 using the Adilib conversational assistant development platform detailed in Sect. 4.1 versus the corresponding Adilib Dialogue Template presented in Sect. 4.2, a comparative analysis is conducted in this section.

Note that the evaluation carried out is quantitative and focuses on the amount of information required to set up a conversational assistant in each scenario. A qualitative evaluation involving platform users has not yet been undertaken given its inherent complexity. Training individuals to use Adilib effectively requires several days of instruction, resulting in a considerable time-intensive process especially when multiple evaluators would need to be involved in order to carry out a robust qualitative assessment.

5.1 Navigation Use Case

The design and implementation of a navigation-type assistant is now examined. The estimation focuses on a specific use case with functionalities restricted to navigating a menu containing the options displayed in Fig. 8. In addition to allowing navigation through the different levels of the menu, the conversational assistant must be able to:

- Trace and save the user's path from the start node to the end node.
- Provide next options.
- Skip intermediate nodes if the user requests so and there are no paths to disambiguate.

Table 1. Interaction model of a sample Navigation use case.

		Description
Intents	1	To inform about an entity.
Entities	9	One for each node of the graph. Each entity has 1 value.
User Examples	∼90	About 10 per intent + entity value.
Attributes	9	One for each entity.
Memory Rules	9	To activate the selected attribute plus the attributes of the parent nodes.
System Responses	6	4 to list the options of the nodes that have children; 1 to inform that an end node has been reached; 1 to inform that the user has not been understood (fallback).
Interaction Rules	5	One for each system response (minus fallback).
Total Items	129	

A conversational assistant that allows this interaction and is implemented in Adilib must follow the interaction model reflected in Table 1.

After designing Table 1 and in order to develop the conversational assistant, an expert in the field would need to enter the 129 items that make up the defined interaction model in the corresponding sections of the Adilib User Interface previously described and shown in Fig. 2. Note that some of these items, such as memory or dialogue rules, require an average of 10 fields to be filled in order to be completed. Instead, a non-expert end-user would only need to fill the Navigation Template User Interface of Fig. 4 with the 9 values of the navigation menu in Fig. 8 to implement a conversational assistant with the same capabilities. In addition to reducing by 93% the number of elements that need to be defined and entered for developing the assistant, the knowledge necessary to do so is limited to the application domain. This also facilitates maintenance and evolution of the conversational speech interface, in case the defined navigation menu changes.

5.2 Questionnaire Use Case

Next, the design and implementation of a questionnaire-type conversational speech interface is evaluated. The analysis is performed for a particular use case with functionalities restricted to a questionnaire that follows the flow of Fig. 9. The resulting conversational assistant must be able to guide the user through the questionnaire in compliance with the following instructions:

– The user cannot skip the mandatory questions.
– The answers to each question must be of the appropriate type.

Table 2 shows an interaction model that meets these requirements.

After designing Table 2 and in order to develop the conversational assistant, an expert in the field would need to enter the 142 items that make up the defined interaction model in the corresponding sections of the Adilib User Interface previously described

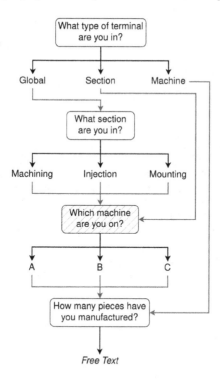

Fig. 9. Questionnaire menu. The striped question is not compulsory, the remaining questions are.

Table 2. Interaction model of a sample Questionnaire use case.

		Description
Intents	3	1 to skip a question; 1 to report entities; 1 to report the value of the last question.
Entities	3	One per each choice type question. In this particular case, each entity also has 3 associated values
User Examples	~110	About 10 per intent/intent + entity value.
Attributes	4	One for each question.
Memory Rules	4	One to activate each attribute based on what the user says.
System Responses	7	4 for the questions; 1 to inform that the question cannot be skipped; 1 to report completion; 1 to inform that the user has not been understood (fallback).
Interaction Rules	11	6 for questions (depending on the answer to the first question, one rule or another will be activated and the second question will change); 2 for questions that can be reached skipping the previous ones; 1 to inform that the question cannot be skipped; 1 to report completion; 1 to report completion after skipping the last question
Total Items	142	

and shown in Fig. 2. Note that some of these items, such as memory or dialogue rules, require an average of 10 fields to be filled in order to be completed. Instead, a non-expert end-user would only need to fill the Questionnaire Template User Interface of Fig. 5 with the 13 values of the questionnaire diagram in Fig. 9 to implement a conversational assistant with the same capabilities. In addition to reducing by 91% the number of elements that need to be defined and entered for developing the assistant, the knowledge necessary to do so is limited to the application domain. This also facilitates maintenance and evolution of the conversational speech interface, in case the defined questions and/or answers change.

5.3   Slot Filling Use Case

Finally, the design and implementation of a slot-filling conversational speech interface is examined. Once more, the analysis is performed for a particular form that follows the structure of Fig. 10. The resulting conversational assistant must be able to help the user to complete the form in compliance with the following instructions:

- The user cannot skip the mandatory slots.
- The values given to each slot must be of the appropriate type.
- Slot values can be overwritten.
- The user can ask information about a specific slot.
- The user can ask information about the remaining empty slots.

Table 3 shows an interaction model that meets these requirements.

Table 3. Interaction model of a sample Slot Filling use case.

		Description
Intents	11	4 to report each slot and its value; 1 to assent to overwrite; 1 to deny overwriting; 1 to ask what options remain; and 4 to ask what type a particular slot is.
Entities	4	One for each slot. In this case, the "color" entity will have 3 possible values.
User Examples	∼130	About 10 per intent/intent + entity value.
Attributes	4	One for each entity.
Memory Rules	8	4 to activate each attribute based on what the user says and 4 to override each attribute.
System Responses	39	4 to inform that a particular slot has been registered; 4 to inform what type a particular slot is; 4 to ask to overwrite a particular slot; 1 to inform that the form has been completed; 1 to inform that the "date" field is mandatory; 24 to inform which slots are still to be filled; 1 to inform that the user has not been understood (fallback).
Interaction Rules	43	One for each system response defined above (except fallback) plus 4 to report that the response has been recorded after overwriting the field value
Total Items	239	

After designing Table 3 and in order to develop the conversational assistant, an expert in the field would need to enter the 239 items that make up the defined interaction model in the corresponding sections of the Adilib User Interface previously described and shown in Fig. 2. Note that some of these items, such as memory or dialogue rules, require an average of 10 fields to be filled in order to be completed. Instead, a non-expert end-user would only need to fill the Slot Filling Template User Interface of Fig. 6 with the 7 values of the slot-filling diagram in Fig. 10 to implement a conversational assistant with the same capabilities. In addition to reducing by 97% the number of elements that need to be defined and entered for developing the assistant, the knowledge necessary to do so is limited to the application domain. This also facilitates maintenance and evolution of the conversational speech interface, in case the defined slots and/or values change.

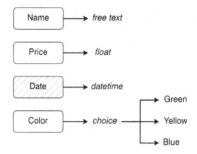

Fig. 10. Slot Filling menu. The striped slot is not compulsory, the remaining slots are.

As observed in the conducted analysis, the advantage provided by Dialogue Templates to develop conversational interfaces is very large. Despite the analyzed sample use cases being quite straightforward, the complexity of their development using conventional platforms such as Adilib scales considering the depth of the navigation menus or the number of questions/answers or form fields. However, the complexity of implementing those using Dialogue Templates remains the same. Another convenience provided by Dialogue Templates is that no expert linguistic knowledge is demanded. The only requirement to develop conversational interfaces is domain expertise in the specific use case.

6   Conclusions and Future Work

The main contribution of this work is the conception and implementation of Dialogue Templates, compact conversational interfaces with specific capabilities aimed at facilitating the development, maintenance and evolution of conversational speech interfaces by non-expert end-users. As a field of application, work has focused on the industrial environment in which three use cases related to navigating maintenance management systems, recording manufacturing plant activity data and registering warehouse inventory have been identified as real concrete examples which can clearly benefit from spoken conversational interaction. The concept of the proposed Dialogue Templates has been introduced in detail and Dialogue Template designs have been described for each of the considered use cases, specifying both their dialogue logic and the main characteristics of their components. Additionally, a comparative analysis of the effort required to implement a conversational interface using our conventional assistant development platform versus the considered Dialogue Templates has been carried out. Results have shown that implementation gains for simple interaction examples are above 90%, while further gains are expected for more complex real interaction scenarios including deeper navigation structures, higher number of questions/answers or additional form fields. Another very important contribution is that expert linguistic knowledge is not required to develop assistants using Dialogue Templates. Thus, companies can be autonomous when it comes to developing, maintaining and evolving their conversational speech interfaces. Having an accessible way to develop and maintain these tools shall help increase the popularity of conversational interfaces in the industrial sector. Finally, it is also relevant to note that in addition to covering the use cases described in this article, the presented Dialogue Templates also serve to cover many more potential application scenarios that require their navigation, question-answering and slot-filling capabilities such as e.g. searching for information in instruction manuals with nested sections and subsections; filling patient follow-up questionnaires or conducting product testing and verifying specifications, among others.

As future work, a qualitative validation of conversational assistants implemented using the proposed Dialogue Templates in industrial environments is expected to be carried out. The goal is for end-user companies to use the presented Dialogue Templates to develop conversational spoken assistants for their particular use cases and to pilot those in real application scenarios. In addition, we also aim to qualitatively compare end-user experience when implementing assistants using the Adilib platform versus the implemented Dialogue Templates in terms of ease of use, versatility, time required and subjective perception, among others. Another line of future work includes detecting additional interaction use cases that cannot be solved using the Dialogue Templates presented in this article and designing and implementing their corresponding Template User Interfaces, APIs and Engines. Additionally, it would be interesting to explore how to intercommunicate the Engines of the Templates among themselves. For example, in order to allow navigating to a form or questionnaire and then completing it.

Acknowledgments. This project has received funding from the Department of Economic Development and Infrastructure of the Basque Government under grant number ZL-2022/00560 (GEVO).

References

1. Altarif, B., Al Mubarak, M.: Artificial intelligence: chatbot-the new generation of communication. In: Hamdan, A., Harraf, A., Arora, P., Alareeni, B., Khamis Hamdan, R. (eds.) Future of Organizations and Work After the 4th Industrial Revolution: The Role of Artificial Intelligence, Big Data, Automation, and Robotics, pp. 215–229. Springer, Cham (2022). https://doi.org/10.1007/978-3-030-99000-8_12
2. del Pozo, A., et al.: EKIN: towards natural language interaction with industrial production machines. In: Annual Conference of the Spanish Association for Natural Language Processing 2021: Projects and Demonstrations, SEPLN-PD, 5–8 (2021)
3. Saenz, M. S.: Contributions to attributed probabilistic finite state bi-automata for dialogue management, Doctoral dissertation, Universidad del País Vasco-Euskal Herriko Unibertsitatea (2021)
4. Google Dialogflow ES - Basics. https://cloud.google.com/dialogflow/es/docs/basics. Accessed 18 May 2023
5. Google Dialogflow CX - Basics. https://cloud.google.com/dialogflow/cx/docs/basics. Accessed 18 May 2023
6. Amazon LEX V2 - How it works. https://docs.aws.amazon.com/lexv2/latest/dg/how-it-works.html. Accessed 18 May 2023
7. Alexa Skills - Create the interaction model for your skill. https://developer.amazon.com/en-US/docs/alexa/custom-skills/create-the-interaction-model-for-your-skill.html. Accessed 18 May 2023

8. Microsoft Power Virtual Agents - Key concepts for bot framework composer users. https://learn.microsoft.com/en-us/power-virtual-agents/preview/composer-concepts. Accessed 18 May 2023

9. Microsoft LUIS - Application design. https://learn.microsoft.com/en-us/azure/cognitive-services/luis/concepts/application-design. Accessed 18 May 2023

10. Rasa - Playground. https://rasa.com/docs/rasa/playground. Accessed 18 May 2023

11. Devlin, J., Chang, M.-W., Lee, K., and Toutanova, K.: Bert: pre-training of deep bidirectional transformers for language understanding. arXiv preprint arXiv:1810.04805 (2018)

12. IBM Watson Assistant - Overview. https://cloud.ibm.com/docs/watson-assistant?topic=watson-assistant-build-actions-overview. Accessed 18 May 2023

13. Shukla, S., et al.: Conversation learner-a machine teaching tool for building dialog managers for task-oriented dialog systems. arXiv preprint arXiv:2004.04305 (2020)

14. Rasa - Stories. https://rasa.com/docs/rasa/stories. Accessed 18 May 2023

15. Rasa - Writing Conversation Data. https://rasa.com/docs/rasa/writing-stories. Accessed 18 May 2023

16. Google Dialogflow ES - Mega Agents. https://cloud.google.com/dialogflow/es/docs/agents-mega. Accessed 18 May 2023

17. Amazon LEX V2 - Network of Bots. https://docs.aws.amazon.com/lexv2/latest/dg/network-of-bots.html. Accessed 18 May 2023

18. Alexa Skills - Understand How Users Invoke Custom Skills, https://developer.amazon.com/en-US/docs/alexa/custom-skills/understanding-how-users-invoke-custom-skills.html. Accessed 18 May 2023

19. OpenAI - ChatGPT. https://openai.com/chatgpt. Accessed 6 Sept 2023

20. Google - Bard. https://bard.google.com/. Accessed 6 Sept 2023

21. Rasa - Using LLMs. https://rasa.com/docs/rasa/next/llms/large-language-models/. Accessed 6 Sept 2023

22. Peng, B., Li, C., Li, J., Shayandeh, S., Liden, L., Gao, J.: Soloist: building task bots at scale with transfer learning and machine teaching. Trans. Assoc. Comput. Linguist. **9**, 807–824 (2021)

23. Hudeček, V., Dušek, O.: Are LLMs All You Need for Task-Oriented Dialogue? arXiv preprint arXiv:2304.06556 (2023)

24. Basque Industrial Sector. https://www.basquecountry.eus/t32-sectores/en/contenidos/noticia/sectores_industria_08/en_s_ind/sectores_ind.html. Accessed 18 May 2023

25. Serras, M., Torres, M.I., del Pozo, A.: User-aware dialogue management policies over attributed bi-automata. Pattern. Anal. Applic. **22**, 1319–1330 (2019)

26. Sanh, V., Debut, L., Chaumond, J., Wolf, T.: DistilBERT, a distilled version of BERT: smaller, faster, cheaper and lighter. arXiv preprint arXiv:1910.01108 (2019)

Multiparty Dialogic Processes of Goal and Strategy Formation in Hybrid Teams

Andreas Wendemuth[1]($\boxtimes$) and Stefan Kopp[2]

[1] Institute for Information Technology and Communications, Otto-Von-Guericke-University, 39016 Magdeburg, Germany
andreas.wendemuth@ovgu.de
[2] Social Cognitive Systems, Bielefeld University, 33501 Bielefeld, Germany
stefan.kopp@uni-bielefeld.de

Abstract. A current trend which is already prevalent in highly structured (e.g. industrial) working environments is the cooperation of people, intelligent physical agents (robots) and, in parts, intelligent information agents (AIs, chatbots) in hybrid teams, mostly in paired settings. This position article discusses a major generalization and extension of this concept: (a) the goals, strategies, and actions are not fully prespecified, but develop in the course of a dialogic process; (b) the agents are not merely tools or assistants, but proactively intervene as peers; (c) the hybrid teams are multiparties with several humans and (situated or remote) intelligent agents, exhibiting and modelling pronounced group behavior. Cognitive, dialogic systems are the technical backbone of such team settings, bringing together techniques of multimodal processing, information retrieval, situated action planning and autonomous action generation, recognizing and anticipating task-related states of the actors.

Keywords: Spoken dialog systems and conversational analysis · Multiparty human-machine interaction · Information retrieval

1 Introduction

To date, we witness a wide variety of approaches for managing professional and everyday tasks. There exist highly structured, often verbal or formal descriptions advising how a combination of actions lead to an exactly specified goal. These descriptions are to be found in e.g. building or production processes, involving multiple human and technical actors and being fixed for longer periods of time, and are the consequence of thorough preliminary analysis and planning. While this may allow for high quality and efficiency, it is inherently limited in agility and robustness of the goal-achievement processes.

In contrast, in many tasks rigid planning approaches are either not optimal, as conditions may constantly change, or not suitable, as the goal-finding process and the results of actions are interdependent. The latter is e.g. the case in many design or development related settings, which demand an interplay of partial planning, testing in action etc., where multiple, not fully predetermined goals are negotiated based on the outcome of

© The Author(s), under exclusive license to Springer Nature Switzerland AG 2023
H. P. da Silva and P. Cipresso (Eds.): CHIRA 2023, CCIS 1996, pp. 110–120, 2023.
https://doi.org/10.1007/978-3-031-49425-3_7

intermediate findings. These highly interactive cognitive and social processes do not just take place amongst humans (with other humans, but also with themselves), but are also conditioned to the capabilities of participating intelligent physical agents (robots) and, in parts, intelligent information agents (AIs, chatbots) in hybrid teams. While to date this happens mostly in paired settings, hybrid teams of the near future are *multiparties* with several humans and (situated or remote) intelligent agents, exhibiting and modelling pronounced group behavior.

Humans excel in such underspecified situations, exhibiting learning-by-doing or trial-and-error strategies, in which byways are explicitly expected and even desired in finding a solution, and such exploratory approaches meet the human creativity potential. Equally desired is the interaction among actors, including humans but also the mentioned intelligent agents, which are not merely tools or assistants, but in future proactively intervene. It is still an open question how intelligent agents can be enabled to engage in continuous coordination in a socially cooperative and dynamic environment. It is envisaged that today's technical aids will transform into *peers*, increasingly assuming a formative role at the levels of actions, plans, and goals.

In this position paper, we first discuss related concepts (2), before describing the problem space of assisting in cooperative goal or strategy finding (3). We specifically lay out and discuss scenarios in which cognitive systems provide dialogic support for centralized or multiparty interactions in hybrid teams (4). We will then identify future questions and research approaches (5). We conclude in proposing a novel kind of cooperative cognitive system which can assist humans in open and underspecified situations (6), thus extending future human-machine interaction to multiparty dialogic processes amongst peers.

2 Related Concepts

In a traditional setting since the 1990's, collaboration was defined as shared plans, with the ability to plan and act together through some process of group decision-making [13, 14], where goals or strategies are coordinated among the actors beforehand, and merely adaptations in the action phase. More recently, the interlinked problems of understanding what the collaborator's intent, and foreseeing actions to support them, has been addressed [21]. This should be pursued on the basis of user states which are classified from sensory observations. Companion technology [7] aims to complement the functional intelligence of technical actors with an equivalent intelligence in human-machine interaction. To do so, the user's preferences, capabilities, requirements and needs must be matched with the user's current situation and emotional state, with the help of appropriate planning, reasoning and decision-making. For the first time, here the role of interaction and dialog have stressed the dynamic evolution of problem-solving [32].

In the related area of human-robot systems, several roadmaps [10, 28] see a development towards collaborative robotics, with safe, close and dependable physical interaction between robot and human in a shared workspace. Therefore, human-compatibility is a core design concept, which entails that future robots must sense, reason, learn, and act in close contact with humans in a partially unknown world. This includes dialogic capabilities, such as social context-defined human-robot interaction patterns and collaborative manipulation based on estimated user intent [26].

Where these interactions mainly see a paired collaboration, recently group inter-actions have come into focus. Groups are being described as complex and adaptive dynamical systems [2], in which global patterns from local interactions emerge and at the same time structure them. Important interaction processes, such as formation of coali-tions or in-group/out-group behavior, cannot be derived solely from dyadic interactions, but requires taking into account more complex interactions. For example, the action of a third agent on the interaction within a dyad (e.g. strengthening or weakening of the possibility of cooperation, exchange of information) is already an example of a "group interaction" [20]. Although tools for a mathematical description of such interaction, such as hypergraphs or simplicial complexes [5], have been known for a long time and are already being used, for example, for a network analysis of social interactions [19], a deeper understanding of the role of higher-order interactions in regulation networked activities, such as team dynamics, is just beginning [4].

3 Problem Space

Open questions derive from partially open-plot situations which cannot be covered by classical planning and current human-machine interaction systems. In classical planning models, loops of planning and acting, possibly in multi-agent systems with centralized or decentralized monitoring, are adjusted through parametric or process-related vari-ables. In contrast, open-goal situations demand interacting levels of cooperation (real-ization, negotiation, reflection) where the actors dynamically coordinate their activity. This involves the distribution and modularization of competence in the problem space, and their influence at the three levels of cooperation processes. We distinguish problems and cooperation structures along the following dimensions:

- *locality* of actions and competences: from many actions and competences (extremely local) of individual actors (human, intelligent agent) to a hierarchically active mediator with rich competence (global).
- *centralization* of processes: from a process of cooperation with all stake- holders (central) to cooperation (at several levels) between different actors (distributed). The latter entails process modularization and standardization.
- *dynamics* of team structures and roles: from functional groups or teams with a given distribution of responsibilities, size, and life span (rigid), to flexible sizes with temporal functions and roles (dynamic).

Interaction is based on the hypothesis that in functioning hybrid teams there must be sufficient coordination on three interacting levels of cooperation [15] and that different coordinative or communicative mechanisms can be used for this (see Fig. 1): At the *realization* level, the operational implementation of separate or joint actions must be coordinated (e.g. through observation, feedback or intervention); at the *negotiation* level, the objective or larger implementation plan must be coordinated with strategies and role assignments (e.g. by proposing or negotiating based on new information); Finally, on a *reflection* level, the process itself can be coordinated, if necessary with an alternative choice, according to changeable criteria and dispositions [16].

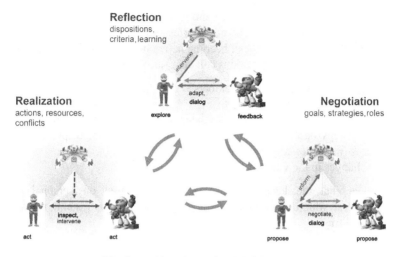

Fig. 1. Problem Space for Hybrid Teams.

4 Cognitive System Support

4.1 Centralized Setting

A typical problem space with centralized support can be envisaged as an interface assistive agent, specified in the introduced dimensions as follows:

1. Actions and competencies are distributed, where actors have specialized process-related knowledge.
2. Cooperation is supported by a centralized cognitive system.
3. Rigid (functional) team setting.

The centralized cognitive system acts as an independent mediator and moderator at all cooperation levels. Such a setting can for example be given by product construction (e.g. a tool) under given specifications. The team contains intelligent agents both for mechanical purposes as well as specification interpretation, also with external information sources. The agents understand meta-requests such as "hand me the four-inches-wrench" and "a manual of the drill is needed". Such requests are parsed, technically interpreted and checked for availability and specification conformity, and action is taken or clarification is sought. Those actions are only query-specific, goal determination is not an issue. The interaction with the cognitive support system can however provide exactly such assistance.

In this centralized setting the cognitive support system is a personal companion of the team's agents. It is endowed with procedural memory. It knows the team member's preferences and can assess their current task-related, cognitive and dispositive (emotional, intentional, traits) state. Situation assessment is realized through multimodal sensors and scene interpretation. Dialogic abilities are used to clarify situations. Understanding is realized by knowledge models to map the goal finding process. Environmental processes are observed, as well as actions by the team members. The cognitive support system can capture both human-machine interaction and machine-machine interaction (M2M) by direct access to status variables, while not interfering with the M2M.

The cognitive support system can become active itself, or by request, to foster the goal-finding process. Such interventions can take various forms, for example:

- act exactly as requested by team members,
- pro-actively propose further support,
- express doubt that team members have the required competences or focus for action or planning steps, based on the observation of the cognitive and dispositive states, or preferences (not necessarily factually based),
- propose changes in the working process.

It is clear that the level of intervention, also based on personal observations/preferences, which is allotted to the cognitive support system, is subject to negotiation and trust.

4.2 Multiparty Setting

Another type of problem setting arises when considering cooperation in larger and more heterogeneous teams, which can be cast in the problem dimensions as follows:

1. Different and local competences of actors, heterarchies of agents and users.
2. Modularized and possibly distributed cooperation processes between (sub- groups of) actors at different levels.
3. Variable group(s) of many actors, having individual roles, functions and action autonomies.

In such a setting, cooperation among multiple agents and users takes place, with underspecified goals. Examples are involved negotiations, medical teams or complex assembly tasks. This entails problems of incremental decision processes in cooperation of humans, intelligent physical agents and intelligent information agents under underspecified targets and varying conditions. A central mediator (with superior position) is not suitable (as in the centralized setting), but rather, local competencies, manifested by the intentional, anticipatory and cooperative contributions of the individual agents, lead to distributed cooperation between (groups of) actors and form the outcome of the team as a whole. This form of cooperation consist of separate phases, which occur either sequentially or in parallel: negotiating or briefing, joint solving of subtasks, group work which combines and advances individual solutions. In hybrid teams, these phases form and resolve in an ad-hoc fashion, where autonomy, consolidation, binding of results, and assignment of responsibilities are subject to negotiation. This also extends to personal factors such as preferences, abilities, functions and dispositions. External factors play an equal role, such as availability of resources, information, location, etc., and must be balanced by the team. These negotiation processes occur at the realizational, negotiation and reflection levels.

The role of the cognitive system support here changes to supervising the complex dynamics (varying rates, lags, and delays), structure (subgroups of cooperation) and work results (accomplished subtasks, state of planning). In particular, lack of coherence or diverging planning will lead to a point where the need for strategy changes arises, which must be mediated between several actors. Since good teams generally are characterized by long periods of coordinated and conflict-free cooperation of the members, the support of the cognitive system must not be a "repair mode", but rather be particularly foreseeing and integrative, reducing centrifugal or partitioning tendencies at an early stage.

4.3 Peer Level

The premise of hybrid teams is that intelligent physical agents and intelligent information agents are seen as peers to humans. We therefore discuss the consequences of such a setting. Several extensions to current approaches come to play. Traditional support sees the non-human agents as assistants, and follows a controller-like paradigm, where humans are positioned as natural leaders, and non-human agents are given a subsidiary role. As an example, a smart home environment will have a controlling unit which follows patterns predefined by humans (e.g. increase temperature at a specific time of day) and assigns corresponding tasks to technical system (i.e. advise the heater to activate). In contrast, under the peer paradigm, the technical system becomes an intelligent actor who has more options under his own responsibility (e.g. fix the heating times according to user preferences and usage patterns which have been estimated on his own account). As a team member, intelligent actors have own goals, such as minimizing energy consumption or costs, or acting in a sustainable mode which prefers gentle treatment of material (e.g. slow rise of temperature). The peer may in general act / react individually and pursue (optimised) strategies. Such responsibilities and goals may either be assumed on the actor's own accord, be negotiated within the hybrid team, or be supervised by cognitive system support. The adaptation of responsibilities and goals again will be subject to user preferences, usage patterns and changing conditions. Should the cognitive system support detect or anticipate conflicts (e.g. between human interests and technical actor's goals), a dialogue-based resolving process is initiated [32]. This again reflects the role of all hybrid team members as peers, rather than commanding the technical actors to change specific behavior patterns.

It is foreseeable that humans will not be comfortable which such team roles at once, but rather need to develop trust that technical systems behave as peers. Actions, plans and goals of all team members therefore should be transparently communicated, explained if necessary, and confirmed. Privacy and security should be considered naturally at all phases. It is important that the team is the defining entity, i.e. goals should not be set under hidden agendas of third parties such as companies or institutions [6, 12]. Comfort, trust and general agreeableness therefore are based much less on the team constellation and task at hand, but rather by the way decision processes are expressed and disclosed. Cognitive support systems should therefore pro-actively engage team members in dialogues to find agreeable courses of action.

4.4 Suitable Support for Strategy Finding

Under varying conditions, hybrid team cooperation under underspecified goals is maintained by suitable support, as described in the above scenarios. Humans and intelligent actors may take individual actions and drive the goal-finding process. A crucial point arises when – even under suitable support – the current approach is deemed infeasible.

This demands a change in (partial) strategy. Such strategy changes do not come easy: major changes in planning become necessary, which results in high extra effort and possibly severe personal resistances. There may not be one obvious new strategy, but a lengthy negotiation process must compare alternatives and their success expectancy. Cognitive support systems should help explore these alternatives, and keep record of their assessment. Even worse, in case of further failure, reversal to the original strategy may be necessary, which demands even more support.

Overall, cognitive support systems can be characterized by the following features: given sensory and informational input, actions, intentions and plans of team members and the team as a whole must be (automatically) identified. Consequences and success expectancy of plans and actions should be assessed based on team member states and external information sources. Cooperation with team members, taking into account their personal preferences and skills, is necessary in a peer-like manner. Having sketched these core features, one can conclude that the performance of such cognitive support systems exceed the current by far the state-of-the-art of today's personal assistants or information search engines.

5   Research Questions and Corresponding Work

For cognitive systems to provide the outlined support efficiently and acceptably, **future research questions** can be specified, and corresponding (existing) research can be identified to answer these questions, which can be cast as follows:

- Which relevant states and traits (motoric, perceptual, dispositional, cognitive) of human actors can be recognized? Which multimodal sensory information and inferential methods are required? Which description of the state of the cooperation process, including markers of (anticipated or actual) conflicts, is suitable?
- How is coordination and negotiation at the three layers governed by overarching principles and mechanism? How can cognitive support systems follow them?
- Which semantic or ontological formalism acts as a basis for modeling strategies, goals and tasks? How are alternative, predictive or anticipatory actions identified to explore various subgoals and strategies? When and how is strategy change recognized and moderated?
- How are compromises or new directions in hybrid teams initiated and supported? Under which competing rationales (e.g. transparency, efficiency, autonomy and fairness) can a team work conciliably?
- Which are suitable datasets, generated, annotated and enriched from empirical cooperation studies? How do cognitive support systems learn preferences and strategies from such datasets?

Answering these questions is possible only through transdisciplinary, basic and applied research. Some existing approaches can be grouped into the following **work categories**:

Team Members' Dispositions and Action Intentions can be automatically detected from mimics, gestures, pose and speech. For gesture recognition, several methods are available based on structured dynamic time warping [31] and deep learning techniques such as bidirectional recurrence and temporal convolutions [23]. Image sequences and optical flow also allows for action recognition with very high accuracy [22]. Mimic expressions can be rated on a categorical and dimensional scaling with the help of facial action coding (FACS) units [25]. Speech-phonetic and prosodic features are used for disposition recognition, with maximum accuracy in the differentiation between valence and arousal, which has been shown for various speakers and corpora [27]. Expressiveness of interaction can be induced [9] and amplified by accompanying, variable gestures [17]. Discourse particles (DP) and para-linguistic features allow for identifying relevant statements in the dialog, where complex situations have DPs as markers (e.g. hesitations, filler words). The involvement of a team member can be identified in temporal passages of passive, passive-participatory and active terms [9]. A person's expression can be specified by generative [3] and discriminative [35] models.

Information Finding Dialogs are fundamental in problem solving. For example, so-called Technology Scouting [34] identifies methods and technologies in a specific industrial sector. When complex queries (in contrast to simple ad-hoc questions) are formulated, current (information search) systems still fail to come up with adequate support. Here, exploratory search [33] can tackle such problems. Different information seeking methods are discussed in [1]. The dynamics of search processes can be described by complex behavioral models based on Markov chains [30]. Collaborative search is also determined by personality traits and emotional states of team members, in success and failure settings [29].

Multimodal Communication and Adaptive Dialog Strategies can flexibly support cooperation. Extensive studies exist on situated communication with cognitive systems. Here, important factors are communicative functions of task-related actions, and the shared action context for, e.g., verbal or gestural references. The latter have been analysed as social signals and their role for dialog adaptation and user model update in [8]. Exploration and negotiation processes are highly dynamic and adaptive, where cognitive support systems can analyse and catalyse cooperative behavior with dialogic conversational agents [18].

Mental states and Reciprocal Cooperation should be modelled for assessing the course of negotiation. For improved collaboration and coordination, and for resolving problems and conflicts, it is possible to detect other actors plans to better predict future arguments and actions [11]. Hidden states, such as beliefs, intentions, or goals, can be modeled by Bayesian theory of mind. This can be applied in diagnostic (understanding) and causal inference (prediction). Unavoidable states of intractability appear when aiming at complete modeling, which leads to the introduction of satisficing (good-enough) models. They are able to balance adaptation in accuracy and efficiency [24].

6 Innovation and Effect, Conclusions

Based on the previous discussions, a new paradigm has been proposed, and steps for implementation detailed, for hybrid teams as peer cooperations of people, intelligent physical agents and intelligent information agents. These teams excel in situations where goals, strategies, and actions are not fully prespecified. Dialogic processes are at the core of cognitive support systems which recognize and anticipate the formation and alteration of multiparty team actions and strategies. The application scenarios are manifold, and will increase in future, e.g. in (driver) assistance systems, collaborative robotics in industry 4.0, medical teams, or smart homes. Hybrid teams benefit from the different capabilities of their actors, while at the same time a certain cohesion is necessary. Technical agents must exhibit robust machine information acquisition and processing, which may conflict with simplified, intuitive, even emotional operations by humans. By moving to peer level and to cooperative learning and strategy formation, the management of high complexity tasks, error tolerance and knowledgeability can be the future hallmarks of hybrid teams.

Acknowledgements. The author A. Wendemuth would like to thank the Center for Behavioral Brain Sciences, Magdeburg, and the German Federal State of Sachsen Anhalt, for continued support.

References

1. Al-Suqri, M., Al-Aufi, A.: Information Seeking Behavior and Technology Adoption: Theories and Trends. IGI Global (2015). https://doi.org/10.4018/978-1-4666-8156-9
2. Arrow, H., McGrath, J., Berdahl, J.: Small Groups As Complex Systems: Formation, Coordination, Development, and Adaptation. Sage Publishing Group (2000). https://doi.org/10.4135/9781452204666
3. Baak, A., Müller, M., Bharaj, G., Seidel, H.P., Theobalt, C.: A data-driven approach for real-time full body pose reconstruction from a depth camera. In: Consumer Depth Cameras for Computer Vision: Research Topics and Applications, pp. 71–98 (2013)
4. Battiston, F., et al.: The physics of higher-order interactions in complex systems. Nat. Phys. **17**(10), 1093–1098 (2021)
5. Battiston, F., et al.: Networks beyond pairwise interactions: structure and dynamics. Phys. Rep. **874**, 1–92 (2020)
6. Beldad, A., de Jong, M., Steehouder, M.F.: How shall I trust the faceless and the intangible? A literature review on the antecedents of online trust. Comput. Hum. Behav. **26**(5), 857–869 (2010). http://dblp.uni-trier.de/db/journals/chb/chb26.html#BeldadJS1
7. Biundo, S., Wendemuth, A. (eds.): Companion Technology. CT, Springer, Cham (2017). https://doi.org/10.1007/978-3-319-43665-4
8. Buschmeier, H., Kopp, S.: Communicative listener feedback in human-agent interaction: Artificial speakers need to be attentive and adaptive. In: Proceedings of the 17th International Conference on Autonomous Agents and Multiagent systems, pp. 1213–1221 (2018)
9. Böck, R., Siegert, I.: Recognising emotional evolution from speech. In: Proceedings of the International Workshop on Emotion Representations and Modelling for Companion Technologies (ERM4CT 2015) at ICMI, pp. 13–18 (10 2015). https://doi.org/10.1145/2829966.2829969
10. Christensen, H., et al.: A roadmap for us robotics– from internet to robotics 2020 edition. Found. Trends® Robot. **8**(4), 307–424 (2021). https://doi.org/10.1561/2300000066
11. Diaconescu, A.O., et al.: Inferring on the intentions of others by hierarchical Bayesian learning. PLoS Comput. Biol. **10**(9), e1003810 (2014)
12. Gol Mohammadi, N., et al.: Trustworthiness Attributes and Metrics for Engineering Trusted Internet-based Software Systems. In: Helfert, M., Desprez, F., Ferguson, D., Leymann, F. (eds.) Cloud Computing and Services Science, pp. 19–35. Springer International Publishing, Cham (2014)

13. Grosz, B., Hunsberger, L., Kraus, S.: Planning and acting together. AI Mag. **20**, 23–34 (1999)
14. Grosz, B.J., Kraus, S.: Collaborative plans for complex group action. Artif. Intell. **86**(2), 269–357 (1996)
15. Hollnagel, E.: Cognition as control: a pragmatic approach to the modelling of joint cognitive systems. Control **9**, 1–23 (2002)
16. Konradt, U., Otte, K.P., Schippers, M.C., Steenfatt, C.: Reflexivity in teams: a review and new perspectives. J. Psychol. **150**(2), 153–174 (2016). https://doi.org/10.1080/00223980.2015.1050977
17. Kopp, S., Bergmann, K.: Less time to speak leads to less speech-gesture redundancy. In: Proceedings of the 7th International Gesture Conference (ISGS 7) (2016)
18. Kopp, S., van Welbergen, H., Yaghoubzadeh, R., Buschmeier, H.: An architecture for fluid real-time conversational agents: integrating incremental output generation and input processing. J. Multimodal User Interfaces **8**, 97–108 (2014)
19. Li, P., Dau, H., Puleo, G., Milenkovic, O.: Motif clustering and overlapping clustering for social network analysis. In: IEEE INFOCOM 2017-IEEE Conference on Computer Communications, pp. 1–9. IEEE (2017)
20. Lyons, J.B., Sycara, K., Lewis, M., Capiola, A.: Human–autonomy teaming: Definitions, debates, and directions. Front. Psychol. **12**, 589585 (2021). https://doi.org/10.3389/fpsyg.2021.589585
21. Macindoe, O.: Sidekick agents for sequential planning problems. PhD thesis, Massachusetts Institute of Technology (2014)
22. Mayer, N., et al.: What makes good synthetic training data for learning disparity and optical flow estimation? Int. J. Comput. Vision **126**, 942–960 (2018)
23. Pigou, L., Van Den Oord, A., Dieleman, S., Van Herreweghe, M., Dambre, J.: Beyond temporal pooling: recurrence and temporal convolutions for gesture recognition in video. Int. J. Comput. Vision **126**, 430–439 (2018)
24. Pöppel, J., Kopp, S.: Satisficing models of Bayesian theory of mind for explaining behavior of differently uncertain agents: Socially interactive agents track. In: Proceedings of the 17th International Conference on Autonomous Agents and Multiagent Systems, pp. 470–478 (2018)
25. Saeed, A., Al-Hamadi, A., Handrich, S.: Advancement in the head pose estimation via depth-based face spotting. In: 2016 IEEE Symposium Series on Computational Intelligence (SSCI), pp. 1–6. IEEE (2016)
26. Schmidtler, J., Knott, V., Hoelzel, C., Bengler, K.: Human centered assistance applications for the working environment of the future. Occup. Ergon. **12**, 83–95 (2015). https://doi.org/10.3233/OER-150226
27. Schuller, B., Vlasenko, B., Eyben, F., Rigoll, G., Wendemuth, A.: Acoustic emotion recognition: a benchmark comparison of performances. In: Proceedings of Automatic Speech Recognition and Understanding Workshop (ASRU 2009), Merano, Italy, pp. 552–557. IEEE (2009)
28. SPARC, E.: Robotics 2020 multi-annual roadmap for robotics in Europe, call 2 ict24. Horizon (2020). https://doi.org/10.3030/688441
29. Stange, D., Kotzyba, M., Nürnberger, A.: Professional collaborative information seeking: towards traceable search and creative sensemaking. In: Transactions on Computational Collective Intelligence XXVI, pp. 1–25. Springer (2017). https://doi.org/10.1007/978-3-319-59268-8_1
30. Steichen, B., Ashman, H., Wade, V.: A comparative survey of personalised information retrieval and adaptive hypermedia techniques. Inf. Process. Manag. **48**, 698–724 (2012). https://doi.org/10.1016/j.ipm.2011.12.004
31. Tang, J., Cheng, H., Zhao, Y., Guo, H.: Structured dynamic time warping for continuous hand trajectory gesture recognition. Pattern Recogn. **80**, 21–31 (2018)

32. Wendemuth, A., Böck, R., Nürnberger, A., Al-Hamadi, A., Brechmann, A., Ohl, F.W.: Intention-based anticipatory interactive systems. In: 2018 IEEE International Conference on Systems, Man, and Cybernetics (SMC). pp. 2583–2588 (2018). https://doi.org/10.1109/SMC.2018.00442
33. White, R., Roth, R.: Exploratory Search: Beyond the Query-Response Paradigm. Synthesis Lectures on Information Concepts, Retrieval, and Services, vol. 1 (2009). https://doi.org/10.2200/S00174ED1V01Y200901ICR003
34. Wolff, M.: Scouting for technology. Research Technology Management **35**, 10–12 (1992). https://doi.org/10.1080/08956308.1992.11670801
35. Yub Jung, H., Lee, S., Seok Heo, Y., Dong Yun, I.: Random tree walk toward instantaneous 3D human pose estimation. In: Proceedings of the IEEE Conference on Computer Vision and Pattern Recognition, pp. 2467–2474 (2015)

Adaptive Network Modelling of Informal Learning Within an Organization by Asking for Help and Getting Help

Debby Bouma and Jan Treur[✉]

Social AI Group, Department of Computer Science, Vrije Universiteit Amsterdam, Amsterdam, The Netherlands
d.bouma@student.vu.nl, j.treur@vu.nl

Abstract. This paper contributes a computational analysis of how informal learning within organizations often takes place. The approach covers asking questions, the influence of approachability and presence, and direct and indirect answering of questions asked. This is done by modeling different people with their mental states, internal mental models, and communication. The results show that both direct and indirect answering of questions to a help-seeker can improve or complete their mental model. However, when questions need to be passed to other people, this slows down the mental model learning process. These results laid the foundation for further research and confirms intuitive results.

Keywords: Adaptive network model · Communication · Learning within an organization · Asking for help · Mental models · Organizational learning

1 Introduction

Within an organization, asking for help is not always easy, it comes with several social costs. Help seekers might be afraid to come across as 'incompetent, dependent, and inferior to others' (Lee, 2002). This can negatively influence their self-esteem, and one's assumed position in an organization (Lee, 2002; Argyris, 1993; Tedeschi & Melburg, 1984). It is also mentioned that asking for help on an important task might come with higher costs as compared to a less important task (Lee, 2002).

In this paper, there will be taken a deeper dive into the mental models of persons and organizational learning of them based on asking for help. This will be done with the help of several computational models. The use of computational models prevents the creation of unethical and/or hostile workplaces, while also giving a (simplified) idea of how this thought process happens.

When this is done, there will be a clearer understanding of how both the idea and the reality of approachability and presence influence asking for help. Based on a computational analysis of this, it might be easier to know how to lower the social costs of asking for help. This improves organizational learning and can improve the workplace. By researching what the cost is of asking for help, a workplace can work on lowering

H. P. da Silva and P. Cipresso (Eds.): CHIRA 2023, CCIS 1996, pp. 121–142, 2023.
https://doi.org/10.1007/978-3-031-49425-3_8

these costs. This decreases the job demands, thereby lowering the pressure, and therefore increasing the motivation and lowering the strain leading to improved organizational outcomes (Bakker & Demerouti, 2007).

This paper consists of eight sections. First, in Sect. 2 we will discuss the background information about organizational learning, mental models, asking for help, and approachability, and presence. In Sect. 3 we will discuss a scenario where someone might ask one or two people for help. Thereafter, in Sect. 4 the self-modeling network modeling approach used for computational analysis and simulation is briefly introduced. In Sect. 5 the adaptive network model is introduced, here the underlying assumptions for the model are discussed. After that, in Sect. 6 the simulation results are shown and discussed. The paper ends with a discussion in Sect. 7, while limitations and further research that can be done in Sect. 8.

2 Background Knowledge

Organizational Learning and Mental Models. Humans possess the capacity to engage in collective behavior and collaborate through joint action. In these joint actions, groups develop shared understanding and knowledge exchanged through various forms of communication. This includes verbal and nonverbal means, as well as through actions and objects. Communication within a group encompasses metaphors, myths, and other shared concepts. Initially, new members of the group may have limited shared knowledge due to the group's specific communication practices, but over time, they acquire this understanding through learning, this happens by taking more and more part in communication (Bouma, Canbaloğlu, Treur, & Wiewiora, 2023; Cook & Yanow, 1993). Such learning takes place through the sharing of mental models; 'They are working models of situations or processes from the world, and include information we know, as well as our beliefs' (Bouma et al., 2023). When asking for help, mental models are improved, and thus organizational learning occurs.

Asking for Help. Currently, organizations are very complex, and asking for help is seen as an important step to learning within the organization. However, like mentioned previously, taking the step to ask for help is not always easy. To lower the threshold for this, it is important to understand what mechanisms influence help-seeking. In (Van der Rijt et al., 2013), several variables. Such as accessibility, awareness of expertise, trust, and hierarchy were explored. The authors concluded that the perception of the help providers provide, trust and accessibility had a positive association with asking for help. It was also shown that people are more likely to ask help from higher-up than from lower-down. Asking for help is seen as an interesting and valuable process because it helps you acquire knowledge and explanations. When you consult with knowledgeable people, missing knowledge can be filled in, it can be used to organize thoughts, it can shine light on previously unconsidered options, it can be used to avoid mistakes, solve problems, gain confidence, and receive social support (Heath & Gonzalez, 1995; Yaniv, 2004).

Approachability. As mentioned in the previous paragraph, if people are asking for help, it is usually from someone higher up the hierarchy than the help-seeker. Searching 'approaching someone is scary' on Google gave almost 70 million results, on sites such as Quora, Reddit, or theexceptionalskills people are discussing how scary it is to approach someone. The irrational fear of talking to someone gets even higher when it is to someone higher up the hierarchy. Approachability has mainly been reviewed in the student-teacher relation, and not as much on the workfloor. However, the student-teacher and the subordinate-supervisor relation are somewhat similar. Approachability is a word that can take a lot of attributes, among others: open-minded, engaging, communicative, reachable, professional, positive body language. Kind-hearted, authentic (Karnita, Woodcock, Bell, & Super, 2017). 'Until recently non-Western education has been dominated by (Confucian) teacher led approaches, with teachers viewed as experts.' This means that the teachers were not meant to be questioned. This lowered the teacher's approachability since the student's fear of being wrong was heightened. This can lead to students being disengaged, or falling behind (Karnita et al., 2017). It was concluded by Reid and Johnston that approachability is a characteristic of a high-quality student-teacher relationship (Reid & Johnston, 1999). Since approachability involves the tendency to exhibit elements of caring and goodwill, a help-seeker who believes that the colleague cares for their wellbeing may view the colleague as more approachable, and this can lower the bar for someone to seek help.

Presence and Availability. It has been shown that the availability of help, either through online or physical support, has a positive relation to someone's well-being. Whether it is through blogging, social capital in your neighborhood, or social support (Rains & Keating, 2011; Kawachi, Kennedy, Lochner, & Prothrow-Stith, 1997; Cohen & Wills, 1985; DeLongis & Holtzman, 2005). The perception of availability can help with coping mechanisms (DeLongis & Holtzman, 2005). An example of where availability of help, or lack thereof, can negatively impact people, is at train stations. Travelers who write down their trip and run into changes which makes them unable to follow their original planning, report various ways of coping, such as: 'fare evading, postponing the trip, accepting potentially longer journeys, travelling less with public transport or going back home.' (Durand et al., 2023). This shows the importance of the availability of help. An increase in availability of recreational resources for sports, conditioning activities, and individual activities also was positively associated with participation of these activities (Roux et al., 2007). It is also shown that the presence of resource availability has a positive relation with affective commitment (Moss, McFarland, Ngu, & Kijowska, 2007). It would make sense if this were true not only for resources, but also for help-seeking. While these examples do not necessarily show the importance of availability/ presence for help-seeking on the workfloor, they do show that people are more likely to use something when it is available to them.

3 Scenario

The scenario considered in this paper is as follows. There is a company that develops pictures of space. This company has several employees, but these scenarios focus on three of the employees specifically: Anna (A), Ben (B), and Carlos (C).

Anna is the newest employee and is not completely sure about the entire process. The job consists of three steps:

- **Step a:** Setting up the camera and aligning it with a telescope to capture the desired part of space. This includes securely attaching the camera and properly focusing it.
- **Step b:** Taking the pictures. This includes adjusting camera settings.
- **Step c:** Editing the pictures. This includes moving them from the camera to a computer and using post-processing software to enhance the quality, this can be done by adjusting exposure, color balance, etc.

In Scenario 1, Anna completes steps 1 and 2 successfully, but has some issues with the completion of step 3. Anna knows that Ben can do step 3, so she approaches him. Ben explains step 3 to her, and after that, Anna can do step 3.

In Scenario 2, Anna is not sure who knows how to do step 3, so she approaches both Ben and Carlos, to ask them for help. In this scenario, Carlos does not know how to finalize step 3, but Ben does. After acquiring this information, Ben helps Anna understand the last step.

In Scenario 3, Anna has issues with step 3, and like Scenario 1, asks Ben for help. However, in this scenario, Ben does not know how to help Anna, but knows that Carlos can help her. Ben transfers the question to Carlos. Carlos can get the information to Anna in two ways:

- He tells Anna directly: Scenario 3a
- He tells Ben, who then tells Anna: Scenario 3b

In this scenario, there are three steps, and the focus will be on the third step. The first two steps are added for context, logical flow, and enhancing clarity. By making the process take three steps, the mental models became clearer, and gives a completer and more realistic picture.

4   Self-modeling Network Modelling Approach

In this section, the network-oriented modelling approach used is briefly introduced. A temporal causal network model is characterized as follows here: X and Y denote nodes of the network, also called states (Treur, 2020a), (Treur, 2020b):

- *Connectivity characteristics*: Connections from state X to Y and their weights $\omega_{X,Y}$
- *Aggregation characteristics*: For any state Y, some combination function c_Y defines the aggregation that is applied to the impacts $\omega_{X,Y}X(t)$ on Y from its incoming connections from states X.
- *Timing characteristics*: Each state Y has a speed factor η_Y defining how fast it changes for given causal impact.

The following canonical difference equation is used for simulation purposes (Treur, 2020b):

$$Y(t + \Delta t) = Y(t) + \eta_Y \left[c_Y \left(\omega_{X_1,Y} X_1(t), \ldots, \omega_{X_k,Y} X_k(t) \right) - Y(t) \right] \Delta t \qquad (1)$$

Here, Y is any state Y and X_1 to X_k are the states from which Y gets its incoming connections.

This equation calculates the difference between the aggregated impact $c_Y \left(\omega_{X_1,Y} X_1(t), \ldots, \omega_{X_k,Y} X_k(t) \right)$ on state Y and the current value $Y(t)$ and adds a fraction of this difference to this current value $Y(t)$. This makes that from t to $t + \Delta t$ the value of Y changes in the direction of the value of the aggregated impact. How fast it changes in that direction is specified by speed factor η_Y.

The software environment used is described in (Treur, 2020b), Chapter 9. In the scenarios described here, the advanced logistic sum function was used as combination function (Treur, 2020b), which is also often used for neural networks:

$$\mathbf{alogistic}_{\sigma,\tau}(V_1, ..., V_k) = \left[\frac{1}{1 + e^{-\sigma(V_1+...+V_k-\tau)}} - \frac{1}{1 + e^{\sigma\tau}} \right] (1 + e^{-\sigma\tau})$$

Realistic network models are typically adaptive, where both the states and certain network characteristics change over time. To address this, self-modeling networks (also known as reified networks) provide a network-centric conceptualization for adaptive networks. These self-modeling networks enable the formulation of declarative descriptions using mathematically defined functions and relations. For more details see (Treur, 2020a; Treur, 2020b). For more information, and an example see (Bouma et al., 2023) Sect. 5.

5   The Adaptive Network Model

The introduced adaptive model addresses the communication between two or three colleagues within a company who share a mental model. This either goes directly, or through someone else. In this paper, the mental model of someone is completed by asking colleagues for help. In this model, we have made several assumptions:

- **Communication:** The three colleagues only communicate with each other, there is no outside influence, and these three colleagues end up with the same mental model,
- **Approachability:** As mentioned before, approachability has two options (idea and reality). These have an influence on the approachability of the asked colleague. These are a spectrum from completely on to completely off and can be adjusted. For the sake of simplicity, we have decided to keep it completely off or completely on.
- **Presence:** Similar to approachability, it has reality and idea. These have an influence on the approachability of the asked colleague. These are either completely on or off, someone is present, or they are not.
- **Willingness to Help:** It is assumed that all colleagues are willing to assist and support each other. They can also rely on each other for guidance, advice, and encouragement.
- **Knowledge:** Every person in this model possesses a certain level of knowledge in their area. Some are more experienced, and some are not, and they ask each other for help.
- **Learning Environment:** This model assumes a friendly learning environment among the colleagues. There is a willingness to share experiences, ask questions, and learn from more experienced colleagues.
- **Varied Perspectives:** It is assumed that there is only one correct way to do this scenario. Therefore, there are no varied perspectives and approaches.

This paper shows four different types of learning scenarios within an organization. Every node in this model can be adjusted separately, which makes the model more realistic. The graphical connectivity picture can be seen in Fig. 1 and Tables 1, 2 and 3 show the specification for Scenario 1. The graphical connectivity pictures and tables of Scenario 2–4 can be found in the Appendix in Sect. 9.

In Fig. 1 and Table 1, at the base level (lower plane), the internal simulation of a mental model by the different individuals is modelled: Anna (A), Ben (B), and Carlos (C). Every person has their own mental model of the same situation. In this model, following Sect. 3 a_X, where X can be swapped out for any team member, stands for the mental model state (at the base level: the lower plane in Fig. 1) for setting up the camera, b_X for making the pictures. Finally, c_X stands for mental model states for the editing of pictures. Solid arrows represent a connection the team member is sure off, and a dotted arrow represents a connection the team member does not know about.

The first-order self-model level includes self-model states $\mathbf{W}_{X,Y}$ where X and Y are two base level mental model states; for example, $\mathbf{W}_{a\_A,b\_A}$, see Table 2 and the middle plane in Fig. 1. Such self-model states represent that the person has knowledge about the (causal) connection from a to b. The upward connections are depicted by blue arrows, and the downward arrows shows how the value from $\mathbf{W}_{X,Y}$ is used in the activation of base state Y. Changes in values for these $\mathbf{W}$-states represent adaptation or learning. To this end, the $\mathbf{W}_{X,Y}$ states from all dyads of different team members are linked by black arrows. This means that they in principle can learn from each other. How much they learn from each other is determined by the second-order self-model level.

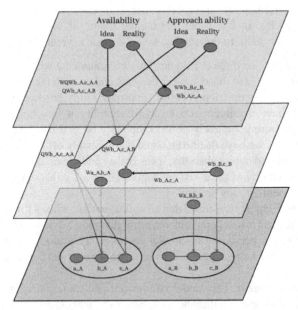

Fig. 1. Graphical representation of the connectivity for Scenario 1.

The second-order self-model level models the control for how the colleagues learn from each other; see Table 3 and the upper plane in Fig. 1. This directly relates to how learning is represented in the first-order self-model level. The $\mathbf{W}_{\mathbf{WW}}$-states represent

Table 1. Base states.

	Nr	State	Explanation
Individual mental states of Anna	X_1	a_A	Setting up the camera for Anna
	X_2	b_A	Making the pictures for Anna
	X_3	c_A	Editing the pictures for Anna
Individual mental states of Ben	X_4	a_B	Setting up the camera for Ben
	X_5	b_B	Making the pictures for Ben
	X_6	c_B	Editing the pictures for Ben

Table 2. First-order self-model states.

	Nr	State	Explanation
Question states of the self-model	X_7	$QW_{b\_A,c}$ $_{A,A}$	First-order self-model state of Anna representing her question for the weight of the connection from b to c within her mental model
	X_8	$QW_{b\_A,c}$ $_{A,B}$	First-order self-model state of Ben representing Anna's question for the weight of the connection from b to c within her mental model
Self-model states of Anna	X_9	W_{a_A,b_A}	First-order self-model state representing the weight of the connection from a to b within the mental model of Anna
	X_{10}	W_{b_A,c_A}	First-order self-model state representing the weight of the connection from b to c within the mental model of Anna
Self-model states of Ben	X_{11}	W_{a_B,b_B}	First-order self-model state representing the weight of the connection from a to b within the mental model of Ben
	X_{12}	W_{b_B,c_B}	First-order self-model state representing the weight of the connection from b to c within the mental model of Ben

the weights of the (communication) channels between the **W**-states for different mental models.

Every $\mathbf{W_{QWQW}}$-state has incoming arrows that provide the context information that is relevant for the processes it controls, and a downward (control effectuating) arrow to the second order self-model level to determine how it influences the processes for the respective **W**-states. The fact that all these states, and their effect on other states can be adapted individually, ensures that this network model is highly adaptive.

Table 3. Second-order self-model states.

	Nr	State	Explanation
Context states	X_{13}	AI	The idea of approachability
	X_{14}	AR	The reality of approachability
	X_{15}	PI	The idea of presence
	X_{16}	PR	The reality of presence
Second-order self-model states from one person to another	X_{17}	$\mathbf{W}_{W_{b\_B,c\_B,}W_{b\_A,c\_A}}$	Second-order self-model state for the weight of the connection from the first-order self-model state $\mathbf{W}_{b\_B,c\_B}$ of the mental model of Ben to the first-order self-model state $\mathbf{W}_{b\_A,c\_A}$ of the mental model of Anna.
Second-order self-model states from one person to another	X_{18}	$\mathbf{W}_{QW_{b\_A,c\_A,A'}\,QW_{b\_A,c\_A,B}}$	Second-order self-model state for the weight of the connection from the first-order self-model state of the mental model of Anna to the first-order self-model state of the mental model of Ben

6 Simulation Results

The available dedicated software environment in MATLAB was used to run several simulations, particularly the scenarios described in Sect. 5. For the most important matrices, see the Appendix in Sect. 9. For the full specifications, see https://www.researchgate.net/publication/371755063.

6.1 Scenario 1: Anna Asks Ben

As can be seen in Fig. 2, Anna surely learns upon posing her question. The first step is indeed asking the question, represented by $\mathbf{QW}_{b\_A,c\,A,A}$ (which is X_7) getting a high activation level: the red line starting around time 3.

Upon this, Ben receives this question which is represented by $\mathbf{QW}_{b\_A,c\,A,B}$ (which is X_8) getting a high activation level: the blue line starting immediately after the previous red line, around time 4. The yellow lines represent Anna. The most left yellow line which starts rising at around timepoint 10 is X_{17} which represents state $\mathbf{W}_{W_{b\,B,c\,B,}W_{b\,A,c\,A}}$. This state shows that Ben is teaching Anna the link between state b and c. The middle yellow line, which starts rising around timepoint 12, represents the first order self-model

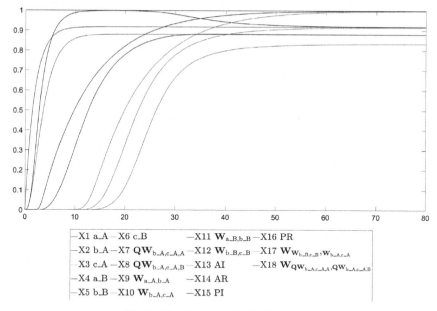

Fig. 2. Simulation results for Scenario 1.

state $\mathbf{W}_{b\_A,c\ A}$, and shows Anna is learning. Then the most right yellow curve, which starts rising at around time point 15 shows that the connection between states b and c in Anna's mental model actually works in the base level: c_A indeed gets a high activation level which did not happen before.

6.2 Scenario 2: Anna Asks Both Ben and Carlos

Scenario 2 is not that different from Scenario 1. Only, in this case Anna asks both her coworkers Ben and Carlos for answers. Ben knows the answer and tells her, thus the same rising lines as in Scenario 1 can be seen. However, Carlos does not know the answer, thus his mental state for the link between task b and c stays 0, explaining why this line stays on 0. The graph is shown in Fig. 3.

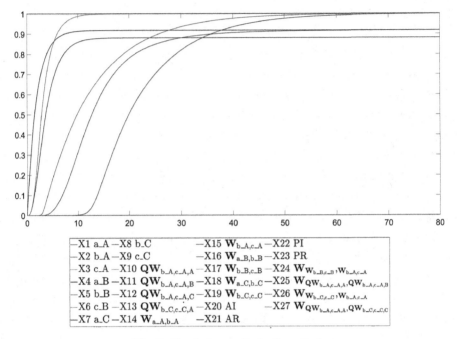

Fig. 3. Simulation results for Scenario 2.

6.3   Scenario 3a: Anna Asks Ben, Ben Asks Carlos, and Carlos Gives the Answer to Anna

In Scenario 3a, Anna asks Ben for the answer to her question. However, Ben does not know the answer. However, Ben knows that Carlos knows the answer, so Ben decides to ask Carlos. Carlos replies to Anna to teach her. At the end of this course of interaction, Ben is still missing the link between task b and c in his mental model, explaining the line that stays on 0 in Fig. 4.

6.4   Scenario 3b: Anna Asks Ben, Ben Asks Carlos, and Carlos Tells Ben, so Ben Can Tell Anna

In the last scenario, 3b, Anna asks Ben for the answers to her question. In this scenario, Ben does not know the answer but knows Carlos does, so Ben asks Carlos. However, instead of telling Anna directly, Carlos tells Ben, who tells Anna. At the end of this interaction, which is shown in Fig. 5, everyone has a complete mental model.

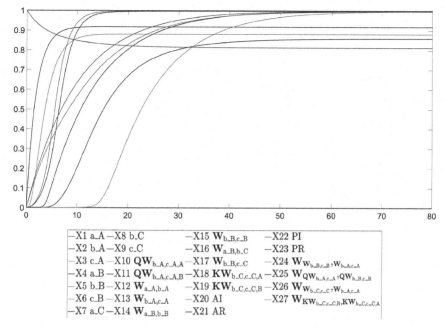

—X1 a_A	—X8 b_C	—X15 $\mathbf{W}_{b\_B,c\_B}$	—X22 PI
—X2 b_A	—X9 c_C	—X16 $\mathbf{W}_{a\_B,b\_C}$	—X23 PR
—X3 c_A	—X10 $\mathbf{QW}_{b\_A,c\_A,A}$	—X17 $\mathbf{W}_{b\_B,c\_C}$	—X24 $\mathbf{W}_{\mathbf{W}_{b\_B,c\_B},\mathbf{W}_{b\_A,c\_A}}$
—X4 a_B	—X11 $\mathbf{QW}_{b\_A,c\_A,B}$	—X18 $\mathbf{KW}_{b\_C,c\_C,A}$	—X25 $\mathbf{W}_{\mathbf{QW}_{b\_A,c\_A},\mathbf{QW}_{b\_B,c\_B}}$
—X5 b_B	—X12 $\mathbf{W}_{a\_A,b\_A}$	—X19 $\mathbf{KW}_{b\_C,c\_C,B}$	—X26 $\mathbf{W}_{\mathbf{W}_{b\_C,c\_C},\mathbf{W}_{b\_A,c\_A}}$
—X6 c_B	—X13 $\mathbf{W}_{b\_A,c\_A}$	—X20 AI	—X27 $\mathbf{W}_{\mathbf{KW}_{b\_C,c\_C,B},\mathbf{KW}_{b\_C,c\_C,A}}$
—X7 a_C	—X14 $\mathbf{W}_{a\_B,b\_B}$	—X21 AR	

Fig. 4. Simulation results Scenario 3a.

7 Discussion

This paper addressed the influence of approachability and presence, as well as direct and indirect answering of questions. This is done by an example where a person (Anna) had to ask Ben (and Carlos) for help with her work. The results show that when someone is present and approachable, the help-seeker gets to fulfil their mental model. This process is slower when the help-seeker gets their answer indirectly. This makes sense intuitively, however by showing this is also computationally substantiated, it can establish a foundation for future work, and identify gaps.

The differences of this paper to (Bouma et al., 2023) are as follows. In (Bouma et al., 2023) the focus is on people getting information as soon as possible. It is focused on both (feed forward and feedback) organizational learning and communication between colleagues and their team leader. The current paper focuses on the details of communication, addressing the role of asking for help and the control of the communication steps. When asking for help, people have to check their own mental models, then teach someone else. All this was not addressed in (Bouma et al., 2023). As can be seen in the graphs in Sect. 6, learning from colleagues takes place, but slower when it is indirect. In all scenarios, there was someone who could provide the help-seeker with answers, either directly or indirectly.

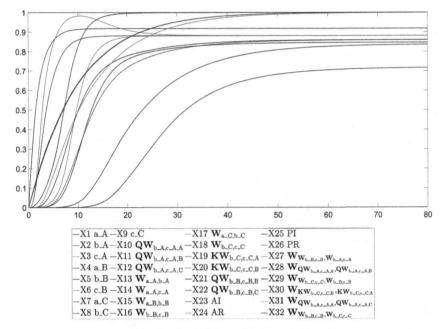

Fig. 5. Simulation results Scenario 3b.

In Sect. 2 it was discussed that asking for help has several factors, however, the difficulty of the task also can play a role in asking for help. According to DePaulo and Fisher, the harder the task, the easier it is to ask for help (DePaulo & Fisher, 1980). Another paper found a positive correlation between someone's expertise, accessibility, and trust and the likelihood of the help-seeker to come to them, the frequency the help-seeker would come to them, and the help-seeker's perceived quality of the found help. This paper also claims that strengthening relations between colleagues, and thereby ensuring accessibility, can help with this (Van der Rijt et al., 2013).

8   Limitations and Further Research

Like any other computational model, the introduced model does not cover reality in full. In an organization there are many factors that influence the communication between colleagues. There are also other factors being simplified; the amount of people in the model, personality traits, and several other factors. There are many options for further research, such as adding more people, adding more context states, and differentiating the dyad values more, the level of difficulty of the task that someone needs help with. Most of these options were not considered for this paper for the sake of simplicity. Empirical information about asking for help in a professional setting is also scarce, and something that could be improved upon with further research.

While this paper has shown things that intuitively make sense, such as answering the help-seeker directly, instead of having the answer be passed through, speeds up the completion of mental models. It has laid the foundation for further, specified, research.

This research could be related to teaching more than one person at a time. Another option is that the question is not answered after the first try, would the help-seeker go back to the person who answered their question the first time, or would they find someone else? And if they would find someone else, how would their mental model be completed if they get taught a connection by someone else, or several different people (who may do it a little different).

As can be seen, there are a lot of options for further research, but by laying the foundation in this paper, hopefully his will become more accessible, and in workplaces, the motivation can be increased, and the strain can be lowered, thereby creating a better work environment. In the Appendix more details of the different variants of the model that have been explored are included; e.g., Figs. 6, 7 and 8.

Appendix

Scenario 1

Table 4a. Role matrix **mb** for Scenario 1.

mb	Scenario 1			
X_1	a_A	X_1		
X_2	b_A	X_1		
X_3	c_A	X_2		
X_4	a_B	X_4		
X_5	b_B	X_4		
X_6	c_B	X_5		
X_7	$\mathbf{QW}_{b\_A,c\_A,A}$	X_2	X_3	X_7
X_8	$\mathbf{QW}_{b\_A,c\_A,B}$	X_7		
X_9	$\mathbf{W}_{a\_A,b\_A}$	X_9		
X_{10}	$\mathbf{W}_{b\_A,c\_A}$	X_{12}		
X_{11}	$\mathbf{W}_{a\_B,b\_B}$	X_{11}		
X_{12}	$\mathbf{W}_{b\_B,c\_B}$	X_{12}		
X_{13}	AI	X_{13}		
X_{14}	AR	X_{14}		
X_{15}	PI	X_{15}		
X_{16}	PR	X_{16}		
X_{17}	$\mathbf{W}_{Wb\_B,c\_B,Wb\_A,c\_A}$	X_8	X_{13}	X_{15}
X_{18}	$\mathbf{W}_{QWb\_A,c\_A,A,QWb\_A,c\_A,B}$	X_7	X_{14}	X_{16}

Table 4b. Role matrix **mcw** for Scenario 1.

mcw	Scenario 1			
X_1	a_A	1		
X_2	b_A	1		
X_3	c_A	X_{10}		
X_4	a_B	1		
X_5	b_B	1		
X_6	c_B	1		
X_7	$\mathbf{QW}_{b\_A,c\_A,A}$	1	-1	1
X_8	$\mathbf{QW}_{b\_A,c\_A,B}$	X_{18}		
X_9	$\mathbf{W}_{a\_A,b\_A}$	1		
X_{10}	$\mathbf{W}_{b\_A,c\_A}$	X_{17}		
X_{11}	$\mathbf{W}_{a\_B,b\_B}$	1		
X_{12}	$\mathbf{W}_{b\_B,c\_B}$	1		
X_{13}	AI	1		
X_{14}	AR	1		
X_{15}	PI	1		
X_{16}	PR	1		
X_{17}	$\mathbf{W}_{Wb\_B,c\_B,Wb\_A,c\_A}$	1	1	1
X_{18}	$\mathbf{W}_{QWb\_A,c\_A,A,QWb\_A,c\_A,B}$	1	1	1

Scenario 2

Table 5a. Role matrix **mb** for Scenario 2.

mb	Scenario 2			
X_1	a_A	X_1		
X_2	b_A	X_1		
X_3	c_A	X_2		
X_4	a_B	X_4		
X_5	b_B	X_4		
X_6	c_B	X_5		
X_7	a_C	X_7		
X_8	b_C	X_7		
X_9	c_C	X_8		
X_{10}	**QW**$_{b\ A,c\ A,A}$	X_2	X_3	X_{10}
X_{11}	**QW**$_{b\ A,c\ A,B}$	X_{10}		
X_{12}	**QW**$_{b\ A,c\ A,C}$	X_{10}		
X_{13}	**QW**$_{b\ C,c\ C,A}$	X_{13}		
X_{14}	**W**$_{a\ A,b\ A}$	X_{14}		
X_{15}	**W**$_{b\ A,c\ A}$	X_{15}	X_{17}	
X_{16}	**W**$_{a\ B,b\ B}$	X_{16}		
X_{17}	**W**$_{b\ B,c\ B}$	X_{17}		
X_{18}	**W**$_{a\ C,b\ C}$	X_{18}		
X_{19}	**W**$_{b\ C,c\ C}$	X_{19}		
X_{20}	AI	X_{20}		
X_{21}	AR	X_{21}		
X_{22}	PI	X_{22}		
X_{23}	PR	X_{23}		
X_{24}	**W**$_{Wb\ B,c\ B,Wb\ A,c\ A}$	X_{11}	X_{20}	X_{22}
X_{25}	**W**$_{QWb\ A,c\ A,A,Wb\ A,c\ A,B}$	X_{10}	X_{21}	X_{23}
X_{26}	**W**$_{Wb\ C,c\ C,Wb\ A,c\ A}$	X_{12}	X_{20}	X_{22}
X_{27}	**W**$_{QWb\ A,c\ A,A,Wb\ C,c\ C,C}$	X_{10}	X_{21}	X_{23}

Table 5b. Role matrix **mcw** for Scenario 2.

mcw	Scenario 2			
X_1	a_A	1		
X_2	b_A	1		
X_3	c_A	X_{15}		
X_4	a_B	1		
X_5	b_B	1		
X_6	c_B	1		
X_7	a_C	1		
X_8	b_C	1		
X_9	c_C	1		
X_{10}	**QW**$_{b\ A,c\ A,A}$	1	-1	1
X_{11}	**QW**$_{b\ A,c\ A,B}$	X_{25}		
X_{12}	**QW**$_{b\ A,c\ A,C}$	X_{27}		
X_{13}	**QW**$_{b\ C,c\ C,A}$	1		
X_{14}	**W**$_{a\ A,b\ A}$	1		
X_{15}	**W**$_{b\ A,c\ A}$	1	X_{24}	
X_{16}	**W**$_{a\ B,b\ B}$	1		
X_{17}	**W**$_{b\ B,c\ B}$	1		
X_{18}	**W**$_{a\ C,b\ C}$	1		
X_{19}	**W**$_{b\ C,c\ C}$	1		
X_{20}	AI	1		
X_{21}	AR	1		
X_{22}	PI	1		
X_{23}	PR	1		
X_{24}	**W**$_{Wb\ B,c\ B,Wb\ A,c\ A}$	1	1	1
X_{25}	**W**$_{QWb\ A,c\ A,A,Wb\ A,c\ A,B}$	1	1	1
X_{26}	**W**$_{Wb\ C,c\ C,Wb\ A,c\ A}$	1	1	1
X_{27}	**W**$_{QWb\ A,c\ A,A,QWb\ C,c\ C,C}$	1	1	1

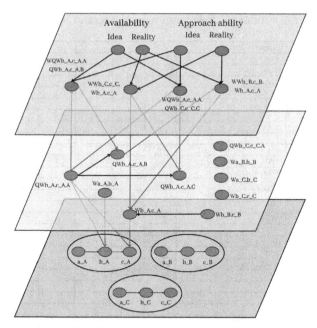

Fig. 6. Graphical representation of the model for Scenario 2.

Scenario 3a

Table 6a. Role matrix **mb** for Scenario 3a.

mb	Scenario 3a				
X_1	a_A	X_1			
X_2	b_A	X_1			
X_3	c_A	X_2			
X_4	a_B	X_4			
X_5	b_B	X_4			
X_6	c_B	X_5			
X_7	a_C	X_7			
X_8	b_C	X_7			
X_9	c_C	X_8			
X_{10}	**QW**$_{b\ A,c\ A,A}$	X_2	X_3	X_{10}	
X_{11}	**QW**$_{b\ A,c\ A,B}$	X_{10}			
X_{12}	**W**$_{a\ A,b\ A}$	X_{12}			
X_{13}	**W**$_{b\ A,c\ A}$	X_{13}	X_{17}		
X_{14}	**W**$_{a\ B,b\ B}$	X_{14}			
X_{15}	**W**$_{b\ B,c\ B}$	X_{15}			
X_{16}	**W**$_{a\ C,b\ C}$	X_{16}			
X_{17}	**W**$_{b\ C,c\ C}$	X_{17}			
X_{18}	**KW**$_{b\ C,c\ C,A}$	X_{18}	X_{19}		
X_{19}	**KW**$_{b\ C,c\ C,B}$	X_{19}			
X_{20}	AI	X_{20}			
X_{21}	AR	X_{21}			
X_{22}	PI	X_{22}			
X_{23}	PR	X_{23}			
X_{24}	**W**$_{Wb\ B,c\ B,}$**W**$_{b\ A,c\ A}$	X_{11}	X_{20}	X_{22}	
X_{25}	**W**$_{QWb\ A,c\ A,A,}$**QW**$_{b\ A,c\ A,B}$	X_{10}	X_{21}	X_{23}	
X_{26}	**W**$_{Wb\ C,c\ C,}$**W**$_{b\ A,c\ A}$	X_{11}	X_{19}	X_{21}	X_{23}
X_{27}	**W**$_{KWb\ C,c\ C,B,}$**KW**$_{b\ C,c\ C,A}$	X_{19}	X_{11}		

Table 6b. Role matrix **mcw** for Scenario 3a.

mcw	Scenario 3a				
X_1	a A	1			
X_2	b A	1			
X_3	c A	X_{13}			
X_4	a B	1			
X_5	b B	1			
X_6	c B	1			
X_7	a C	1			
X_8	b C	1			
X_9	c C	1			
X_{10}	$\mathbf{QW}_{b\ A,c\ A,A}$	1	-1	1	
X_{11}	$\mathbf{QW}_{b\ A,c\ A,B}$	X_{25}			
X_{12}	$\mathbf{W}_{a\ A,b\ A}$	1			
X_{13}	$\mathbf{W}_{b\ A,c\ A}$	1	X_{26}		
X_{14}	$\mathbf{W}_{a\ B,b\ B}$	1			
X_{15}	$\mathbf{W}_{b\ B,c\ B}$	1			
X_{16}	$\mathbf{W}_{a\ C,b\ C}$	1			
X_{17}	$\mathbf{W}_{b\ C,c\ C}$	1			
X_{18}	$\mathbf{KW}_{b\ C,c\ C,A}$	1	X_{27}		
X_{19}	$\mathbf{KW}_{b\ C,c\ C,B}$	1			
X_{20}	AI	1			
X_{21}	AR	1			
X_{22}	PI	1			
X_{23}	PR	1			
X_{24}	$\mathbf{W}_{\mathbf{W}b\ B,c\ B,\mathbf{W}b\ A,c\ A}$	1	1	1	
X_{25}	$\mathbf{W}_{\mathbf{QW}b\ A,c\ A,A,\mathbf{QW}b\ A,c\ A,B}$	1	1	1	
X_{26}	$\mathbf{W}_{\mathbf{W}b\ C,c\ C,\mathbf{W}b\ A,c\ A}$	1	1	1	1
X_{27}	$\mathbf{W}_{\mathbf{KW}b\ C,c\ C,B,\mathbf{KW}b\ C,c\ C,A}$	1	1		

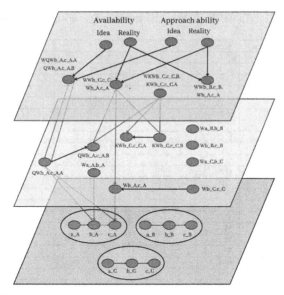

Fig. 7. Graphical representation of the model for Scenario 3a.

Scenario 3b

Table 7a. Role matrix **mb** for Scenario 3b.

mb	Scenario 3b			
X_1	a_A	X_1		
X_2	b_A	X_1		
X_3	c_A	X_2		
X_4	a_B	X_4		
X_5	b_B	X_4		
X_6	c_B	X_5		
X_7	a_C	X_7		
X_8	b_C	X_7		
X_9	c_C	X_8		
X_{10}	$\mathbf{QW}_{b\ A.c\ A.A}$	X_2	X_3	X_{10}
X_{11}	$\mathbf{QW}_{b\ A.c\ A.B}$	X_{10}		
X_{12}	$\mathbf{QW}_{b\ A.c\ A.C}$	X_{10}		
X_{13}	$\mathbf{W}_{a\ A.b\ A}$	X_{13}		
X_{14}	$\mathbf{W}_{b\ A.c\ A}$	X_{16}	X_{18}	
X_{15}	$\mathbf{W}_{a\ B.b\ B}$	X_{15}		
X_{16}	$\mathbf{W}_{b\ B.c\ B}$	X_{16}	X_{18}	
X_{17}	$\mathbf{W}_{a\ C.b\ C}$	X_{17}		
X_{18}	$\mathbf{W}_{b\ C.c\ C}$	X_{18}		
X_{19}	$\mathbf{KW}_{b\ C.c\ C.A}$	X_{19}	X_{20}	
X_{20}	$\mathbf{KW}_{b\ C.c\ C.B}$	X_{20}		
X_{21}	$\mathbf{QW}_{b\ B.c\ B.B}$	X_{11}		
X_{22}	$\mathbf{QW}_{b\ B.c\ B.C}$	X_{21}		
X_{23}	AI	X_{23}		
X_{24}	AR	X_{24}		
X_{25}	PI	X_{25}		
X_{26}	PR	X_{26}		
X_{27}	$\mathbf{W}_{Wb\ B.c\ B.}Wb\ A.c\ A}$	X_{24}	X_{26}	X_{29}
X_{28}	$\mathbf{W}_{QWb\ A.c\ A.A.}Wb\ A.c\ A.B}$	X_{23}	X_{25}	
X_{29}	$\mathbf{W}_{Wb\ C.c\ C.}Wb\ B.c\ B}$	X_{24}	X_{26}	
X_{30}	$\mathbf{W}_{KWb\ C.c\ C.B.}KWb\ C.c\ C.A}$	X_{10}	X_{20}	X_{30}
X_{31}	$\mathbf{W}_{QWb\ A.c\ A.A.}QWb\ A.c\ A.C}$	X_{10}	X_{31}	
X_{32}	$\mathbf{W}_{Wb\ B.c\ B.}Wb\ C.c\ C}$	X_{21}	X_{32}	

Table 7b. Role matrix **mcw** for Scenario 3b.

mcw	Scenario 3b			
X_1	a A	1		
X_2	b A	1		
X_3	c A	X_{14}		
X_4	a B	1		
X_5	b B	1		
X_6	c B	1		
X_7	a C	1		
X_8	b C	1		
X_9	c C	1		
X_{10}	$QW_{b\ A,c\ A,A}$	1	-1	1
X_{11}	$QW_{b\ A,c\ A,B}$	X_{28}		
X_{12}	$QW_{b\ A,c\ A,C}$	X_{31}		
X_{13}	$W_{a\ A,b\ A}$	1		
X_{14}	$W_{b\ A,c\ A}$	X_{27}	X_{29}	
X_{15}	$W_{a\ B,b\ B}$	1		
X_{16}	$W_{b\ B,c\ B}$	1		
X_{17}	$W_{a\ C,b\ C}$	1		
X_{18}	$W_{b\ C,c\ C}$	1		
X_{19}	$KW_{b\ C,c\ C,A}$	1	X_{30}	
X_{20}	$KW_{b\ C,c\ C,B}$	1		
X_{21}	$QW_{b\ B,c\ B,B}$	1		
X_{22}	$QW_{b\ B,c\ B,C}$	X_{32}		
X_{23}	AI	1		
X_{24}	AR	1		
X_{25}	PI	1		
X_{26}	PR	1		
X_{27}	$W_{Wb\ B,c\ B.Wb\ A,c\ A}$	1	1	1
X_{28}	$W_{QWb\ A,c\ A,A.QWb\ A,c\ A,B}$	1	1	
X_{29}	$W_{Wb\ C,c\ C.Wb\ B,c\ B}$	1	1	
X_{30}	$W_{KWb\ C,c\ C,B.KWb\ C,c\ C,A}$	1	1	1
X_{31}	$W_{QWb\ A,c\ A,A.QWb\ A,c\ A,C}$	1	1	
X_{32}	$W_{Wb\ B,c\ B.Wb\ C,c\ C}$	1	1	

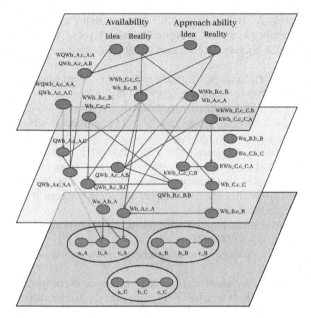

Fig. 8. Graphical representation of the model for Scenario 3b.

References

Argyris, C.: Actionable knowledge: Changing the status quo. San Francisco: JosseyBass (1993).
Ashford, S., & Northcraft, G. (1992). Conveying more (or less) than we realize: The role of impression–management in feedback-seeking. Organizational Behavior & Human Decision Processes, 53(3), 310334

Bakker, A.B., Demerouti, E.: The job demands-resources model: state of the art. J. Manag. Psychol. **22**(3), 309–328 (2007)

Bouma, D., Canbaloğlu, G., Treur, J., Wiewiora, A.: Adaptive network modeling of the influence of leadership and communication on learning within an organization. Cogn. Syst. Res. **79**, 55–70 (2023)

Cohen, S., Wills, T.A.: Stress, social support, and the buffering hypothesis. Psychol. Bull. **98**(2), 310 (1985)

Cook, S.D., Yanow, D.: Culture and organizational learning. J. Manag. Inq. **2**(4), 373–390 (1993)

DeLongis, A., Holtzman, S.: Coping in context: the role of stress, social support, and personality in coping. J. Pers. **73**(6), 1633–1656 (2005)

DePaulo, B.M., Fisher, J.D.: The costs of asking for help. Basic Appl. Soc. Psychol. **1**(1), 23–35 (1980)

Durand, A., Zijlstra, T., Hamersma, M., van Oort, N., Hoogendoorn-Lanser, S., Hoogendoorn, S., et al.: "Who can I ask for help?": Mechanisms behind digital inequality in public transport. Cities **137**, 104335 (2023)

Heath, C., Gonzalez, R.: Interaction with others increases decision confidence but not decision quality: evidence against information collection views of interactive decision making. Organ. Behav. Hum. Decis. Process. **61**(3), 305–326 (1995)

Karnita, R., Woodcock, A., Bell, S., Super, K.: Approachability as a Prerequisite of Student Reflection. In: Kantola, J.I., Barath, T., Nazir, S., Andre, T. (eds.) Advances in human factors, business management, training and education, pp. 493–502. Springer International Publishing, Cham (2017)

Kawachi, I., Kennedy, B.P., Lochner, K., Prothrow-Stith, D.: Social capital, income inequality, and mortality. Am. J. Public Health **87**(9), 1491–1498 (1997)

Lee, F.: The social costs of seeking help. J. Appl. Behav. Sci. **38**(1), 17–35 (2002)

Moss, S.A., McFarland, J., Ngu, S., Kijowska, A.: Maintaining an open mind to closed individuals: the effect of resource availability and leadership style on the association between openness to experience and organizational commitment. J. Res. Pers. **41**(2), 259–275 (2007)

Rains, S.A., Keating, D.M.: The social dimension of blogging about health: Health blogging, social support, and well-being. Commun. Monogr. **78**(4), 511–534 (2011)

Reid, D., Johnston, M.: Improving teaching in higher education: Student and teacher perspectives. Educ. Stud. **25**(3), 269–281 (1999)

Roux, A.V.D., et al.: Availability of recreational resources and physical activity in adults. Am. J. Public Health **97**(3), 493–499 (2007)

Tedeschi, J.T., Melburg, V.: Impression management and influence in the organization. Res. Soc. Organ. **3**, 31–58 (1984)

Treur, J.: Modeling multi-order adaptive processes by self-modeling networks. In: In: Antonio J. Tallón-Ballesteros, Chi-Hua Chen, (eds.) Proceedings of the 2nd International Conference on Machine Learning and Intelligent Systems, MLIS'20, Frontiers in Artificial Intelligence and Applications, vol. 332, pp. 206 - 217, IOS Press (2020a)

Treur, J.: Network-oriented modeling for adaptive networks: designing higher-order adaptive biological, mental and social network models. Springer (2020b). https://doi.org/10.1007/978-3-030-31445-3

Van der Rijt, J., Van den Bossche, P., van de Wiel, M.W., De Maeyer, S., Gijselaers, W.H., Segers, M.S.: Asking for help: a relational perspective on help seeking in the workplace. Vocat. Learn. **6**, 259–279 (2013)

Yaniv, I.: Receiving other people's advice: influence and benefit. Organ. Behav. Hum. Decis. Process. **93**(1), 1–13 (2004)

Trust, Perspicuity, Efficiency: Important UX Aspects to Consider for the Successful Adoption of Collaboration Tools in Organisations

Anna-Lena Meiners[1]([✉]) [ID], Andreas Hinderks[2] [ID], and Jörg Thomaschewski[2] [ID]

[1] Karlsruhe Institute of Technology, Karlsruhe, Germany
`meiners@kit.edu`
[2] University of Applied Sciences Emden/Leer, Emden, Germany
`andreas@hinderks.org`, `joerg.thomaschewski@hs-emden-leer.de`
`https://hci.anthropomatik.kit.edu`

Abstract. Collaboration tools are heavily used in work, education, and leisure. Yet, what makes a good collaboration tool is not well researched. This study focuses on what users expect of collaboration tools by investigating how they are used and which UX aspects are important to users when using them. In a survey, 184 participants described their use of collaboration tools and then rated the importance of 19 given UX aspects in their specific scenario. Results show that seven UX aspects are almost universally seen as most important. Additionally, five aspects seem to be especially relevant in specific usage domains. It is indicated that the context of use, especially the usage domain, influences which UX aspects are important to users. These results can be used by organisations as a guideline when selecting a collaboration tool suitable for their members in order to successfully adopt a tool.

Keywords: UX aspects · Collaboration tools · UX evaluation

1 Introduction

Digital collaboration tools are used in a variety of domains: For example, Microsoft Teams is used to collaborate professionally, Discord to connect during gaming sessions, and Moodle to learn online. These all-encompassing usage possibilities, for work, leisure, as well as education, make these tools relevant to a large amount of humans and organisations. The use of collaboration tools is currently even on the rise, driven especially by the increased relevance of remote collaboration in the Covid-19-pandemic [3].

HCI and organizational researchers have addressed challenges that hybrid and remote collaboration bring [12], yet little research exists on what makes a good collaboration tool and how to select one to adopt, if an organisation is about to switch to hybrid or remote collaboration. This may be challenging due to a

H. P. da Silva and P. Cipresso (Eds.): CHIRA 2023, CCIS 1996, pp. 143–162, 2023.
https://doi.org/10.1007/978-3-031-49425-3_9

rapidly growing market of collaboration tools, that leaves organisations facing an increasing number of options to choose from. If they want to sustainably adopt a tool, it is advisable to meet the users' expectations. Understanding the users' needs and preferences when using collaboration tools is a crucial prerequisite to select a tool that will be broadly accepted and used.

Research has been done to understand which UX aspects are important for specific tools and categories of tools [10,14]. For instance, usefulness and dependability are perceived most important for text processing tools like Microsoft Word, whereas for messengers such as WhatsApp, trust and intuitiveness of the interface are the top aspects. So far though, the category of collaboration tools has not been investigated like this. Therefore, the aim of this research is to create some insight into UX properties of these tools. The specific research questions for this study are:

- RQ1: How are collaboration tools used?
- RQ2: Which UX aspects do users find important for collaboration tools?

More specifically, in this article, different usage domains and contexts of use in which collaboration tools are being used are investigated, as this influences the overall UX [16]. Furthermore, it is surveyed how users rate the importance of different UX aspects for collaboration tools in their specific use case, to comprise a ranking of the most relevant ones.

In conclusion, the main goal of this work is to create a ranked list of important UX aspects for the use of collaboration tools. These results can be used by UX researchers to focus evaluation of UX of collaboration tools on the most important aspects, for example by indicating which scales to measure in a questionnaire. They also aid UX practitioners designing collaboration tools to lead knowledgeable discussions about their products' UX and support informed design decisions in product development. These findings also enable researchers to gain a deeper understanding of the correlates of context of use and UX and can be used as starting points for further evaluations in this field of study. Lastly, they can be used to decide on a specific tool to adopt in an organisation to meet the users' expectations and therefore enable a lasting adoption of a new tool.

2   Related Work

UX as a whole covers a large number of different quality aspects concerning the interaction of a user and technology. For a good UX impression the product should be easy to learn or even intuitive to use, it should react as the user expects, be visually appealing, fun to use, etc. [5] So, to guarantee a high level of UX quality, several semantically distinct UX quality aspects must be considered. In reality, all these aspects cannot be assessed in one study. At the same time, not all UX aspects may be relevant in all scenarios. Research shows that in certain contexts, different UX aspects show higher relevance than in others [17]. For example, in leisure activities, beauty seems to be of more relevance than in work activities [17].

When surveying perceived UX, standardized questionnaires with a defined set of items are a proven method [13, p. 185 f.]. They can be distributed to large numbers of participants via the internet and allow for comparable results. The modular extension of the User Experience Questionnaire (UEQ) [7], the UEQ+ framework [15], offers the possibility to compile a product-specific questionnaire from different scales measuring individual UX aspects and build such a questionnaire. Each UEQ+ scale can be combined with a scale that assesses the importance of this UX aspect for the participant, which in turn enables the calculation of a single UX KPI by factoring each scale rating with the personal importance of the scale for the user [6, 11]. Furthermore, the importance ratings give intriguing insights into the perception of UX. The UEQ+ scales, and thus UX aspects, to be measured must be selected in advance. It is advisable not to select the scales solely based on the subjective feelings, so as not to distort the results through preconceptions and biases. User surveys are one way to determine the perceived importance of UX factors which supports a more objective and thus appropriate selection of scales.

For this reason, e.g. [10] conducted studies that surveyed the importance of UX factors for specific software products as well as the possibility to generalise results for specific products to a higher level of product types. The results suggest that in most cases importance ratings for product types (e.g. "Is this UX aspect important for word processing software"?) highly corresponded to ratings for specific products (e.g. "Is this UX aspect important for Microsoft Word?"), basically meaning that what is important for a specific product from a category will also be important for any other product of the same category and vice versa. Still, there are some exceptions where results did not match perfectly, for example when surveying the product Instagram and the product type "social networks". Importance ratings for different UX aspects corresponded somewhat but not nearly as good as with other product types.

One explanation for this inconsistency could be that the product type "social networks" contains a great variety of products offering very different feature sets. Additionally, they are being used in very different contexts, which in turn affects the importance of different UX aspects. For example, a social network mainly used in a professional context such as LinkedIn might score lower in importance of its stimulating capabilities than a social network mostly used for leisure like TikTok. The same could be true for collaboration tools as they include software products with very different feature sets and use cases, the only unifying feature being that all are used to support human collaboration in some way or another, whether it may be for work, education, or leisure. This makes it especially difficult to choose the right UX aspects to focus on when assessing the UX quality of a collaboration tool for a specific use case.

When adopting a new technology the Technology Acceptance Model (TAM) is a way to predict future use of technology [2]. This model proposes that users' perceptions of system capabilities, such as ease of use, usefulness, can be used as indicators of the future use and thus sustainable integration of a tool in an existing organisation. Research has shown that this model might not be fully applicable for collaboration tools, though [1]. [4] also suggest further aspects to consider when adopting a collaboration tool. E.g., learning platforms need to integrate into existing infrastructure and the adoption must be timed suitably.

Ultimately, there still is a research gap regarding which UX aspects are the important ones in different scenarios, so in this study, a survey was planned to examine the most relevant UX aspects for collaboration tools specifically.

3   Method

The aim of the study is to evaluate usage modes and typical contextual characteristics of collaboration tool usage (RQ1). It furthermore serves to evaluate the importance of different UX aspects for the use of collaboration tools (RQ2) to generate a ranked list of important UX aspects. To answer the research questions an online survey was planned and conducted.

First, a questionnaire was developed in line with other similar studies [10,14]. The survey thus included the following questions: Participants were asked to choose one specific collaboration tool they worked with. This was followed by questions about how frequently and since when they used it, in which activity domain - i.e. for work, education, a hobby, etc. -, which features they typically used, and which tasks they fulfilled with it. All the single-choice questions were accompanied by text input fields, where participants could leave a comment to specify their choice, or add an "other"-alternative. After that, participants rated the importance of 19 UX aspects for their selected tool on a 7-point Likert scale of -3 (not important at all) to 3 (very important). Participants could choose not to answer if they did not see the UX aspect fit at all. In the end, participants were asked to state their age and gender and could leave a general comment.

The UX aspects and their specific item question were ("How important is it to you that ..."):

- Adaptability: "... the tool can be adapted to personal preferences and working styles?"
- Aesthetics: "... the tool looks beautiful and appealing?"
- Attractiveness: "... the overall impression of the tool is good?"
- Clarity: "... the visual design of the tool is clearly structured and easy to grasp?"
- Dependability: "... the tool is easy to control and operates predictably?"
- Efficiency: "... users can solve their tasks with little effort using the tool?"
- Identification: "... users can personally identify with the tool? For example, that users feel up-to-date or professional when using the tool?"
- Intuitive Use: "... the tool can be used immediately without any training or help?"
- Novelty: "... the tool's design is creative and interesting?"
- Perspicuity: "... it is easy to get familiar with the tool and to learn how to use it?"
- Quality of Content: "... the information provided by the tool is actual and well-prepared? This refers to all audiovisual media, texts, documents, etc. that you have not fed into the tool yourself."

- Social Acceptance: "... the tool has a good reputation and that users can be proud to use the tool and are not ashamed of it?"
- Social Interaction: "... the tool supports users to communicate, collaborate and help each other?"
- Social Stimulation: "... the tool enables users to have engaging, positive experiences with other people?"
- Stimulation: "... using the tool is fun and motivates users?"
- Trustworthiness of Content: "... the information provided by the tool is reliable? This refers to all audiovisual media, texts, documents, etc. that you have not fed into the tool yourself."
- Trust: "... the user's data is in safe hands with the tool?"
- Usefulness: "... using the tool brings advantages such as saving time or effort?"
- Value: "... the tool's design looks professional and of high quality?"

The questionnaire was pre-tested by a panel of 7 UX experts. After revision, the questionnaire was again pre-tested, but this time by two persons without any technological or UX background whatsoever. The questionnaire was then slightly revised again. The distribution of the final versions via social media, forums, and collaboration platforms took place in September 2022. The questionnaire was made available in an English and a German language version. The full, final version of the questionnaire is found in the research protocol [8].

The collected data was cleaned via the following steps:

1. Removing empty rows, renaming columns and encoding answers (e.g. converting importance ratings to 1–7 integer values) for easier use
2. Removing useless entries, such as duplicates (0) and not fully submitted answers (71)
3. Removing non-serious answers
   - according to time spent on importance rating less than 44 s (2)
   - all importance ratings answered the same or in a "knitting pattern" (0)
   - checking for non-serious comments (0)
   - plausibility check of age (1 person stated to be eleven years old, but the rest of their entry seemed very plausible and detailed, so it is an assumed typo. Only the age entry was removed from the data set.)

Overall, of 257 entries, 184 could be kept for analysis. The cleaned data set was then analysed using descriptive statistics and rank correlation analysis as well as t-tests. The data was clustered and split into meaningful groups according to the usage domain and the tools to enable in-depth comparison of different usage modes and possible overlaps with product-related idiosyncrasies. In addition, a short test was conducted comparing the new data on two tools to inventory data. In the inventory data sets, the importance of a subset of the UX aspects was rated for software products also apparent in this study: Microsoft Teams and Discord. This was done to roughly check stability of importance ratings over time.

4   Results

In the following, the results of the data analysis are presented. First, there is a section on specifics of the participants. Second, answers on the use of the collaboration tools are presented. Lastly, the importance data is analysed with a focus on different tools and usage domains.

4.1   Participants

The 184 participants' ages ranged from 18 to 63 years with a median of 34 years. 111 participants (60.3%) identified as male, 66 (35.9%) as female and 3 (1.6%) as diverse/other. 4 (2.2%) participants chose not to answer. 10 (5.4%) participants used the English version of the questionnaire, 174 (94.6%) completed the survey in the German version.

4.2   Use of Collaboration Tools

The use of collaboration tools was evaluated from different perspectives: Which tools participants used, how frequently and for how long they used them, in which domains, and for which tasks. The research protocol offers a more detailed insight into these answers, but a general overview is given here.

Selected Tools. Participants chose a specific collaboration tool they had used before. Most participants (67, 36.4%) chose Microsoft Teams. 24 participants (13.0%) chose Discord. Other options were picked much less frequently. Overall, more than 60 tools were mentioned by participants. The fill list can be found in the research protocol.

Frequency and Duration of Use. About half of the participants used their selected tool daily (96, 52.2%), 55 (29.9%) used it weekly, 24 (13%) monthly. 103 participants (56%) have been using their selected tool for 1 to 3 years. Another 52 (28.3%) stated they have been using it for 4 to 6 years.

Usage Domains. Most participants (129, 70.1%) used their chosen tool for work, 57 (31%) for studies, 36 (19.6%) for a hobby, and 20 (10.9%) for an honorary office. 6 "other" entries (3.2%) stated that people used the tool for secondary employment (3 times) or for informal meetings with friends and family (3 times). On median, participants used their selected tool for one domain only.

Tasks. Additionally, participants used their selected tool on median for 3 distinct tasks. 140 (76.1%) used the tool to communicate in general. 138 (75%) used the tool to hold online meetings. 125 (67.9%) used the tool to share information. 98 (53.3%) used the tool to organize activities of a group or team. 77 (41.8%) created documents collaboratively.

4.3   Importance Ratings

The importance ratings were analysed with a focus on different groups of participants or usage domains. To find meaningful groups in the overall pool of data entries, data was partitioned in an exploratory way, starting with the group that chose Microsoft Teams, as they were the largest group (N = 67, 36.4% of participants). The same was done with entries that selected Discord as the second most often rated tool with (N = 24, 13%). Then, different usage domains were picked and analysed. The resulting groups were: usage for work only, usage for education only, usage for work and/or education, and mixed usage (meaning participants indicated they used the tool for work, education, as well as leisure), using Microsoft Teams, and using Discord. The appropriate counter-events were analyzed, too.

In the following subsections the rankings of the UX aspects per group are presented, where the aspect with the highest mean importance rating ranked 1st and the one with the lowest rating ranked 19th. The first 7 aspects are highlighted as in almost all cases, after the top 7, there was a meaningful gap in the average rating until the next most important aspect. Also, the top 7 overall do not differ as much in their rating, so it is reasonable to handle them as a group. In the following, this circumstance is elaborated on the basis of selected examples. More details can be found in the research protocol.

Overall Importance Rating. Figure 1 shows the overall means of the importance ratings for the 19 given UX aspects as well as their 95% confidence intervals. The most important aspects in the overall data set are: trust, perspicuity,

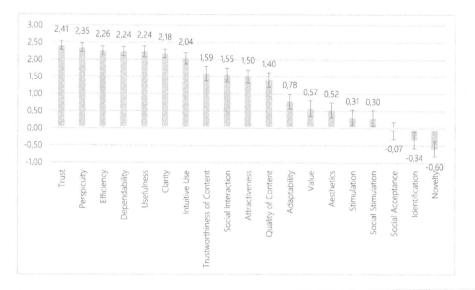

Fig. 1. Overall ratings for importance of UX aspects to all collaboration tools (N = 184; scale ranges from −3 to +3; 95% confidence interval shown).

efficiency, dependability, usefulness, clarity, and intuitive use. Rated as least important are: novelty, identification, social acceptance, and social stimulation. Details can be found in Table 1.

Work and Non-work Use. Table 2 shows the importance rating for all participants that indicated they used their selected tool for work only (N = 89, 48.37% of participants). The entries indicating usage of the tool for anything but work were also evaluated. Ranks of aspects were compared via correlation analysis and the average ratings were compared using t-tests. The aspect rankings correlate with a coefficient of 0.96, and there is a significant difference in the rating of one aspect, value, which is rated significantly more important in the work domain than in others. In both cases though, rated as most important are: trust, perspicuity, usefulness, efficiency, dependability, clarity, and intuitive use. Deemed least important are: novelty, identification and social acceptance.

Educational and Non-educational Use. Table 3 shows the importance rating for all participants that indicated they used their selected tool for their education only (N = 24, 13% of participants). The counter-group of non-educational

Table 1. Descriptive statistics and null indications (i.e. number of times where a participant chose not to rate this aspect) for the overall data (N = 184).

UX Aspect	Mean	Conf. Interval		Std. Dev.	Variance	Null indications
Trust	2.41	1.53	3.29	0.13	0.78	1
Perspicuity	2.35	1.47	3.23	0.13	0.77	0
Efficiency	2.26	1.39	3.14	0.13	0.77	2
Dependability	2.24	1.35	3.13	0.13	0.80	1
Usefulness	2.24	1.14	3.33	0.16	1.20	0
Clarity	2.18	1.30	3.05	0.13	0.76	2
Intuitive Use	2.04	0.89	3.18	0.17	1.32	0
Trustworthiness of Content	1.59	0.11	3.06	0.21	2.18	15
Social Interaction	1.55	0.16	2.94	0.20	1.94	2
Attractiveness	1.50	0.22	2.78	0.19	1.64	3
Quality of Content	1.40	-0.05	2.85	0.21	2.11	19
Adaptability	0.78	-0.71	2.28	0.22	2.24	0
Value	0.57	-1.00	2.15	0.23	2.48	3
Aesthetic	0.52	-0.99	2.04	0.22	2.28	1
Stimulation	0.31	-1.19	1.82	0.22	2.27	2
Social Stimulation	0.30	-1.31	1.90	0.23	2.59	2
Social Acceptance	-0.07	-1.80	1.66	0.25	2.99	3
Identification	-0.34	-2.02	1.34	0.24	2.82	6
Novelty	-0.60	-2.10	0.90	0.22	2.25	3

use (N = 127) was analyzed in the same way as before: Ranks of aspects and average ratings were compared using correlation analysis and t-tests. The aspect ranking of the study group correlate with the non-study group with a coefficient of 0.95. There are no aspects that were rated significantly different between study use and non-study use. Rated as most important in every case were: trust, perspicuity, usefulness, efficiency, dependability, clarity, and intuitive use. Deemed least important were: novelty, identification, and social stimulation. The educational use was also contrasted with the work use. The correlation coefficient in aspect rankings was 0.97. Again, there were no significantly differently rated aspects.

Leisure and Non-leisure Use. Another category of usage was evaluated, usage for neither work nor studies, i.e. leisure activities. Table 4 shows the importance rating for all applicable entries, with N = 19, as well as the counter-event of usage for work and/or education, with N = 128 (69.6% of participants).

Table 2. Mean importance rating (M) and according ranking (R) per UX aspect for the Work (N = 89) and Non-Work Domain (N = 55) as well as t-value (two-tailed, alpha-level of 0.05, significant differences highlighted with *).

| UX Aspect | Work | | Other | | |
	M	R	M	R	T-Value
Trust	2.47	1	2.36	1	0.534
Perspicuity	2.36	2	2.16	3	0.234
Usefulness	2.34	3	2.04	6	0.144
Efficiency	2.32	4	2.11	5	0.234
Dependability	2.23	5	2.24	2	0.954
Clarity	2.16	6	2.15	4	0.941
Intuitive Use	1.99	7	2.00	7	0.959
Trustw. of Cont	1.57	8	1.38	9	0.496
Attractiveness	1.56	9	1.20	10	0.151
Quality of Cont	1.52	10	1.19	11	0.216
Soc. Interaction	1.45	11	0.65	8	0.392
Adaptability	0.67	12	0.91	12	0.375
Value	0.63	13	0.04	16	0.030*
Aesthetics	0.51	14	0.47	13	0.901
Stimulation	0.45	15	0.13	15	0.220
Soc. Stimulation	0.04	16	0.39	14	0.230
Soc. Acceptance	0.04	17	−0.49	17	0.070
Identification	−0.25	18	−0.72	18	0.093
Novelty	−0.62	19	−0.76	19	0.574

The aspect rankings of groups correlate with a coefficient of 0.31. There are 9 aspects that were rated significantly different between the two according to two-tailed t-tests with an alpha level of 0.05: dependability, clarity, intuitive use, social interaction, and stimulation were rated significantly more important in the work/education domain, whereas adaptability, social stimulation, identification, and novelty were rated significantly more important in the leisure domain. For the leisure domain, the seven aspects rated most important are: efficiency, trust, social stimulation, adaptability, quality of content, perspicuity and attractiveness, whereas in the non-leisure domain usefulness, dependability, intuitive use, and clarity replace social stimulation, adaptability, quality of content, and attractiveness. In fact, clarity is rated the least important by one in the leisure domain. Dependability and intuitive use receive negative importance scores in the leisure domain as well.

Table 3. Mean importance rating (M) and according ranking (R) per UX aspect for the Education (N = 24) and Non-Education Domain (N = 127) as well as t-value (two-tailed, alpha-level of 0.05, significant differences highlighted with *).

| | Edu. | | Other | | |
UX Aspect	M	R	M	R	T-Value
Perspicuity	2.46	1	2.33	2	0.476
Trust	2.42	2	2.40	1	0.916
Efficiency	2.25	3	2.24	5	0.476
Usefulness	2.21	4	2.27	4	0.820
Clarity	2.21	5	2.17	6	0.817
Intuitive Use	2.17	6	2.02	7	0.601
Dependability	2.08	7	2.28	3	0.444
Quality of Cont	1.76	8	1.36	11	0.209
Trustw. of Cont	1.64	9	1.56	10	0.787
Soc. Interaction	1.38	10	1.56	9	0.600
Attractiveness	1.33	11	1.56	8	0.514
Aesthetics	0.67	12	0.50	14	0.628
Adaptability	0.58	13	0.73	12	0.650
Stimulation	0.25	14	0.37	15	0.709
Value	0.13	15	0.58	13	0.173
Soc. Stimulation	0.00	16	0.23	16	0.576
Soc. Acceptance	−0.33	17	−0.03	17	0.379
Identification	−0.67	18	−0.30	18	0.238
Novelty	−0.75	19	−0.59	19	0.635

Table 4. Mean importance rating (M) and according ranking (R) per UX aspect for the Leisure (N = 19) and Non-Leisure Domain (N = 128) as well as t-value (two-tailed, alpha-level of 0.05, significant differences highlighted with *).

UX Aspect	Leisure M	R	Other M	R	T-Value
Efficiency	2,37	1	2,32	3	0,081
Trust	2,11	2	2,44	1	0,126
Soc. Stimulation	2,11	3	0,13	16	0,000*
Adaptability	2,00	4	0,70	12	0,001*
Quality of Cont	2,00	5	1,56	9	0,242
Perspicuity	1,89	6	2,38	2	0,081
Attractiveness	1,74	7	1,52	10	0,504
Usefulness	1,58	8	2,31	4	0,083
Aesthetics	1,16	9	0,55	14	0,177
Value	1,11	10	0,62	13	0,356
Identification	0,68	11	−0,30	18	0,030*
Trustw. of Cont	0,67	12	1,61	8	0,062
Novelty	0,21	13	−0,61	19	0,049*
Dependability	−0,05	14	2,19	5	0,000*
Soc. Acceptance	−0,05	15	-0,05	17	0,991
Intuitive Use	−0,21	16	1,96	7	0,000*
Soc. Interaction	−0,65	17	1,46	11	0,000*
Clarity	−0,71	18	2,15	6	0,000*
Stimulation	−1,00	19	0,38	15	0,000*

Using Microsoft Teams. Table 5 shows details for the importance rating for the tool selected most often by participants with N = 67 (36.4% of participants): Microsoft Teams. To contrast, the same evaluation was conducted with every data entry that did not rate Microsoft Teams but any other tool. Between these groups, differences were evaluated using rank correlation analysis as well as two-tailed t-tests with an alpha level of 0.05. The results show a fairly high correlation coefficient of 0.91 for the ranking of UX aspects, and significant differences in the ratings of four aspects - attractiveness, quality of content, usefulness, and value -, which were all deemed more important for MS Teams than other tools. Regardless, the 7 aspects rated most important were the same in both use cases: usefulness, perspicuity, trust, efficiency, dependability, clarity and intuitive use. Furthermore, identification and novelty were rated least important in both cases.

Table 5. Mean importance rating (M) and according ranking (R) per UX aspect for Microsoft Teams (N = 67) and Not Microsoft Teams (N = 117) as well as t-value (two-tailed, alpha-level of 0.05, significant differences highlighted with *).

UX Aspect	MS Teams		Others		T-Value
	M	R	M	R	
Usefulness	2.52	1	2.08	7	0.003*
Perspicuity	2.42	2	2.30	2	0.321
Trust	2.41	3	2.41	1	0.993
Efficiency	2.39	4	2.19	4	0.321
Dependability	2.27	5	2.22	3	0.706
Clarity	2.17	6	2.18	5	0.919
Intuitive Use	1.90	7	2.12	6	0.210
Attractiveness	1.77	8	1.35	10	0.017*
Quality of Cont	1.72	9	1.22	11	0.027*
Trustw. of Cont	1.71	10	1.51	9	0.386
Soc. Interaction	1.36	11	1.66	8	0.179
Value	1.00	12	0.32	16	0.003*
Aesthetic	0.76	13	0.39	14	0.102
Adaptability	0.61	14	0.88	12	0.246
Stimulation	0.23	15	0.36	15	0.544
Soc. Acceptance	0.10	16	−0.18	17	0.307
Soc. Stimulation	0.09	17	0.41	13	0.201
Identification	−0.32	18	−0.35	18	0.935
Novelty	−0.52	19	−0.64	19	0.613

Using Discord. Table 6 shows similar data for Discord with N = 24 (13% of participants) and its counter-event "anything but Discord" (N = 160). Here, the rankings correlate with a coefficient of 0.88, and two-tailed t-tests with an alpha level of 0.05 show significant differences in the ratings of one aspect, social interaction, which was deemed significantly more important for Discord than other tools. This is reflected in the assessment of the top 7 aspects rated most important for the groups. For Discord these are: efficiency, trust, clarity, dependability, social interaction, perspicuity and intuitive use. With other tools, usefulness takes social interaction's place in the top 7.

Comparison with Inventory Data. To roughly test the stability of ratings over time, two subsets of data were compared to corresponding inventory data: the importance ratings of Microsoft Teams and Discord. The full data set can be found in a corresponding research protocol [9]. In the inventory data, importance of UX aspects was measured for specific software products. A questionnaire

Table 6. Mean importance rating (M) and according ranking (R) per UX aspect for Discord (N = 24) and Not Discord (N = 160) as well as t-value (two-tailed, alpha-level of 0.05, significant differences highlighted with *).

UX Aspect	Discord		Others		T-Value
	M	R	M	R	
Efficiency	2.33	1	2.19	4	0.289
Trust	2.29	2	2.41	1	0.645
Clarity	2.25	3	2.18	6	0.650
Dependability	2.25	4	2.22	5	0.962
Soc. Interaction	2.21	5	1.66	11	0.006*
Perspicuity	2.13	6	2.30	2	0.289
Intuitive Use	1.96	7	2.12	7	0.766
Usefulness	1.92	8	2.08	3	0.226
Attractiveness	1.42	9	1.35	9	0.768
Adaptability	1.21	10	0.88	12	0.153
Trustw. of Cont	0.95	11	1.51	8	0.130
Aesthetic	0.88	12	0.39	14	0.261
Quality of Cont	0.84	13	1.22	10	0.204
Soc. Stimulation	0.52	14	0.41	16	0.517
Stimulation	0.25	15	0.36	15	0.855
Value	−0.05	16	0.32	13	0.110
Soc. Acceptance	−0.35	17	−0.18	17	0.435
Novelty	−0.75	18	−0.64	19	0.619
Identification	−0.78	19	−0.35	18	0.217

was distributed solely focusing on one product but otherwise asking participants about the importance of aspects in the same way as in this study. One difference was that only 15 UX aspects were polled; four aspects measured in this study were not part of the collection then: identification, social interaction, social stimulation, and social acceptance. Nonetheless, the rest of the aspects can be compared regarding their mean rating and according ranks.

30 participants rated the importance of 15 UX aspects for Microsoft Teams in a previous survey. The scales missing in the inventory data were left out when comparing both data sets per rank correlation analysis. The rankings correlated with a very high coefficient of $r = 0.97$. The left-out aspects were rated rather low in the ranking in the new data: social interaction was 11th, social acceptance 16th, social stimulation 17th, and identification 18th. There were 3 aspects rated significantly differently according to two-tailed t-tests with an alpha level of 0.05: perspicuity, clarity, and attractiveness, all of which were rated significantly less important in the inventory data set.

Furthermore, in the inventory data, 23 participants surveyed the importance of 15 UX aspects. When comparing the importance rankings, the four aspects not measured in the inventory data set were left out. The test for rank correlations between the two data sets resulted in a correlation coefficient of $r = 0.89$. Note that social interaction was ranked 5th most important in the new data but was left out in the comparison. The other 3 left out aspects ranked considerably lower: social stimulation ranked 14th, social acceptance 17th, and identification least important. Two-tailed t-tests with an alpha level of 0.05 revealed 3 aspects were rated significantly different: clarity was rated more important in the new data, whereas value and novelty were rated less important than in the inventory data.

5   Discussion

This research has given insights into the general usage of collaboration tools (RQ1) and the UX aspects important to collaboration tools (RQ2). In the following, the research questions are answered in detail and some issues with this data set are discussed.

5.1   RQ1: How Are Collaboration Tools Used?

A wide variety of tools was named by participants when asked which collaboration tools they used. A total of 60 tools were mentioned in this study. In addition to 'classic' collaboration tools, that offer a wide variety of features to accommodate needs of teams working collaboratively, such as Microsoft Teams, several chat and conferencing tools were named, like Discord or Slack. Furthermore, tools to share and synchronously work on documents were listed, such as HedgeDoc or git tools. Video conferencing tools like Zoom and Skype were mentioned as well. Apart from these, participants also counted conventional messengers like WhatsApp into the group of collaboration tools. This emphasises the task-relatedness of this specific type of software products - anything that is used to collaborate is seen as a collaboration tool, whether it was designed as one or not.

Participants in this survey mostly used collaboration tools for their work and/or their studies. Some also used them recreationally or for voluntary work. The participants were frequent and heavy users of collaboration tools with almost none using tools less than weekly or for less than a year's time.

The vast majority of users used more than one tool to fulfill their tasks and also rarely used them for one task only - especially communicating with others and coordinating a group of people as well as sharing information were often mentioned together. Apart from that, video conferencing was noted as an especially big part of collaboration tool usage, too.

In this study, the users' focus area seems to be the work and/or study domain. It should be mentioned that many participants were acquired via the professional network LinkedIn, though, which might be the cause for the high number of professional users. Nonetheless, some accounts were given by participants that used the tools outside of work. This could be in the form of using the same tool in different domains. Mostly, though, different tools were used in differing domains. For example, Discord was used almost exclusively in the leisure domain, whereas Microsoft Teams was used predominantly in the work domain.

Overall, the results highlight the diversity of use cases and corresponding contexts of use in which collaboration tools play a role.

5.2   RQ2: Which UX Aspects Do Users Find Important for Collaboration Tools?

The data collected in this survey shows that 7 UX aspects were perceived as especially important for collaboration tools in almost all the scenarios we considered. For most of our usage groups, these were the top 7 highest rated UX aspects with some distance to the next most important aspects, albeit mostly in different orders. These are:

1. Trust
2. Perspicuity
3. Efficiency
4. Dependability
5. Usefulness
6. Clarity
7. Intuitive use

This research also indicates that there are significant differences in which UX aspects are considered as important in different contexts of use and domains: In cases where participants used the tool for work and/or studies, they rated different aspects as important than when they used the tool for leisure activities, such as hobbies or honorary offices. It is therefore advisable to add five more aspects to the list of important UX aspects, which were considered especially important in the leisure domain:

1. Social stimulation
2. Social interaction
3. Adaptability
4. Quality of Content
5. Attractiveness

The product itself did not impact the rating of UX aspects as much, as seen in the comparison of Microsoft Teams vs Non-Microsoft Teams usage, and Discord vs Non-Discord Usage.

It might thus be recommendable to stop focusing on specific software products and start shifting to differentiation of usage modes to determine which UX aspects might be most important. An organisation whose members will use the collaboration tool educationally only, such as a school, might therefore concentrate on other UX properties of a tool than a leisure organisation such as a chess club.

Still, it is noteworthy that the data presented here only constitutes the participants perception of what is important for a collaboration tool when polling a list of given UX aspects. These results should therefore be used cautiously as there may be more important aspects, which have not been polled in this survey. It could also be hard for participants to admit that social acceptance may factor into their experience, for example. There could also be management decisions that dictate a focus on other UX aspects, such as novelty - for instance to stand out from the competition.

Nevertheless, with the results of this study, organisations can gain an understanding of what is important to their members when using collaboration tools and employ this as a guideline in the process of selecting a collaboration tool for their specific use case. These results will also be valuable to designers and researchers dealing with collaboration tool, as they allow them to evaluate in a more focused manner and develop more valuable features.

5.3   On the Importance Ranking of Aspects

For interpretation of the data, rankings of the aspects were generated. The aspect that was rated highest on average was given 1st place, the second highest 2nd place, third highest 3rd place, etc. until the 19th or lowest rated aspect. This approach contains some inherent issues that need to be kept in mind when interpreting the ranks:

Firstly, only the mean of ratings gets represented by the ranks. But in reality, these come with error bars. Even with small confidences, and thus small error bars, it is not highly unlikely that ranks might switch, especially in cases where a group of aspects are rated in a very similar way.

For example, with the non-leisure group being relatively big, confidence intervals are small, but still especially with similarly rated aspects, ranks could vary a lot. With bigger confidence intervals, rankings can seem to become almost arbitrary as visible with the leisure group ($N = 19$). In Fig. 2, and Fig. 3, the ranges any aspect rank could get assigned in these two groups are illustrated. All of this highlights the importance of a considerate approach to handling rankings derived from the importance ratings.

Secondly, rankings are only an abstracted view on the actual data. Differences between ratings, i.e. how much more important one aspect is than another, become invisible. It becomes difficult to establish which ones are the most important ones to focus on during development or research, for example. In this study, we tried to compensate this difficulty by referencing the absolute ratings and searching for "leaps" between ratings. We found that in almost all usage scenarios evaluated, the top 7 aspects formed a group, which led to their classification as the most important ones. This threshold still could (and should) be revised for other purposes and does not claim to be an absolute truth.

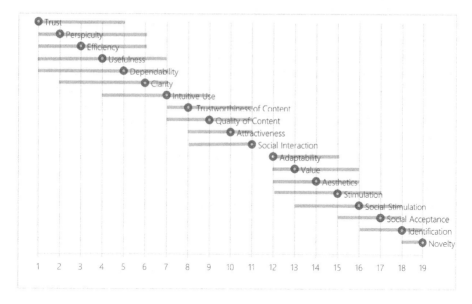

Fig. 2. Ranking range diagram for Non-Leisure Domain (N = 128); 95% confidence ranges for each aspect visualised by green lines; rank as per mean rating visualised by a purple dot.

5.4   On the Stability of the Importance Rankings

For Microsoft Teams and Discord inventory data was available to assess the stability of importance ratings over time. In both cases, ratings were fairly similar though not free from differences: Some aspect ratings were significantly different.

The first survey took place in 2020 [9]. Differences may be caused by a global change in user needs in the meantime - in both cases, clarity was rated significantly higher than two years ago. It is also possible, that features and use cases of both software products changed over time which in turn influences importance ratings. Also, sample sizes of both inventory surveys and the newer Discord survey are relatively small, so should be considered cautiously in general.

Thus, overall, the results can still be interpreted as very stable: In both cases, the top 7 most important UX aspects are the same - with the sole exception that in this Discord survey, the newly included aspect social interaction ranked 5th, but wasn't included in the inventory survey. This emphasizes the relativity of the portrayed rankings regarding the study design and calls for caution when interpreting the importance data. It also highlights a constant need to expand on the list of aspects influencing UX adapting to new use cases and priorities of users.

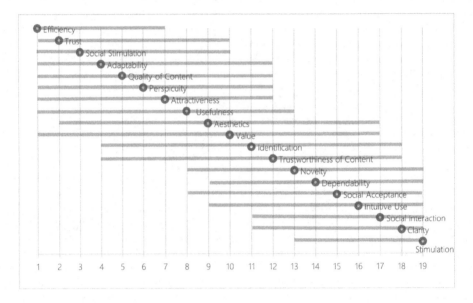

Fig. 3. Ranking range diagram for the Leisure Domain (N = 19); 95% confidence ranges for each aspect visualised by green lines; rank as per mean rating visualised by a purple dot.

6   Conclusion

This study presents insightful data on usage of collaboration tools and how different usage modes might influence the importance of UX aspects for them. Although the category of collaboration tools includes a wide variety of tools which are being used in very different scenarios for various tasks, there still seems to be a consensus on 7 important UX aspects that fit for most scenarios: trust, perspicuity, efficiency, dependability, usefulness, clarity, and intuitive use. In some use cases outside of the work/study domain, the aspects social stimulation, social interaction, adaptability, quality of content, and attractiveness can be added to the list of especially important aspects. The specific product does not seem to be the predicting factor here but rather the usage domain. This list can be used as a guideline for organisations to select collaboration tools that will be adopted successfully in their scenario.

Limiting in this study is the small percentage of participants that used collaboration tools recreationally only. It would be interesting to be able to differentiate professional from leisure users better with more representable sample sizes. It might also be useful to measure the participants' usage motivation specifically to not derive it from usage domains, such as usage for work or usage for a hobby, only.

There was also a great number of tools evaluated in this study with a small sample size which did not allow for generalizing interpretation but demonstrated interesting starting points for further research. The Discord data is especially mentionable in this regard.

Furthermore, it would also be intriguing to find a more concise definition of what makes a UX aspect important for a software product. In this survey, a rather practical approach was chosen, to rank aspects and pick the top ones as important and disregard the others, but in other scenarios it might be more suitable to find discrete metrics for importance. An investigation of which aspects are regarded as unimportant - and if they really are - would also seem promising with respect to a better understanding of influencing factors in UX of collaboration tools.

At last, it is necessary to transfer these findings to practical applications to be able to recommend concrete design decisions that support the relevant UX aspects. This way, our findings will not only be useful in evaluation but also in user-centered development of collaboration tools.

References

1. Dasgupta, S., Granger, M., McGarry, N.: User acceptance of e-collaboration technology: an extension of the technology acceptance model. Group Decis. Negot. **11**(2), 87–100 (2002). https://doi.org/10.1023/A:1015221710638
2. Davis, F.D.: Perceived usefulness, perceived ease of use, and user acceptance of information technology. MIS Quart. **13**(3), 319 (1989). https://doi.org/10.2307/249008
3. De Klerk, J.J., Joubert, M., Mosca, H.F.: Is working from home the new workplace panacea? Lessons from the COVID-19 pandemic for the future world of work. SA J. Ind. Psychol. **47** (2021). https://doi.org/10.4102/sajip.v47i0.1883
4. Gatwood, J., Hohmeier, K., Kocak, M., Chisholm-Burns, M.: Acceptance of productivity software as a course management and collaboration tool among student pharmacists. Curr. Pharm. Teach. Learn. **13**(4), 361–367 (2021). https://doi.org/10.1016/j.cptl.2020.11.019
5. Hassenzahl, M.: The effect of perceived hedonic quality on product appealingness. Int. J. Hum.-Comput. Interact. **13**(4), 481–499 (2001). https://doi.org/10.1207/S15327590IJHC1304_07
6. Hinderks, A., Schrepp, M., Domínguez Mayo, F.J., Escalona, M.J., Thomaschewski, J.: Developing a UX KPI based on the user experience questionnaire. Comput. Stand. Interfaces **65**, 38–44 (2019). https://doi.org/10.1016/j.csi.2019.01.007
7. Laugwitz, B., Schrepp, M., Held, T.: Konstruktion eines Fragebogens zur Messung der User Experience von Softwareprodukten. In: Heinecke, H., Paul, H. (eds.) Proceedings of the Mensch und Computer 2006, pp. 125–134. Oldenbourg Wissenschaftsverlag (2006). https://doi.org/10.1524/9783486841749.125
8. Meiners, A.L.: Which UX aspects are important for collaboration tools? Research protocol identifying important UX aspects influencing the user's experience when using collaboration tools. Technical report, University of Applied Sciences Emden/Leer (2023). https://doi.org/10.13140/RG.2.2.21382.55361/1
9. Meiners, A.L., Kollmorgen, J., Schrepp, M., Thomaschewski, J.: Protocol: ranking of important UEQ+ factors for established products. Technical report, University of Applied Sciences Emden/Leer (2021). https://doi.org/10.13140/RG.2.2.34986.95688

10. Meiners, A.L., Kollmorgen, J., Schrepp, M., Thomaschewski, J.: Which UX aspects are important for a software product?: importance ratings of UX aspects for software products for measurement with the UEQ+. In: Mensch und Computer 2021, Ingolstadt, Germany, pp. 136–139. ACM (2021). https://doi.org/10.1145/3473856.3473997

11. Meiners, A.L., Schrepp, M., Hinderks, A., Thomaschewski, J.: A benchmark for the UEQ+ framework: construction of a simple tool to quickly interpret UEQ+ KPIs. Int. J. Interact. Multimedia Artif. Intell. (In Press) (2023). https://doi.org/10.9781/ijimai.2023.05.003

12. Newman, S.A., Ford, R.C.: Five steps to leading your team in the virtual COVID-19 workplace. Organ. Dyn. **50**(1), 100802 (2021). https://doi.org/10.1016/j.orgdyn.2020.100802

13. Sauro, J., Lewis, J.R.: Quantifying the user experience: practical statistics for user research. Elsevier/Morgan Kaufmann, Amsterdam (2012)

14. Schrepp, M., Kollmorgen, J., Meiners, A.L., Hinderks, A., Winter, D., Thomaschewski, J.: On the importance of UX quality aspects for different product categories. In: International Journal of Interactive Multimedia and Artificial Intelligence, p. 15 (2023). https://doi.org/10.9781/ijimai.2023.03.001

15. Schrepp, M., Thomaschewski, J.: Design and validation of a framework for the creation of user experience questionnaires. Int. J. Interact. Multimedia Artif. Intell. **5**(7), 88 (2019). https://doi.org/10.9781/ijimai.2019.06.006

16. Simsek Caglar, P., Roto, V., Vainio, T.: User experience research in the work context: maps, gaps and agenda. In: Proceedings of the ACM on Human-Computer Interaction, vol. 6, no. CSCW1, pp. 1–28 (2022). https://doi.org/10.1145/3512979

17. Tuch, A.N., Schaik, P.V., Hornbæk, K.: Leisure and work, good and bad: the role of activity domain and valence in modeling user experience. ACM Trans. Comput.-Hum. Interact. **23**(6), 1–32 (2016). https://doi.org/10.1145/2994147

Tracing Stress and Arousal in Virtual Reality Games Using Players' Motor and Vocal Behaviour

Susanna Brambilla(✉) ⓘ, Giuseppe Boccignone ⓘ, N. Alberto Borghese ⓘ,
Eleonora Chitti ⓘ, Riccardo Lombardi, and Laura A. Ripamonti ⓘ

University of Milan, 20133 Milan, Italy
susanna.brambilla@unimi.it

Abstract. In this study, we tackle the integration of stressors and voice interaction in a Virtual Reality game to assess players' arousal and stress levels. The selected game genre and its characteristic components are used as a basis to create stress-inducing elements. Additionally, a voice interaction module has been created using a voice assistant called Minerva. The module allows for real-time detection and recording of players' emotional responses based on variations in pitch and intensity of speech. The game consists of a single level divided into four areas with increasing levels of stress. The experiment involved 16 volunteer students who played the game while their prosodic and behavioral movement data were collected. Participants also completed questionnaires and produced ratings to assess their perceived stress and arousal levels. The collected data were analyzed to evaluate the effectiveness of the real-time estimation of arousal and stress.

Keywords: Virtual reality · Arousal · Stress · Video game · Prosodic features · Motion behavioral data

1 Introduction

As technology advances and VR becomes increasingly prevalent, the focus on creating engaging and emotionally resonant gaming experiences becomes paramount. Voice-driven interactions and their implications for Virtual Reality (VR) gaming hold great significance in the realm of immersive entertainment and user experience, offering a unique avenue to tap into players' emotions and engagement levels in real-time.

The chief concern of this work is to delve into the intricacies of voice-driven interactions and their profound implications for VR players' engagement and affective/emotional resonance. Cogently, here we address the close interplay between stress and arousal levels along the game, estimated from the player's motor and vocal behaviours, respectively.

The motivation for embarking on such endeavour lies in the fact that, despite remarkable advancements in visual and haptic technologies, the potential of voice

H. P. da Silva and P. Cipresso (Eds.): CHIRA 2023, CCIS 1996, pp. 163–186, 2023.
https://doi.org/10.1007/978-3-031-49425-3_10

as a medium for enhancing the gaming experience remains untapped. By and large, video games struggle to take full advantage of such technologies. Yet, microphones are now an integral part of every player's equipment, given the growing popularity of voice chat in games.

The relevance of such a concern stems from the very fact that, *ceteris paribus*, the success of a video game feeds on its ability to maintain a large amount of players interested in the game and immersed in the experience. A growing body of studies contends with making such experiences adaptive (e.g., [20,28,33]), but a limited number capitalise on voice to unveil the player's affective state beyond its instrumental service as a control tool for video games.

Engagement and immersion call for the key construct of "flow". When a person is completely absorbed in the activity he/she is carrying out, that person is deemed to be in a state of flow [17]. It is difficult to identify precisely what characteristics of a game lead the player to be in the flow, a broad and subjective state of mind. Generally speaking, it can be experienced when the challenge posed by the game grows in proportion to the player's skills. When challenge levels and skills are unbalanced, emotional states, such as boredom and frustration, typically take place. Boredom (or apathy) arises when the skills of the player exceed the challenge imposed by the game. By contrast, frustration (or anxiety) emerges when the challenge overwhelms the player's skills.

Crucially, flow is closely related to stress, which intertwines with the player's arousal (the degree of activation/deactivation). In the presence of low-stress levels, players can lose interest and motivation to continue the experience. Conversely, high levels of stress bring players into a state of anxiety. In a crude summary, the player's stress and arousal are closely interconnected and together shape the player's emotional experience (but see Sect. 3). Thus, it goes without saying that studying models capable of estimating the players' affective inner states, such as their arousal, as well as their stress level, can be useful for correctly identifying the real-time level of involvement and dynamically adapting the proposed challenge to improve players' overall experience (cfr. Fig. 1).

Under such circumstances, the present work investigates the player's arousal and its relationship with stress to prospectively put such information in the service of game experience dynamic adaptation (see Fig. 1). To the best of our knowledge, this provides a novel contribution to the field.

Such efforts raise specific research questions (RQs):

1. whether and to what extent the player's stress and arousal dynamics are intertwined along the gaming experience (RQ1);
2. if this is the case, how can stress and arousal dynamics be estimated from the player's behaviour (here, gaming actions and voice), and to what extent do such outcomes correlate with the actual dynamics (RQ2).

To address the above RQs, we build on the VR game and the system developed by Brambilla et al. [12], in which the authors demonstrated how motion behavioral data can be used to recognize the VR players' continuous stress level with Machine Learning (ML) techniques.

Here, a layer of voice interaction has been added to the game, under the rationale that, by constraining the player to speak while progressing, it becomes possible to estimate the arousal expressed via vocal behaviour. To such an end, relevant prosodic features are considered, such as pitch, and volume.

Preliminary results indicate a strong correlation between self-assessed stress and arousal ratings, as well as a medium correlation between estimated stress and arousal levels, highlighting the potential for using voice interaction as a non-invasive method to assess players' emotional states during gameplay.

The subsequent sections unfold as follows. Section 2 analyzes the state-of-the-art with a particular emphasis on affective state recognition from voice in gaming. Section 3 lays out the rationales behind this research and our working assumptions. Section 4 will describe the video game and all the introduced vocal interactions. In Sect. 5, the experiment carried out with real players is described. Section 6 illustrates the techniques used in this work and the methodology with which the recognition model was created: the speech data are described in detail. In Sect. 7, the results so far achieved are presented and discussed. Finally, Sect. 8 draws some conclusions.

2   State-of-the-Art

Numerous studies in the literature regarding the analysis and estimation of affective states start from capturing the two dimensions of core affect in games (e.g., [21,28,41]); some of them have focused on estimating the emotional state from the voice and the related vocal parameters.

Balzarotti et al. [2] have proposed a series of activities in the form of games in which prosodic data are recorded in order to identify the user's emotional response. The activities are specifically designed to make the user move through different affective states: the exploration of a not particularly interesting web page to obtain a neutral response and a low level of interaction; a boring, repetitive game with a low level of challenge to recognize boredom in the player; a game with an opponent from whom the user has to escape and several levels of increasing difficulty, with the aim of recognizing frustration or satisfaction; a quiz game with a series of general knowledge questions in which easy questions alternate with difficult questions in order to recognize both player's frustration and satisfaction. The experiment showed that players were more engaged and satisfied in the activity related to the quiz game having a structure of quick questions and answers, similar to a natural conversation.

In the video game industry, a growing trend can be glimpsed regarding the inclusion of vocal interactions, especially in the indie market. Examples are titles such as *In Verbis Virtus* (Indomitus Games, 2015), where the player controls a magician and casts spells by pronouncing the formulas with his voice, or the more recent *Phasmophobia* (Kinetic Games, 2020), where the player plays a ghost hunter who must interact with the voice to locate the ghost. These vocal interactions are limited to recognizing the commands to use vocal interaction as a gameplay mechanics. In no case, they exploit the prosodic information to estimate the affective state of the player.

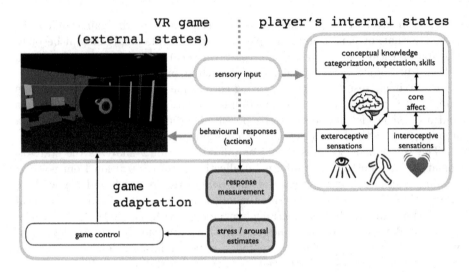

Fig. 1. Conceptual framework of the present work. The external state dynamics of the VR game elicits the player's internal state dynamics. The latter involves conceptual, affective, interoceptive and exteroceptive components, yielding to behavioural responses (here, gamer's motor and vocal behaviour are considered). Grey-shaded boxes highlight components this work specifically addresses: response measurements estimate the player's stress level and arousal dynamics. In perspective, such estimates can be potentially exploited, in future works, for game adaptation.

Differently from these studies, as stated from the beginning, our main contribution is in addressing the problem of gauging user's arousal by analyzing his vocal behaviour while playing a video game in VR, starting from the analysis of the prosodic characteristics, and to explore arousal entanglement with the stress level experienced by the player. The rationales behind our approach are outlined in the following Section.

3   Rationales

Stress and arousal are closely intertwined and influence one another. Therefore, understanding the dynamic interplay between them can provide insights into how the individual adapts to and copes with stressful situations in general, and specifically in the context of VR games.

From a broad standpoint, living organisms, including the brain, strive to minimize the discrepancy between their internal models of the world and the actual sensory input they receive, both from the world and the body. To such end, the brain continuously generates predictions about incoming sensory data and updates them based on the sensory input it receives [5,16,19,35].

Stress, in this framework, can be seen as a disruption or perturbation to the system's internal models. It can arise from various sources such as external threats, environmental changes, or internal psychological factors, e.g., the discrepancy between the individual's expectation and the actual situation [26]. Stress activates the body's stress response system, which involves the release of stress hormones such as cortisol and adrenaline [35]. These hormones can impact the brain's functioning, particularly the regions involved in prediction and perception. When faced with stress, the system's internal models may no longer accurately predict the sensory input, leading to increased prediction errors [26,27,30].

Arousal, on the other hand, refers to the level of physiological and psychological activation or alertness experienced by an individual; in other terms, it is related to the individual's readiness to respond to the environment. It is a psychological construct that, in its minimal form, refers to the physiological state of the organism, particularly with respect to the activity of the sympathetic branch of the autonomous nervous system [3]; more generally, after the seminal work by Russell [32], arousal is a fundamental dimension of the core affect, the other dimension being represented by valence (degree of pleasure/displeasure). The core affect (cfr., Fig. 1), in turn, builds on interoception and is grounded in the *internal milieu* of the individual, providing an integrated sensory representation of the physiological state of the body: the somatovisceral, kinesthetic, proprioceptive, and neurochemical fluctuations that take place within the core of the body. As such, in emotion theory, the core affect represents a basic ingredient for constructing emotion (the latter not being reducible to the former) [6]. Further, evidence from current results in neuroscience suggests that, if interoception plays a role in allostasis (the brain-centered predictive regulation of the *internal milieu* [35]) and allostasis is at the core of the brain's computational architecture, then the properties of affect - valence and arousal - are best thought of as basic features of consciousness, rather than properties of emotion *per se* [7,39]. In this view, according to recent advancements in theoretical neuroscience [5,39], arousal can be operationalised as the system's attempt to reduce prediction errors and minimize surprisal. Higher levels of arousal imply a greater allocation of resources to reduce the mismatch between predictions and sensory input (thereby minimizing surprisal).

Clearly, stress can modulate arousal levels, leading to increased or decreased arousal depending on the context. Acute stressors may initially lead to increased arousal as the system mobilizes resources to adapt to the perceived threat. This heightened arousal can enhance the system's ability to update its internal models and reduce prediction errors.

To recap the above discussion, the consequences of the close interplay between stress and arousal are far-reaching and involve the construction of the individual's affective experience. Stress can influence the construction of emotions by altering the interpretation and appraisal of sensory information. Stressful situations can trigger physiological changes associated with arousal, such as increased heart rate, sweating, and heightened vigilance. These bodily changes provide signals interpreted by the brain during the process of emotion construction. Indeed, arousal plays a critical role in shaping emotional experiences. Increased arousal levels can influence the construction of emotions by amplifying certain bodily sensations and influencing the brain's interpretation of these sensations. In summary, studying the interplay between stress, arousal, and emotion construction, which highlights the dynamic nature of affective experiences, is crucial in characterizing the player's experience. (see Fig. 1)

Under such circumstances, with reference to research question RQ1, we expect that, for the reasons discussed above, a statistically significant degree of correlation can be measured.

To address RQ2, for what concerns stress level inference, here we draw on the study presented by Brambilla et al. [12]. As to arousal estimation, we shall consider vocal behaviour.

The use of vocal cues has an impressive and long-standing tradition both in emotion theory [3,34] and in engineering [10]. Indeed there is considerable evidence that emotion/affect states produce changes in respiration, phonation and articulation, which in turn partly determine the parameters of the acoustic signal. Much of the consistency in the findings is linked to differential levels of arousal gauged via acoustic measurements such as energy, fundamental frequency of phonation (referred to as $F0$), and speech rate (eg., in terms of number of syllables per second, syll/s).

The vocal energy or amplitude is perceived as the intensity of the voice. The fundamental frequency $F0$ reflects the frequency of the vibration of the vocal folds and is related to the pitch; it is worth noting that most phoneticians distinguish between pitch and the fundamental frequency [22]. The first corresponds to the subjective impression of how voiced sounds, particularly sonorants and vowels, are perceived on a scale going from low to high, as on a musical scale of notes. In contrast, the second corresponds to the physiological parameter of the vibration frequency of the vocal folds (or cords) or the equivalent acoustic parameter $F0$ of fundamental frequency measured in hertz (Hz). Yet, the term pitch is, however, often loosely applied to the acoustic or physiological measurement (e.g., "pitch detection", "pitch range"). [4]. Overall, the intonation, tone, timing, and energy of speech are all jointly influenced in a nontrivial manner to express the emotional message [23].

In the affective computing literature, these are often referred to as prosodic features. Clearly, within this field, there has been a tremendous development of techniques for inferring affect and emotions from speech (see [1,24,36–38], for in-depth reviews). However, for the purposes of the work presented here that specifically deals with arousal, in order to keep things simple either conceptually and computationally, we will predominantly rely on the findings previously discussed in [10,14,23]. In this particular work, the framework for estimating arousal uses an unsupervised approach, meaning it does not rely on pre-labeled data with arousal scores to train the model. Instead, it employs specific prosodic features, such as pitch and volume, to extract relevant information from the players' vocal behaviors. By analyzing these features, the model derives an arousal score or index, bounded in the range $[-1, 1]$, without any prior knowledge of the true arousal levels of the players. The approach is formally simple, but it has the advantage of being interpretable, since the model's focus is on discovering inherent patterns in the data without being influenced by predefined labels, and does not require learning. Within the scope of this work, game adaptation is not addressed; rather, our emphasis is directed towards one of the numerous aspects that could be taken into consideration for the purpose of game adaptation.

4   Video Game Description

To find an answer to our research questions, we have designed and prototyped an *ad-hoc* first-person survival horror VR game, which we used as the testing environment with actual players. The game is set in a spatial station under alien attack. Consequently, the player goal is to stay alive and escape the damaged station using a safety pod. During the game, players interact with Minerva, the space station's Artificial Intelligence (AI), which acts as a voice assistant.

The choice of the game genre has been inspired by the work of Vachiratamporn et al. [40], which underlines its effectiveness in eliciting strong emotional responses. In a similar vein, we decided to deploy the game on VR headsets because of the enhanced immersion and sense of presence these devices can provide, as well as their ability to elicit stronger emotional responses, characterized by higher peaks of anxiety and fear, but also of joy deriving from overcoming challenges (Pallavicini et al. [29]).

As said, when an individual's expectations and the game scenario he/she is dealing with do not match, the situation is perceived as stressful and self-threatening due to insufficient resources to cope with it. Therefore, exploiting peculiar features of the survival game-genre and drawing on [26] and on [12], we have added ad hoc stressors to the game, such as: the feeling of isolation, the presence of terrifying enemies, scary music and sound effects, poor lighting, low oxygen levels, and a general shortage of resources.

While playing, players' stress is estimated through motion behaviour data, tracked using sensors built-in in the head-mounted display [12]. At the same time, the voice interaction module (Minerva) we have added to the game detects in a non-obtrusive way and in real-time fluctuations in their arousal level by analysing variations in their voice pitch, intensity and speed.

4.1   Game Level

The game consists of a single level, composed of six consecutive rooms connected by corridors and divided into four areas characterized by stressors aimed at gradually increasing the player's stress level. The level structure is linear and its content is always presented in the same way to all the testers so as to obtain consistent data to effectively compare the gaming sessions of different players. The four areas and the level's elements are represented in Fig. 2.

The first area (*non-stress* or *baseline* room) is a small room containing just a computer terminal. Its purpose is to acquire neutral data, which will then be used to track variations in prosodic data collected from players. In this room, players meet Minerva for the first time and are asked to introduce themselves

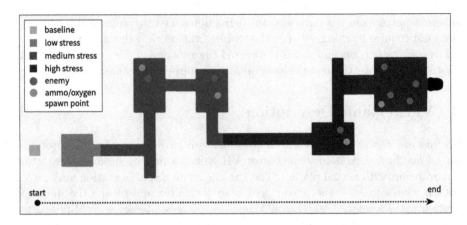

Fig. 2. The map of the game level with the area divided by the stress level to be elicited. Enemies and resources spawn points are also represented.

briefly. In that way, we make sure that players speak clearly and calmly, with an arousal level close to 0 due to the absence of anxiety and any expectation about the game, conditions necessary to obtain prosodic data as neutral as possible.

The second area (*low-stress* room) is set in the safe room of the station. The room is well-lit, there are no enemies, and there is no oxygen shortage. Here players will be able to familiarize themselves with the resources available (e.g., ammo, medikits, gun, etc.), as well as to learn and practice with the voice commands useful to interact with Minerva to advance in the game. Minerva also begins to hint obscurely to the player about the dangers lurking ahead, thus setting the tone for the later stages of the game. As a result, we obtain a slight increase in arousal due to the surprise and excitement of the unknown that awaits beyond the closed door. By asking Minerva to open it, the player gains access to the next area.

The third area (*medium-stress* area) consists of two corridors and two rooms connected to the safe room. From this moment on, the oxygen reserve in the spacesuit worn by the players will gradually start to drop, and they will need to replenish their reserve using oxygen cylinders they can find scattered across the rooms. If oxygen drops to zero, players will suffer constant damage to their health. Moreover, the light is dimmed and players will have to use the flashlight to look around. It will also be possible to hear noises coming from the innermost rooms of the space station. All of this is intended to put players in a state of stress and arousal that forces them to move quickly, but with caution. Here, in fact, the players will face the first two enemies. Once the creatures have been defeated, Minerva will ask the players to describe them, thus allowing us to identify variations in the tone of voice, and, consequently, any increase in arousal.

The last area (*high-stress* area) is composed of two corridors and two rooms, nearly completely dark, thus making it impossible to see without a flashlight. In this area, the oxygen will start to decrease much faster, thus forcing players to constantly check their oxygen levels. As players get closer to the final goal (the escape pod), the noises produced by alien creatures will become more frequent and louder and a siren will start to scream to produce an even more stressful experience. Meanwhile, players must also face a lot of enemies that are blocking the path toward the escape pod.

4.2 Vocal Interaction Layer

A fundamental element of the gameplay is interacting with Minerva, the AI of the space station. The speech interaction is based on the *Unity Speech Recognition* library, which - by performing a *Speech To Text* operation - returns the sentence(s) recognized from the players' speech in the form of text strings, which can then be analyzed to spot specific keywords that players can use to activate a command or to provide information to the AI.

Every moment of the gameplay requiring vocal interaction with Minerva is codified in the Question and Answer structure shown in Fig. 3. Every line of dialogue corresponds to an object"Question" connected to 0 or more possible answers: if there are no answers to give, Minerva provides information to the players and once the line of dialogue has ended, it automatically switches to the next step; in the case of a question with 1 or more possible answers, Minerva waits for the players to answer. At this point, a string comparison operation is performed by comparing each word expressed by the players with the keywords related to all possible answers to that specific question. Note that each keyword has been reduced to its theme through a stemming operation (the process of reducing the inflected form of a word to its root form, as typically performed in natural language processing algorithms). If necessary, a majority vote is used to elect the answer closest to the phrase expressed by the players. In other words, each word in the phrase expressed by the players, also present in an answer expected by Minerva, contributes to increasing a similarity counter between the expressed phrase and the answer under consideration. After examining all the possible answers, the one with the highest value for the similarity counter is selected. The value of the similarity counter of the selected answer is then compared with a similarity threshold. If it does not reach the threshold value, Minerva will consider the answer provided by the player insufficient and will return appropriate feedback.

Due to this structure - based on questions and answers - players can interact only in two modes with Minerva: either they can pose a question to Minerva or they have to answer a question posed by Minerva.

Players Ask Something to Minerva. Players can ask for Minerva's help with a set of predefined commands: it is the most common type of interaction during the game and is almost always feasible. By pronouncing the keyword"Minerva" and any sentence containing one or more keywords among all possible commands, the player can trigger the assistance of the AI. Minerva will then execute the requested command to help the player. Possible commands are:

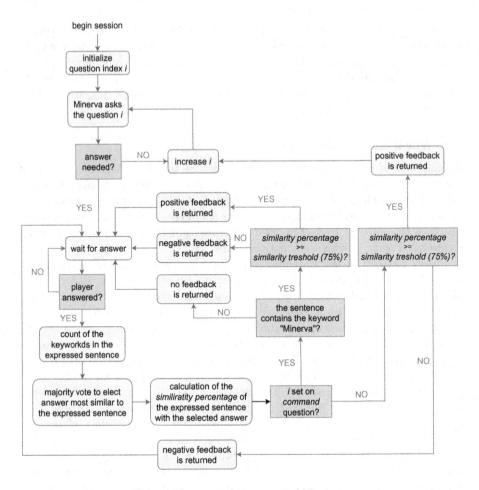

Fig. 3. The general structure of Minerva.

- *open the door*: aiming at a door while asking Minerva to open it, will unlock it. The light above the door will turn from red to green to give appropriate feedback to the player;
- *ammo spawn*: one ammo clip will spawn in the nearest spawn point unless Minerva is recharging this ability (30" cooldown);
- *oxygen generation*: a cylinder of oxygen is generated in the nearest spawn point, unless Minerva is recharging this ability (90" cooldown);
- *hit enemy*: targeting an enemy while asking Minerva for help triggers an electric discharge that damages and stuns the creature for 2" unless Minerva is recharging this ability (60" cooldown);
- *command list*: Minerva lists all possible commands, giving a brief description of their effects and of which are the correct keywords to activate them.

Minerva Asks Something to Players. In order to analyze longer sentences, whose information content (in terms of prosodic data) is therefore more substantial, there are three moments during which Minerva asks the players to describe something. In this cases, it is not necessary to trigger the attention of Minerva (whose attention is obtained by saying "Minerva" before any possible request), since the AI is already "listening" to the player. Moreover, the interaction is seamlessly intertwined with the gameplay, to avoid disrupting the immersivity. The player's answer is valid if it contains at least 5 words and includes at least 1 keyword among those expected by Minerva in the specific situation. If the sentence does not match these constraints, an appropriate feedback is given and iterated until the player produces a sentence with the expected characteristics. The first time Minerva asks a description to the player is in the baseline room: it is the very first interaction with the AI and the player is prompted to introduce him/herself. Subsequently, Minerva asks the player to describe the first alien monster encountered. The description is asked immediately after the end of the combat the player has to sustain with the monster, hence when the excitement of the fight is still alive. The last occasion to collect long sentences takes place in the high-stress area, when Minerva warns the player about damage in the spacesuit and asks for a description of the problem. This moment is particularly relevant since it offers the opportunity to track fluctuations (if any) of the arousal from the voice of players experiencing an extremely anxious and stressful situation.

4.3 Devices Used to Collect Data

The VR devices used to collect data are *Meta Quest 2*[1] headset, its built-in microphones, and its two controllers. *Meta Quest 2* has numerous built-in sensors that allowed us to collect several types of information through:

- tracking function: its 6 degrees of freedom (6DoF) tracking system allows to effectively translate head and hands movements into the VR world;
- touch control: each controller has a series of capacitive sensors on its buttons aimed at understanding the exact position of the players' fingers;
- stereophonic audio: it fosters a deeper immersion in the virtual environment without requiring headphones;
- high-precision microphones: they can catch the player's voice even when he/she is whispering while at the same time cancelling environmental noise.

5 Experimental Setting

The experiment, which involved 16 volunteer students (age mean 24.94) for approximately 40' each, was structured as depicted in Fig. 4. To avoid collecting biased data, no tester suffering from motion sickness was included in the sample.

Participants read and signed the informed consent form for handling personal data collected during the experiment. Then, they were asked to respond

---

[1] https://store.facebook.com/it/quest/products/quest-2/.

Fig. 4. Flowchart of the testing session.

to two questionnaires: the first one is a specifically designed demographic questionnaire, while the second is a standard psychological questionnaires that aims to assess the level of stress perceived during the last month, namely, the Perceived Stress Scale (PSS) [15]. Once the questionnaires were completed, they started the gaming session, during which prosodic data for arousal estimation and behavioral movement data for stress estimation were collected. The final step required the participants to self-assess the perceived level of arousal and stress, using DANTE (Dimensional ANnotation Tool for Emotions) [8], by watching their gameplay recorded during the game session.

5.1   Demographic Data of the Sample

From the demographic standpoint, it is important to underline that all the participants declared to play video games regularly during the week (five of them playing more than 20 h a week). Therefore, they are regular video gamers, thus, we can reasonably be sure that none of them would have experienced stress deriving from a poor familiarity with the medium. The majority of the participants stated that their favorite game genre was action, closely followed by adventure. Furthermore, half of the participants claimed they had no experience with VR devices, while the other half had only limited experience.

Last but not least, all the subjects reported feeling very lightly stressed before beginning the experiment.

5.2   Self-annotation

To label the collected data, players' real arousal and stress ratings were needed. Therefore, participants were asked to self-report their perceived stress and arousal levels during the gaming session by rating them on a recording of their gameplay, using an *ad-hoc* version of DANTE. DANTE is an online annotation tool featuring an interactive Self-Assessment Manikin (SAM) questionnaire [11] that allows users to continuously annotate valence and arousal with a slider scale ranging from -1 to 1. In this project, a stress slider (presented as a coloured bar) was added, enabling participants to report their perceived stress levels on a range from low to high stress (-1 to 1).

6   Methods: Model-Based Analysis

Fig. 5 presents at a glance a functional view of our model-based analysis. Its core relies on two models/systems: the stress estimation system developed in [12] (Fig. 5, box a), and the real-time arousal estimation model proposed here (Fig. 5, box b).

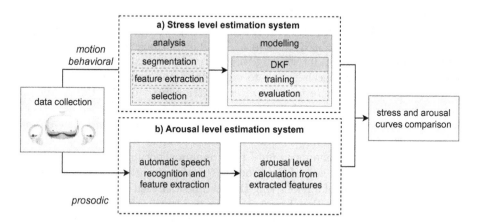

Fig. 5. Estimation of stress and arousal levels of the gamer. The system operationalises the highlighted components of the conceptual framework outlined in Fig. 1 that are specifically addressed in this work

The two models allow real-time inference of continuous stress and arousal level dynamics from the data collected via VR controllers and headset. Results can be eventually analyzed and compared with one another, as well as those obtained from players' self-assessments concerning the actual perceived stress and arousal.

6.1   Stress Estimation

The stress estimation system is based on [12]. The raw data was obtained by tracking the movements of the Quest 2 devices, as well as the pressure on the buttons, and which buttons were pressed. These data were acquired with a sampling frequency of 64 Hz. Once the raw data were obtained and analyzed, a set of statistical features were extracted for all the data obtained from head and left/right hands: mean, standard deviation, minimum and maximum values are used, as well as the average number of times the buttons were pressed within the designated time period (see [12] for more details).

In particular, the system assessed the stress level by means of a Discriminative Kalman Filter (DKF)[13]. A DKF is able to predict the continuous level of players' stress. It works in a supervised way: the DKF model was trained using players' motion behavioral features and self-reported stress ratings assessed using DANTE. The model has been tested via Leave-One-Out-Cross-Validation (LOOCV) by iterating on the number of subjects. At each iteration, the data relating to one of the subjects were chosen to be part of the test set, while the remaining subjects were part of the training set.

6.2   Arousal Estimation

Speech Recognition. Speech recognition, also known as Automatic Speech Recognition (ASR) or Speech-to-text, is a feature that allows a program to process human speech into a written format. The most advanced speech recognition solutions use AI and ML, integrating the grammar, syntax, structure and composition of audio and speech signals to understand and process human speech.

Here we use the *DictationRecognizer* functionality[2] of the Unity Speech Recognition library, which exploits the *Windows Online Speech Recognition* technology to perform the Speech-To-Text operation. The dictation function allows, as soon as the individual players start speaking, to make a series of hypotheses on the sentence they pronounced until they remain silent for a certain period of time (about 2 s). At the end of the process, the sentence uttered by the players is returned in the form of a text string that can be analyzed at will. Most important here the Speech-To-Text function allows to identify the instant in time in which the user started speaking and the instant in time in which he stopped speaking.

Arousal from Voice. Given the standard $f_S = 44.1$KHz sampling frequency and voiced-interval time stamps, the audio signal y_n is windowed, $\tilde{y}_n = w_n y_n$ via a Blackmann-Harris sliding function w_n, of length $\Delta t_w = 40$msec, thus considering $N_w = \frac{\Delta t_w f_s}{1000} = 1744$ samples. Each voiced frame is obtained by applying a sliding window with $\tau_w = 30$msec overlap. Each utterance varies in its duration, thus each utterance is chunked into $(\Delta t_w - \tau_w) \times N_f + \tau_w \approx 1$sec, (a duration which is assumed to be an adequate duration for estimating affective information from audio [25],) resulting in ≈ 100frame/sec. Under such conditions, point estimates of the two chosen prosodic features, namely the voice fundamental frequency F_0(Hz) and voice intensity I(dB), are computed at a rate of 100Hz. Estimation was performed by specifically porting the pitch and intensity base calculation methods in Unity from Praat [9]. All unvoiced frames were assigned as a missing value.

At each frame, parameters are computed, ignoring missing values, in terms of the feature statistics necessary for the arousal estimate [4,10,14,23]; a window of 15-frame length is used to derive the following statistics. As to F_0:

- μ_{F_0}: the mean of the F_0 values,
- σ_{F_0}: the standard deviation F_0 ,
- min F_0: the minimum F_0 value of the voice recording,

---

[2] https://docs.unity3d.com/ScriptReference/Windows.Speech.DictationRecognizer.html.

- $\max F_0$: the maximum F_0 value of the voice recording,
- R_{F_0}: the F_0 range, namely, the difference $\max F_0 - \min F_0$,

Analogously, for the intensity I(dB) the parameters $\mu_I, \sigma_I, \min I, \max I, R_I$ are obtained.

Eventually, the time-varying vector of parameters $X(k) = [x_1(k)\, x_2(k) \cdots x_K]$ is obtained with $x_1(k) = \mu_{F_0}, x_2(k) = \sigma_{F_0}, \cdots, x_{N_x}(k) = R_I$. Here k is the frame index obtained at discrete time steps $t_n \rightarrow t_n + \tau_w$

Raw feature values are rarely informative without a reference, the variability between speakers being often larger than that within speakers [14]. Thus, at every voiced frame, we rely on a baseline to assess deviations in feature values, and, thus, variations in vocal arousal. The baseline reference was preliminarily obtained, following the same procedure described above on the data acquired from the baseline evaluation of the gamer, and summarised as the baseline mean vector of parameters $\underline{X} = \begin{bmatrix} x_1 \, x_2 \cdots x_{N_x} \end{bmatrix}$ to be used for the online estimation of the arousal score. A score, denoted $a_i(n)$, is first computed for each parameter $x_i(n)$,

$$a_i(n) = \mathrm{sgn}(x_i(n) - \underline{x_i}), \tag{1}$$

where $\mathrm{sgn}(\cdot)$ stands for the signum function that here maps the difference $x_i(n) - \underline{x_i}$ between a parameter x_i and its baseline $\underline{x_1}$ to the parameter score $a_i \in \{-1, 0, 1\}$.

Then, the expected arousal score, $\overline{a_i(n)}$ is estimated via the empirical mean

$$\overline{a(n)} = \frac{1}{N_x} \sum_{i=1}^{N} a_i(n) \tag{2}$$

Eventually, the arousal index trace $\overline{a(n)}$ is downsampled to a 60Hz sampling rate in order to match the sampling rate of the stress estimate trace.

6.3   Data Pre-processing

Once the different types of data (voice, movement-behavioral, self-assessed stress and arousal ratings) have been collected, they have been first synchronized using previously saved timestamps. Next, stress and arousal labels obtained from DANTE were assigned to differentiate between two datasets: (a) arousal dataset, containing prosodic data, arousal values estimated in real-time during the game session and real arousal values reported during the self-assessment phase; (b) stress dataset - containing the movement data acquired by the Quest 2 device and the real stress values tracked during the self-assessment phase.

Since voice features were extracted in real-time to estimate arousal levels during the game session, it was necessary to extract features from motion-behavioral data. These features were then used to train the DKF model, allowing the validation of real-time arousal estimation and comparison of its results with the DKF model's performance in stress estimation.

All the different types of collected data (voice, self-assessed stress and arousal ratings, movement-behavioral) have been synchronized using previously saved timestamps.

Stress Feature Extraction and Selection. The subsequent step involved extracting and selecting the most relevant features to feed the DKF model. To perform this step, a segmentation operation was carried out using a sliding window method: this allows the dataset to be divided into fixed-size windows. Each individual window represents a short time interval, from which the features were extracted. After extracting the features from one window, the window is

Table 1. List of the features, the one selected be given as input for the learning models are checked with a ✓. Abbreviations: min = minimum, max = maximum, # = number. Adapted from [12].

TYPE	DATA	FEATURE				
		μ	σ	min	max	$\mu\#press$
head	velocity	✓	✓			
	angular velocity					
	acceleration	✓		✓		
	angular acceleration	✓	✓	✓	✓	
left hand	velocity	✓		✓		
	angular velocity	✓	✓	✓	✓	
	acceleration			✓		
	angular acceleration	✓	✓	✓	✓	
	grip pressure	✓	✓	✓	✓	
	trigger pressure	✓	✓		✓	
	thumbstick position x		✓	✓	✓	
	thumbstick position y	✓				
	grip pressed					✓
	trigger pressed					✓
right hand	velocity	✓	✓	✓	✓	
	angular velocity	✓	✓	✓	✓	
	acceleration	✓	✓	✓	✓	
	angular acceleration	✓	✓	✓	✓	
	grip pressure	✓		✓		
	trigger pressure		✓	✓	✓	
	thumbstick position x					
	thumbstick position y					
	grip pressed					✓
	trigger pressed					✓

moved or slid to the next segment of the dataset, with some degree of overlap in order to capture the temporal dynamics and relationships between time intervals. In this study, the chosen window had a 6 s size, with an overlap of 1 s. Regarding the motion behavioral data, the extracted features were the most commonly used in statistics, i.e., mean, minimum value, maximum value and standard deviation. In relation to the button pressed, the average number of presses in the established time window was used.

Finally, Pearson's correlation coefficients between each feature and the self-reported stress level were calculated. This made it possible to identify the features with a higher average degree of correlation, which would then be used for model training. At the same time, it is was possible to identify unrelated features and remove them from the dataset, so as not to negatively affect the training process. The process consisted of a univariate feature selection with a p-value threshold equal to 0.05. All the motion behavioral features selected to be given as input to the ML model are shown in Table 1. In total, 55 features were selected.

7   Results

In order to offer a qualitative grasp of the results achieved, we present the data of several different testers we deem particularly representative of the overall outcomes (see Fig. 6, 9, 8, and 7). The curves plotted in the figures compare stress and arousal dynamics, either self-assessed and estimated, of the different subjects.

It is worth remarking that, since during the game session, understandably, the players did not talk constantly, the prosodic features were not always available. Silence intervals were excluded from the analyses.

Curves were compared in pairs:

1. self-assessed stress level vs. self-assessed arousal level ;
2. self-assessed stress vs. DKF-predicted stress; [12]
3. self-assessed arousal vs. estimated arousal;
4. DKF-predicted stress vs. estimated arousal;

Results over different players are proposed to highlight individual variability. For a quantitative evaluation of results, Pearson correlation was used to compute correlation matrices, first for every single subject, and then averaging over all the subjects. This method allows to measure the statistical relationship between two continuous variables based on their covariance. Results are summarised in Fig. 10.

In brief, on average, we have measured the following:

1. a strong positive correlation between self-assessed stress and self-assessed arousal levels;
2. a medium positive correlation between self-assessed stress and DKF-predicted stress;
3. a medium positive correlation between self-assessed arousal and estimated arousal;
4. a medium positive correlation between DKF-predicted stress and estimated arousal;

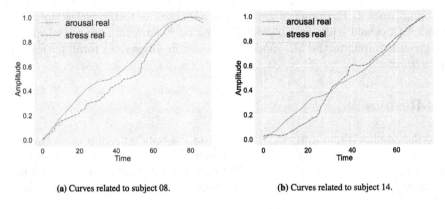

(a) Curves related to subject 08.   (b) Curves related to subject 14.

Fig. 6. Curves of the stress and arousal ratings.

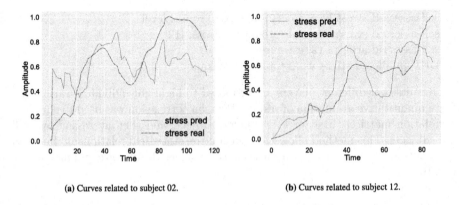

(a) Curves related to subject 02.   (b) Curves related to subject 12.

Fig. 7. Curves of the stress ratings and levels predicted by the DKF model using motion behavioral data.

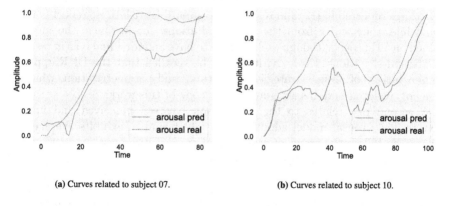

(a) Curves related to subject 07.   (b) Curves related to subject 10.

Fig. 8. Curves of the arousal ratings and the arousal level predicted using prosodic data.

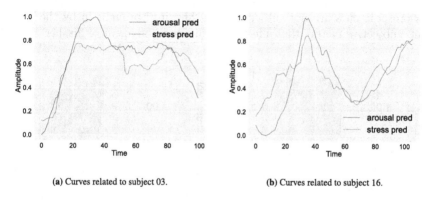

(a) Curves related to subject 03.   (b) Curves related to subject 16.

Fig. 9. Curves of the arousal and stress levels predicted by the models.

7.1 Discussion

The strong positive correlation observed between perceived stress and arousal levels align with general theoretical assumptions and experimental results reported in the psychological realm. Yet, here it is eventually obtained in a real VR context.

It is worth noticing that the reported matrices refer to a value averaged over all subjects' data. This clearly entails that individual results can exhibit a correlation range from strong to weak. For the sake of generality and comparison purposes, the analyses conducted here did not specifically account for within-subject factors (e.g., in the learning procedure and parameters). Such between-subject variations can be readily appreciated in detail from plots presented in Figs. 7, 8, and 9.

Also, at the same level of detail, some discrepancies between compared levels can be observed. The first concerns the DKF prediction of stress (Figs. 7). For the purposes of this work, we straightforwardly adopted the inference and learning procedures reported in [12] and results are compatible with those reported there; meanwhile, they suffer from the same limitations: for instance, the model is trained on all subjects, though each is likely to have an individual bias in response to stressful situations. However, it should be recalled that the DKF approach offers a variety of design strategies for learning and parametrization, which we have not explored here because out of the scope of this work.

A second one relates to the comparison between perceived and inferred arousal. The arousal model adopted here, albeit simple, exhibits average estimates that follow the trend of real arousal ratings. However, an overestimate can be noticed within and between subjects. On the one hand, one should recall that, differently from DKF, the model provides a time-point local estimate of perceived arousal, which does not take advantage of time-series constraints. On the other hand, arousal levels were self-rated by subjects using the video-stream only, without audio for fairness' sake, to prevent them from using audio as a proxy for arousal rating. *Prima facie*, it is likely that direct arousal estimates from prosodic cues are not subject to the "filtering" brought in by the several latent, subjective factors that affect the individual judgment of his/her arousal.

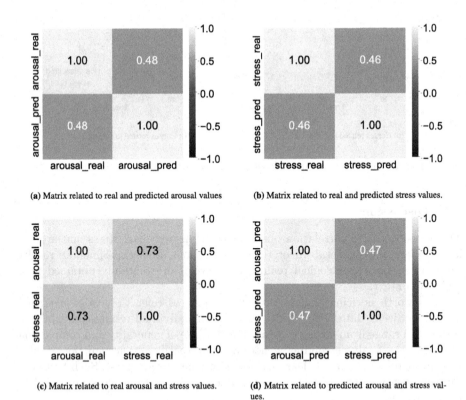

(a) Matrix related to real and predicted arousal values

(b) Matrix related to real and predicted stress values.

(c) Matrix related to real arousal and stress values.

(d) Matrix related to predicted arousal and stress values.

Fig. 10. Correlation matrices obtained using all subjects' data, related to the different comparisons between arousal and stress labels.

Yet, such effect is moderated when only model predictions are compared (Fig. 9), albeit still present in specific time intervals.

In conclusion, these limitations have the potential to impact the results by introducing biases, complexities, and variations that need to be considered when interpreting the study's findings. A cautionary note should be stated at this point. Obviously, self-ratings could be prone to individual biases, lacks recalling the experienced situation, errors and time delays in employing the rating tool, fatigue and mind wandering of the player after the VR gaming session. Yet, one must consider that the alternative, represented by an "external" human rater, is not an innocent one. Though often adopted in the affective computing realm with the aim of providing an "objective ground-truth", such a deceptively straightforward setting hides a complex state of affairs and may turn into a slippery route [18]. Unfortunately, in this realm, we are far from the standard conditions we encounter, for instance, in computer vision, where classes of objects and events of interest can be objectively sensed and categorized (e.g., by assigning a "label"). Indeed, measuring affective and, more specifically, emotional changes is complex and fraught with difficulties. This caveat should always be taken seriously, as scrutinized in depth in terms of validity by [31].

8   Conclusions

Integrating stressors and voice interaction in the game provided valuable insights into players' arousal. The chosen stressors successfully induced stress and anxiety in players, as evidenced by their affective responses captured through voice interactions and motion behavioral data. The game level design allowed for controlled and comparable experiences across different gaming sessions. The voice interaction module, facilitated by the AI assistant Minerva, quite effectively detected and recorded prosodic data, enabling the estimation of players' arousal levels. The experimental results showed promising potential for using voice interaction as a non-invasive method to assess players' emotional states during gameplay.

In particular, the study provided evidence of a strong correlation between actual stress and real arousal ratings acquired through participants' self-assessments (RQ1). Preliminary results suggest that such outcome is reflected in a medium correlation between the estimated stress and arousal levels (RQ2), in spite of the simplicity of the arousal model devised here. Yet, the individual variability observed in responses to the game experience calls for further investigation into system personalization.

8.1   Final Conclusions and Further Work

While the results of our study provide a fresh insight into these problems, several limitations should be acknowledged. Firstly, the sample size was relatively small, consisting of 16 volunteer students. A larger and more nuanced sample would enhance the external validity/generalizability of our findings. Further, refinement of the voice interaction module and analysis algorithms could enhance the accuracy and reliability of arousal and stress recognition. On the one hand, the arousal estimation model, being completely real-time and unrelated to the self-assessments provided by the participants, could find wide use in applications that adapt to the affective state of the players.

On the other hand, from a more theoretical perspective, a model accounting for a principled integration of stress and arousal, in the vein of Fig. 1, can provide key insights into the problem, which goes beyond VR games *per se*, but from which VR game design could benefit.

Also, we have only considered here player's game actions and vocal behaviour. Exploring, for instance, additional physiological cues, such as heart rate and skin conductance, is likely to provide a more comprehensive understanding of players' affective states. Moreover, investigating the long-term/longitudinal effects of gaming-induced stress and exploring potential interventions or adaptive game design strategies to mitigate excessive stress could represent a valuable research direction.

The study focused on a specific game genre and stress-inducing elements; exploring the effects of different stressors and game genres could provide a more comprehensive understanding. Indeed, the approach can be potentially employed in different contexts: VR games and applications with similar structure and elements to the one developed. In particular, a reliable baseline phase for acquiring of neutral values of prosodic data and movement data is needed, as well as elements that generate stress, as underlined in the research of Lebois et al. [26].

Overall, in spite of current limitations, this study contributes to the field of affective gaming by demonstrating the importance and the feasibility of integrating stressors and voice interaction for real-time assessment of players' arousal and stress levels. The ultimate goal is to develop affective gaming systems that enhance players' experience, promote well-being, and contribute to the field of emotion-aware computing.

Acknowledgement. This work has been partially supported by EC H2020 ESSENCE project, Grant number 101016112.

References

1. Akçay, M.B., Oğuz, K.: Speech emotion recognition: emotional models, databases, features, preprocessing methods, supporting modalities, and classifiers. Speech Commun. **116**, 56–76 (2020)
2. Balzarotti, S., Piccini, L., Andreoni, G., Ciceri, R.: "I know that you know how I feel": Behavioral and physiological signals demonstrate emotional attunement while interacting with a computer simulating emotional intelligence. J. Nonverbal Behav. **38**, 283–299 (2014)
3. Banse, R., Scherer, K.R.: Acoustic profiles in vocal emotion expression. J. Pers. Soc. Psychol. **70**(3), 614 (1996)
4. Bänziger, T., Scherer, K.R.: The role of intonation in emotional expressions. Speech Commun. **46**(3–4), 252–267 (2005)
5. Barrett, L.F.: The theory of constructed emotion: an active inference account of interoception and categorization. Soc. Cogn. Affect. Neurosci. **12**(1), 1–23 (2017)

6. Barrett, L.F., Bliss-Moreau, E.: Affect as a psychological primitive. Adv. Exp. Soc. Psychol. **41**, 167–218 (2009)
7. Barrett, L.F., Satpute, A.B.: Historical pitfalls and new directions in the neuroscience of emotion. Neurosci. Lett. **693**, 9–18 (2019)
8. Boccignone, G., Conte, D., Cuculo, V., Lanzarotti, R.: Amhuse: a multimodal dataset for humour sensing. In: Proceedings of the 19th ACM International Conference on Multimodal Interaction, pp. 438–445 (2017)
9. Boersma, P.: Praat, a system for doing phonetics by computer. Glot. Int. **5**(9), 341–345 (2001)
10. Bone, D., Lee, C.C., Narayanan, S.: Robust unsupervised arousal rating: a rule-based framework with knowledge-inspired vocal features. IEEE Trans. Affect. Comput. **5**(2), 201–213 (2014)
11. Bradley, M.M., Lang, P.J.: Measuring emotion: the self-assessment manikin and the semantic differential. J. Behav. Ther. Exp. Psychiatry **25**(1), 49–59 (1994)
12. Brambilla, S., Boccignone, G., Borghese, N., Ripamonti, L.A.: Between the buttons: stress assessment in video games using players' behavioural data. In: Proceedings of the 6th International Conference on Computer-Human Interaction Research and Applications - CHIRA, pp. 59–69. INSTICC, SciTePress (2022). https://doi.org/10.5220/0011546400003323
13. Burkhart, M.C., Brandman, D.M., Franco, B., Hochberg, L.R., Harrison, M.T.: The discriminative Kalman filter for Bayesian filtering with nonlinear and non-gaussian observation models. Neural Comput. **32**(5), 969–1017 (2020)
14. Busso, C., Lee, S., Narayanan, S.: Analysis of emotionally salient aspects of fundamental frequency for emotion detection. IEEE Trans. Audio Speech Lang. Process. **17**(4), 582–596 (2009)
15. Cohen, S., Kamarck, T., Mermelstein, R.: A global measure of perceived stress. J. Health Soc. Beh. 385–396 (1983)
16. Corcoran, A.W., Pezzulo, G., Hohwy, J.: From allostatic agents to counterfactual cognisers: active inference, biological regulation, and the origins of cognition. Biol. Philos. **35**(3), 32 (2020)
17. Csikszentmihalyi, M., Csikszentmihalyi, M.: Toward a psychology of optimal experience. Flow and the foundations of positive psychology: the collected works of Mihaly Csikszentmihalyi, pp. 209–226 (2014)
18. D'Amelio, A., Patania, S., Buršić, S., Cuculo, V., Boccignone, G.: Inferring causal factors of core affect dynamics on social participation through the lens of the observer. Sensors **23**(6), 2885 (2023)
19. Friston, K.: The free-energy principle: a unified brain theory? Nat. Rev. Neurosci. **11**(2), 127–138 (2010)
20. Frommel, J., Fischbach, F., Rogers, K., Weber, M.: Emotion-based dynamic difficulty adjustment using parameterized difficulty and self-reports of emotion. In: Proceedings of the 2018 Annual Symposium on Computer-Human Interaction in Play, pp. 163–171 (2018)
21. Frommel, J., Schrader, C., Weber, M.: Towards emotion-based adaptive games: emotion recognition via input and performance features. In: Proceedings of the 2018 Annual Symposium on Computer-Human Interaction in Play, pp. 173–185 (2018)
22. Hirst, D.J., de Looze, C.: Measuring Speech. Fundamental Frequency and Pitch., pp. 336–361. Cambridge University Press (2021)
23. Juslin, P.N., Scherer, K.R.: Vocal Expression of Affect. Oxford University Press, Oxford (2005)

24. Khalil, R.A., Jones, E., Babar, M.I., Jan, T., Zafar, M.H., Alhussain, T.: Speech emotion recognition using deep learning techniques: a review. IEEE Access **7**, 117327–117345 (2019)
25. Kim, Y., Provost, E.M.: Emotion classification via utterance-level dynamics: a pattern-based approach to characterizing affective expressions. In: 2013 IEEE International Conference on Acoustics, Speech and Signal Processing, pp. 3677–3681. IEEE (2013)
26. Lebois, L.A., Hertzog, C., Slavich, G.M., Barrett, L.F., Barsalou, L.W.: Establishing the situated features associated with perceived stress. Acta Psychol. **169**, 119–132 (2016)
27. Linson, A., Parr, T., Friston, K.J.: Active inference, stressors, and psychological trauma: a neuroethological model of (mal) adaptive explore-exploit dynamics in ecological context. Behav. Brain Res. **380**, 112421 (2020)
28. Nogueira, P.A., Torres, V., Rodrigues, R., Oliveira, E., Nacke, L.E.: Vanishing scares: biofeedback modulation of affective player experiences in a procedural horror game. J. Multimodal User Interfaces **10**(1), 31–62 (2016)
29. Pallavicini, F., Ferrari, A., Pepe, A., Garcea, G., Zanacchi, A., Mantovani, F.: Effectiveness of virtual reality survival horror games for the emotional elicitation: preliminary insights using resident evil 7: biohazard. In: Antona, M., Stephanidis, C. (eds.) UAHCI 2018. LNCS, vol. 10908, pp. 87–101. Springer, Cham (2018). https://doi.org/10.1007/978-3-319-92052-8_8
30. Peters, A., McEwen, B.S., Friston, K.: Uncertainty and stress: why it causes diseases and how it is mastered by the brain. Prog. Neurobiol. **156**, 164–188 (2017)
31. Quigley, K.S., Lindquist, K.A., Barrett, L.F.: Inducing and measuring emotion and affect: tips, tricks, and secrets. In: Reis, H.T., Judd, C.M. (eds.) Handbook of Research Methods in Social and Personality Psychology, pp. 220–252. Cambridge University Press, New York (2014)
32. Russell, J.A.: Core affect and the psychological construction of emotion. Psychol. Rev. **110**(1), 145 (2003)
33. Schell, J.: The Art of Game Design: A book of lenses. CRC Press (2008)
34. Scherer, K.R.: Vocal communication of emotion: a review of research paradigms. Speech Commun. **40**(1–2), 227–256 (2003)
35. Schulkin, J., Sterling, P.: Allostasis: a brain-centered, predictive mode of physiological regulation. Trends Neurosci. **42**(10), 740–752 (2019)
36. Schuller, D.M., Schuller, B.W.: A review on five recent and near-future developments in computational processing of emotion in the human voice. Emot. Rev. **13**(1), 44–50 (2021)
37. Shah Fahad, M., Ranjan, A., Yadav, J., Deepak, A.: A survey of speech emotion recognition in natural environment. Digit. Signal Proc. **110**, 102951 (2021)
38. Singh, Y.B., Goel, S.: A systematic literature review of speech emotion recognition approaches. Neurocomputing **492**, 245–263 (2022)
39. Solms, M., Friston, K.: How and why consciousness arises: some considerations from physics and physiology. J. Conscious. Stud. **25**(5–6), 202–238 (2018)
40. Vachiratamporn, V., Legaspi, R., Moriyama, K., Numao, M.: Towards the design of affective survival horror games: an investigation on player affect. In: 2013 Humaine Association Conference on Affective Computing and Intelligent Interaction, pp. 576–581 (2013)
41. Yang, W., Rifqi, M., Marsala, C., Pinna, A.: Physiological-based emotion detection and recognition in a video game context. In: 2018 International Joint Conference on Neural Networks (IJCNN), pp. 1–8. IEEE (2018)

Electro-oculographic Discrimination of Gazing Motion to a Smartphone Notification Tone

Masaki Omata[⊠][iD] and Shingo Ito[iD]

University of Yamanashi, Kofu, Yamanashi, Japan
{omata,itoh20}@hci.media.yamanashi.ac.jp

Abstract. This paper describes an experiment to validate whether unconscious responses or conscious gazing motions to notification tones can be discriminated from skin conductance responses or electro-oculograms. Our goal is to solve a problem that a smartphone cannot discriminate that a user has noticed a notification from the smartphone unless the user directly operates it or speaks to it when the user noticed the notification. In our experiment, participants were presented with notification tones while they were watching a video or reading orally as a main task, and their physiological signals were recorded during the task. As the results, we found that it took approximately four seconds to discriminate the response from skin conductance responses, whereas it took only one second to discriminate the response from the electro-oculogram. Furthermore, we found that the recall was 92.5% and the precision was 96.1% for discriminating the conscious gazing motions to the notification tones from the electro-oculograms between upper and lower of an eye.

Keywords: Electro-oculogram · Skin conductance response · Gazing motion · Notification tone

1 Introduction

In view of recent notification functions of smartphones, a smartphone unilaterally generates sound, light, or vibration of a notification, regardless of user's state. Therefore, a smartphone cannot detect whether a user is aware of a notification without an explicit response from the user. Some problems that arise in the situation include the following: in the case of an incoming phone call, even if a user is aware of the notification, it continues to ring until the user responds by operating the smartphone. In addition, in the case of an email notification or a calendar schedule notification, a user may miss an important notification or message due to the short duration of sound or vibration, regardless of whether or not the user is aware of the notification.

At present, user's primary methods of responding to smartphone notifications are to operate a smartphone directly and to respond with the user's voice. Therefore, when a smartphone is in a bag, in a remote location where the user cannot pick it up directly, or in a situation where the user cannot speak, it takes time for the user to operate the smartphone after a notification occurs. On the other hand, with the spread of wearable terminals in recent years, a user can receive notifications via a device worn on the user's body. However, even with wearable devices, a method of responding to notifications is the same: either by operating the device directly or by voice. Therefore, when the device cannot be operated directly, such as when user's hands are occupied, when driving a car, or when riding a bicycle, there remains the problem of not being able to respond immediately to a notification.

We point out that smartphone notifications should be presented with a persistence that ensures that the user notices them, but we also point out that it is important not to present them unnecessarily persistently. Andersen et al. [1] and Blum et al. [2] showed a method for determining a probability that a user perceives a notification based on the intensity of the notification and the user's actions. Fortin et al. proposed a method to estimate the user's awareness of notifications based on the skin conductance change that appears after a notification [3].

In this paper, we examined a possibility of using electro-oculography, which reflects user's eye movements, as a physiological signal other than skin conductance that Fortin et al. used. The reason is that we hypothesized that the electro-oculogram would be useful as a channel other than a hand that could easily respond when presented with a notification from a smartphone. A notification control system, which we have envisioned, uses physiological signals to discriminate whether the user is aware of a notification or not, and if so, stops the notification, and if not, repeats the notification.

We conducted an experiment to determine whether a user's awareness of a notification can be discriminated from changes in skin conductance and electro-oculogram before and after presentation of a notification tone under conditions of unconscious or conscious attention to the notification, in order to validate the hypothesis. The contributions of this paper based on the results are as follows.

- Electro-oculogram can shorten a time from the start of presentation of a notification tone to discrimination of user's gazing motion to one second, compared with the average time of 4 s by skin conductance response.
- Electro-oculogram between the upper and lower of one eye shows a more pronounced change in a user's gazing motion toward a notification tone than electro-oculogram between temples.

2 Related Work

In a study on the perception of smartphone notifications, Poppinga et al. developed a model that could predict opportune moments to issue notifications with approximately 77 percent accuracy by observing 6,581 notifications from 79 different users over 76 days [4]. Yao et al. conducted an experiment to study the effect of weight and underlying vibration frequency on perceived strength [5]. The results showed that for the same measured acceleration, a heavier box is perceived to vibrate with greater strength. Furthermore, signals with higher underlying frequency were perceived to be weaker for the same measured acceleration. Andersen et al. showed that logistic regression was indeed a suitable candidate for quantification of, in this instance vibrotactile information, and for the future design of user-adaptive vibrotactile displays by creating a dataset with ages spanning from seven to 79 years under indoor and outdoor experimental settings [1].

One problem, however, is that their experiments used data based on specific activities and conditions that were determined, and thus are insufficient to discriminate or estimate various situations of users at any given moment in time as real-time processing. To solve the problem, it is necessary to continue measuring the user's activities. Blum et al. presented a user study that took into account the amount of motion, as measured by an accelerometer, at the site of vibration immediately preceding the stimulus, and showed that a logistic regression model including prior acceleration is significantly better at predicting vibration perception [2]. However, the method is only a prediction before the notification is presented, and is not sufficient to check whether the user actually noticed the notification after it was presented.

Fortin et al. reported that both vibrotactile and auditory smartphone notifications induce skin conductance responses (SCR), and that they could be employed to predict perception of smartphone notifications after the presentation, as a method to estimate whether a user noticed a notification after the notification and to control a notification based on the estimated result [3]. They used the maximum value of the phasic activity (PhasicMax) of the SCR for the estimation. As the results of their estimation method, an accuracy of 0.61, recall value of 0.75 and specificity of 0.38 were obtained. However, the method of Fortin et al. requires a window of up to 6 s to calculate PhasicMax, which is rather long considering the time between a smartphone notification and a detection of the user's response. This is due to the physiological characteristics of SCR, which slowly rises and then decays after stimulus presentation.

We have used electro-oculogram in order to solve the problem of discrimination time. Electro-oculogram is an electric potential recorded by electrodes attached around an eye. It has been reported that startle blinks [7] and eye movements occur [8] in response to auditory perception, and Yamanaka et al. showed a hearing test method using eye movements that appear after sound stimulation [9]. The results of Yamanaka et al. showed that eye movements appeared within two seconds at most after sound stimulation, suggesting that the use of electro-oculography to discriminate whether or not a user has noticed a notification tone can be processed in a shorter time than use of SCR. However, the experiments by Yamanaka et al. were conducted in a seated or supine position in a dark soundproof room, so our study was conducted under conditions similar to everyday life.

3 Experiment: Physiological Signals in Response to Notification Tone

In this experiment, participants were asked to watch a video and read a text orally as experimental tasks, during which electro-oculogram and skin conductance were measured and recorded. The physiological signals were analyzed when the participants were presented with a notification tone during the tasks. The participants' unconscious responses were recorded without any specific instructions during the first block, and the conscious responses were recorded during the second block, in which participants were instructed to gaze toward the notification tone. The experimental environment was considered to be an everyday environment in which smartphones are actually used, which was different from Yamanaka et al.'s experiment in which participants were seated or supine in a dark soundproof room [9].

3.1 Task, Procedure and Participant

The two experimental tasks were video viewing and oral reading. Each trial of both tasks lasted eight minutes. In the video viewing task, participants watched one of six different animal documentary videos, and they were instructed to answer questions about the content of the video after watching it, in order to have them concentrate on the video. In the oral reading task, participants read orally a text consisting of several stories that could not be completed in eight minutes. The reason for the oral task was to validate whether the electro-oculogram could be used to discriminate attention to a notification tone, even if it was affected by changes in facial EMG potentials due to the mouth movements. Figure 1 shows a participant during the reading task. As shown in the figure, the participants were instructed to hold the manuscript with the hand that was not attached to skin conductance electrodes during the reading task.

Fig. 1. Experimental environment and a participant during the oral reading task.

During the tasks, the participants were presented with four types of notification tones 15 times at random timing with a minimum interval of 30 s. The notification tones were the opening iPhone ringtone (1.8 s), the iPhone tri-tone (0.6 s), the ringtone of LINE (4.0 s), and one of the following notification tones from the LINE application that each participant uses daily: whistle (0.4 s), simple bell (1.0 s), Pokipoki (0.5 s), or metallophone (1.2 s). All notification tones were output from a loudspeaker at a sound pressure of 50 dB.

All participants performed an unconscious block with no specific instructions followed by a block that instructed conscious gazing, as the within-subjects design. The participants performed one trial of the video viewing task and one trial of the text reading task in each block. The order in which the two trials were performed in each block was designed to be counterbalanced. Immediately before the conscious gazing block, the participants were instructed to perform a gazing motion when they hear a notification tone. Before the block, the participants practiced the gazing motion.

The experiment was conducted in a room in the laboratory where the sounds of daily life were heard. The room temperature was kept at a constant 22 °C using an air conditioner in order to minimize the influence of changes in room temperature on the physiological signals. Two pairs of EMG electrodes were attached to the participant's face to measure the electro-oculogram, and one pair of electrodes was attached to the non-dominant hand to measure the skin conductance response. The loudspeaker outputting the notification tones was placed 50 cm to the right of a participant at waist height when the participant was seated (as shown Fig. 1).

The participants were ten male college students (20–23 years old) who use an iPhone on a daily basis. Informed consent was obtained from all of the participants.

3.2 Physiological Signals

Electro-oculogram. Two pairs of electromyogram (EMG) electrodes for measuring the two types of electro-oculograms were attached to the participant's face, as shown in Fig. 2. One set was used to measure the potentials between the participant's right and left temples (Hereafter referred to as horizontal electrodes), and the other set was used to measure the potentials between the upper and lower of the participant's right eye (Hereafter referred to as vertical electrodes). It is known that the amplitude and frequency of EMG potentials show an almost linear relationship with strength of contraction of the whole muscle. The horizontal electrodes in Fig. 2 can measure the electrical potential of movement of the eyeball to the right and left, and the vertical electrodes can measure the electrical potential of movement of the eyeball up and down [10–12]. The frequency of measurement was 2048 Hz and the unit of measurement was microvolts (μV). The electrodes and sensors were MyoScan from Thought Technology Ltd.

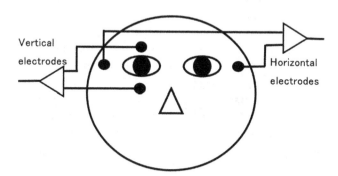

Fig. 2. Positioning of horizontal and vertical electrodes for measuring electro-oculograms.

Because the raw EMG data for the electro-oculogram take positive and negative values, a root mean square (RMS) was calculated from the raw data. Data for an RMS are data for each two seconds before and after the start of stimulus presentation. The reason for the time period is based on the results of Yamanaka et al. who observed oculomotor responses within a maximum of two seconds after the presentation of a sound stimulus [9].

The maximum voluntary contraction (MVC) of each participant was recorded, and a normalized muscle activity (%MVC) was calculated by dividing an RMS muscle activity by an MVC. The %MVCs were integrated for two seconds before and two seconds after the start of the tone presentation, respectively, and the values were used as data for analysis, which is defined as integrated EMG (iEMG). In this analysis, the MVC of each participant is defined as the amount of RMS muscle activity when the participant closed his/her own eyes with full force.

Skin Conductance Response. A pair of electrodes to measure skin conductance response (SCR) was attached to the fingertips of index and middle fingers of the participant's non-dominant hand, as shown in Fig. 3. The electrodes measure the conductance change between the two fingers due to mental sweating. In general, mental sweating is known to show transient changes with a latency of one to two seconds from the time of stimulus presentation. The frequency of measurement is 256 Hz and the unit of measurement is micro siemens. The electrodes and sensor are SC-Flex by Thought Technology.

In the analysis of experimental results, maximum of phasic activity (PhasicMax) for each participant was extracted, as in Fortin et al. [3]. PhasicMax is the time from the start of presentation to the peak of the phasic activity in the time series of raw data of SCR after the start of a tone presentation.

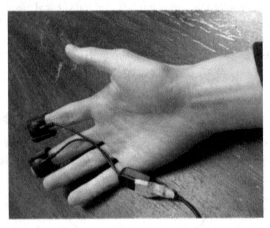

Fig. 3. Attachment of electrodes to measure skin conductance response.

3.3 Result of Electro-oculogram

Unconscious Condition. Figure 4 shows the box-and-whisker plots of each participant's iEMG values for the iEMG value in the two seconds after the start of the notification tone presentation minus the iEMG value in the two seconds before the start of the presentation. Figure 4a shows the horizontal electrode values during video viewing, Fig. 4b shows the horizontal electrode values during text reading, Fig. 4c shows the vertical electrode values during video viewing, and Fig. 4d shows the vertical electrode values during text reading. For each of the four conditions shown in Fig. 4, a two-factor analysis of variance (significance level 5%, $F(1, 77)$) was conducted for the type of notification tones and before and after the presentation. The results indicate that there were no significant differences in the iEMG values before and after the tone presentation in the four conditions. Furthermore, there were no significant differences in the iEMG values for the interaction between the type of tones and before and after the presentation of the notification tones (significance level 5%, $F(3, 77)$).

Conscious Gazing Condition. We conducted a paired t-test ($t(79)$) to test the difference in mean iEMG values before and after the presentation of notification tones for each combination of different electrodes (horizontal and vertical) and different tasks (viewing and reading), regardless of the type of notification tones. The results show that there was a significant difference in iEMG between before and after presentation of the tones in all of the combinations ($p < .05$). In addition, we conducted an unpaired t-test ($t(158)$) to test the difference in mean values of the iEMGs for the four seconds from two seconds before to two seconds after the presentation of the tones and for the same number of four seconds randomly selected from periods during which the tones were not presented. Significant differences were found of the horizontal and vertical electrodes during the viewing task and of the vertical electrodes during the reading task ($p < .05$). However, no significant difference was found of the horizontal electrodes during the reading task ($p > .05$).

3.4   Logistic Regression Analysis to Discriminate Gazing Using iEMG

As in Andersen et al. [1] and Fortin et al. [3], we performed logistic regression analyses to test the accuracy of discriminating whether iEMG data were generated by the gazing motions or not. The accuracy is a metric that measures how often the logistic regression model correctly predicts the outcome. We used iEMG difference data for two seconds before and two seconds after the presentation of the tones for each combination of electrodes (horizontal and vertical) and tasks (viewing and reading) for all the participants as data during a gazing motion. On the other hand, we used the difference of iEMG data between the first two seconds and the second two seconds of a random four-second period during which no tones were presented, for each pair of the electrodes and task combination of all the participants, as data while they were not performing the gazing motion.

The accuracy of discriminating gazing or otherwise based on iEMG differences was checked for each of the following pairs of electrodes: horizontal and vertical, horizontal only, and vertical only. Table 1 shows the precision and recall for discriminating gazing and non-gazing motions for both the viewing and reading tasks, combining data from both the horizontal and vertical electrodes. The precision is a metric that measures how often the logistic regression model correctly predicts the positive class, and the recall is a metric that measures how often the model correctly identifies positive instances from all the actual positive samples. As shown in the table, the recall for gazing discrimination is as high as 0.95, while the precision is as low as 0.69. Table 2 shows the precision and

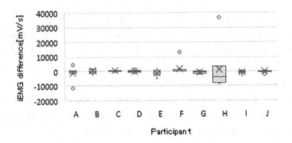

(a) iEMG differences for horizontal electrodes in the video viewing task.

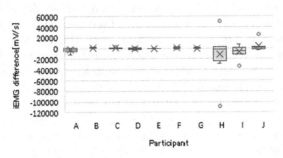

(b) iEMG differences for horizontal electrodes in the reading task.

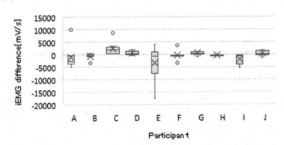

(c) iEMG differences of vertical electrodes in the video viewing task.

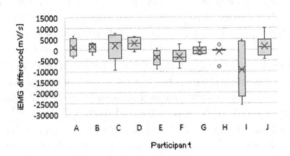

(d) iEMG differences of vertical electrodes in the reading task.

Fig. 4. iEMG differences of each electrode pair before and after the presentation of the notification tones in each task.

recall for gazing and non-gazing discrimination for both the viewing and reading tasks, the viewing task only, and the reading task only, using only the data from the horizontal electrodes. In each task, the recall for gazing discrimination is high, ranging from 0.93 to 0.99, while the precision is low, ranging from 0.57 to 0.64. Table 3 shows the precision and recall of the gazing and non-gazing discrimination for the viewing and reading tasks, the viewing task only, and the reading task only, using only the data from the vertical electrodes. For all tasks, each recall for gazing discrimination is high, ranging from 0.95 to 0.96, and each precision is high, ranging from 0.89 to 0.96.

Table 1. Precision and recall by logistic regression analyses of discrimination of gazing motion from both horizontal and vertical electrodes.

	Video viewing and reading	
	Gazing	Non-Gazing
Precision	0.69	0.92
Recall	0.95	0.57

Table 2. Precision and recall by logistic regression analyses of discrimination of gazing motion from horizontal electrodes.

	Video viewing and reading		Viewing		Reading	
	Gazing	Non-Gazing	Gazing	Non-Gazing	Gazing	Non-Gazing
Precision	0.57	0.84	0.64	0.97	0.57	0.80
Recall	0.94	0.29	0.99	0.44	0.93	0.30

Table 3. Precision and recall by logistic regression analyses of discrimination of gazing motion from vertical electrodes.

	Video viewing and reading		Viewing		Reading	
	Gazing	Non-Gazing	Gazing	Non-Gazing	Gazing	Non-Gazing
Precision	0.93	0.96	0.96	0.98	0.89	0.95
Recall	0.96	0.93	0.98	0.96	0.95	0.89

Figure 5 shows receiver operating characteristic (ROC) curves for determining a threshold value that discriminates between gazing and non-gazing. The vertical axis represents the sensitivity, and the horizontal axis represents the 1-specificity. Of the two curves, the solid line represents plots for the horizontal electrodes and the dashed line represents plots for the vertical electrodes. From the ROC curves, a cutoff value that serves as a threshold for discriminating gazing motion is obtained using the Youden index. The time from the presentation of the notification tones until the difference between the iEMG values before and after the presentation exceeded the cutoff value was calculated to be 1.68 s for the horizontal electrodes and 1.00 s for the vertical electrodes.

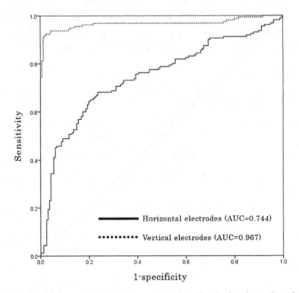

Fig. 5. ROC curves for each pair of electrodes for discrimination of gazing motion.

3.5 Result of Skin Conductance Response

Figure 6 shows box-and-whisker plots representing the time until PhasicMax was observed in the SCR of each participant for each type of task, integrating the unconscious and conscious blocks. The horizontal axis indicates each participant and the vertical axis indicates the time in seconds, with the video viewing task and the reading task color-coded. The data for two of the ten participants were excluded because we could not observe any change, suggesting that the electrode contact was insufficient in this experiment.

The number of times that the phasic activities of the skin conductance were not observed after a tone was presented was 10.2% of the total number of times that the tones were presented. The minimum and maximum time from the start of the tones to PhasicMax were 3.0 and 7.0 s. The average time was 4.2 s for the video viewing task and 4.0 s for the reading task.

3.6 Discussion

Comparing the time to detect gazing motion between the electro-oculogram and SCR, the electro-oculogram was about one second and the SCR was four seconds, clearly

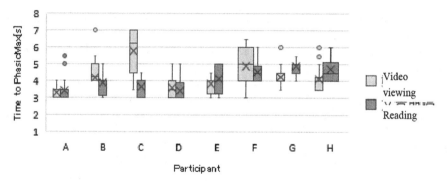

Fig. 6. Time to PhasicMax of SCR per participant in each task.

indicating that the electro-oculogram is shorter and more useful. The time of the SCR is similar to that in previous studies, and we therefore consider that SCR is not suitable for extracting the user's response immediately after the presentation of a notification. On the other hand, SCR is useful as a second detection index to improve the detection accuracy after the electro-oculogram, because the change is remarkable though it takes time.

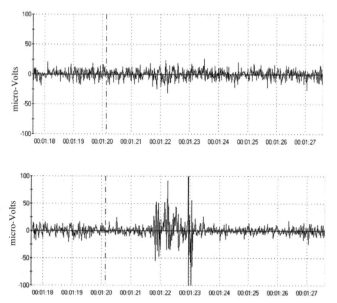

Fig. 7. Electro-oculograms of horizontal electrodes (top) and vertical electrodes (bottom) during a gazing motion.

As the result of the analysis of the electro-oculogram, the vertical electrode data were found to be more useful than horizontal electrode data for discriminating gazing motion with higher accuracy. Figure 7 shows the EMG of the horizontal and vertical electrodes before and after the gazing motion. The vertical dashed line in the graph indicates the start time of the presentation of a notification tone. As shown in Fig. 7, even in situations where no significant changes due to gazing motion can be observed in the horizontal EMG, significant changes can be observed in the vertical EMG.

The reason why the vertical electrodes are useful is that the vertical electrodes were attached upper and lower of the participant's eye, so that even when the gazing motion is small, the eye movement has a greater effect on the vertical electrodes than on the horizontal electrodes. Because the horizontal electrodes cannot acquire EMG of eye movements significantly, they are easily affected by EMG caused by daily facial muscle movements and blinking of eyes. On the other hand, the vertical electrodes can acquire a prominent EMG of eye movements even though they are affected by daily EMG.

4 Conclusions

In this study, we examined whether unconscious responses or conscious gazing behavior can be detected from physiological signals in order to solve the problem that a smartphone cannot identify when a user notices a notification unless the user directly manipulates the smartphone. If the responses can be detected or estimated, we believe it will be possible to provide users with a natural response method that does not involve an operation.

The experimental results of skin conductance response showed that the skin conductance response increased after the presentation of the notification tones, similar to the previous study by Fortin et al. [3]. The time between the presentation of the notification tone and the observation of PhasicMax was found to be unaffected by the participants' video viewing and reading behaviors. We also found that the variation in the time between the presentation of the tones and the PhasicMax for each participant was small.

Regarding the results of the electro-oculogram, we could not observe a response to the notification from changes in the electro-oculogram caused by the participant's unconscious eye movements or blinking. From the result, we conclude that it is difficult to detect that a user is aware of a notification using changes in the electro-oculogram caused by an unconscious response to the notification. On the other hand, when the participants consciously gazed at the notification tones, we were able to detect the gazing motion from the changes in the electro-oculogram, so we conclude that it is possible to detect the gazing motion by which the user consciously notices the notification from the changes in the electro-oculogram.

We measured the EMG between the temples and between the upper and lower of eyes of the participants, and found that the electrodes between the temples showed only small changes in potential due to gazing motions, and sometimes gazing could be detected, and sometimes it could not. In addition, it was sometimes difficult to distinguish whether or not a gazing motion was performed due to changes in the facial muscles during oral reading. Therefore, we conclude that it is difficult to detect or estimate the user's gazing motion from the potentials of the electrodes between the temples. On the other hand, we found that the potentials of the electrodes the upper and lower of one eye could discriminate gazing motion regardless of whether the participant was watching a movie or reading orally. In addition, we found that the average time from the start of presentation of the notification tones to the changes in EMG that could discriminate gazing motion was about one second. Therefore, we conclude that electro-oculogram can shorten the time from the start of presentation of a notification tone to the discrimination of gazing motion, compared with the average time of four seconds for the conventional skin conductance response.

However, when electrodes are attached to the upper and lower parts of one eye, the current method is expected to cause a tendency to blink more than usual, or the user may find the electrodes obtrusive. From the standpoint of practicality, it is important to incorporate the electrodes as part of everyday tools, rather than to wear them independently as stand-alone devices. One possible example of a device design that solves the problems is a glasses-type device such as JINS MEME [13]. As a specific example, Usui et al. used the EMG sensor on the nose-pad of the JINS MEME to estimate the direction of gaze [14]. As our future work, we plan to redesign the location of the electrodes and to incorporate the electrodes into a wearable device, while maintaining the high discrimination accuracy for gazing.

References

1. Andersen, H. J., Morrison, A., Knudsen, L.: Modeling vibrotactile detection by logistic regression. In: Proceedings of the 7th Nordic Conference on Human-Computer Interaction: Making Sense Through Design (NordiCHI 2012), New York, NY, USA, pp. 500–503. Association for Computing Machinery (2012). https://doi.org/10.1145/2399016.2399092
2. Blum, J.R., Frissen, I., Cooperstock, J.R.: Improving haptic feedback on wearable devices through accelerometer measurements. In: Proceedings of the 28th Annual ACM symposium on user interface software & Technology (UIST 2015), New York, NY, USA, 31–36. Association for Computing Machinery (2015). https://doi.org/10.1145/2807442.2807474
3. Fortin, P.E., Sulmont, E., Cooperstock, J.: Detecting perception of smartphone notifications using skin conductance responses. In: Proceedings of the 2019 CHI Conference on Human Factors in Computing Systems (CHI 2019), New York, NY, USA, Paper 190, 1–9. Association for Computing Machinery (2019). https://doi.org/10.1145/3290605.3300420
4. Poppinga, B., Heuten, W., Boll, S.: Sensor-based identification of opportune moments for triggering notifications. IEEE Pervasive Comput. **13**(1), 22–29 (2014). https://doi.org/10.1109/MPRV.2014.15
5. Yao, H., Grant, D., Cruz, M.: Perceived vibration strength in mobile devices: the effect of weight and frequency. IEEE Trans. Haptics **3**(1), 56–62 (2010). https://doi.org/10.1109/TOH.2009.37
6. Miyata, Y. (ed.).: New Physiological psychology. Kitaohji Shobo, p328, Kyoto, (1998)
7. Hori T.: Physiological psychology. Baifukan, p. 164 (2008)
8. Widmann, A., Engbert, R., Schröger, E.: Microsaccadic responses indicate fast categorization of sounds: a novel approach to study auditory cognition. J. Neurosci. **34**(33), 11152–11158 (2014). https://doi.org/10.1523/JNEUROSCI.1568-14
9. Yamanaka, Y.: Objective Hearing Test using Eye Movements [Translated from Japanese.]. Practica Oto-Rhino-Laryngologica **58**(6), pp. 313–319 (1965). https://doi.org/10.5631/jibirin.58.313
10. Ono, Y.: Non-invasive biosignal processing and analysis IV, electromyogram and electrooculogram: measurement and signal analysis for bioengineering. Contents Syst. Control Inf. **62**(8), 337–342 (2018)
11. Bulling, A., Ward, J.A., Gellersen, H., Tröster, G.: Eye movement analysis for activity recognition using electrooculography. IEEE Trans. Pattern Anal. Mach. Intell. (TPAMI) **33**(4), 741–753 (2011)

12. Benedek, M., Kaernbach, C.: A continuous measure of phasic electrodermal activity. J. Neurosci. Methods **190**(1), 80–91 (2010). https://doi.org/10.1016/j.jneumeth.2010.04.028
13. JINS. JINS MEME. https://jinsmeme.com/en. Accessed 21 Jun 2023
14. Usui, T., Ban, Yamamoto, T.: A study on estimating eye direction using smart eyewear. In: Proceedings of Multimedia, Distributed, Cooperative, and Mobile Symposium 2016, pp. 1172–1174 (2016)

Why Career Orientation is Often Difficult and How Digital Platforms Can Support Young People in This Process

Jessica Brandenburger[(✉)] [ID] and Monique Janneck [ID]

Institute for Interactive Systems (ISy), Technische Hochschule Lübeck, Lübeck, Germany
{Jessica.Brandenburger,Monique.Janneck}@th-luebeck.de

Abstract. Countless career options and support services make it difficult for young people to choose a career. Within a research project (JOLanDA), we are developing a digital platform that is intended to support decision-making processes in the context of career choice at an early stage and, thanks to a playful approach and a novel interaction concept, to be used in a self-motivated manner outside of school if possible. In a German-wide online survey (n = 1044) among school and university students (14–35 years), requirements for career orientation platforms were collected. The results show that the *decision-making* and *planning knowledge* as well as the *exploration* and the *occupational knowledge* are rather low. The young people seem to have little knowledge of application processes and the organization of a course of study or in-company training. Choosing a career seems to be difficult, as almost one in two does not know what interests him or her. One-third do not know about corresponding offers and one-fifth state that existing platforms do not contain enough offers. We have summarized implications for developers so that platforms for skills acquisition can be made more attractive and also more conducive to young people.

Keywords: Career orientation · Online learning platforms · Human-centered design

1 Introduction

Young people today have countless career choices due to a wide range of study subjects and training opportunities [1, 2] - deciding on a career is often not easy. Career guidance services are increasingly digitized and digital applications are designed to support career choices [3].

For the development of a digital career guidance platform with a playful approach and novel interaction concept, in the research project (JOLanDA) funded by the German Federal Ministry of Education and Research (BMBF), we collected requirements for digital career guidance platforms by means of an online survey (n = 1044). First, career choice competence was assessed by means of the ThüBOM questionnaire (short version of the Career Choice Adaptability Questionnaire [4, 5]), based on the Thuringian Career

H. P. da Silva and P. Cipresso (Eds.): CHIRA 2023, CCIS 1996, pp. 201–215, 2023.
https://doi.org/10.1007/978-3-031-49425-3_12

Choice Competence Model [6], of school students as well as of university students (14–35 years) in Germany, in order to obtain an assessment of how the general career choice competence of young people currently stands. Furthermore, young people were asked why they think it is difficult to find a career nowadays. We presented a new platform to support career orientation that metaphorically resembles a career choice jungle and includes a playful journey of discovery about personal strengths and interests. Young people were asked what else they would like to see on a career guidance website, or if and why they would visit the presented career guidance platform with a gamified approach. Design and gamification elements of the platform were examined in terms of their usefulness and motivating effect. Furthermore, students' self-assessed motivational regulation was surveyed [7] to find out about the important aspect of Self-Regulated Learning (SRL), which can have a significant impact on performance [8]. Finally, implications for the development of online learning platforms for skill acquisition were identified from the findings and considered for the further development of this platform.

2   Career Orientation

Occupational field explorations, potential analyses and company internships are a standard part of vocational orientation [9]. According to a study by the Bertelsmann Stiftung (2022), young people find it difficult to find their way through the wealth of information on choosing a career [9]. According to the study, one in four young people does not engage with the topic of career guidance without being prompted to do so. Therefore, the attractive design of career guidance offers is very important. New developments, particularly in the area of online platforms for the acquisition of competencies in the context of career orientation, include the Berufswahlapp[1], which was developed as part of the Berufswahlpass 4.0 research project [10]. Using a playful approach, users have a cockpit (dashboard) at their disposal in which they can view the successes and data they have achieved. Furthermore, users can choose the color scheme themselves and thus individualize the user interface (choice between: candy, cool, normal). Meanwhile, it is also possible to get to know apprenticeship occupations and companies in the computer game Minecraft®[2] (project of Grundleger e.V.). Here, students can also add new occupations to the environment while they play. Furthermore, there is a ChatGPT study program search[3]: Based on personal interests, suitable professions and study programs are suggested here. The app DEEP![4] with many self-reflection tasks and the platform future.self[5] (launched in 2023) also support career and study choices. The ChoiceLab platform[6] [11], launched in 2021, provides information on the frequency of occurrence of occupations, income and satisfaction of a particular desired occupation; one can view more detailed information on currently 325 occupations, for example, how the quality of work and work-related stresses are assessed. Overall, only a few platforms take a

---

[1] https://berufswahlapp.de/.

[2] https://grundleger.de/projekte/gaming.

[3] https://grundleger.de/projekte/webapp.

[4] https://begabungsvielfalt.de/.

[5] https://futureself.education/.

[6] https://www.choicelab.de/.

gamified approach, mostly using occupation-based quizzes, yet the use of gamification, for example, can motivate and make knowledge acquisition and decision-making fun, useful, and interactive [12]. We will therefore integrate a gamified approach into the development of a career guidance platform, in addition to tests that focus on identifying e.g. personal strengths to support individual career choice decisions.

3   Presentation of a Career Orientation Platform for Young People

In iterative development cycles, we have developed a career guidance platform in close collaboration (workshops and field phases) with young people. The platform is specifically designed to sensitize young people to biographical decision-making processes related to career choice as well as their own needs and abilities at an early stage, even before the actual process of career guidance. The platform metaphorically represents the career choice jungle and thus the often opaque many options for career orientation (see Fig. 1). Students can go on a voyage of discovery on the platform, travel on different expeditions by means of a trip on a raft across a river and complete different discovery paths (with learning content) that help them to get to know their own strengths and interests (see demo video [13]). The goal of platform use is to become a "guide of one's own life path".

4   Method

We collected data from school and university students (n = 1044) aged 14–35 years in Germany as part of an online study. The questionnaire was distributed via a panel (Bilendi/respondi) in August 2022. Included was a screencast video (01:19 min.) of the newly developed platform so that school students and university students could get an overview of the platform's home page. After watching the video, a further button appear on the platform to the further questions, so we could ensure some dwell time on the video. The current status of the developed career guidance platform was presented (see Fig. 1) and the following research questions were investigated within the study;

1 What is the career choice competence of young people?
   (Information about the initial situation, section 5.1)
2 Why is/was it difficult for young people to make career choices?
   (Problem identification, section 5.2)
3 What do young people want in a digital platform for career guidance?
   (Needs of the target group, section 5.3)
4 Which functional, design, and gamification elements are useful and also motivating?
   (Design instructions, Sect. 5.4)
5 What would be a good outcome after using the platform?
   (Goal definition, section 5.5)
6 Why do young people visit a career guidance platform?
   (Motivational Regulation, section 5.6)

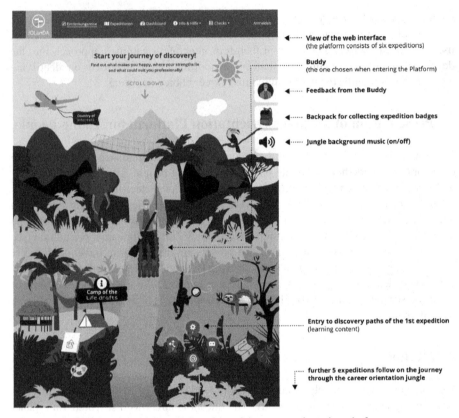

Fig. 1. View of the web interface of the career orientation platform.

5   Results

A total of n = 585 school students (female = 55.6%, male = 44.4%, aged M = 16.2 years (SD = 1.477, range 14–19 years)) and n = 459 university students (female = 51%, male = 49%, aged M = 23.65 years (SD = 4.522, range 18–35 years)) participated in the survey.

5.1   Career Choice Competence

Career choice competence was assessed based on the Thuringian Career Choice Competence Model [6], consisting of three central aspects; *knowledge, motivation,* and *action* using a short questionnaire. A 4-point Likert scale (1 = does not apply at all/does not apply to 4 = applies strongly/completely/very often) was used to assess various facets of career choice competence ([14], Appendix E). The internal consistency of the facet scales of the brief questionnaire on career choice competence is good overall (school students Mα = .778, university students Mα = .748), but lowest with respect to students' *Openness* (α = .678) (see Table 1).

Career choice competence is higher among university students than among school students (see Table 1 & Fig. 2). As shown by a Mann-Whitney U test (data are not normally distributed), university students have significantly higher *Self-knowledge* ($U(N_1 = 585, N_2 = 459) = 110201.500$; $z = -5.004$; $p < .001$; $r = 0.15$), *Knowledge on prerequisites* ($U(N_1 = 585, N_2 = 459) = 109994.500$; $z = -5.051$; $p < .001$; $r = 0.16$), *Knowledge on planning and deciding* ($U(N_1 = 585, N_2 = 459) = 95193.000$; $z = -8.184$; $p < .001$; $r = 0.25$), *Openness* ($U(N_1 = 585, N_2 = 459) = 124569.500$; $z = -2.051$; $p = .040$; $r = 0.06$), *Exploration* ($U(N_1 = 585, N_2 = 459) = 101533.000$; $z = -6.831$; $p < .001$; $r = 0.21$) and *Self-regulation* ($U(N_1 = 585, N_2 = 459) = 120169.500$; $z = -2.935$; $p = .003$; $r = 0.09$) than school students.

Table 1. Cronbach's alpha, means, and standard deviation of the career choice competence scale.

	Facets of professional competence (items)	School students (n = 585)			University students (n = 459)		
		α	M (SD)	Σ (SD)	α	M (SD)	Σ (SD)
Knowledge	Self-knowledge (1–4)	.793	2.76 (.706)	11.04 (2.83)	.718	2.97 (.643)	11.86 (2.57)
	Occupational (concept) knowledge (5–6)	.796	2.35 (.837)	4.70 (1.67)			
	Knowledge on prerequisites (7–9)	.864	2.52 (.868)	7.57 (2.60)	.823	2.80 (.795)	8.39 (2.38)
	Knowledge on planning and deciding (10–11)	.798	2.43 (.915)	4.85 (1.83)	.738	2.89 (.830)	5.79 (1.66)
Motivation	Career concern (12–13)	.729	3.21 (.719)	6.41 (1.44)	.772	3.23 (.734)	6.46 (1.47)
	Career curiosity (Openness) (15–16)	.678	2.94 (.725)	6.06 (1.46)	.704	3.03 (.728)	6.06 (1.46)
Action	Exploration (17–19)	.828	2.43 (.734)	7.29 (2.20)	.776	2.75 (.739)	8.26 (2.22)
	Self-regulation (14, 20–22)	.711	2.96 (.619)	11.84 (2.48)	.716	3.07 (.607)	12.28 (2.43)
	Problem solving (23–25)	.807	3.19 (.617)	9.56 (1.85)	.742	3.21 (.598)	9.63 (1.79)
	Mean	.778	2.75 (.748)	69.16 (12.43)	.748	2,99 (.709)	68.73 (11.17)

The largest effect, but also only a medium one according to Cohen (1992)[15], is in *Knowledge on planning and deciding* ($r = 0.25$). Only very small differences between school students and university students are found in the areas of *Career concern* and

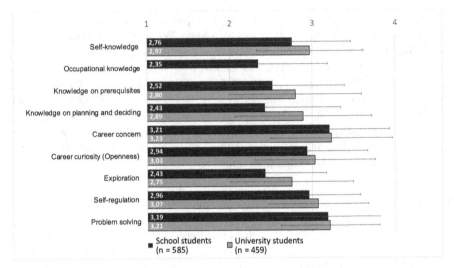

Fig. 2. Results (Mean values) of the short questionnaire on career choice competence.

Problem solving, but the highest competencies seem to be found here. In the area of *Problem solving* (items such as "I can get to the bottom of problems and make reasonable decisions" (item 23)), school students (M = 3.19, SD = .617) and university students (M = 3.21, SD = .598) were more likely to report being able to make reasonable decisions (Min = 1, Max = 4). The subfacet *Career concern* (items such as "It is important for me to clarify what career options are available to me" (item 12)) is also rated similarly high. This shows that it is important for school students and university students to clarify what career options they have.

In comparison, school students show the lowest level of competence in the area of *Occupational knowledge*, i.e., they do not seem to know very well what application processes for studies/training look like or how in-company training or studies are organized. University students were not asked about concept knowledge because they have already made a decision to study and the results would not be comparable. Furthermore, *Knowledge on planning and deciding*, which encompasses goal setting in the context of career entry, and *Exploration*, i.e., how often the young people have obtained information on occupations and employment opportunities, appear to be only moderately developed.

5.2 Difficulties in Choosing a Profession

Career orientation seems difficult, as 40.5% of university students and 54% of school students do not know what interests them (Fig. 3).

In addition, about 30% of the respondents (school students: 34.7%, university students: 27.9%) do not know the relevant offers and do not know where they can get information. About one fifth of the respondents state that the existing platforms (websites) do not contain sufficient offers. Still, 23.3% of the university students and 16.1% of the school students state that career orientation is not difficult for them. Further reasons

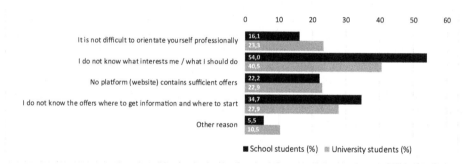

Fig. 3. Why career orientation is/was difficult according to school students and university students in percent (%).

why vocational orientation seems to be difficult can be taken from the paraphrased free text answers (evaluated with MAXQDA2022) (see Table 2).

Table 2. Other reasons why career orientation is/was difficult (data provided by school students + university students (n) > = 2).

	School students (n = 585)		University students (n = 459)	
	N	%	N	%
Other reasons (free text)	32	5.5	48	10.5
(Too) much choice / many possibilities	10	1.71	22	4.79
(Too) many interests	4	0.68	6	1.31
Offers (school, career days) only target standard professions			3	0.65
Insufficient career counseling in schools	4	0.68	2	0.44
Few offers / bad job situation			3	0.65
Corona (omission of offers)	2	0.34	1	0.22
Desired profession does not seem realistic (salary etc.)			2	0.44
Interesting offers not in the vicinity	2	0.34		
Search for information difficult / complicated / unclear	1	0.17	1	0.22

5.3 Better Support for Career Guidance

Every second young person (>50%) would like tips on how to achieve his/her goals, knowledge about finances and motivational tips. This is closely followed by tips on how to make better decisions (school students: 51.7%, university students: 48.7%).

Table 3. What would school students & university students like to see on career guidance platforms (data school students + university students (n) > = 2).

	School students (n = 585)		University students (n = 459)	
	N	%	N	%
Motivation tips	301	51.7	245	53.5
Concentration tips	302	51.9	204	44.5
Creativity techniques	149	25.6	142	31.0
Tips on how to achieve goals	322	55.3	237	51.7
Tips on how to make better decisions	301	51.7	223	48.7
Knowledge about finances	319	54.8	246	53.7
Planning tools (budget/holiday/process planning)	228	39.2	186	40.6
List of other sources of information/support	197	33.8	115	25.1
Other (free text)	8	1.37	6	1.31
Knowledge about taxes	2	0.34		
Info about good companies / jobs	2	0.34	1	0.22

For school students (51.9%), concentration tips and planning tools (39.2%) are also very good. Fewer university students but still also 44.5% want concentration tips and 40.6% planning tools. For university students, creativity techniques (31%) are slightly more important than for school students (25.6%). In turn, lists of other information sources are more important for school students (33.8%) than for university students (25.1%).

5.4 Preferred Functional, Design and Gamification Elements

On a 5-point Kunin scale, university students (n = 585) and school students (n = 459) were able to use asterisks to indicate how useful and smileys to indicate how motivating they found individual presented elements (via image and explanatory text) of the career guidance platform. Differences in terms of preference of design elements and support mechanisms between school students and university students should thus be identified. Mann-Whitney U tests show that significant differences regarding the usefulness of; 1) a *Certificate* ($U(n_1 = 585, n_2 = 459) = 124647.500, z = -2.047, p = .041, r = .06$), 2) the *Story* ($U(n_1 = 585, n_2 = 459) = 123799,000, z = -2.238, p = .025, r = .07$) and of 3) *Items* ($U(n_1 = 585, n_2 = 459) = 121038,500, z = -2.813, p = .005, r = .09$) exist between school students and university students (Fig. 4).

Regarding the motivational effect, significant differences only exist for *Items* ($U(n_1 = 585, n_2 = 459) = 122598.000$, $z = -2.510$, $p = .012$, $r = .08$) between school students and university students. If we look at the overall motivational effect and the usefulness of the elements, it becomes clear that the motivational effect is strongly related to the usefulness of the elements. According to Cohen (1992) [15], the effects are strong everywhere ($r = .50$) (see Table 4).

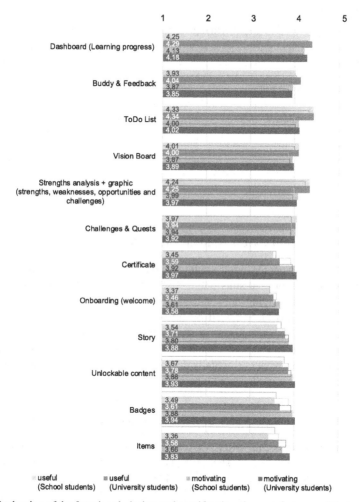

Fig. 4. Evaluation of the functional, design and gamification elements in terms of their usefulness and motivating effect.

Table 4. Spearman rank correlation of functional, design and gamification elements.

	Functional, design and gamification elements	motivating
useful	Dashboard	.500***
	Buddy with Feedback function	.596***
	ToDo List	.574***
	Vision Board	**.700*****
	Strengths analysis + graphic (strengths, weaknesses, opportunities and challenges)	**.646*****
	Certificate	.558***
	Onboarding (welcome)	**.608*****
	Story	.590***
	Challenges & Quests	**.641*****
	Unlockable content	.592***
	Badges	.597***
	Items	**.630*****

Correlation coefficients, *** < .001, ** = < .01, * = < .05 (two-sided)

5.5 What Goals Should Career Guidance Websites Achieve?

According to the young people, good results after using a career guidance website include identifying an occupation that suits one (school students: 71.1%, university students: 64.2%), as well as identifying personal interests and skills (school students: 59.6%, university students: 54.6%), followed by information, especially for school students (44.7%), about which school subjects or further training opportunities are now already important for the respective dream occupation. Around 40% of young people would like to know more precisely what one actually deals with in the individual professions (e.g., computer work, working outdoors/with people).

5.6 Motivational Regulation of School Students and University Students

Using the four subscales of the SRQ-A (Academic Self-Regulation Questionnaire) [7], based on the Self-Determination Theory (SDT), young people's self-assessed motivational regulation was surveyed on a 4-point Likert scale (1 = not at all true to 4 = very true) with 8 items. The questionnaire was developed for students and in its original form includes 32 items and, among others, the question why students do their homework. We rephrased questions 1–8 to ask why students would attend the career guidance platform. Two items each were used to elicit a subfacet.

With regard to motivational regulation, it was observed that the highest scores of students appeared to be in the *identified regulation* style (behavior to achieve a self-rated goal/topic wants to be understood [16]. That means, they would visit the platform because they find the topic of career guidance important and want to learn more about the topic. The lowest scores appeared to be in the *introjected regulation* style (behavior to avoid guilt, anxiety/get adult approval [16]́ (Table 5). This means that young people would be less likely to visit the platform because they want the teacher/lecturer/parent to think they are good students, or because they would feel bad if they did not.

Independent samples t-test was used to examine self-reported regulation between students. There is no variance homogeneity in *introjected regulation*, so the Welch test was interpreted here. There are statistically significant differences between university students and school students in *intrinsic motivation* (behavior performed for pleasure [16] ($t(1037) = -4.145$, $p < .001$, (95%-CI[-.269, -.096], d = -0.259 (small effect according to (Cohen, 1992), [15])) regarding platform use. *Intrinsic motivation* is higher in university students. That means, they would have more fun using the platform and more fun in general learning about future topics. There were no statistically significant differences between school and university students on *introjected regulation, external regulation* (engagement in activities to avoid external consequences/to follow rules [16], and *identified regulation.*

Table 5. Results of the subscales of the academic self-regulation questionnaire and comparison of mean values.

Facetten (Items)	School students (n = 581)		University students (n = 458)					
	M	SD	M	SD	T	df	p	Cohen's d
Introjected Regulation (1, 4)	2.22	0.769	2.31	0.901	-1.612	898.590	.107	-0.103
External Regulation (2, 6)	2.92	0.682	2.96	0.650	-.996	1037	.319	-0.062
Intrinsic Motivation (3, 7)	2.88	0.715	3.06	0.688	-4.145	1037	**< .001**	-0.259
Identified Regulation (5, 8)	3.31	0.642	3.38	0.599	-1.759	1037	.079	-0.110

6 Discussion, Implications and Limitations

Overall, the university students' career choice competence is higher than that of the school students, as expected. It is interesting to note that school students and university students rate their *Problem-solving* skills as good according to their own assessment, which indicates good self-confidence. They also rate *Career concern* highly, which means that it is generally important for school students and university students to clarify which career options are suitable for them.

The biggest difference between school students and university students is in terms of *Knowledge about planning and decision-making*. These items were about whether young people already have a plan or have set clear goals to prepare themselves for entering the workforce. Since this is still a long way off, especially for younger students, the results are not surprising, as well as the results on less *Exploration* and less *Occupational knowledge*.

The choice of occupation seems to be difficult for young people due to the large number of occupational offers/employment opportunities and also many personal interests - young people need support in the decision-making process.

In Germany, a decision is often made before entering fifth grade as to which school-leaving certificate to pursue (whether the certificate of secondary education after ninth or tenth grade or A-level after twelfth or thirteenth grade), and the choice of secondary school is made thereafter. Students who choose to stay in school longer often also plan to go on to study at a university. Here, other school systems in other countries may have different influences.

Below, we have summarized the main findings that answer our research questions and can support the developers of skills acquisition platforms in the context of career guidance (Table 6).

The platform was shown within the online study via video and the individual functional, design and gamification elements via graphics. Therefore, we can assume that, for example, certain elements seem to be motivating, but the results do not guarantee that the motivational effect is given with long-term (and real) use of the platform. An intensive examination of elements during field phases (school workshops) would have to follow and can provide more profound results. Furthermore, the online study asked for ideas that were derived from workshop results with students at the beginning of the platform development. This means that there may be other important functional elements that were not considered in this study.

Table 6. Implications resulting from core results.

User needs	• Younger students need more support with decision-making and planning knowledge
	• Application processes for studies/training as well as the organization of studies or in-company training should be made known to young people
	• Existing offers should reach the target group
	• Young people should be supported in finding out what they are interested in and need support with regard to decision-making, because they sometimes have many interests
	• Existing platforms seem to need additions to provide sufficient support
	• Many options today make it difficult to see through and require clear representations and a high degree of accuracy of fit
Supporting functional, design & gamification elements	• Tips on how young people can achieve their goals
	• Impart knowledge about finances
	• Motivational tips
	• Tips on how to make better decisions
	• Focus tips and planning tools (budget- vacation/ process planning)
	• Very useful seem; *ToDo lists, Dashboards* (with e.g. learning progress), *Strengths / Weaknesses / Opportunities / Challenges Analysis*, creating a *Vision Board*, a *Story/Framing* of the learning environment and also a *Buddy who can give feedback* on learning behavior
	• These elements also seem to be the most motivating plus *Challenges & Quests*
	• The motivational impact of a gamification and design element depends on its usefulness
	• School students probably need to be more intrinsically motivated than university students, since university students in general already seem to have more desire to engage with future topics
Platform goals	• Young people wish to find a profession that suits them
	• Young people want to find out about their personal interests and skills
	• Information about which school subjects or further training opportunities are already important/interesting for the respective dream job should be known at an early stage
	• A description of what one actually does in the individual occupations (e.g. computer work, working outdoors/with people) is helpful

7 Conclusion

For the development of a digital platform that is intended to support important decision-making processes, such as career choice, school and university students (14–35 years) were questioned in a Germany-wide online survey (n = 1044) regarding their career choice competence and why career orientation is difficult for them. This allowed us to define the initial situation and also the problem space.

Overall, career choice competence is higher among university students than among school students. The young people rate their problem-solving competence very highly. They also consider it important to inform themselves about their occupational options, even though they often do not know what they actually want.

Furthermore, we were able to identify requirements (user needs) for digital platforms and which functional, design and gamification-elements seem to be useful and also motivating for young people.

For most young people, tips on how to better achieve their goals, motivational tips and tips on finances would be helpful, followed by tips on how to make better decisions.

The motivational effect of functional, design and gamification elements seems to be strongly related to the usefulness of the elements. ToDo lists, dashboards, and strengthen analyses seem to be most useful in the context of career guidance for young people.

By asking what would be a good outcome after using a career orientation platform, we were able to sharpen the goal definition.

According to the young people, a good outcome after platform use would be if they had found an occupation that suited them and identified personal interests and skills.

The results of the study will inform the development of our platform and can provide design guidance to developers of online learning platforms for skills acquisition (see Sect. 6).

In the future, we will further investigate user preference for different design elements and dependent factors so that the platform can be designed to be as adaptive and user-friendly as possible. A particular focus will be on fostering intrinsic motivation among young people. Furthermore, within field studies, the young people are continuously surveyed on the actual platform usage (e.g. usability (weak points), user experience and perceived intrinsic motivation).

Acknowledgements. This work was funded by the Federal Ministry of Education and Research of the Federal Republic of Germany (BMBF FKZ 13FH033SA8/THL 13FH033SB8).

References

1. Fink, B. (2021). Berufswahl – Welche Informationsquellen gibt es? Bildungsexperten Netzwerk. https://www.bildungsxperten.net/bildungschannels/berufswahl-welche-informationsquellen-gibt-es/
2. Bundesagentur für Arbeit. (2023). Lexikon der Ausbildungsberufe. https://www.arbeitsagentur.de/datei/dok_ba014834.pdf
3. Cedefop; ETF; European Commission. (2021). Investing in career guidance. https://www.cedefop.europa.eu/en/publications/2230
4. Kaak, S., Driesel-Lange, K., Kracke, B., & Hany, E. (2013). Diagnostik und Förderung der Berufswahlkompetenz Jugendlicher. In bwp@ Spezial 6 – Hochschultage Berufliche Bildung 2013 (pp. 1–13). Driesel-Lange, K. / Dreer, B. http://www.bwpat.de/ht2013/ws14/kaak_etal_ws14-ht2013.pdf
5. Dehne, M., Kaak, S., Lipowski, K., & Kracke, B. (2020). Berufsorientierung in bewegung. berufswahlkompetenz ökonomisch erfassen. kurzversion des fragebogens berufswahlkompetenz. In: K. Driesel-Lange, Ulrike Weyland, & Birgit Ziegler (Eds.), Zeitschrift für Berufs-und Wirtschaftspädagogik, pp. 81–105. Franz Steiner Verlag

6. Driesel-Lange, K., Hany, E., Kracke, B., & Schindler, N. (2010). Ein Kompetenzentwicklungsmodell für die schulische Berufsorientierung. In: Ursula Sauer-Schiffer & Tim Brüggemann (Ed.), Der Übergang Schule-Beruf. Beratung als pädagogische Intervention, pp. 157–175. Waxmann

7. Ryan, R.M., Connell, J.P.: The Self-Regulation Questionnaires Scale Description. J. Pers. Soc. Psychol. **57**(1989), 749–761 (1989)

8. Cheng, E.C.K.: The role of self-regulated learning in enhancing learning performance. Int. J. Res. Rev. **6**(1), 1–17 (2011)

9. Barlovic, I., Burkard, C., Hollenbach-Biele, N., Lepper, C., Ullrich, D. (2022). Berufliche Orientierung im dritten Corona-Jahr. Eine repräsentative Befragung von Jugendlichen 2022. www.chance-ausbildung.de/jugendbefragung/berufsorientierung2022%0A39

10. Brüggemann, T., et al :(2020). Vom Berufswahlpass zur Berufswahlapp.

11. Busch, F. (2022). ChoiceLab – eine neue Online-Ressource zur Berufsorientierung. Immaterielle Faktoren der Berufswahl im Fokus. BWP, 51(2/2022), 44–45. https://www.bwp-zeitschrift.de/dienst/publikationen/de/17840

12. Saleem, A.N., Noori, N.M., Ozdamli, F.: Gamification applications in E-learning: a literature review. Technol. Knowl. Learn. January. (2021). https://doi.org/10.1007/s10758-020-09487-x

13. Brandenburger, J., Mergan, H., Schametat, J., Vergin, A., Engel, A., & Janneck, M. (2022). A Digital Application for Digital Natives to Improve Orientation Competence and Career Choice Decisions. Proceedings of Mensch und Computer 2022. https://doi.org/10.1145/3543758.3547511https://doi.org/10.1145/3543758.3547511

14. Lipowski, K., Kaak, S., Kracke, B.: Handbuch Schulische Berufliche Orientierung - Praxisorientierte Unterstützung für den Übergang Schule - Beruf (2. Friedrich-Schiller-Universität Jena, Auflage) (2021)

15. Cohen, J. (1992). A Power Primer Psychol Bull 112:155–159. Psychological Bulletin [PsycARTICLES], 112(July), 155–159. http://www2.psych.ubc.ca/~schaller/528Readings/Cohen1992.pdf

16. Grolnick, W.S., Ryan, R.M., Deci, E.L.: Inner resources for school achievement: motivational mediators of children's perceptions of their parents. J. Educ. Psychol. **83**(4), 508–517 (1991). https://doi.org/10.1037/0022-0663.83.4.508

3D Reconstruction Using a Mirror-Mounted Drone: Development and Evaluation of Actual Equipment

Ayumi Noda(✉) ⓘ, Kimi Ueda ⓘ, Hirotake Ishii ⓘ, and Hiroshi Shimoda ⓘ

Kyoto University, Yoshida-honmachi, Sakyo-ku, Kyoto-shi, Kyoto, Japan
{ayumi,ueda,hirotake,shimoda}@ei.energy.kyoto-u.ac.jp

Abstract. A possible method to support work inside a nuclear power plant (NPP) would be to take images of the environment with an RGB-D camera and conduct 3D reconstruction. The reconstructed model is useful for confirming the site in advance. However, in imaging inside an NPP, a lot of areas are occluded by pipes or machinery, resulting in omissions in the reconstructed model. We have proposed a method to fly a small mirror-mounted drone instead of a large drone equipped with an RGB-D camera and to capture the occluded area using mirror reflection. In this paper, we examined the feasibility of mirror-mounted drone by fabricating the actual equipment. With the flight test, the proposed drone was shown to fly stably even with the mirror. In addition, we developed a method for 3D reconstruction using images obtained in the imaging with the mirror-mounted drone. The proposed method estimates the mirror pose, reduce the noise of depth images and generate the reconstructed model. The evaluation showed that although noise remained in the reconstructed model, the imaging with fewer omissions was achieved with the mirror-mounted drone.

Keywords: 3D reconstruction · Drone · Nuclear Power Plant (NPP) · RGB-D camera

1 Introduction

In order to support works inside a Nuclear Power Plants (NPP), acquiring the data of the environment using an 3D sensor such as an RGB-D camera and generating the 3D reconstructed model may be a possible solution [1,2]. In this solution, in addition to the color image, information on the distance to the object is used to generate a 3D model. Therefore, this model faithfully reproduces the latest conditions inside an NPP including the scale, and it is useful for confirming the site in advance before entering the site. However, the interior of the NPP is complex and intricate, and occlusion can easily occur. When imaging by a hand-held camera, it is difficult for the worker to be aware of occlusion, and there are areas that cannot be directly captured because they are out of the reach of the workers, which causes omissions in the reconstructed model. It is expected that

H. P. da Silva and P. Cipresso (Eds.): CHIRA 2023, CCIS 1996, pp. 216–231, 2023.
https://doi.org/10.1007/978-3-031-49425-3_13

an autonomous drone equipped with an RGB-D camera can be used to take the images of the site with fewer omissions, but with current technology, the drone has to be large to equip with the high-resolution RGB-D camera. Therefore, it is difficult for the RGB-D camera-mounted drone to fly inside the NPP.

To solve these problems, we have proposed a method of flying an autonomous drone equipped only with a mirror and using the mirror reflection of the mirror surface to capture the occluded areas. Conceptual diagram of the imaging and 3D reconstruction using a mirror-mounted drone is shown in Fig 1. Since small mirror is lighter than an RGB-D camera, it can be mounted on small drones. In our previous work, the path planning problem was studied by simulation, assuming cooperative imaging with the worker [3]. In this paper, we verify whether it is possible to fly a small drone equipped with a mirror using actual equipment, and furthermore, we develop a 3D reconstruction method using the mirror reflection. This paper focuses only on 3D reconstruction and does not deal with autonomous flight path planning of the mirror-mounted drone.

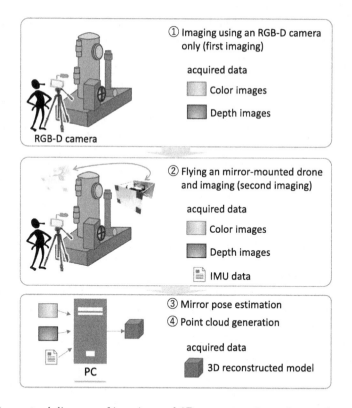

Fig. 1. Conceptual diagram of imaging and 3D reconstruction using a mirror-mounted drone.

2   Related Works

2.1   Imaging and 3D Reconstruction with Drones

In recent years, many studies have reported on the use of drones equipped with cameras to fly and take images, and then use the obtained images to perform 3D reconstruction. Using these methods, it is possible to take the images of even the environments that are inaccessible to humans. In addition, imaging with fewer omissions is expected to be achieved by monitoring the imaging situation and adjusting the drone flight plan according to the situation.

Zhang et al. [4] proposed a method to explore caves using a drone equipped with an RGB-D camera as a "Co-Archaeologists". In this method, an archaeologist with a computer acts as a supervisor of the drone and monitors it. The drone flies and takes the images of the cave while autonomously sensing and avoiding collisions. The computer uses the data obtained by the drone to determine the drone's path and perform 3D reconstruction. The system yields a 3D model of the cave interior. Inzerillo et al. [5] tested a method for inspecting road pavement that uses a hand-held camera and a camera-mounted drone to take the images of the road and to generate a 3D model. Conventionally, pavement evaluation has been done visually by humans, which leaves room for subjectivity, exposes humans to danger, and low productivity. However, a semi-automated method using drones has enabled more efficient and reliable evaluations. Kim et al. [6] proposed a method in which a drone and an unmanned ground vehicle (UGV) work together to collect data for the autonomous operation at intricate environments such as construction sites and disaster sites. In those environments, it is difficult for UGV to monitor the site situation alone because the view from UGV is obstructed by obstacles. In this method, a drone takes the images of the environment from the sky and generates a rough 3D model. Then, based on the rough 3D model, the location where the UGV should move to obtain more detailed information and the route to that point are generated, and the UGV moves through the environment according to the route. Tests in the real outdoor environments have shown that this method can produce highly accurate 3D models. Zhao et al. [7] proposed a method to generate a 3D model of a dam from aerial images obtained by a drone for emergency monitoring and inspection. Since dams are complex and huge, manual inspection is hazardous. The method of setting up multiple fixed observation points has been proposed, but it is inefficient because there are many areas that cannot be observed. Drones can be operated remotely and can inspect a wide area. Tests on several dams have shown that the 3D models obtained are accurate enough for inspection, and the efficiency of dam inspections has increased. Marks et al. [8] proposed a method to generate 3D reconstructed models of plants to record the shape of plants in crop cultivation. Conventionally, plant shape has been measured and recorded manually by humans, which is time-consuming. In this method, accurate 3D models are generated by applying bundle adjustment and template matching techniques to images obtained by drones.

However, the drones used in these methods are large drones, making it difficult to fly them inside the NPP for safety reason. For example, Zhao et al. [7] used DJI M210 and DJI Phantom 4 Pro, whose diagonal lengths are 643 mm and 350 mm, respectively. There are also restrictions on the environment in which the drones can fly, with environments with few obstacles being assumed, such as outdoor high-altitude areas or large indoor areas. The interior of the NPP has a large discrepancy from the assumed environment because of the pipes and machinery. For these reasons, it is difficult to apply the conventional methods to imaging inside the NPP.

On the other hand, methods have been proposed to imaging in the environment using a small drone. For example, Gautam et al. [9] validated Visual SLAM using a small drone called Tello. They applied the convolutional neural network SLAM method developed for ground vehicles to the drone and compared it with other Visual SLAM methods. Experiments on simulators and an actual drone showed that their method produced relatively accurate model.

However, in these methods, 3D reconstruction is basically conducted based on feature points of captured objects in the images, making it difficult to achieve the localization and to obtain detailed model of objects with few feature points, such as monochromatic walls or pipes. In particular, since the interior of the NPP is intricate and narrow, the only way to take the images of objects is often to get close to them, which leads to few feature points in the obtained images. In addition, these methods cannot directly obtain accurate size information of the objects, and must be combined with another method to obtain size information.

2.2   3D Reconstruction with Mirrors

In several studies, the use of mirrors has been proposed as a technique for capturing areas that cannot be directly captured by a single camera. This technique has several advantages over the use of multiple cameras, including lower cost and no need for synchronization between cameras.

For example, Akay et al. [10] proposed a method for 3D reconstruction using an RGB-D camera, a color camera, and mirrors. In this method, the object to be captured is placed between cameras and the mirror. The area containing the mirror is extracted from the obtained image by an RGB-D camera, and the information in that area is integrated with the information in the other areas to realize the imaging without omissions. Furthermore, the information from the color camera can give a high-resolution texture. Kontogianni et al. [11] proposed using mirrors to capture the entirety of the artifact as a quicker method for 3D reconstruction of small artefacts, and developed reconstruction methods for both laser scanners and for image-based modeling methods. These methods enable the calculation of the mirror's position and orientation by attaching markers to the mirror that can be identified from the laser scanner or camera. Experimental results show that these methods allow reconstruction of the entire artefacts with less effort than without the use of mirrors. Yin et al. [12] proposed a method of imaging without omissions by introducing a plane mirror to a technique called fringe projection profilometry. Fringe projection profilometry is a method in which structured light is projected onto an object by a projector, and the light is captured by a camera to estimate the shape of the object from light distortion. This method had the disadvantage of not being able to measure the entire circumference of the object at once because the light is projected by a projector, but this problem was overcome with the introduction of mirrors. Masumura et al. [13] also proposed a method of capturing the entire object using a specular surface in range image reconstruction. The unique feature of their method is that not only the mirror surface but also the floor surface is captured during imaging, and the position of the mirror surface relative to the image sensor is estimated using the information from the floor surface. This eliminates the need for rigorous prior calibration and enables easy reconstruction of the entire object.

However, in these methods, at least either the camera or the mirror is fixed and only a single object is often the subject of the image. In the case of imaging the interior of the NPP assumed in this paper, it is necessary to capture the occluded areas while moving the mirror around in the environment because the environment is vast. There are few reports assuming the reconstruction of the vast environment using mirrors.

3   Design and Fabrication of the Mirror-Mounted Drone

In this section, drone types, mirror shapes and methods of mounting on drones are considered and the mirror-mounted drone is fabricated. Various required specifications are assumed for a mirror-mounted drone to be used inside the NPP.

3.1   Drone Types

Drones used for imaging inside the NPP need to get close to complex structures. Compared to larger drones, smaller drones can pass between objects and have a better chance of getting close to the target structure. In addition, smaller drones cause less damage if they should collide with an object in the NPP. Therefore, the drone used for imaging inside the NPP should be small. For this reason, we used the Tello of Ryze Tech, Inc. The size of Tello is 98 mm × 92.5 mm × 41 mm. The weight of Tello itself is about 80 g. The maximum flight time is 13 min. In this study, how much weight Tello could carry stably was evaluated by flying Tello and maximum weight turned out to be about 50 g. Therefore, the weight of additional equipment must be less than this weight. No current high-resolution RGB-D camera can be loaded with additional batteries and storage media at a lighter weight than 50 g yet.

3.2   Design of the Mirror

The mirror used in the proposed method must not only be able to be mounted on a small drone in terms of both weight and shape, but must also the shape should be rigid enough not to be deformed and should be large enough in order to keep the quality of the 3D reconstructed model. In this paper, we examined the specifications required of the mirror from both perspectives.

Regarding the possibility of mounting the mirror on a drone, the mass of the mirror must be less than the payload of the drone, so in this paper, the mirror was limited to about 50 g. The mounting position of the mirror must also be considered. Examples of a design with a mirror mounted in inappropriate positions are shown in Fig. 2. In the flight test, the drone with those design could not fly stably. If the mirror was mounted above or below the center of gravity of the drone, the balance of the center of gravity would change significantly and the drone would become uncontrollable. Furthermore, the infrared sensor used for positioning is located below the Tello, and mounting the mirror below the drone may interfere with the operation of the infrared sensor. Therefore, in this paper, a mirror and its counterweight were mounted on the side of the drone as shown in Fig. 3. This allows the mirror to be mounted while minimizing changes in the center-of-gravity balance.

Focusing on 3D reconstruction, the mirror should have a shape that is rigid and does not deform during flight. This is because deformation of the mirror may lead to distortion of the mirror image, which may lead to distortion or failure of the reconstruction. Furthermore, the mirror surface should be as large as possible to reflect a large area at a time. A convex mirror satisfies the above two conditions, but the number of points that can be obtained is sparse, and the reconstruction process is complex. Therefore, a planar mirror was used in this study, and a X-shaped frame was used to reinforce the planar mirror to increase its rigidity as shown in Fig. 4. In addition, the mirror surface is prone to vibration during flight due to the rotation of the drone's motor and air currents. To prevent blurring of the mirror reflection obtained by the mirror surface vibration, reinforcement rods were added between the mirror and the counterweight to further increase rigidity as shown in Fig. 3.

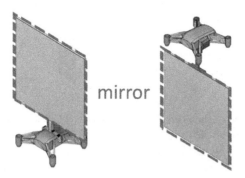

Fig. 2. Examples of a drone design with a mirror mounted above or below the drone. The areas enclosed by the red dashed line indicate the mirror surface. Flight tests with an actual drone showed that they could not fly stably due to an imbalance in the center of gravity.

Besides, for 3D reconstruction using the mirror reflection, it is necessary to estimate the mirror pose. Therefore, in this paper, red cloths cut into 30 mm squares were attached to the four corners of the mirror. The distance between the centers of these cloths was measured before the flight and used to estimate the position of the mirror. The distance between the centers of the top left and bottom left cloths was 82.5 mm, and the distance between the top left and top right cloths was 150.0 mm. In addition, data from Inertial Measurement Unit (IMU) equipped with the drone were used to estimate the mirror orientation. Estimation of the mirror position and orientation (hereafter jointly referred to as "pose") are described in detail in the next section.

3.3   Fabrication of the Mirror-Mounted Drone

Based on the above design, a mirror-mounted Drone was fabricated as shown in Fig. 5. A 0.5 mm thick, 180 mm wide × 112.5 mm height mirror sheet was used as the mirror surface in this paper. The frame was made of PLA and fabricated by a 3D printer, Replicator +. The overall weight of the mirror-mounted drone was 119g. When this drone was flown by manual operation, oscillation was observed in the drone pose, but decayed within about 10 s after takeoff.

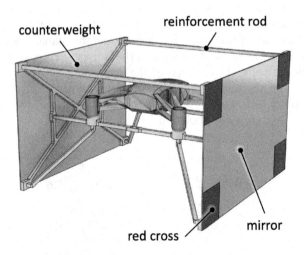

Fig. 3. The final design of the mirror-mounted drone. The mirror and its counterweight are placed on the sides of the drone. They are reinforced and made rigid by X-shaped and rod-shaped frames. In addition, red clothes are attached to the mirrors, which are used to estimate the mirror position.

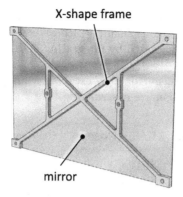

Fig. 4. The design of the mirror and X-shaped frame.

4 Imaging and 3D Reconstruction Using the Mirror-Mounted Drone

In order to obtain the reconstructed model with fewer omissions, imaging and 3D reconstruction of the environment are performed in the following sequence. First, an RGB-D camera is fixed inside an environment using a tripod and begins imaging. Next, a mirror-mounted drone is operated to fly near occluded areas. At this time, the RGB-D camera takes color and depth images of the mirror-mounted drone, and at the same time, orientation data from the IMU of the mirror-mounted drone is recorded. After the imaging is completed, the mirror pose at the time each image was taken is estimated from the obtained images and the IMU data. Then, noise in the depth image is removed. Finally, 3D reconstruction is performed using mirror reflection.

Fig. 5. The mirror-mounted drone fabricated in this paper.

Although the area that can be captured through the mirror surface in a single pair of color and depth image is small, a reconstructed model with few missing points is expected to be generated by integrating multiple images captured over a long period of time.

In subsequent sections, mirror pose estimation and 3D reconstruction considering the mirror reflection are described.

4.1 Estimation of the Mirror Pose

In order to perform 3D reconstruction using the mirror reflection, the mirror pose is required.

In the proposed method, the pose is estimated using markers attached to the mirror and the IMU data from the drone. As described in Sect. 2.1, conventional methods which uses drone's onboard camera for drone pose estimation and 3D reconstruction are not applicable in the imaging inside the NPP. In the proposed method, instead of using drone's onboard camera, the RGB-D camera is placed outward and takes images that include the drone using an outside-side-in method. Then, the mirror position is estimated from the markers' positions and depth values. In this estimation, the orientation is also obtained. However, while the position is obtained with high accuracy, the estimated orientation varies greatly due to errors in the depth values. Therefore, in the proposed method, the orientation is estimated using IMU data from the drone. In theory, the position can be also obtained using IMU data, but estimation accuracy is low because errors in the data accumulate due to integration. By using markers to estimate the position and IMU data to estimate the orientation, it is expected that the mirror pose estimation with higher accuracy is achieved than when estimating the pose using either markers or IMU data.

Position estimation using markers is conducted in the following steps. First, red regions are extracted from the images by thresholding with HSV values. Next, the distances between the extracted regions are measured and then are compared to the distances between the actual markers that were measured beforehand. From these comparisons, a group of the four regions is detected such that the distances match the distances between the real markers. This group of the regions is determined to be the regions of the markers. Finally, the coordinates of the regions of the markers in the image and the positional relationships between the markers are used to solve the Perspective-4-Point (P4P) problem and estimate the mirror pose. Of this mirror pose information, considering the accuracy, the proposed method uses only the position information.

4.2 3D Reconstruction Considering the Mirror Reflection

3D reconstruction using an RGB-D camera is basically accomplished by using the depth value, the coordinates of each pixel in the image, and the focal length of the camera to calculate where the object in each pixel is located. For images containing a mirror surface, 3D reconstruction considering mirror reflection is achieved by assuming that there is a virtual camera with a pose that is plane-symmetrical with the actual RGB-D camera respect to the mirror surface, and applying the basic 3D reconstruction method by assuming that an image of the mirror surface is obtained with this virtual camera as shown in Fig. 6.

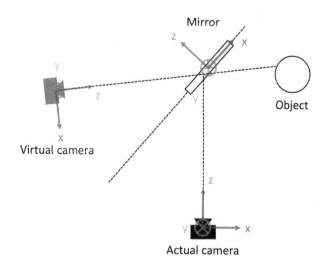

Fig. 6. The principle to reconstruct the real object using the virtual camera.

In the proposed method, 3D reconstruction considering the mirror reflection is conducted in the following steps. First, the area of the mirror surface is extracted from the depth image, then depth values of the other areas are set to 0, which means that the depth value was not measured. Next, the virtual camera pose is calculated using the pose of the actual RGB-D camera and the mirror. In the proposed method, a mirror coordinate system is defined as a right-handed coordinate system with the origin at the center of the mirror, the x-axis corresponding to the direction from left to right of the mirror, and the y-axis corresponding the direction from top to bottom of the mirror. When the pose of the actual RGB-D camera is P_c and relative pose of the mirror to the actual camera is P_{mc}, the pose of the actual camera as seen from the mirror is expressed as $P_{mc}^{-1}P_c$. Given that the mirror surface is on the xy-plane as shown in Fig. 6, the relative pose of the virtual camera to the mirror, which is plane-symmetric with $P_{mc}^{-1}P_c$, is obtained by the following formula:

$$P'_{mc} = \begin{bmatrix} 1 & 0 & 0 & 0 \\ 0 & 1 & 0 & 0 \\ 0 & 0 & -1 & 0 \\ 0 & 0 & 0 & 1 \end{bmatrix} P_{mc}^{-1}P_c \tag{1}$$

Converting the pose in the mirror coordinate system to that in the actual camera coordinate system, virtual camera's pose is calculated as $P_c^{-1}P'_{mc}$. In the next step of 3D reconstruction, because depth images obtained by RGB-D cameras contain a lot of noise, these noises are reduced using Murayama's method. Murayama et al. [14] proposed a method to reduce random noise by modifying the depth values using information from other depth images which take the similar areas and camera poses at the time those images were taken. Even for the images taken of a mirror-mounted drone, random noise can be eliminated as long as the same region is captured in a sufficiently large number of multiple images. In the last step, the conventional 3D reconstruction method is applied to the virtual camera pose and noise-reduced depth images.

5   Evaluation of the Proposed Method

In this section, an evaluation of the proposed method in a mockup of an NPP using an actual mirror-mounted drone is described.

5.1   Outline of the Evaluation

The purpose of this evaluation is to assess whether the proposed method can conduct 3D reconstruction with fewer omissions. To achieve this purpose, the mirror-mounted drone was manually operated in an environment which replicated the interior of an NPP and the environment was filmed. Then, 3D reconstructed models were created from the images obtained from the imaging and their quality was investigated.

5.2   Method

Environment. This evaluation was conducted in Room 255, Research Building 10 on the main campus of Kyoto University. The size of the environment was approximately W 2 m × L 2 m × H 3 m. In order to mock up the inside of the NPP, a pipe with diameter of 0.1 m and a height of 2.0 m was installed. The floor plan of the room is shown in Fig. 7.

Process Flow of the Evaluation. First, the RGB-D camera was fixed at the position indicated by the camera symbol in Fig. 7 to take the images of the environment. The environment was then captured without flying the drone, and a pair of color and depth image (hereafter referred to as "first images") was obtained preliminary to the flight. In these images, the far side of the pipe as seen from the RGB-D camera was not captured, so it was expected to be missing from the reconstructed model. Next, while imaging with the RGB-D camera, the mirror-mounted drone was flown by manual operation. At this time, while viewing the taken images, the mirror-mounted drone was controlled so that it flew near the occluded areas and those areas could be captured by the RGB-D camera using mirror reflection. The mirror-mounted drone was moved from drone launch site to approximately 0.3 m to the left rear of the pipe, and the

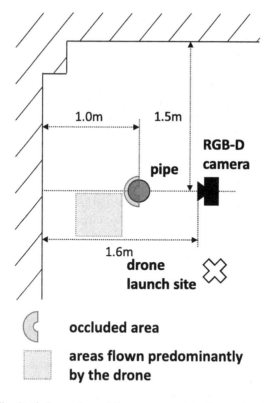

Fig. 7. A floor plan of the room used in the evaluation.

drone was moved up and down approximately 1 m. IMU data from the mirror-mounted drone was also recorded. The sampling rate of imaging and IMU data recording was approximately 10 frames per second. 1460 pairs of color and depth image and IMU data were captured in the imaging, and 564 pairs, in which all four markers of the mirror were captured, were used for 3D reconstruction. Last, point clouds were generated in two different method. The first one (hereafter referred to as "first imaging point cloud") was generated only from first images, which was taken before the drone flight. The other one (hereafter referred to as "second imaging point cloud") was generated from the other pairs of color and depth image using the proposed method, which were taken during the drone flight. In "first imaging point cloud", the far side of the pipe was expected to be missing, whereas in "second imaging point cloud", that area was expected to be captured and reconstructed because the mirror-mounted drone was flown near the area. By comparing the degree of omission in these point clouds, we evaluated whether the proposed method was able to capture images with fewer omissions.

Used Equipment. Xtion Pro Live was used as the RGB-D camera to take the images of the environment. The specification of Xtion Pro Live is shown in Table 1. A laptop PC was used to operate the RGB-D camera and record the IMU data from the mirror-mounted drone. The OS of laptop PC was Windows 10 Pro 64bit, CPU was Intel(R) Core(TM) i7-8550U. A program to generate point clouds was developed and executed on a desktop PC. The OS of desktop PC was Windows 10 Pro 64bit, CPU was Intel(R) Core(TM) i7-10700, GPU was NVIDIA GeForce GTX 1060, and RAM was 32 GB.

Table 1. The specifications of Xtion Pro Live.

Resolution of color image	640 × 320 pixels (30 fps)
Resolution of depth image	640 × 320 pixels (30 fps)
Depth range	0.3 ∼ 10 m
FOV	Horizontal 58 deg, Vertical 45 deg, diagonal 70 deg

Implementation. The programs were developed with Visual Studio 2019. In the programs, Boost (Ver.1.80.0), Eigen (Ver.3.4.0) were used. In addition, OpenCV (Ver.4.7.0) was used for mirror position estimation by image processing, Point Cloud Library (Ver.1.12.0) was used for point cloud generation, and CUDA (Ver.11.2) was used for parallel processing.

5.3 Results

An example of the image obtained in the imaging with mirror-mounted drone is shown in Fig. 8. It can be seen that the occluded area is filmed through the mirror surface. The generated point clouds are shown in Fig. 9, 10. Compared to "first imaging point cloud", "second imaging point cloud" includes points on the far side of the pipe from the RGB-D camera and has fewer missing areas. Therefore, 3D reconstruction using a mirror-mounted drone is considered effective for imaging with fewer omissions. However, the "second imaging point cloud" still contains noise and appears blurred. The reason that the noise was not fully removed

Fig. 8. Examples of the images obtained in the imaging with mirror-mounted drone.

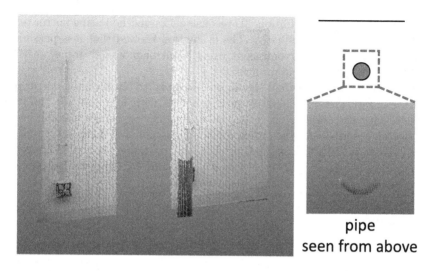

Fig. 9. The overview of "first imaging point cloud".

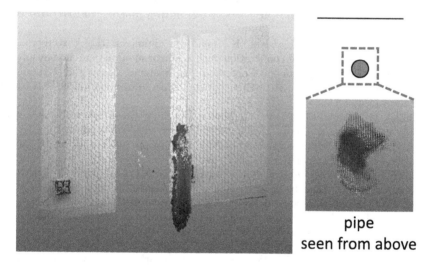

Fig. 10. The overview of "second imaging point cloud".

may be the error in the estimated value of the mirror pose. In order to reduce this error, red cloth marker attached to the mirror may be replaced with other markers such as LEDs.

6   Conclusion and Future Work

In this paper, a mirror-mounted drone was fabricated for imaging for 3D reconstruction of an NPP. With the flight test, it was confirmed that mirror-mounted drone could fly stably. In addition, 3D reconstruction method using mirror reflection was developed and evaluated. The evaluation showed that it is possible to achieve imaging with fewer omissions using a mirror-mounted drone, although the obtained 3D models contain noise.

In the future, a new method should be developed to estimate the mirror pose more accurately and to generate the 3D models with less noise. In addition, it is necessary to complete the cooperative imaging system by combining the path planning method for the autonomous mirror-mounted drone introduced in a previous study with the method proposed in this paper. It is also important to verify the effectiveness of the cooperative imaging by flying the autonomous mirror-mounted drone inside the NPP.

References

1. Ishii, H.: Plant maintenance and dismantling work support based on three-dimensional scanning technology. Int. J. Nucl. Saf. Simul. **4**(2), 97–104 (2013)
2. Harazono, Y., Ishii, H., Shimoda, H., Taruta, Y., Kouda, Y.: Development of AR-based scanning support system for 3D model reconstruction of work sites. J. Nucl. Sci. Technol. **59**(7), 934–948 (2022). https://doi.org/10.1007/978-3-030-11051-2_69
3. Noda, A., Harazono, Y., Ueda, K., Ishii, H., Shimoda, H.: A study on 3D reconstruction method in cooperation with a mirror-mounted autonomous drone. In: 2022 IEEE International Conference on Systems, Man, and Cybernetics (SMC), Prague, pp. 305–310. IEEE (2022). https://doi.org/10.1109/SMC53654.2022.9945519
4. Zhang, G., Shang, B., Chen, Y., Moyes, H.: SmartCaveDrone: 3D cave mapping using UAVs as robotic co-archaeologists. In: 2017 International Conference on Unmanned Aircraft Systems (ICUAS), Miami, pp. 1052–1057. IEEE (2017). https://doi.org/10.1109/ICUAS.2017.7991499
5. Inzerillo, L., Mino, G.D., Roberts, R.: Image-based 3D reconstruction using traditional and UAV datasets for analysis of road pavement distress. Autom. Constr. **96**, 457–469 (2018). https://doi.org/10.1016/j.autcon.2018.10.010
6. Kim, P., Park, J., Cho, Y.K., Kang, J.: UAV-assisted autonomous mobile robot navigation for as-is 3D data collection and registration in cluttered environments. Autom. Constr. **106**, 102918 (2019). https://doi.org/10.1016/j.autcon.2019.102918
7. Zhao, S., Kang, F., Li, J., Ma, C.: Structural health monitoring and inspection of dams based on UAV photogrammetry with image 3D reconstruction. Autom. Constr. **130**, 103832 (2021). https://doi.org/10.1016/j.autcon.2021.103832
8. Marks, E., Magistri, F., Stachniss, C.: Precise 3D reconstruction of plants from UAV imagery combining bundle adjustment and template matching. In: 2022 International Conference on Robotics and Automation (ICRA), Philadelphia, pp. 2259–2265. IEEE (2022). https://doi.org/10.1109/ICRA46639.2022.9811358
9. Gautam, A., Mahangade, S., Gupta, V. I., Madan, R., Arya, K.: An experimental comparison of visual SLAM systems. In: 2021 International Symposium of Asian Control Association on Intelligent Robotics and Industrial Automation (IRIA), Goa, pp. 13–18. IEEE (2021). https://doi.org/10.1109/IRIA53009.2021.9588784
10. Akay, A., Akgul, Y. S.: 3D reconstruction with mirrors and RGB-D cameras. In: 2014 International Conference on Computer Vision Theory and Applications (VISAPP), Lisbon, pp. 325–334. IEEE (2014)

11. Kontogianni, G., Thomaidis, A., Chliverou, R., Georgopoulos, A.: Exploiting mirrors in 3D reconstruction of small artefacts. Int. Arch. Photogramm. Remote. Sens. Spat. Inf. Sci. **42**(2), 531–537 (2018). https://doi.org/10.5194/isprs-archives-XLII-2-531-2018

12. Yin, W., Xu, H., Feng, S., Tao, T., Chen, Q., Zuo, C.: System calibration for panoramic 3D measurement with plane mirrors. In: Zhao, Y., Barnes, N., Chen, B., Westermann, R., Kong, X., Lin, C. (eds.) ICIG 2019. LNCS, vol. 11902, pp. 15–26. Springer, Cham (2019). https://doi.org/10.1007/978-3-030-34110-7_2

13. Masumura, H., Ji, Y., Umeda, K.: Shape reconstruction using a mirror with a range image sensor – detection of mirror in a range image. In: Duan, B., Umeda, K., Hwang, W. (eds.) Proceedings of the Seventh Asia International Symposium on Mechatronics. LNEE, vol. 589, pp. 994–1000. Springer, Singapore (2020). https://doi.org/10.1007/978-981-32-9441-7_103

14. Harazono, Y., Ishii, H., Shimoda, H., Kouda, Y.: Development of a scanning support system using augmented reality for 3D environment model reconstruction. In: Karwowski, W., Ahram, T. (eds.) IHSI 2019. AISC, vol. 903, pp. 460–464. Springer, Cham (2019). https://doi.org/10.1007/978-3-030-11051-2_69

Do Users Tolerate Errors? Effects of Observed Failures on the Subjective Evaluation of a Gesture-Based Virtual Reality Application

Lisa Graichen[1]([✉]) and Matthias Graichen[2]

[1] TU Berlin, Berlin, Germany
lisa.graichen@web.de
[2] Independent Researcher, Munich, Germany

Abstract. Recently, virtual reality (VR) has received increasing attention in science, research, and industry, as well as in consumer electronics. Together with this hardware, innovative interaction modes such as mid-air gestures are being developed and employed. Because these setups are complex and less established than traditional buttons and touch-based interfaces, there is a higher risk that users will perceive errors, failures, and technical malfunctions. This raises the question of how popular, accepted, and trusted such systems are among users and whether observed errors influence this subjective assessment. Previous studies have shown that trust typically increases with usage duration and may decay after system failures. We conducted a study using an HTC Vive headset on which we mounted a Leap Motion device for gesture detection. Participants performed basic tasks with a "blocks" application using a set of gestures. Afterwards, they were asked to rate their levels of trust in and acceptance of the system. We investigated the correlation between the number of observed errors and reported levels of trust and acceptance to determine whether malfunctions directly influence subjective assessment. We found no effect of errors on acceptance but a significant correlation between number of errors and overall trust score.

Keywords: User experience · Virtual reality · Gestures · Malfunction

1 Introduction

In recent years, extended reality applications have emerged rapidly, finding their way into users' everyday lives as well as professional applications, science, and research. The term "extended reality" (XR) comprises different levels of immersion, including virtual reality (VR), augmented reality (AR), and mixed reality (MR). Although XR systems have existed for decades, recent technological advances have catalyzed the development of various applications and research questions. Consequently, low-cost systems such as the Oculus Rift and HTC Vive have entered the market, making the VR experience affordable and widely accessible.

Typically, XR applications are implemented using head-mounted displays (HMDs). HMD systems are usually equipped with a set of controllers that users can hold in their

H. P. da Silva and P. Cipresso (Eds.): CHIRA 2023, CCIS 1996, pp. 232–243, 2023.
https://doi.org/10.1007/978-3-031-49425-3_14

hands to control or manipulate the virtual environment. However, using such additional devices to interact with the virtual environment may not be suitable for several reasons. For example, holding the controllers for an extended period may cause discomfort for the user, and some applications require the user's hands to be free. Furthermore, if the controllers are employed by many users and/or frequently changing users, additional hygiene-related challenges arise. As an alternative to these controllers, gesture and voice control can be used. However, these interaction types are still infrequently used in combination with VR (Rakkolainen et al., 2021). Therefore, we built a prototype application using gesture-based interaction (GBI). As a device for gesture detection, we used a Leap Motion (ultraleap.com), which is a well-functioning, inexpensive tool that can be connected to a laptop or VR headset and comes with developer documentation and plugins. Despite its simplicity and usefulness, it is still challenging to implement gestures such that every potential user, regardless of hand size, muscle tone, or movement habits, experiences perfect gesture detection. This observation raises the question of how users react to errors. Is there a correlation between observed errors and subjective assessment of the application based on interaction mode? That is to say, do users rate the system more negatively when they observe more malfunctions?

2 Theory

In the domain of human–machine interaction, there are a wide range of interaction activities that are referred to as "gestures," beginning with clicking, pointing, and moving a traditional computer mouse. In this domain, the term "gesture" is most frequently employed to refer to the use of touch screens, with their well-established set of gestures including swiping, zooming, and tapping in different contexts and dimensions (Saffer, 2008). However, bodily movements that are performed in the air without making contact with a surface and hence without haptic feedback are also considered to be gestures. Such mid-air gestures have applications in vehicles, where they may be used for interaction with in-vehicle information systems, as well as in smart homes and VR. Even systems that use gaze interaction (where "gaze" is defined as a directional movement that triggers a predefined action) are referred to as "gesture-based systems" (e.g., Rakkolainen et al., 2021). Finally, use of the classical controllers that usually ac-company VR HMDs is referred to as a "gesture-based interaction" (GBI).

In this paper, we use the term "GBI" to denote mid-air gestures that do not require physical contact with a surface (Saffer, 2008). According to O'hara et al. (2013), these gestures are defined by specific characteristics, namely 1) a distance from all surfaces is maintained, 2) no pressure is exerted on any surface, 3) no matter is transferred, 4) no momentum occurs, 5) freedom of movement is high, 6) there is no attrition or wear, and 7) no haptic feedback is applied.

The detection and recognition of gestures can be achieved using various technologies. For example, there are several hardware solutions that can be attached to the user's body, such as motion-capture suits, which are typically used for gestures that involve the whole body (e.g., Pfeiffer, 2013b). Additionally, there are gloves for hand gesture recognition (e.g., Pfeiffer, 2013a), wristbands (e.g., Myo wristband, He et al., 2017), finger rings, and small sensors that can be attached to the fingers of the hand (Kao et al., 2015). Moreover, there are camera-based devices that record images of the hand or body, such as the Microsoft Kinect and the Leap Motion. The recorded images are then processed using a variety of algorithms (see Premaratne, 2014 for an overview).

At present, concepts such as the "natural user interface" are at the forefront of technical developments (Wigdor & Wixon, 2011). This term refers to the creation of an interaction that resembles everyday communication and conveys a feeling of boundlessness and intuitiveness. GBI involving mid-air gestures is already in use and has long been investigated, at least since Bolt's (1980) "Put that there" approach (Bolt, 1980). However, despite the long history of this type of GBI, there is currently no set of gestures that is established across different applications or domains or even within a single do-main or area of application. Therefore, researchers must determine what gestures to use for each new system that they wish to build. This process demands considerable effort from the researchers and introduces a steep learning curve for potential users. It creates a barrier to the use of such systems in vehicle and smart home applications, and users need to remember the gestures when they stop using the application for a period. Moreover, this may result in a lack of training, which makes it more difficult for users to perform the gestures correctly. For developers, it is important to obtain insight into how users perform the relevant gestures.

Another important question is how many gestures an application should incorporate. Using more gestures allows for the gestures to be better adapted to the task and (hopefully) for them to be perceived as more natural and intuitive. However, having more gestures also requires more learning and memory effort from the user. Using fewer gestures reduces the learning effort for users and the implementation effort for developers, but the gestures adopted might be less suitable and intuitive. These is-sues remain unsolved, although effort has been made to elicit comprehensive gesture sets from user groups and experts (e.g., Leng et al., 2017; Loehmann et al., 2013; Piumsomboon et al., 2013; Seeling et al., 2018; Seeling et al., 2016).

Currently, there are few studies that combine GBI and VR. Therefore, research in this field, especially with a focus on user interaction, is relevant. Some studies have asked users to interact with virtual avatars. In Narayana et al. (2019), the authors built a prototype using an avatar. Users were required to perform a task with blocks, and it was found that they considered social, deictic, and iconic gestures to be important to employ when they could not use speech as a mode of interaction. Furthermore, users considered iconic gestures less important for communication directed towards solving the task when they could use speech interaction. A similar approach is VoxWorld by Pustejovksy et al. (2020), in which a virtual avatar was also employed. Deictic, action, and affordance gestures were used together with facial expressions and could be detected and per-formed by the virtual agent. In Rodriguez et al. (2017), the authors implemented a VR system using data gloves for gesture detection and investigated how quickly users could adapt to this system. They found that experienced users adapted more quickly than inexperienced users.

With regard to observed technical failures and errors, it is of particular interest how users react to these occurrences and how they affect acceptance of and trust in the system. Without acceptance and trust, users will not be willing to use a system. It is known from human–robot interaction that trust is not stable but changes over time, and it can be reduced when users perceive system failures (Esterwood & Robert, 2022). However, trust seems to stabilize after longer periods of use (Tolmeijer et al., 2021; Yu et al., 2018), reaching a level that matches the capabilities of the system. Thus, high system performance leads to high trust, and if performance falls below a certain threshold, trust decreases. The level of this threshold seems to be particular to the individual (Yu et al., 2018). The results of Dorton et al. (2022) demonstrated that when interacting with AI, users may increase or decrease their level of trust after certain experiences and consequently adapt their workflow by adding or removing certain tasks. Studies show that when confronted with errors in an auto-mated vehicle, users seem to decrease their level of trust, but this effect is temporary. After perceiving accurate system performance, trust recovers, a process termed "trust repair" (Dorton & Harper, 2022; Kraus et al., 2020; Lee et al., 2021). In Mishler and Chen (2023), similar results were obtained using a similar de-sign. However, although the findings showed that trust recovered after an observed failure, it was not restored to the levels measured before the failure.

In this study, we investigate how errors and system malfunctions affect user trust and acceptance. We used a VR setup in which participants were asked to perform basic tasks using mid-air gestures. A Leap Motion device was used for gesture recognition. Although this approach is well established and works well, it can still lead to errors, either because the system does not detect the hand movement correctly or because the user performs an incorrect gesture or the correct gesture in an imprecise way. We defined an error as any malfunction that did not result in the de-sired outcome.

We documented observed errors for each participant to answer the following re-search questions:

1) How do observed errors affect user trust? Is there a correlation between observed errors and reported trust?
2) How do observed errors affect user acceptance? Is there a correlation between observed errors and reported acceptance?

3 Methods

3.1 Design

We chose a one-way repeated measures design with interaction mode (controller vs. mid-air gestures) as the factor. We employed the controller interaction mode because it is the device that comes standard with the HTC Vive and is used to allow participants to familiarize themselves with the VR setting and practice performing tasks in the environment. Use of the standard controllers would also be considered GBI, but performing mid-air gestures feels more natural to users because no tool needs to be touched, as in human communication. Therefore, we refer to this interaction mode as "GBI."

3.2 Participants

An opportunity sample of 35 participants (21 females and 14 males, mostly students) was selected. The participants' mean age was 25.97 years ($SD = 7.41$, min = 15, max = 48). Four of them had no prior experience with GBI, while 31 had experience with

GBI. None reported low interest in GBI, 18 reported medium interest in GBI, and 17 reported high interest in GBI. There were no restrictions on participation based on VR experience or visual aids; however, participants were not able to wear glasses during the study. This research complied with the tenets of the Declaration of Helsinki, such that informed consent was obtained from each participant.

3.3 Facilities and Apparatus

We used an HTC Vive headset equipped with standard controllers and a built-in eye-tracking system. To implement GBI, we used a Leap Motion controller (https://www.ult raleap.com) that was connected to the HTC Vive and mounted to its front (see Fig. 1). We used a simple application that allows users to perform basic tasks, such as creating 3D blocks, resizing them, and grabbing and moving the created objects (see Fig. 2). We used Unity to implement the blocks application. The experimenter was able to follow all the participants' actions on the connected laptop. We used a video camera to record the performed gestures and the laptop screen to enable analysis of participants' gesturing behavior and the reactions of the system.

3.4 Interaction Tasks

Six tasks were designed for controller and GBI. These tasks were derived from basic tasks that can cover a wide range of possible activities (see Table 1 for details). To ensure that the chosen gestures were appropriate for the selected interaction tasks, a pre-test was conducted with 17 participants using an online questionnaire. Participants were presented with images of different gestures and asked to rate the appropriateness of each gesture for each task. In the present study, we selected six gestures that were rated as highly appropriate for the selected interaction tasks. Table 1 presents the task descriptions and the corresponding gestures or controller actions.

3.5 Procedure

Upon arrival, participants were introduced to the VR device and familiarized with the general usage of the system and devices (see Fig. 1). Each participant was given as much time as necessary to learn and practice all the interaction tasks. Participants were tested repeatedly on their interaction performance to reduce training effects during the experiment and reduce their likelihood of making an incorrect gesture during an interaction task. The functionality of gesture recognition was demonstrated on-screen using an online visualization tool included with the Leap Motion. This demonstration illustrated the device's tracking of the participant's fingers and palm. In the first phase, participants used a small application to familiarize themselves with the HTC Vive.

In the second phase, participants performed tasks using the controllers (as a baseline condition) or using gestures using the Leap Motion device. In the third phase, participants used the other interaction mode to initiate the tasks (see Table 1 for details on the tasks and gestures). Prior to each experimental trial, participants were instructed to perform the interaction task when they felt safe and comfortable doing so (see Fig. 2).

Table 1. Tasks with Corresponding Mid-Air and Controller Gestures.

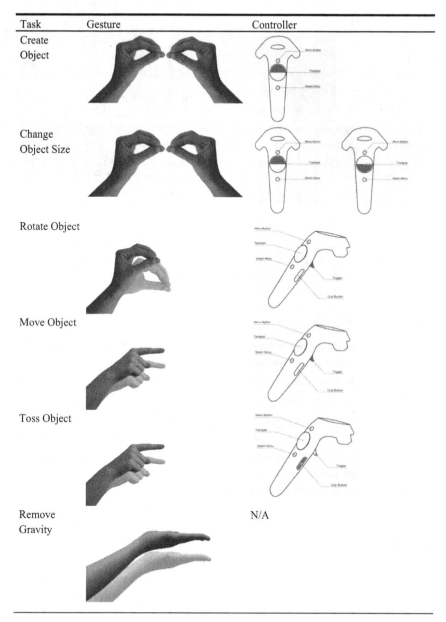

Task	Gesture	Controller
Create Object		
Change Object Size		
Rotate Object		
Move Object		
Toss Object		
Remove Gravity		N/A

After each phase, participants completed a questionnaire about their subjective impressions regarding their most recent interaction, including their trust in and acceptance of the system. At the end of the experiment, participants completed additional

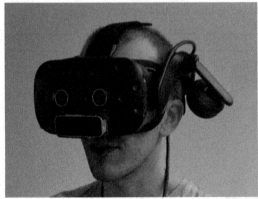 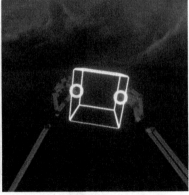

Fig. 1. Setup of HTC Vive with Leap Motion mounted to the front.

Fig. 2. View of the participant in VR

demographic questionnaires, which elicited hand measurements and data on the participant's sense of immersion and simulator sickness. In total, the experiment took approximately 1.5 h per participant.

3.6 Dependent Variables

Participants assessed their trust in the system on a 12-item unidimensional scale (ranging between 1 and 5) from a questionnaire that measures trust in automation (Körber, 2019). The Cronbach's alpha reliability analysis yielded low-to-excellent (cf. Cronbach, 1951) values between $.53 > \alpha < .95$.

Acceptance was measured using a 9-item questionnaire (with a 5-point rating scale ranging from -2 to 2) developed by (Van der Laan et al., 1997). It consists of two subscales: "usefulness" (five items) and "satisfying" (four items). The Cronbach's alpha reached acceptable-to-excellent values of $\alpha = .8$ for the usefulness subscale and $\alpha = .67$ for the satisfying subscale.

Error rates were documented by the examiner during the study. A video recording was made in case analysis was necessary after the study.

4 Results

One task from one participant had to be excluded from the analysis due to a system crash. Because the data were not normally distributed, we calculated Spearman correlations. Correlations were interpreted according to Cohen (1988).

For documented errors, we found very similar rates across genders, with $M = 0.82$ and $SD = 1.18$ for female participants and $M = 0.78$ and $SD = 1.28$ for male participants. We conducted a t-test and found the difference to be non-significant, with $t(33) = 0.29$, $p = .77$. This result indicates that there was no systematic variation in errors between male and female participants. However, it also shows that each participant observed almost one error or malfunction per task performed (see Table 2).

Table 2. Error rates for female and male participants.

Hand measure	Female		Male	
	M = 0.82	1	M = 0.78	SD = 1.28

For acceptance we found $M = 12.9$ and $SD = 4.69$ for overall score and $M = 6.97$ and $SD = 2.94$ for subscale usefulness and $M = 5.97$ and $SD = 2.08$ for subscale satisfying (see Table 3).

Table 3. Score and subscores for acceptance.

Acceptance Scale		
Overall score	$M = 12.9$	$SD = 4.69$
Usefulness	$M = 6.97$	$SD = 2.94$
Satisfying	$M = 5.97$	$SD = 2.08$

For trust we found $M = 53.3$ and $SD = 9.91$ for the overall score, see Table 4 for values for all subscales.

Table 4. Score and subscores for trust.

Trust Scale		
Overall score	$M = 53.3$	$SD = 9.91$
Reliability/ Competence	$M = 21.1$	$SD = 4.16$
Understanding/ Predictability	$M = 15.6$	$SD = 3.96$
Intention of developers	$M = 8.86$	$SD = 2.24$
Familiarity	$M = 5.37$	$SD = 3.14$
Propensity to trust	$M = 10.1$	$SD = 10.58$
Trust in automation	$M = 7.74$	$SD = 1.85$

Table 5 presents Spearman correlations for overall scores and acceptance subscores in relation to trust and error rates, respectively. All correlations between acceptance and error rates were non-significant. We found a significant correlation between overall score for trust and error rates and the perceived trustworthiness subscale and error rates. We obtained non-significant correlations between all other trust subscales and error rates. These correlations were negative, which indicates that higher error rates are associated with lower trust scores.

Table 5. Correlations for acceptance respective trust and error rates.

Correlation investigated	ρ and p values	
Overall acceptance x error rates	$\rho = -0.19$	$p = .253$
Usefulness x error rates	$\rho = -0.17$	$p = .323$
Satisfying x error rates	$\rho = -0.29$	$p = .086$
Overall trust x error rates	$\rho = -0.35$	$p = .041$
Reliability/ competence x error rates	$\rho = -0.32$	$p = .06$
Understanding/ predictability	$\rho = -0.23$	$p = .188$
Intention of developers x error rates	$\rho = -0.17$	$p = .324$
Familiarity x error rates	$\rho = -0.09$	$p = .62$
Propensity to trust x error rates	$\rho = -0.15$	$p = .406$
Trust in automation x error rates	$\rho = -0.02$	$p = .903$
Perceived Trustworthiness x error rates	$\rho = -0.43$	$p = .01$

5 Discussion

In the presented study, we investigated whether errors influence user acceptance and trust in relation to mid-air gestures. As previous studies have shown, gestures are difficult to implement and, therefore, error rates tend to be relatively high. We calculated correlations between error rates and acceptance and trust, respectively. We found no correlation between acceptance and error rates. This result indicates that users' judgements of the acceptability of GBI in our VR setting did not vary based on how many errors they observed. However, we observed a significant negative correlation between overall trust and error rates, which reflects that trust dropped when users observed more errors. This result is interesting, as it shows that gestures remain appealing to users but that there is a need for developers to mitigate issues that lead to system malfunction.

The use of gestures for human–computer interaction is complicated. In previous studies, we found that gestures are attractive, stimulating, well accepted, and trusted by users (Graichen et al., 2019). However, large anatomical differences in hand size and shape, myotonus, and movement performance can make robust gesture recognition difficult. With regard to technological advances and availability of the necessary hardware and software, GBI devices can easily be implemented in different contexts by developers and researchers. Nevertheless, recognition rates for gestures are significantly lower than those obtained when using more traditional interaction modes, such as interfaces with haptic elements or touchscreens. Interestingly, participants do not seem to be significantly disrupted by these errors and maintain positive subjective feelings towards gestures. Nevertheless, gestures take longer than other interaction modes for users to learn. They may have to consult a user manual when implementing them, and they have to remember the gestures used by the system. Unlike touch-based systems, which have applied standards, gesture-based systems do not have an established set of gestures. Thus, the gestures employed may also differ across different systems or applications.

Developers must choose between two paths when implementing GBI. They can design an interaction system with a small number of gestures that users can remember more easily but that are limited in terms of their adaptability to different tasks. Alternatively, they can implement a larger number of gestures, which are more difficult for users to remember but are more adaptable to different tasks.

The present study is limited in scope due to its exploratory nature. Further research is needed to identify why the gesture recognition rate is lower than desired and to find new technical solutions to these problems. Since participants in such studies are often students, it would be important to investigate how attractive and acceptable gestures are to older users, and how gesture recognition works with these user groups. In addition, it would be interesting to examine how hand muscle parameters affect gesture recognition; how users generally perform gestures; how this performance compares to what is expected by gesture recognition developers, algorithms, and devices; and how improvements can be made based on these insights.

References

1. Bolt, R.A.: "Put-That-There": Voice and gesture at the graphics interface. ACM SIGGRAPH Comput. Graph. **14**(3), 262–270 (1980). https://doi.org/10.1145/965105.807503
2. Cohen, J. (1988). Statistical power analysis for the behavioral sciences (2nd ed.). Taylor and Francis. http://gbv.eblib.com/patron/FullRecord.aspx?p=1192162
3. Cronbach, L.J.: Coefficient alpha and the internal structure of tests. Psychometrika **16**(3), 297–334 (1951). https://doi.org/10.1007/BF02310555
4. Dorton, S.L., Harper, S.B.: Self-Repairing and/or buoyant trust in artificial Intelligence. Proc. Hum. Factors Ergonomics Soc. Annu. Meet. **66**(1), 162–166 (2022). https://doi.org/10.1177/1071181322661098
5. Dorton, S.L., Harper, S.B., Neville, K.J.: Adaptations to trust incidents with artificial intelligence. Proc. Hum. Factors Ergonomics Soc. Annu. Meet. **66**(1), 95–99 (2022). https://doi.org/10.1177/1071181322661146
6. Esterwood, C., Robert, L. P. (2022). A literature review of trust repair in HRI. : In 2022 31st IEEE International Conference on Robot and Human Interactive Communication (RO-MAN), pp. 1641–1646. IEEE. https://doi.org/10.1109/RO-MAN53752.2022.9900667
7. Graichen, L., Graichen, M., Krems, J.F.: Evaluation of gesture-based in-vehicle interaction: user experience and the potential to reduce driver distraction. Hum. Factors: J. Hum. Factors Ergonomics Soc. **61**(5), 774–792 (2019). https://doi.org/10.1177/0018720818824253
8. He, S., Yang, C., Wang, M., Cheng, L., Hu, Z. (2017). Hand gesture recognition using MYO armband. : In 2017 Chinese Automation Congress (CAC), pp. 4850–4855. IEEE. https://doi.org/10.1109/CAC.2017.8243637
9. Kao, H.L., Dementyev, A., Paradiso, J. A., Schmandt, C. (2015). NailO: Fingernails as an input surface. : In B. Begole, J. Kim, K. Inkpen, W. Woo (Eds.), Proceedings of the 33rd Annual ACM Conference on Human Factors in Computing Systems, pp. 3015–3018. ACM. https://doi.org/10.1145/2702123.2702572
10. Körber, M.: Theoretical considerations and development of a questionnaire to measure trust in automation. In: Bagnara, S., Tartaglia, R., Albolino, S., Alexander, T., Fujita, Y. (eds.) IEA 2018. AISC, vol. 823, pp. 13–30. Springer, Cham (2018). https://doi.org/10.1007/978-3-319-96074-6_2
11. Kraus, J., Scholz, D., Stiegemeier, D., Baumann, M.: The more you know: trust dynamics and calibration in highly automated driving and the effects of take-overs, system malfunction,

and system transparency. Hum. Factors: J. Hum. Factors Ergonomics Soc. **62**(5), 718–736 (2020). https://doi.org/10.1177/0018720819853686

12. Lee, J., Abe, G., Sato, K., Itoh, M.: Developing human-machine trust: Impacts of prior instruction and automation failure on driver trust in partially automated vehicles. Transport. Res. F: Traffic Psychol. Behav. **81**, 384–395 (2021). https://doi.org/10.1016/j.trf.2021.06.013

13. Leng, H. Y., Norowi, N. M., Jantan, A. H. (2017). A user-defined gesture set for music interaction in immersive virtual environment. : In E. Sari A. B. Tedjasaputra (Eds.), Proceedings of the 3rd International Conference on Human-Computer Interaction and User Experience in Indonesia, pp. 44–51. ACM. https://doi.org/10.1145/3077343.3077348

14. Loehmann, S., Knobel, M., Lamara, M., Butz, A.: Culturally independent gestures for in-car interactions. In: Kotzé, P., Marsden, G., Lindgaard, G., Wesson, J., Winckler, M. (eds.) Human-Computer Interaction – INTERACT 2013: 14th IFIP TC 13 International Conference, Cape Town, South Africa, September 2-6, 2013, Proceedings, Part III, pp. 538–545. Springer Berlin Heidelberg, Berlin, Heidelberg (2013). https://doi.org/10.1007/978-3-642-40477-1_34

15. Mishler, S., Chen, J.: Effect of automation failure type on trust development in driving automation systems. Appl. Ergon. **106**, 103913 (2023). https://doi.org/10.1016/j.apergo.2022.103913

16. Narayana, P., et al.: Cooperating with avatars through gesture, language and action. In: Arai, K., Kapoor, S., Bhatia, R. (eds.) Intelligent Systems and Applications: Proceedings of the 2018 Intelligent Systems Conference (IntelliSys) Volume 1, pp. 272–293. Springer International Publishing, Cham (2019). https://doi.org/10.1007/978-3-030-01054-6_20

17. O'hara, K., Harper, R., Mentis, H., Sellen, A., Taylor, A.: On the naturalness of touchless: Putting the "interaction" back into NUI. ACM Trans. Comput.-Hum. Interact. **20**(1), 1–25 (2013). https://doi.org/10.1145/2442106.2442111

18. Pfeiffer, T.: 54. Documentation of gestures with data gloves. In: Müller, C., Cienki, A., Fricke, E., Ladewig, S., McNeill, D., Tessendorf, S. (eds.) Handbücher zur Sprach- und Kommunikationswissenschaft / Handbooks of Linguistics and Communication Science (HSK) 38/1:, pp. 868–879. DE GRUYTER (2013). https://doi.org/10.1515/9783110261318.868

19. Pfeiffer, T. (2013b). Documentation of gestures with motion capture. In C. Müller, A. Cienki, E. Fricke, S. Ladewig, D. McNeill, S. Teßendorf (Eds.), Handbücher zur Sprachund Kommunikationswissenschaft: Band 38.2. Body - Language - Communication: An International Handbook on Multimodality In Human Interaction. Volume 1, pp. 857–867. Walter de Gruyter GmbH

20. Piumsomboon, T., Clark, A., Billinghurst, M., Cockburn, A. (2013). User-defined gestures for augmented reality. In: W. Mackay, S. Brewster, S. Bødker, & W. E. Mackay (Eds.), Proceedings of the SIGCHI Conference on Human Factors in Computing Systems (CHI '13). Extended Abstracts. 27 April - 2 May 2013, Paris, France, p. 955. ACM. https://doi.org/10.1145/2468356.2468527

21. Premaratne, P.: Human computer interaction using hand gestures. Springer Singapore, Singapore (2014)

22. Pustejovksy, J., et al.: Interpreting and generating gestures with embodied. Hum. Comput. Interact. (2020). https://doi.org/10.5281/zenodo.4088625

23. Rakkolainen, I., et al.: Technologies for multimodal interaction in extended reality - A scoping review. Multimodal Technol. Interact. **5**(12), 81 (2021). https://doi.org/10.3390/mti5120081

24. Rodriguez, G., Jofre, N., Alvarado, Y., Fernández, J., Guerrero, R.: Gestural interaction for virtual reality environments through data gloves. Adv. Sci., Technol. Eng. Syst. J. **2**(3), 284–290 (2017). https://doi.org/10.25046/aj020338

25. Saffer, D. (2008). Designing gestural interfaces. O'Reilly Media, Inc.

26. Seeling, T., Dittrich, F., Bullinger, A. C. (2018). Digitales Gestenmanual zur Gestaltung einer natürlichen gestenbasierten Interaktion zwischen Mensch und Maschine. In Gesellschaft für Arbeitswissenschaft (Chair), Frühjahrskongress 2018, Frankfurt am Main

27. Seeling, T., Fricke, E., Lynn, U., Schöller, D., Bullinger, A.C. (2016). Gestenbasierte Google-Earth-Bedienung: Implikationen für ein natürliches Gesten-Set am Beispiel einer 3D-Topographieanwendung. In Gesellschaft für Arbeitswissenschaft (Ed.), Dokumentation des 62. Arbeitswissenschaftlichen Kongresses: Arbeit in komplexen Systemen - Digital, vernetzt, human?!. GfA-Press

28. Tolmeijer, S., Gadiraju, U., Ghantasala, R., Gupta, A., Bernstein, A. (2021). Second chance for a first impression? Trust development in intelligent system interaction. In: J. Masthoff, E. Herder, N. Tintarev, & M. Tkalčič (Eds.), Proceedings of the 29th ACM Conference on User Modeling, Adaptation and Personalization, pp. 77–87. ACM. https://doi.org/10.1145/3450613.3456817

29. LaanVan der, J.D., Heino, A., de Waard, D.: A simple procedure for the assessment of acceptance of advanced transport telematics. Transp. Res. Part C: Emerg. Technol. 5(1), 1 (1997). https://doi.org/10.1016/S0968-090X(96)00025-3

30. Wigdor, D., Wixon, D. (Eds.). (2011). Safari Tech Books Online. Brave NUI world: Designing natural user interfaces for touch and gesture. Morgan Kaufmann/Elsevier

31. Kun, Y., Berkovsky, S., Conway, D., Taib, R., Zhou, J., Chen, F.: Do I Trust a Machine? Differences in User Trust Based on System Performance. In: Zhou, J., Chen, F. (eds.) Human and Machine Learning, pp. 245–264. Springer International Publishing, Cham (2018). https://doi.org/10.1007/978-3-319-90403-0_12

A Bi-national Investigation of the Needs of Visually Disabled People from Mexico and Japan

Alexandro del Valle$^{(\boxtimes)}$, Zilu Liang, and Ian Piumarta

Kyoto University of Advanced Science, Ukyo Ward, Kyoto 615-8577, Japan
`2022mm04@kuas.ac.jp`

Abstract. Around 2,200 million (2.2 billion) people have some level of visual disabilities, of which 2 million are in Mexico and 13 million in Japan. These significant communities face challenges in several aspects of their lives including risks when travelling, lack of alternative means of communication, and discrimination in their schools or workspaces. We conducted interviews and focus groups to investigate the needs and frustrations of people with visual disabilities in Mexico (State of Mexico and Mexico City) and Japan (Kyoto city) members of foundations, organizations, schools or acquaintances in the areas of mobility, safety, and everyday interactions within public spaces. According to their responses through thematic analysis we identify several opportunities for technical developments to support their needs, including for the digital devices through which they interface with the real world, and propose several technological solutions to address the problems they confront.

Keywords: Visual disabilities · User centered design · Assistive technology

1 Introduction

According to the World Health Organization in the International Classification of Diseases 11 of 2018 (ICD-11), visual disability is the consequence of an illness or condition that affects the visual system and its functionality, in which they are classified according to their severity. For example, the ICD-11 defines nine categories ranging from "No vision impairment" to "Total Blindness" and a special category for "Near vision impairment", where the focus of this paper is the Severe vision impairment and Total Blindness, meaning that a person has a vision acuity of 20/200 (division of near and distant vision expressed in feet), and Total Blindness where a person has no light perception. Approximately 2,200 million (2.2 billion) people have some level of visual disabilities, ranging from mild to severe. Around two million people in Mexico (415, 800 having total blindness) and 13 million in Japan (397,000 with total blindness) [1] suffer from visual impairment. These two countries have contrasting differences and similarities in terms of technology and society. For instance, Japan is representative of a technologically advanced country offering a high level of health care services, whereas Mexico tends to present areas of opportunity in those aspects.

H. P. da Silva and P. Cipresso (Eds.): CHIRA 2023, CCIS 1996, pp. 244–261, 2023.
https://doi.org/10.1007/978-3-031-49425-3_15

Additionally, their distribution of population is different with Japan having most elderly people unlike Mexico that has a relatively young population. To illustrate the average age in Japan is 48.6 years whereas in Mexico it is 29.3 years with age an important contributing factor to visual disabilities such as Glaucoma. This sector of the community faces challenges in several aspects of daily life including elevated risks when travelling, reduced access to communication media, and discrimination in their schools or workplaces.

In Mexico the NOM-034-STPS-2016 [2] regulation supports disabled people, setting standards of infrastructure, safety, and hygiene to ensure disabled workers can carry out their work in a safe and dignified manner. The Mexican government also provides a monthly stipend (the Bienestar pension) of 1,475 MXN (approximately 86 USD) [3] to disabled people who apply to the program.

The Bienestar pension is insufficient to cover the basic expenses. A basic basket of goods, for example costs 2,144 MXN (17,103 JPY, 120 USD) [4] Several disabled people therefore have difficulty meeting the cost of living without support from other family members. Cities in Mexico also have opportunities to improve accessibility for blind people to parks and sidewalks, which do not have tactile guidelines (such as the ubiquitous raised yellow blocks in Japan) and are often blocked by street stalls.

Subway stations in Mexico City usually do not have guard rails to prevent people from falling onto the tracks [5]. Likewise, in Japan many train stations do not have a barrier between the platform and the train tracks, although more Japanese stations have been installing such barriers in recent years.

In Japan the Convention for People with Disabilities ensures their access to health, privacy, and opportunities for dignified work. The Ministry of Foreign Affairs publishes a declaration of this convention online and articles 24, 25, and 27 (Education, Health, Work and Employment) [6] recognize the rights of disabled people to education, without discrimination and based on equal opportunity, ensuring an inclusive education system. Furthermore, the right to the enjoyment of the highest attainable standard of health is recognized without discrimination based on disability and ensuring access to health services that are gender sensitive, including rehabilitation. Finally, the right to gain a living by working freely, in a labor market and work environment that is open, inclusive and accessible, is also recognized.

Companies in both countries have developed and implemented more policies to include people with disabilities in their work teams, opening employment opportunities to them. In Mexico the automotive companies have created inclusivity programs for hiring professionals with disabilities. Ford of Mexico, for example, has a new facility called GTBC (Global Technology and Business Center) that provides proper accommodations for disabled people [7]. Nissan Mexicana's facilities in Aguascalientes also provide measures and signalling for deaf people [8]. Nonetheless, there are still opportunities to improve aids for blind people. The locations just mentioned do not describe equipment or implement signs in Braille, nor do they have tactile paving to support workers with visual disabilities. In Japan companies such as the FP Company have initiatives to support employees with disabilities by providing inclusive working environments [9]. IBM Japan develops technology to support blind people, for example, a 'smart suitcase' guide that helps its users to navigate airports safely [10].

Mexico and Japan have several Non-Profit Organizations and volunteer groups that support people with visual disabilities in different aspects of their daily lives. In Mexico, for example:

- Halcones Blind Runners Group is a branch of Achilles International where people with visual disabilities learn mobility skills through running with a visually able guide who helps them to avoid collisions [11].
- Fundación Zotoluco A.C (Zotoluco Foundation for Blind Children) is a non-profit foundation that provides visually disabled children and teenagers with afterschool classes and workshops that teach braille, mobility skills without using white canes, mathematics, and informatics [12].
- Fundación Devlyn (Devlyn Foundation) is a non-profit organization founded by Devlyn Opticals, a company that sells prescription glasses and provides optometry services. The foundation organizes awareness campaigns, donating lenses and making optometry services accessible to people with limited resources [13].

    In Japan, for example:

- Kyoto Lighthouse is a Social-Welfare corporation that provides services such as braille publishing, life care, and employment support, among other services [14].
- Porini Company is a Welfare business that trains guide helpers and volunteers to travel with blind people, often to new and unfamiliar places, who cannot find their way easily among other daily life activities [15].
- Hitomachi Koryukan Kyoto (People and Town Exchange Center Kyoto) is a Community facility in Kyoto consisting of four centers: Citizen Activity General Center, Welfare Volunteer Center, Longevity Health Center, and the Landscape and Community Development Center where volunteers from Porini company and other foundations visit to assist people with visual disabilities [16].

In the rest of this paper we explore the needs of people with visual disabilities from a binational perspective gained through interviews that were performed in Mexico and in Japan, with participants that have or are somehow related to visual impairments. Interview questions explored mobility, safety, infrastructure, and the participants' personal concerns when interacting with public spaces. The results of the interviews are analyzed to find technological opportunities for new devices and new infrastructure that would support blind people or others with any degree of vision loss. In Sect. 2 we present a review of related work. Section 3 describes the methodology of our interviews. Section 4 presents our thematic analysis of the results. Section 5 suggests proposals based on the needs identified by the participants of our interviews. Section 6 offers some discussion and conclusions.

2 Related Work

The needs of people with visual disabilities have been a concern throughout the years, more so due to the advance of legislation in favor of their rights and the development of inclusive environments. Moreover, every country has done so according to the Status Quo of their societies, national law and international conventions, and so several efforts have been made to understand their requirements and provide recommendations on policies and technologies to satisfy them. Therefore, in this section, we describe previous publications that have focused on discovering the needs of people with visual disabilities in both countries through interviews, surveys and literature reviews.

Schools in Japan throughout the recent years have made efforts to form environments suitable for children and teenagers with visual disabilities to support their best interest in education. An estimated of 67 schools support students with visual disabilities as of the year 2020, Miyauchi and Matsuda [17] performed a thematic analysis on qualitative data from reports of the APSB and the homepages of the schools mentioned in the publication. The results of their analysis produced a classification of the activities into two themes "Activities targeted to individuals with Visual Impairments" and "Activities targeted to the environment of individuals with Visual Impairments". These themes relate to our work by showing the actions taken to satisfy the needs of people with visual disabilities in education, while our work performs a thematical analysis on the needs of people with visual disabilities interviewed, additionally the second theme "Activities targeted to the environment proposed by Miyauchi and Matsuda is also very relevant to one of the themes proposed in our work, "Infrastructure needs" mentioned in the Methodology section which demonstrates how the environment affects the interviewee and how some of the efforts to assist them rely on the spaces rather than on the person himself/herself. (Miyauchi and Matsuda, 2022).

Additionaly, (Nishimura, et al., 2022) [18] through an interview with teachers of special classes for students with visual disabilities, from elementary to lower secondary school obtained insights on the current situation of the study environment, faculty preparation and tools used by children and teenagers with low vision, namely Braille, magnifying glasses, light blocking filters and ICTs (Information and Communication Technologies) to learn. Their results demonstrated that vision problems are increasing, writing systems like Braille are decreasing, and that further investigation is needed to understand in-depth the influence of the teacher's experience on the students' level of achievement as some of the subjects stated they had no more than three years of training for special class education.

On the other hand, in the Mexican context, García Llamas posited similar research to analyze the needs of students with visual disabilities, however he focused on six elementary students and instead of collecting data through literature reviews, he developed an observation framework and conducted in-depth interviews [19]. As a result, the research obtained the ways in which they learn how to explore the environment, and the strategies to follow when a student is having difficulties learning and socializing. In addition, this information informs the thematic analysis of our work in which the mobility and security needs of the interviewees in both countries were investigated, more so regarding the infrastructural needs where, for example, one group of interviewees explained that their children had difficulties studying in regular schools where the use of a white cane is forbidden for them.

Furthermore, in Mexican universities people with visual disabilities face challenges to achieve higher education with a bachelor's degree or graduate degree, in which several factors determine how educational institutions receive and support students with visual disabilities, namely law regulations, faculty and infrastructure. Villa et al. [20] not that postmodernity does not allow inclusion of democracy when discrimination is still present in jurisprudence social, economic, and political frameworks. Their publication refers to a literature review of the current law in Mexico as well as interviews with the 79 students of the Universidad Autónoma de Guerrero in Mexico who live with disabilities including motor, hearing, cognitive, and two with visual impairments. As a result, the study revealed that this University has room for improvement to provide students with the best strategies and infrastructure to support their education. Therefore, the importance of understanding the needs of people with disabilities and the creation of inclusive environments is evident.

3 Methodology

Material for our thematic analysis was collected through semi-structured, open-ended interviews with blind and visually impaired participants in Mexico and Japan. The interviews and focus groups were conducted in Mexico City and the Metropolitan region of the State of Mexico. In Japan the interviews were conducted in Kyoto City. These cities were selected for being, in the case of Mexico, the main urban area of the country where most of its population is located, where a higher concentration of foundations and organizations can be found. In Japan Kyoto city was selected as being one of the most important cities of the country and as home to several organizations that are close to the community. Kyoto lighthouse, Tokyo lighthouse, etc., are organizations that exist in all major areas of Japan, and function in similar ways, so that the laws that support people with visual disabilities are applied in a uniform manner. Data analysis generated local insight into the needs of people with visual disabilities in these communities and may not necessarily reflect the national trends of both countries.

4 Participants

In Mexico we informally recruited participants from foundations and groups who typically had family members and friends in common. Firstly, the Zotoluco Foundation was contacted through the Monterrey Institute of Technology, where a group of families have children who attended their after-school classes. Secondly, the running group Halcones: Blind Runners and other interviewees in Mexico were contacted through friends and colleagues of the interviewer.

In contrast, the interviewees in Japan were recruited from two institutions that were approached through formal contact from our University. The first institution, Porini Company, supported the interviews by providing five participants who either use Porini to obtain help from sighted guides or who volunteer for the company. The second institution, Kyoto Prefectural High School for the blind, provided three teachers, all of whom have visual disabilities, to participate in the interviews. These interviewees are notable because they are people who, in addition to having visual impairments, also carry out significant activities to support other members of the visually impaired community.

Table 1 presents detailed information about the participants. Participants are anonymized to protect their privacy. Background gives a very brief description of the organization, their activities and, in the case of the interviewees, their occupation and the cause for their loss of vision. Age range places each participant into a general category of child or adult, since more precise identification of age is irrelevant in the scope of the present study. Interactions with participants in both countries were classified into two types, focus groups or interviews, shown in the final columns as the Type of participation. Interviewee 3 was a friend of a person who lives with a visual disability and was included as a secondary but valuable source of relevant information.

Table 1. Participants in Mexico (M = Male, F = Female).

Participant	Background
MX1 (M)	Retired public servant. Blind 7 years ago
MX2 (M)	Singer of the Mexico City Gay Chorus, partially blind
MX3 (F)	Office worker, blind from birth
Zotoluco Foundation	Foundation to support blind children with Braille, IT and mobility after school classes
Halcones: Blind Runners	Group of people with visual disabilities and voluntary helpers that train to run in races and marathons

In the same manner, the participants in Japan are presented in Table 2. Data were collected through semi-structured interviews and no focus groups were organized. All participants were adults.

Table 2 .

Participant	Background
JP1 (M)	Acupuncturist on a self-owned clinic, he had a partial visual disability since he was 6 years old. He became totally blind 5 years ago due to Glaucoma
JP2 (M)	Massagist, guide helper and volunteer on Porini Company. (Care provider)
JP3 (M)	Massagist, guide helper and volunteer on Porini Company. (Care provider)
JP4 (M)	Office worker in a well-being company, totally blind since birth
JP5 (F)	Massagist, she has lived with a visual disability from 20 years on due to Glaucoma, she has still low vision remaining
JP6 (M)	Vice principal of the Kyoto Prefectural School for the Blind (Care provider)
JP7 (F)	Professor at the Kyoto Prefectural School for the Blind, Physiotherapist, develops braille documents and practices eastern medicine. She became totally blind around 2 years ago due to retinoblastoma (Care provider)
JP8 (M)	Professor at the Kyoto Prefectural School for the Blind, he has a partial visual disability due to retinal detachment that caused him to lose one eye. (Care provider)
JP9 (M)	Professor at the Kyoto Prefectural School for the Blind, Physiotherapist (Care provider)

4.1 Data Collection

Our study is qualitative in nature because we aimed to gain a deep and detailed understanding of the preferences, experiences, and frustrations of the interview subjects, by focusing on a representative cohort of reasonable size and conducting interviews of relatively long duration (typically between 60 and 120 min). The data collection process varied slightly between the two countries. Data was collected through semi-structured interviews in both countries, whereas focus groups were only used in Mexico.

The interviews in Mexico were performed with a non-standard approach since some of them were opportunistic, occurring in unplanned circumstances where the interviewee was introduced to us on the same day as their interview. The structure of the questions therefore varied. Conversation was left open to the interviewee and the answers could not be recorded. Moreover, one of the participants was a secondary source, meaning that the person was a friend of someone who lives with a blind person, therefore the answers provided were not from first-hand experience. The two focus groups were also performed with a non-standard approach. For example, the conversation with the running group Halcones was performed in two separate conversations, the first while training with the participants and understanding their difficulties while running and the second as a final discussion with all the member in a round-table format.

In the case of Japan, a language barrier presented an obstacle for the interview process which was therefore conducted with an interpreter who helped to communicate effectively with the participants. The interviews were also implemented using a semistructured approach, using a pre-determined set of seed questions but with the expectation of obtaining open answers, letting the participants speak freely if they wanted to volunteer any information, they thought relevant. The questions asked how the participants travelled daily, whether they used public transportation, if they travelled alone or with a guide helper, if they had a guide dog, and which technologies or electronic devices they use. For example, when discussing technologies participants might talk about white canes, raised tactile 'Tenji' blocks, Braille documents, or about electronic devices that can detect objects or provide users with positional information, or about smartphone applications. To illustrate, white canes are navigation or identification tools that aid people with severe vision loss or total blindness to explore their surroundings. Moreover, canes are divided into different types. Namely, Identification Canes, Mobility Canes, and Support Canes. For example, Identification Canes are long straight and white canes that serve only to identify (with no mobility support to the user) by its white tone and sometimes reflective material so that nearby people can help or walk cautiously next to them. Secondly, Mobility Canes, in contrast with the previous aid supports the users with a thicker body and a sliding tip to help users suffering severe vision loss to identify textures and obstacles on the floor. Thirdly, support canes which are the strongest of the three mentioned, this cane provides stability support for people with a physical disability in addition to vision loss, and also feature a white tone and a reflective material to signal that the user has a visual disability. As mentioned previously, the questions were specific but also open for the interviewees to provide as much detail as they wished and also any additional information that could enrich the conversation such as their likes and dislikes, and the difficulties they encounter related to these topics. We also asked additional questions when interviewing teachers, guides, or health professionals that carry out activities related to visual impairments. For example, their questions also covered the roles, activities, and special training that may be involved, and similarly the types of technologies that they may use such as Braille or specific educational software.

5   Results

The interview responses provided by the participants in both countries were reviewed and subjected to a thematic analysis (Nowell, Norris, et al., 2017) [21].

5.1   Thematic Analysis

Through thematic analysis we identified four prevailing themes: *Mobility*, *Safety*, *Emotional support*, and *Infrastructure*. These themes in particular were identified as covering the largest number of everyday concerns in the most condensed manner, given that life itself is multifactorial with diverse situations such as commuting, buying food, working, studying, and interactions with technologies that we use for many activities that apply equally to people with visual disabilities, perhaps while taking into account the particularities of the challenges or inconveniences they face.

Other themes generated in the analysis were *Independence* and *Technology Interaction*. Independence would consider that people with visual disabilities might lose their independence when travelling because they can be at increased risk and they therefore often travel with someone else when visiting unfamiliar locations. Technology Interaction would cover how the participants interact with all the of the technologies that surround them; for example, the 'apps' that they use to control their mobile phones or social media and the diverse equipment they might use while travelling including a white cane, object detection devices, GPS locators, and so on. These two themes were however rejected because the first one overlapped with other factors such as safety and the material conditions of mobility and therefore it was sub-divided into those two independent themes. Technology Interaction considered only the equipment the participants used or wore, but not what other technologies were present in their environment, meaning things outside of their control or not on their person. For example, raised tactile '*Tenji*' blocks on sidewalks and in other public spaces, speech interfaces in shopping malls, and braille buttons on signs in government buildings. These themes therefore exemplify how the interviewees travel, their security concerns, how they feel about the material conditions of their environment and the technologies they have access to, as well as the deficiencies they found in the infrastructure of the public spaces they encounter daily. Additionally, the convergences of themes was also considered, for example, a situation in which mobility is blocked due to an obstacle that puts the safety of the person at risk is a convergence between Mobility and Safety Needs.

The interview responses were analyzed with the results from the focus groups being considered as complementary. In the following tables we show examples of the classification of needs analyzed from the answers of the participants. In the first column we show the results from the interviews in Mexico, reserving the complementary results from the focus groups for additional consideration in the discussion section later. In the second column we show the results from the interviews with the Japanese participants. The commonalities and differences between the two communities will also be further addressed in the discussion section.

Tables 3, 4, 5 and 6 respectively list the Mobility, Safety, Emotional and Infrastructure needs expressed by the participants from both Mexico and Japan. They itemize the most recurrent specific issues within each theme and illustrate which issues match most closely between the two countries.

Table 3. Examples of Mobility Needs.

Mexico	Japan
Mexican public transportation does not implement enough measurements for blind users (Subway stations only implement braille)	Travelling on public transportation alone to unknown places
White canes get stuck in the sidewalks	White canes break easily and get stuck on sidewalks
There are no Tenji blocks in the streets	Travelling to places with precise guidance from Map applications

Table 4. Examples of Safety Needs.

Mexico	Japan
People with visual disabilities can be targets for robbery	Common accidents with pedestrians and bicycles
Sink holes on streets provoke accidents when walking with a white cane	There are train stations with no gates or fences on the platforms
Street signs and building structures hang low resulting in them hitting their heads	There are stoplights without sound alert

Analyzing the interviewees' needs revealed overlaps whenever responses fit into more than one theme. For example, when the interviewee mentions that they have struggled with walking with the white cane on the streets, because it gets stuck in bicycle wheels, both their mobility and safety are affected at the same time. Similarly, when the participant explains that they cannot use white canes in their schools, requiring their parent to attend the class with them, both an emotional and infrastructure need arises because the child is forced to be dependent on their parents and the conditions in the

Table 5. Examples of Emotional Needs.

Mexico	Japan
Guide dogs provide a sense of companionship	Guide dogs help their owners to communicate with others by overhearing what they say to their dog
Children attending regular schools need their parents to attend classes to take notes	They lose personal belongings easily when they are flat or are printed papers
Some people with visual disabilities do not like to be seen as "disabled"	Guide dogs being living creatures have a finite lifespan whose owners outlive causing them to feel sadness when they pass away

Table 6. Examples of Infrastructure Needs.

Mexico	Japan
Public spaces lack braille signs and other inclusive measurements for people with any disability	Public spaces lack braille signs
Children attending regular schools are not allowed to use white canes	Shopping in convenience stores is difficult as products do not have braille and the clerks are stationed in the counter
Stoplights do not have sound warnings in general	Printed mail from the governments does not have braille text

schools are not regulated to provide learning materials for students with visual disabilities. Figure 1 presents a Venn diagram visually representing how the themes interact with each other.

In Fig. 1, the labels for the overlapping themes are ME for Mobility with Emotional, MS for Mobility with Safety, IS for Infrastructure and Safety, and IE for Infrastructure with Emotional. The overlap of all the needs, which would be MSEI, is not shown because there were no answers which covered all the needs simultaneously.

A thematic analysis of the individual interviewee for participants from Mexico is shown in Table 7. The number of occurrences of each need is indicated for each interview, including overlapping themes.

Complementary results from the focus groups related to the interviews in Table 7 will be addressed in the discussion section.

Table 8 shows the thematic analysis of the needs per interviewee for the participants in Japan.

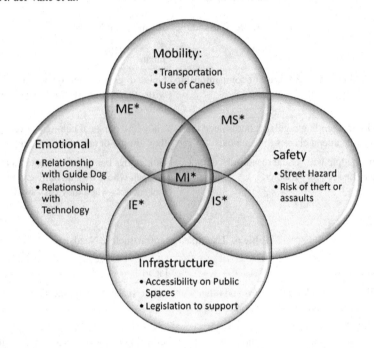

ME:
- Relationship with public transportation
- Feelings when travelling as people with visual disabilities

MS:
- Safety Measures on transportation means
- Hazards when travelling

IE:
- Relationship with public spaces
- Hostile or inclusive architecture

IS:
- Safety Measures on transportation means
- Hazards when travelling

MI:
- Efficiency of Public Transportation
- Hostile or inclusive architecture

Fig. 1. Classification of themes and their correlation.

Table 7. Groups of needs per interviewee in Mexico.

Themes	MX1	MX2	MX3
Mobility	3	1	1
Safety	4	1	1
Emotional	2	1	1
Infrastructure	5	0	1
MI	1	1	1
MS	1	1	1
ME	1	0	0
IE	0	0	1
IS	1	0	0

Table 8. Groups of needs per interviewee in Japan.

Themes	JP1	JP2	JP3	JP4	JP5	JP6	JP7	JP8
Mobility	2	3	2	2	2	3	1	2
Safety	2	1	1	2	2	2	0	1
Emotional	0	0	1	1	1	1	0	1
Infrastructure	3	6	3	4	3	2	1	3
MI	2	0	0	1	1	0	0	0
MS	2	1	1	0	0	0	0	0
ME	0	0	1	0	1	0	0	0
IE	0	0	0	0	0	0	0	0
IS	0	1	0	0	0	0	0	0

6   Discussion

The most common theme found within the responses in both countries was Infrastructure. Most of the difficulties encountered are related to public spaces. In other words, they are lacking in terms of inclusion, or they are designed with hostile architecture (de Fine Licht, 2017) [22], whether intentionally or not, or they are insecure. For example, in both countries some subway stations in some cities do not have barriers on the platforms to prevent people falling onto the rails. Moreover, some streets in both countries lack sidewalks, or the sidewalks are too narrow for people to walk with a white cane. White canes can also become stuck in sewer gratings or collide with trash cans placed in the walker's path or with vehicles parked on the sidewalk.

The most common Mobility need is related to travelling alone to unfamiliar places. People from both countries would like to travel freely without relying on someone to guide them through new locations and public transportation, so they can reduce their living costs and avoid risks. Another commonality is the use, or lack of use, of guide dogs which are not a common means of guidance.

In Mexico none of the participants had a guide dog and some of them mentioned that the cost of supporting one was too high for them to afford. According to the *Escuela para Entrenamiento de Perros Guía para Ciegos I.A.P* (Guide dog Training School, an organization in Mexico and Latin America that raises, trains, and provides dogs for people with any visual disability) the cost for a guide dog from birth to its retirement, assuming nine years of service, is approximately 30,000 USD, a cost that certain sectors of the population cannot afford. Their utility is also often reduced since there are still public spaces and businesses that do not allow guide dogs, despite the 58th Article of the Federal Law of Consumer's Rights Protection that prohibits any business to deny entrance to people accompanied by these dogs.

Among the participants in Japan only JP5 had a guide dog. According to the Japan Guide Dog Association, around 1,000 guide dogs are in active service nationally. As mentioned by the interviewees, some restrictions are imposed on owners of these dogs when entering public spaces. International visitors entering Japan also face restrictions. According to the Ministry of Health, Labour and Welfare, only dogs trained by the International Guide Dog Association are allowed entry to the country. Additionally, guide dogs are a source of companionship and support for both communities. Even though the Mexican participants have not owned one, they mentioned an interest in adopting one in the event they can afford the cost. Moreover, guide dogs also help their owners to communicate indirectly with other people in their surroundings by overhearing the conversation between the owner and their dog. For example, Int 5 mentioned that whenever she needed to ask about a product in a store she talked to the dog about it and then the clerk, or another customer, overheard the conversation and approached her to help her to buy the product.

A difference between Mexico and Japan arises in the use of white canes. Most participants from both countries mentioned that they use a white cane, but significantly fewer people in Mexico use one. For example, two participants that do not use the cane are MX1 and MX3. As mentioned in the participant overview, MX1 is a public servant who had to retire from his position due to glaucoma. He mentioned that he does not like using the white cane for three reasons. Firstly, he learned how to walk around his house without the cane and can navigate any room without aid. Secondly, he suffered accidents due to the cane becoming stuck in the sidewalks.

Thirdly, for his security, he does not want to be visible as a person with disabilities. As described above in the interviewee list, MX3 was born blind. Her friend, who participated in the interview as a secondary source, explains that she does not like using the cane because she always goes out with someone else who can help her to navigate through any space. She therefore has no need to use the white cane. Taking into account the complementary information provided by the focus group at Zotoluco Foundation, they mentioned that the children do not use a cane for two main reasons.

Firstly, the use of canes is not permitted within the premises of the schools they attend (public elementary schools) because the school authorities deem them to be a security risk for both the users and their classmates. The children therefore learn to orient themselves and find their belongings in familiar spaces without using a cane. Furthermore, one participant from the focus group Halcones México explained that he does not like to use a cane because it gets stuck on the sewers in the street and he would prefer a solution that does not require physical contact with the ground. Moreover, he also mentioned that he wears a baseball hat to mitigate the dangers of a white cane not detecting obstacles at head level.

In terms of technological support, another conclusion from the interview responses is that relatively few of the participants mentioned that they know or use any specialized devices such as object detectors, smart white canes, or tactile displays. Only MX1 and JP1 and JP4, mentioned using technical devices of those kinds. MX1said that he knew about object detectors using sonar sensors, as well as smartphone applications. JP1 demonstrated that he was using a "Palm Sonar", a handheld object detection device using ultra-sonic sensors to obtain the distance between the user and an obstacle, and through vibration alerting the user about the object ahead and to proceed with caution. JP4 explained that he uses a braille electronic interface that helps him to take notes and to convert text to audible speech, among other features.

We also observed that our study suffered from some constraints and limitations.

In Mexico the interviews were conducted using a non-standard approach, since some of the conversations took place in unplanned circumstances. Meeting an interviewee and conducting their interview on the same day permitted the structure of the questions to vary. The flow of the conversation was also left open to the interviewees, but their answers could not be recorded. One of the participants was a secondary source, meaning that the interviewee was a friend of someone living with a blind person and their answers were therefore not from direct personal experience.

In Japan the language barrier was an obstacle necessitating the use of an interpreter to help communicate effectively with the participants. Furthermore, the surveys were performed in a semi-structured manner, thus the conversation was kept open to allow the participants to provide information that they considered important or relevant even though the survey might not have a question about the topic that was being discussed.

Finally, the use of the word 'emotional' (as in "Emotional need") may be too broad and extend beyond the scope of technology and human-machine interactions. This term is nevertheless used to have a theme for the needs of people with visual disabilities who mentioned how they felt regarding their mobility or safety, or when they interacted with a specific service, technology, or with a certain public space.

7 Future Work

The first proposals address Mobility, Safety, and Infrastructure. In both countries there are streets without proper sidewalks and, as mentioned by the participants, their white canes become stuck in sewers and collide with other obstacles including trashcans and parked vehicles. A widening of the walkways may improve their mobility and avoid risks of accidents. Moreover, in the case of Mexico, streets could have tactile, raised 'Tenji' blocks installed at crossings to prevent the pedestrians from passing the waiting area without realizing they are now in the middle of the street causing cars to have to stop abruptly. In Japan, specifically in Kyoto, some streets have lampposts in the middle of the sidewalk that risk blocking the path of blind pedestrians who can collide and harm themselves and relocating them may be a solution allowing them to walk freely. Regarding potential technological approaches, object detectors would be reliable only for the front of the user thus not preventing collisions with electric poles or street signals that hang at head level. Therefore, an expansion to the sensors' capabilities and their locations is desirable. A modification to the means of communication to alert the user would also be welcomed. As mentioned by the interviewees, audible alerts can be uncomfortable and may block their hearing and so the use of vibrations and haptic feedback could be a better way of communicating to the user about their surroundings.

Secondly, considering the previous proposals and focusing on the infrastructure of Japan, the enforcement of good transit practices with cyclists and drivers would help visually impaired people to walk freely without the risk of their canes becoming stuck in their wheels. A risk that was mentioned by all the Japanese participants except one (Int 8) was having had accidents in many forms with cyclists as a result of them riding too fast and not noticing that the pedestrian in front of them was visually impaired. An additional technological approach could be object detector devices that use haptic feedback to guide the user to move away from the hazard. If some way could be found to encourage a majority of pedestrians and cyclists to feed information about their location into a map application, visually impaired passersby could be alerted before entering highly populated areas giving them an opportunity to avoid that route or to approach it with extreme caution.

Thirdly, as mentioned previously, some Mexican public schools prohibit visually disabled students from having their parents with them to take notes. A possible solution could be to give students haptic displays, or braille notepads, so they can take notes. This is a multifactorial problem although with the help of crowdfunding and democratic manufacturing in community facilities, open-source devices could be produced locally to support a more independent lifestyle. Even in situations where parents are permitted, having a technological alternative them being present during classes may be beneficial to the personal development of the students.

Finally, a proposal for both countries to provide inclusion into public spaces could be to implement raised, tactile '*Tenji*' blocks that incorporate RFID or QR code technologies for people to scan and then listen to spoken information about the place they are visiting. For example, shopping mall maps usually do not have braille which may be an obstacle to visually impaired people accessing stores and their products comfortably. Train stations in both countries could also benefit from 'smart *Tenji* blocks' to inform the passengers about platform and train information, perhaps updated in real time, that might otherwise be presented only visually and not announced.

8 Conclusions

Visual disability is part of the daily lives of 2.2 billion people around the world. In Mexico 2.24 million people, and in Japan 13 million people, face challenges in several aspects of their lives including mobility risks, reduced access to means of communication, and discrimination in their daily activities. Both countries have made efforts, including legislation, in favor of inclusion in public spaces, education, and work. Previous efforts have been made in both countries, through interviews and reviews, on laws to improve education and workplace conditions. Our study aims to survey the needs of people with visual impairments in terms of their mobility, safety, and their interactions with public spaces, to help identify some potential technological solutions to reduce their frustrations. Information was obtained through interviews performed with participants from Mexico City, State of Mexico, and from Kyoto City who live with a visual disability. Five non-standard interviews were held in Mexico, two with groups and three with individuals, and nine semi-structured interviews were conducted in Japan, totaling 12. The results of the interviews were subsequently reviewed using a thematic analysis and grouped into four types of need, namely, Mobility, Safety, Emotional, and Infrastructure. Several needs relate to the ways that people with visual impairments move and the means of transportation they use. Likewise, other needs relate to how they feel towards their circumstances as well as how they interact with public spaces, and the challenges they face with the design of the infrastructure in their environment.

Four proposals were stated. The first addressed mobility, safety and infrastructure. In both countries there are streets without proper sidewalks putting people at risk of collision accidents, therefore object detectors with extended active ranges including head level may help prevent injury. The second focused on the infrastructure of Japan, where good transit practices with cyclists and drivers would help visually impaired people to travel safely without the risk of their canes becoming stuck in or colliding with wheels, trash cans, and vehicles. An additional technological approach would be to adopt haptic feedback to guide them away from a hazard. Thirdly, Mexican public schools occasionally require visually disabled students to have their parents with them, to take notes. A solution might be to donate haptic displays and interfaces to support their learning, or to use crowdfunding to support the production of opensource devices within the local community. Finally, a proposal for both countries is to install rasied '*Tenji*' blocks with RFID QR code technologies on signs and information sites, so that people can explore and understand their environment easily without necessitating physical contact.

Acknowledgements. We extend our thanks and gratitude to the following institutions and people.

In Mexico, the director of the Fundación Zotoluco A.C for allowing us to form focus groups with tjeir members, all the families that talked with us, and Dr. Enrique Chong Quero, Head of the Mechatronics Department at Monterrey Institute of Technology, for assisting with the talk.

Mr. Ramon Torre Lemus and Ms. Teresa Robledo for the opportunity to approach Halcones and organize a focus group, and Mr. Jonathan Juarez for his helpful contact. Various friends and colleagues, Mr. Ilya Cordova, Mr. Alan Cano, and the Mexico City Gay Chorus for their availability and participation.

In Japan, Ms. Otani for facilitating interviews with members of Porini Co., Ltd. Dr. Yoshimura and Dr. Tabata from Kyoto University of Advanced Science (KUAS) for their support with contacting participants and organizing interviews.

Professor Tabuchi, Vice Principal of the Kyoto Prefectural High School for the Blind, for organizing an interview with their instructors, Mr. Sakaida for liaising with the school, and the Admissions Center at KUAS for their support.

Ms Nakajima, Ms Nakagawa, and Ms Shindo for their invaluable help with translation and interpretation services in support of the interviews.

References

1. ICD-11 for Mortality and Morbidity Statistics. https://icd.who.int/browse11/l-m/en#/http%3a%2f%2fid.who.int%2ficd%2fentity%2f1103667651. Accessed 29 Aug 2023
2. World Economics, Japan's Median Age. https://www.worldeconomics.com/Demographics/Median-Age/Japan.aspx. Accessed 29 Aug 2023
3. Procuraduría Federal del Consumidor. Ojo con tu salud visual. https://www.gob.mx/profeco/documentos/ojo-con-tu-salud-visual?state=published. Accessed 21 June 2023
4. Diario Oficial, NORMA Oficial Mexicana NOM-034-STPS-2016, Condiciones de seguridad para el acceso y desarrollo de actividades de trabajadores con discapacidad en los centros de trabajo. https://www.gob.mx/capacidadesyempleo/documentos/norma-oficialmexicana-nom-034-stps-2016-condiciones-de-seguridad-para-el-acceso-y-desarrollo-deactividades-de-trabajadores-con-discapacidad-en-los-centros-de-trabajo-169519. Accessed 21 June 2023
5. Trejo, Y: PensiónBienestar para personas con discapacidad 2023: fechas, requisitos y cómo registrarse. Actualidad. https://mexico.as.com/actualidad/pension-bienestar-parapersonas-con-discapacidad-2023-fechas-requisitos-y-como-registrarsen/#:~:text=La%20Secretar%C3%ADa%20de%20Bienestar%20inform%C3%B3,de%20los%20adultos%20mayores%20bimestralmente
6. Storecheck: El aumento en los precios de la canasta básica en México. https://blog.storecheck.com.mx/el-aumento-en-los-precios-de-la-canasta-basica-enmexico/. Accessed 23 June 2023
7. DIS-CAPACIDAD. Se desentiendeel Metro de lesiones de un usuario ciego que cayó a las vías. https://dis-capacidad.com/2022/06/22/se-desentiende-el-metro-de-lesiones-de-una-dulto-ciego-que-cayo-a-las-vias/. Accessed 21 June 2023
8. Convention on the Rights of Persons with Disabilities. https://www.mofa.go.jp/files/000449713.pdf. Accessed 21 June 2023
9. Flores, V: Obtiene Ford México distintivo por sus políticas de inclusión. RRHHDigital (2023). https://www.rrhhdigital.mx/secciones/cultura/1293/ObtieneFord-Mexico-distintivo-por-sus-politicas-de-inclusion-s-de-inclusion-
10. Nissan Motor Corporation. Nissan Mexicana reafirmasu compromiso con la inclusión y la diversidad integrando empleados con discapacidad auditiva (2019). https://mexico.nissannews.com/es-MX/releases/release-2426e7a162d023f244395cc0a2052249-nissan-mexicana-reafirma-su-compromiso-con-lainclusion-y-la-diversidad-integrando-empleados-con-discapacidadauditiva#?selectedTabId=releases
11. FP Corporation, Social Initiatives. https://www.fpco.jp/en/en_esg/en_societyeffort.html. Accessed 21 June 2023
12. Japan Times. Firms including IBM Japan to develop AI 'guide suitcase' for the blind (2020). https://www.japantimes.co.jp/news/2020/02/07/national/ibm-japan-ai-guidesuitcase/
13. Halcones Facebook Account. https://www.facebook.com/halconesachillesmexico. Accessed 21 June 2023
14. Fundacion Zotoluco A.C Homepage. http://fundacionzotoluco.org/. Accessed 21 June 2023
15. Fundacion Devlyn Homepage. https://www.fundaciondevlyn.org.mx/. Accessed 21 June 2023
16. Kyoto Lighthouse Homepage. https://www.kyoto-lighthouse.or.jp/. Accessed 21 June 2023
17. Porini Company Ltd Homepage. https://porini.co.jp/jigyou/. Accessed 21 June 2023
18. Hitomachi Koryukan Homepage. http://www.hitomachi-kyoto.jp/. Accessed 21 June 2023
19. Miyauchi, H., Matsuda, E.: Br. J. Vis. Impairment 1–13 (2022)
20. Nishimura, T., Doi, K., Sawada, M., Kaneko, T: Basic survey on children and teachers in special classes for children with low vision in Japan, 40(2), 160–174 (2022)
21. Garcia-Llamas, J.J.: Orientación y movilidad autónoma en niños con discapacidad visual. Tesis de doctorado, Doctorado Interinstitucional en Educación, ITESO, Tlaquepaque, Jalisco (2019)

22. Villa, V., Lorenzo, A., Sáyago, I.: Educación superior incluyente para personas con discapacidad visual en la Universidad Autónoma de Guerrero, México. Revista Saber, Ciencia y Libertad **17**(2), 474–493 (2022)
23. CNIB Foundation: About the White Cane. https://www.cnib.ca/en/about-white-cane?region=on. Accessed 31 Aug 2023
24. Nowell, L., Norris, J., White, D., Moules, N.: Thematic analysis: striving to meet the trustworthiness criteria. Int J Qual Methods **16**, 1–13 (2017)
25. De Fine Licht, K.: Hostile urban architecture: a critical discussion of the seemingly offensive art of keeping people away. Etikk I praksis. Nord. J. Appl. Ethics, 27–44 (2017)

A Three Level Design Study Approach to Develop a Student-Centered Learner Dashboard

Gilbert Drzyzga[⊠] [iD] and Thorleif Harder[iD]

Institute of Interactive Systems, Technische Hochschule Lübeck, Lübeck, Germany
{gilbert.drzyzga,thorleif.harder}@th-luebeck.de

Abstract. Online programs risk higher student dropout rates. Supporting learning tools such as learning analytics dashboards (LADs) can promote self-regulated learning and positively impact student outcomes. In this paper, a three-level design study is presented that demonstrates the reduction of cognitive load at multiple levels when students are involved in the LAD design process. Through a user-centered design process (including requirements analysis and expert interviews), a wireframe was developed using participatory methods and evaluated by 24 university students using the laws of Gestalt psychology, resulting in a clickable, low-fidelity prototype (LFD). This was then evaluated by 24 university students using the interaction principles of EN ISO 9241-110:2020. The refined LFD was further evaluated with university students in an eye-tracking study using the thinking-aloud technique (n = 10). The feedback emphasized the importance of participatory design and provided critical insights into the most effective use of the LAD and its elements, taking into account cognitive aspects. The results showed significant optimization in the small details and the big picture in the use of content elements, e.g., it is a crucial part to create a navigation structure adapted to the needs of an LAD and it is beneficial to present a reduced level of information during the initial access, with the option to add or access additional elements as needed.

Keywords: Design study · User-centered design · Design process · Gestalt laws · Interaction principles · Eye-tacking & thinking aloud · Self-regulated learning · Usability · User experience · Cognitive load

1 Introduction

Online education platforms face the challenge of increasing student dropout rates. However, innovative learning tools such as Learning Analytics Dashboards (LADs) offer a promising solution [41–43]. By creating an environment conducive to self-directed learning, these dashboards can play a part in significantly improving student outcomes [30]. It has been argued [22] that students with higher levels of self-regulation of their learning process will experience greater academic success. LADs enable students to monitor their progress and adjust their learning strategies accordingly by providing personalized, near real-time information about their academic progress. It could help learners monitor their progress, identify areas where they are struggling, and adjust their learning strategies accordingly. Such a user-centered tool would aim to improve online learning experiences and outcomes [32, 33]. This means understanding the cognitive, metacognitive, and motivational processes that underlie self-regulated learning (SRL) and using that understanding to design a tool that supports those processes. The premise is to make the implicit aspects of learning explicit, thereby promoting self-awareness and enhancing SRL.

This paper presents a detailed and in-depth analysis of the different usability methods and approaches used in a three-level design study for the development of an LAD, including a user-centered design (UCD) approach, and how this influenced the design process for the incremental development of the LAD, based on the late-breaking result (LBR)-paper on this study [48]. Feedback from participants at the various levels - based on the design study conducted - played an important role in refining the prototype. By incorporating the UCD approach, the LAD met the needs of its users and increased its effectiveness in supporting the learning process [46]. The process of developing an LAD for an online Learning Management System (LMS) is described in the following using a UCD process. The UCD process includes three key phases, each focusing on specific aspects and involving different groups of students. This allows for an effective step-by-step development of the LAD, with user feedback and iterative refinement. The final design takes into account the needs and preferences of the target audience and ensures an optimal user experience (UX). Involving students in the design process was essential to create a tool that would be accepted and used regularly by students. The study also provides valuable insights for further research and effective integration of the LAD into the LMS. The strength of the study lies in its structured approach, involving students at all levels, providing critical insights into the effective use of dashboard elements, and validating design decisions.

The first stage of development is a Learner Dashboard (LD), which can be used without machine learning or Learning Analytics (LA) methods to give students a first insight into their learning process in the LMS. It shows activities such as click trails, interactions or reading progress in the course material. These are presented on different cards in the LD and combined in a way that gives students insight into their learning progress. For example, activities performed while using the LMS are grouped into meaningful tasks and prepared for output in the LD.

1.1 Background

In recent years, the popularity of digital degree programs has grown significantly, offering students the flexibility to learn at their own pace and from any location. However, these online programs also present challenges, such as the lack of face-to-face interaction and personalized guidance, so they are more isolated [24–26], which could result in suboptimal learning outcomes and higher dropout rates [23]. To address this issue, a collaborative research project has been initiated involving a university network of digital degree programs with over 4,000 enrolled students. The project [47] aims to explore innovative ways to support students in their learning journey and reduce dropout rates [1, 2, 5].

Recent advances in online learning have paved the way for the development of innovative tools and methods that empower students and reduce dropout rates [51–54]. Some of these central advances are LADs, machine learning predictive algorithms, and self-regulation processes. As mentioned by [40], the development of an LAD tool is a complex issue, e.g., privacy concerns, and the technical architecture of such dashboards must be robust and flexible, able to accommodate different learning environments and constantly evolving educational needs. The complexities of LADs, from their operational mechanism to their impact on students' learning experience, need to be thoroughly explored. They highlight the need for advanced assessment methods to improve learning outcomes. However, the effectiveness of these tools depends largely on the environment in which they're used, requiring advanced evaluation methods to measure their performance. Several studies have identified a lack of usability testing or problems associated with LADs, for example Holstein et al. [49] report that users are shown information they are likely to already know. In their study, Schwendimann et al. [50] highlight, among other things, the lack of attention to the nuances of how best to provide information in dashboards and also how best to visualize it, depending on the context and the device being used.

The Mixed Theories of UCD, SRL and Dropout Prediction. A research paper [28] highlights a student-centered perspective that focuses on how students respond to information about their learning behaviors presented on an LAD. The study identifies four design principles that are critical to creating dashboards that support learner agency and empowerment. These principles are: designs that are customizable by students, prioritizing students' sense-making, enabling students to identify actionable insights, and embedding dashboards in educational processes. These principles provide guidance for the ethical use of LA that promotes student agency and empowerment.

With the growth of online education, the issue of Student Dropout Prediction (SDP) has received considerable attention. A survey [23] provides an in-depth analysis of the state-of-the-art literature in SDP, focusing primarily on machine learning predictive algorithms. They propose a comprehensive hierarchical classification of the existing literature and introduce a formal notation for describing alternative dropout models. The survey also addresses other relevant aspects such as evaluation metrics, collected data, and privacy concerns. Interestingly, the survey highlights deep sequential machine learning methods as one of the most effective solutions to the SDP problem.

A similarly article [22] delves into the discoveries about the nature, origins, and development of how students regulate their own learning processes. It is argued that self-regulatory processes lead to success in school, yet few teachers prepare students to learn on their own. In the paper it is defined the essential qualities of academic self-regulation and describes the structure and function of self-regulatory processes. It is concluded that recent advances in online learning have significantly improved students' learning experiences and outcomes. The design principles for learner dashboards, machine learning predictive algorithms for SDP, and self-regulatory processes have played key roles in these advances. However, more research is needed to further improve the tools and methods, especially in terms of adaptability, ethical adoption, and preparing students to effectively use self-regulatory processes.

Improving Online Learning: Development and Integration of a User-Centric LAD/LD into the University's LMS. As part of the solution, the development of an

LAD was identified to promote student SRL, which could aid in the learning process and have a positive impact on student outcomes [7, 8]. The LAD or the LD as a pure LMS tool will be integrated as a plug-in into the university network's Moodle LMS and, when completed, it is planned to release it as open-source software to the wider community [47]. The key is to leverage the learner's pathways of interaction. This means using data collected from the learner's activities and behaviors in the LMS to provide insights and support for their learning process. As mentioned above, to ensure its effectiveness, the LAD is based on and developed using a UCD approach [38]. It involves understanding user needs, preferences and context, and using this understanding to inform all stages of problem solving and design and it emphasizes prototyping, testing, and iteration as the primary methods for improving design. The UCD process typically includes stages such as user research, idea generation and concept development, design, prototyping, user testing and iteration [3, 9, 10, 12]. By following these processes in the approach, continuous iteration and refinement based on user feedback has been achieved.

1.2 Using Design Studies and UCD in the Development of LADs/LDs

Design studies and UCD play an important role in the development of LADs/LDs in general, providing valuable insights and methods for creating effective and user-centered educational tools [27]. By incorporating the principles of UCD, developers can benefit from a systematic and evidence-based approach that is aligned with scientific standards [18, 29]. This alignment is essential in the dynamic design environment of LADs/LDs, where responsiveness and adaptability are important. Design studies provide a structured framework to guide the iterative design process. They promote a deep understanding of learner needs and facilitate the creation of learner-centered designs [27]. Through user research techniques such as interviews, surveys, and observations, design studies help gain insight into learners' preferences, motivations, and challenges. This user-centered approach ensures that the tool meet the diverse needs of learners and provide a positive learning experience. By conducting usability testing and incorporating iterative feedback loops, developers can improve the usability, user experience (UUX), and effectiveness of such a tool. Design research supports intuitive navigation and clear presentation of its elements, which can contribute to improved learning outcomes. Therefore, it was decided to develop a three-stage design study and apply it to the development of the LAD/LD.

This design study follows these approaches and focuses on a UCD process for the development of a software tool that, as an additional application within the LMS, does not overburden the learner, but offers an intuitive and easy access to the software and thus can be a helpful support during the learning phases. Incorporating the principles and framework of design studies can add significant value to the process of developing the LAD/LD through the UCD approach. They are aligned with scientific principles, thereby lending credibility to the knowledge claims they produce [18], which is important in the context of the dynamic design environment of the tool. As Cross [4] points out, 'designerly' ways of understanding are crucial to fully understanding the diverse experiences of end users.

It is also noted [18] that narrative is often used in design studies to communicate and justify findings. Although narratives do not guarantee truth, they provide a relatable and accessible way of sharing findings, thereby enhancing designers' understanding of the user's context and experience. This approach is consistent with Norman's [13] focus on usability and understandability and adds further nuance to the design process. Integrating discovery and validation methods into design studies, as suggested by [18], involves linking evolving research questions with appropriate methods. For the design of an LAD/LD, this approach ensures that new user insights are systematically validated, thereby maintaining robustness and relevance in the design. Finally, given the educational nature of such a tool, insights into educational design research become highly relevant. They guide the integration of educational aspects into the design study [15].

1.3 Focus on an Iterative Approach Within the UCD Process

As mentioned above, in order to develop such a tool, an iterative approach is used within the UCD process, which has been effective in optimizing the content elements and functionalities of the LAD/LD by incorporating expert knowledge throughout the development process. To this end, the design study is divided into the following three phases:

1. Traditional principles such as Gestalt laws
2. Interaction principles
3. Monitoring cognitive load in an eye-tracking study

These three phases should help to improve student engagement and continuous refinement of the tool to provide an integrated and effective dashboard for students. Principles such as the laws of Gestalt [21] and the principles of interaction [6] have been considered. The goal is to improve student engagement, learning outcomes, and overall satisfaction with digital degree programs by providing an LAD/LD that is tailored to students' needs and experiences. This study is guided by two main research questions:

Research Questions (RQ)

- RQ1: How should user interface elements of an online support tool be designed to effectively support learning?
- RQ2: How should user interfaces and content elements of an online support tool be designed to promote usability/user experience?

In the following, the term "LD" is used to refer to the first stage of the development of a technical prototype that only analyzes and prepares data from the LMS.

2 Methodological Approach

The methodological approach, which is a combination of formal research methods and UCD principles, serves as an integrated strategy for the development of the LD. This approach is carefully planned and implemented to ensure a thorough, comprehensive approach that addresses both the technical aspects of the LD and the UUX. This combination is implemented in the mentioned three-level approach. This ensures that not only the current state of the developed LD is examined, but also that it is delved into at various stages. Every step of the process involves active engagement with users to ensure that their voices, opinions and experiences are not only considered, but are an integral part of the final product. Through a carefully designed evaluation process, an LD is delivered that not only achieves efficiency and accessibility, but is also perfectly tailored to the user's preferences, needs and specific context. By designing with the user in mind, it ensures that the LD is not only technologically advanced, but also personally relevant, resulting in higher levels of user satisfaction and engagement. The primary goal is to create an LD that is as intuitive, efficient and engaging as possible, and that enables and supports the user's learning process as described above.

2.1 User-Centered Design

The UCD approach places the needs, preferences, and context of users at the forefront of the design process. By involving students and experts in the development of the LD, it is possible to identify the most relevant indicators, visual representations, information and intervention strategies to optimize the learning process. The UCD approach also ensures that the final product is more accessible, efficient, and satisfying for its intended users. Therefore, the design study of the LD was conducted in three strategic phases to ensure its effectiveness and UUX, gathering valuable insights from students at each step. Each stage aimed to evaluate different aspects of the LD, from its visual appeal to its interaction principles and UX.

2.2 Key Design Study Issues to Consider

The need for a design study in the development of a software tool arises from the recognition of the importance of involving users in the development process, as their feedback can have a significant impact on the effectiveness and usability of the final product. This approach is supported by several studies that have demonstrated its benefits, such as improved user satisfaction or increased engagement [11, 39]. Four key aspects form the basis of this design study (Fig. 1):

Focus on User Experience. This approach, guided by the UUX principles [13], prioritizes user input by involving students in the design process and collecting their feedback at each stage of development. This approach allows for the creation of an LD as a support tool that is specifically tailored to the needs and preferences of students. As a result, the final product is more likely to resonate with the intended audience, resulting in higher usage and overall satisfaction [13]. In addition, it has been suggested that improved UX can increase student engagement and subsequently lead to improved learning outcomes [35].

Visual Appeal and Intuitiveness. By emphasizing the importance of usability and cognitive perspectives, this design study highlights the importance of user interface design and its impact on LD. Based on research [34], the process focuses on developing a visually appealing, easy-to-navigate interface that encourages student engagement with the LD.

Data-Driven Design. The three-level design process uses user behavior data to inform decisions, which is consistent with the principles of evidence-based design [36]. This approach promotes evidence-based decision making, with data collection and analysis occurring at each step. Thus, the process allows for continuous refinement and improvement of the platform, ensuring that the LD remains relevant and effective over time.

Iterative Development. The process is iterative, moving incrementally through the three stages, in line with the principles of agile development [37]. This iterative nature allows to identify and address issues at each stage, ensuring that they are resolved before proceeding to the next stage. As a result, the end product is a more robust and engaging LD.

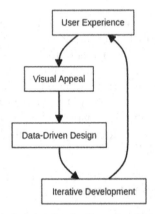

Fig. 1. The underlying four key aspects of the design study.

In summary, the three-level design process is quite effective for developing student-centered LDs. By emphasizing UUX, data-driven decisions, aesthetics, and iterative development, this approach results in an LD that meets student needs, is visually appealing, is evidence-based, and is continually improved as it is tested by the users for the users.

2.3   The Three-Level Evaluation Approach

The design study [48] itself was conceptualized following an in-depth literature review, including the topic of SRL and LADs in general in digital learning environments, and expert interviews (n = 9). Prior to the design study, a paper prototype [44, 45] was developed from the group discussions using different LD views, which was then digitally wireframed (Fig. 2, first arrow). This is the starting point of the design study according to [48].

The three-level design study for the LD began with the first phase of developing and evaluating wireframes based on Gestalt laws to ensure consistency of design (Fig. 2, second arrow/level 1). The result of the study was the creation of a low-fidelity prototype

Fig. 2. Presentation of the three-level design study, according to [48].

(LFP), which took about 19 days (Fig. 2, third arrow). In the second phase of the design study, the interactive prototype was evaluated by a group of 24 students in a half-day workshop using the seven interaction principles (Fig. 2, fourth arrow). This evaluation provided insight into the UUX and the effectiveness of the LD and its elements. The outcome of the study was the creation of a high-fidelity prototype (HFP), which took about 6 days (Fig. 2, fifth arrow). Finally, in the third phase (Fig. 2, sixth arrow), the refined prototype was subjected to an eye-tracking procedure using the thinking-aloud technique with a group of 10 students. This allowed for a deeper understanding of how students interacted with the LD and provided valuable insights into its optimal use. The findings from this study were used to further develop the HFP - in parallel with the implementation of the technical prototype for the LMS (Fig. 2, seventh and eighth arrows).

The 24 students who participated in the first and second phases of the design study are enrolled in the online Media informatics degree program and are studying the Human-Computer Interaction course. They were prepared for the tasks and evaluations by reading the course script and attending weekly one-hour web conferences on these and related course topics. The web conferences were moderated by a university lecturer. Successful completion of the assignments was required to register for the subsequent exam.

The third phase of the study involved students who had already completed two-thirds or more of the usability course in the Information Technology and Design degree program. This ensured that the participants had experience in the field of usability. The advantage of this selection was that the participants already had a basic understanding of usability and could therefore better interpret the results of the eye-tracking study. The participants were informed about the test scenario at the beginning and were given different tasks to complete within the given time limit.

The study followed a systematic, iterative approach with a consistent cycle of evaluation and refinement. The methodology was based on proven design and interaction principles. Advanced eye-tracking technologies were used to achieve a higher level of precision and depth in the evaluation.

The First Level of the Design Study. In the first level, *"Wireframe Evaluation (Evaluating Gestalt Laws)"*, 24 students analyzed the wireframe of the LD according to Gestalt laws. These laws explain human perception of visual elements and their relationships, serving as a tool for students to assess the LD's overall organization, layout, and aesthetics. The feedback from this level identified potential enhancements and refinements for implementation in the next level.

The Second Level of the Design Study. In the second level, the *"Interactive Prototype Workshop (Evaluating Interaction Principles)"*, a half-day workshop was held. Students were provided with the LFP featuring various frames and interaction possibilities based on previous studies. The student group evaluated the dashboard's interactivity according to the EN ISO 9241-110:2020 standard [6]. This hands-on engagement with the LD prototype allowed them to offer feedback on UUX, navigation, and overall experience. Insights from the workshop led to further iterations, enhancing the dashboard's UUX and effectiveness.

The Third Level of the Design Study. The third and final level, *"Eye-Tracking Evaluation"*, involved an in-depth eye-tracking study using the think-aloud technique to examine the cognitive load while using the LD. Ten students participated in a full-day evaluation of the revised interactive prototype, utilizing eye-tracking technology and guided interviews. This approach provided insights into students' eye movements, enabling a better understanding of user navigation and pinpointing areas for further optimization. Additionally, the study collected qualitative feedback from experts and quantifiable feedback on usability, efficiency, and aesthetics of the low-fidelity prototype through the User Experience Questionnaire-Short (UEQ-S) [46].

Summarizing the Design Study. Table 1 below gives an overview of the three evaluations carried out and the development of the LD in between:

Table 1. The entire design study (level 1–3) with the initial setup (level 0), development phases and preparation for programming a first prototype for the LMS.

Level	Evaluation/Activity	Description/Goal
0	Requirements analysis, literature review, and expert interviews	Systematic process to gather, document, analyze, and prioritize user needs and requirements to create an initial wireframe design of the LD
Development	Paper prototyping	
1	Evaluation of the wireframe using Gestalt laws	24 undergraduate students evaluate the visual appeal and understandability of the initial design, laying the groundwork for a user-friendly interface
Development	Low-fidelity prototype	
2	Evaluation against seven interaction principles	Students specializing in human-computer interaction investigate the low-fidelity prototype, ensuring the dashboard's functionality, efficiency, and visual appeal
Development	A first technical prototype for use and evaluation in the LMS	

The LD was systematically evaluated and refined throughout these three levels. This process transformed it from a simple wireframe to a final HFP, with improvements in UUX, navigation, aesthetics and cognitive load achieved through feedback from students and experts.

3 Development and Implementation of the Learner Dashboard Based on the Three-Level Design Study

In order to demonstrate the valuable involvement of students in the design process and the associated benefits for the development of the LD, some of the results from the individual studies (level 1 (in review) & level 2 (in publication)) of this involvement of students in the development process will be highlighted through examples - graphically through the students' designs (level 1 & 2) and on the other hand as results of the eye-tracking study (level 3).

3.1 The Development of a Wireframe for a Learner Dashboard

The literature review played a critical role in identifying the key features and functionalities that the LD should have. This comprehensive analysis of existing research provided valuable insights into the most effective ways to visualize and present data, as well as the potential challenges and pitfalls that might be encountered during the design process. In addition to the literature review, the research team sought the expertise of student stakeholders through a series of interviews. These experts, with their diverse backgrounds and experiences in online learning, offered unique perspectives on their learning process. Their input was invaluable in refining the initial wireframe to ensure that it met the needs of the intended users and addressed any potential concerns.

The initial graphic design of the LD took the form of a wireframe with the main functions and the division of the various content elements such as calendars, learning activities or learning support measures. These different areas were defined as "card" (Fig. 3). This layout served as the basis for subsequent research. By using the paper prototype method, the research team ensured that the initial design was based on established principles and best practices in the field.

Following the paper prototype method, the wireframe was developed as an LFP of the final product. This approach allowed for rapid iteration and improvement, as the research team was able to quickly identify any issues and make the necessary adjustments. As a result, the wireframe served as an effective communication and collaboration tool between the research team and the interviewed experts as they worked together to refine the design and move toward a more polished and functional learning dashboard.

Overall, the initial graphical design of the LD as an initial design laid the groundwork for the research and ensured that the final LD would be both user-friendly and effective in presenting data at this preliminary stage. Through collaboration and iteration, the research team and interviewed experts were able to refine and optimize the design, resulting in an LD that met the needs of its intended users and optimized its UUX and effectiveness for evaluation in the ongoing design process. In the following, the design study shows how this groundwork is a valuable method for developing a student-centered LD with its key features for best SRL and facilitation of the learner's learning process.

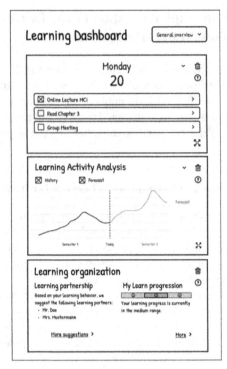

Fig. 3. First version of the LD wireframe (starting point of the design study) [48].

3.2 Evaluation Based on Gestalt Laws and Fact and Interaction Problems (Level 1)

A theoretical evaluation of the design aesthetics is the first step of the presented approach (study in review). It aims to evaluate and understand the visual and functional aspects of the given LD. This is done by considering how the visual elements interact with the functionality and how they can be refined to improve both the aesthetics and the user interface. The investigation of the wireframe shown in Fig. 3 has been divided into two focus areas, accompanied by an additional task. The assignments were carried out over a period of four weeks and formed part of a module in the online study degree program "Media Informatics".

The First Part of the Assignments. In this part, the online students (n = 24), were tasked with evaluating the wireframe in the context of the five basic Gestalt laws: "Law of Proximity", "Law of Similarity", "Law of (Good) Continuation" and the "Law of Good Gestalt" [21]. For each of these laws, students were asked to provide at least one example highlighting either a positive or negative application within the wireframe design. The primary purpose of this exercise was to use the insights of Gestalt psychology to reduce the cognitive effort required to assimilate information in the learning design initially [20]. These laws guide the human eye and brain to perceive visual elements in certain ways, thus influencing how designers organize content and interactive elements for effective comprehension and engagement (study in review).

The second Part of the Assignments. Identifying potential factual problems[1] and also interaction problems, within the wireframe was the second part of the analysis. Here, the assignment encouraged students to support their findings and interpretations with explicit examples in their detailed reports. This process facilitated a deeper understanding of the design principles and their practical implications (study in review).

The Third Part of the Assignment. The students were asked to create alternative design solutions to the wireframe, demonstrating their understanding of Gestalt laws and their ability to apply them creatively (see the section "Students created alternative solutions of the wireframe"). This exercise fostered critical thinking, problem solving, and the ability to translate theoretical knowledge into practical design solutions (study in review).

The Results of This Evaluation. The evaluation was substantial and provides a rich resource for further study and improvement of the wireframe design. The students' evaluations identified issues such as the "Law of Proximity" and illustrate the depth and detail of the students' exploration of the topic (study in review).

Students Created alternative Solutions of the Wireframe. The students were given the additional task of coming up with an alternative solution for a card of their choice based on the "Law of Proximity" that they could imagine in the LD. 11 of the 24 students completed this task. The students' alternative designs illustrate how students perceive such functionalities and what aspects are important to them. It also demonstrates the benefits of the approach taken in the design study, where student involvement leads to a high quality, student-centered outcome (study in review), [48].

Results for Level 1 Refinements. In this part of the design study, for example, the navigation concept was reconsidered because it was found to be counter-intuitive. In addition, editing functionality was added to allow for individual customization. Student feedback revealed shortcomings in the calendar and learning progress elements, particularly in the area of interaction. This feedback was used to redesign the corresponding cards in order to improve the interaction and the graphical presentation (study in review), [48].

3.3   Evaluation Based on the Seven Interaction Principles (Level 2)

The next step (study in publication) was to carry out an interactive analysis of the UUX. This stage involves a detailed evaluation of how users interact with the LD. The goal is not only to map these interactions, but also to identify areas of friction and opportunities for improvement. The UUX analysis provides a deeper understanding of what works and what doesn't, and informs the redesign process with valuable insights. An essential step in the development of such an interactive user interface was the refinement of a wireframe that served as the basic structure for the resulting LFP. The final version of

---

[1] The task used the German term "Sachprobleme", which is used in the context of this paper to mean "factual problems" or "technical problems". It is specifically invoked to describe challenges related to the usability and efficiency of a system or design [11], [19]

the LD prototype was characterized by different views and various modal dialog boxes and key interaction elements such as the question mark icon.

For evaluation purposes, the prototype was made available to 24 students enrolled in a human-computer interaction course during a four-hour online workshop facilitated through an Internet browser. The students, acting as experts in this context, independently tested and evaluated the prototype against the interaction principles in a two-part task. They were given an introduction at the beginning and were able to ask the lecturers questions at any time if they were unclear. There were some questions about how to use the prototype in general, but apart from that the students were able to interact with the prototype and know how to evaluate it. The evaluation process was supervised by three university faculty members to ensure academic rigor. For this purpose, the way of evaluation by the students was supervised by them (following the instructions, collecting the results, moderating the discussions, etc.) (study in publication).

The Results of This Evaluation. The anonymized results of the student evaluations were carefully compiled to further improve the wireframes. The results, which are part of another study in publication, show that the prototype can benefit significantly from refining its user interface and functionality.

3.4 Performing the Eye-Tracking Procedure with Thinking Aloud (Level 3)

The third step [46] is rounded out with the application of cutting-edge eye-tracking technology. This step focuses on assessing cognitive load - the mental effort required by a user to complete a task or comprehend information. By carefully tracking the user's eye movements, it is possible to infer which areas or aspects of the LD are cognitively demanding, helping to refine the design to make it more intuitive and usable. The comprehensive LFP was revised to incorporate the latest findings (see Fig. 4 for an overview of the revised design).

The prototype was then evaluated by a group of students (n = 10) from a usability module. The entire study was conducted within a single day, with each session lasting 30 min. These sessions included a welcome, an introduction to the project, and an explanation of the procedural requirements [46]. The evaluation process was supervised by two university faculty members to ensure academic rigor. During the approximately 20-min test phase, participants were given several subtasks to complete under the guidance of the moderators. Five tasks and scenarios were designed to evaluate the usability and functionality of the prototype, taking into account cognitive load. The tasks involved navigating between different high-level views of the LD, understanding the presentation of information, understanding the functionality of the LD, and understanding the information and whether it was obvious or not. Questions were also asked about understanding and confidence in recommendations for progress in the learning process. The main aim was to identify important directions and areas of gaze, including visualization, heat map, fixation and attention [46]. Following the eye-tracking study, students were asked to evaluate the prototype using the short version of the User Experience Questionnaire (UEQ-S) [16] to assess its overall usability.

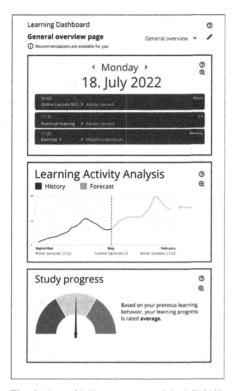

Fig. 4. Low-fidelity prototype of the LD [48].

Findings of the Third Level and Implications for the Design Study. In the ongoing field of UCD, the evolutionary path of the prototype is deeply involved with user feedback and its validation through design modifications. Thus, the third level of the design study has revealed important insights, largely derived from student feedback. These insights, while highlighting several areas for potential improvement, serve to guide the gradual refinement of the prototype towards increased functionality and sophistication, further strengthening the effectiveness of the UCD approach. These insights highlight several key areas for improvement. For example, feedback indicated that the need for a concise, accurate and extensible information format in the LD was an important point to address [46]. Such findings gave important insights for the final step of using the revised and tested LD in level 2. The user feedback in this step also highlighted the need for customization and an intuitive navigation structure, underscoring the importance of a user-centered prototype. After evaluation in level 2 (workshop), these enhancements, including the ability to add personal data to assessments and a shift from a text-based to a visual help page, underscore the ease of use of the developed extended prototype, a critical aspect of this design philosophy. However, they also require a balanced approach to address the associated challenges of complexity and time management.

Furthermore, the differentiation between different views within the prototype, such as the overall view, the semester view, and the module view, requires refinement in order to improve the UUX and thus solidify the prototype's position as a next-level learning tool.

During this phase of the design study, the cognitive processing research gathered a wealth of data from a diverse group of test participants, resulting in a wide range of feedback and some aspects being corroborated by different participants. Subjects' visual engagement was closely monitored, revealing interesting patterns and trends in user attention and interface interaction. This wealth of data provides a solid foundation for critically evaluating the existing prototype and identifying potential changes to refine and improve the UUX for the upcoming HFP.

The full study covers the full range of findings from this research and provides a robust understanding of the overall results. The results of the eye tracking study are not just an end result; they provide a dynamic context for the next development process of the prototype. Based on these findings, a series of refinements and innovations are being prepared that will mark a significant step forward in the prototyping of the LD. The results of the study will be used as a baseline to guide an incremental improvement phase, deeply rooted in user interaction and experience.

Summary. The eye-tracking study [46] provided useful insights that greatly enhanced the understanding of the strengths of the prototype and the areas in which it could be improved. The results of this eye-tracking study presented above, although a small subset of the diverse feedback from the study [46], highlight the potential range of design changes that should be considered and incorporated into the development roadmap. These range from minor tweaks to complete overhauls, all aimed at improving the UUX of the prototype.

4   Summary and Discussion

This paper discussed the various usability methods used during the three-level design study of the LD development. In addition, it reviews the insightful feedback received from a panel of 34 experienced individuals in the field. This feedback was essential in guiding the iterative design process, facilitating the incremental development of the LD, and gaining insight into user needs, particularly in relation to the RQs outlined above. Methodologically, the UCD approach [3, 9, 10, 12] used in the design study played an important role in the development of the LD for university students. Over the course of 60 days in the summer semester, the research gathered essential qualitative feedback from students and experts, leading to a refined and well-optimized LD prototype. The emphasis was on UUX, visual appeal and intuitiveness, followed by data-driven design in an iterative development process. By incorporating the UCD approach, it was ensured that the LD met the needs of its users, thereby increasing its effectiveness in supporting the learning process. The success shown by the feedback of the revised and re-evaluated HFP in another recent study highlights the importance of using an appropriate UCD process in this three-level design study approach when developing tools such as the LD for higher education. This methodology enabled a more effective and engaging product to be created, which could ultimately improve student learning outcomes. In this research, the development of an effective LD was achieved through a systematic design study carried out in three key phases. Each of the phases focused on a specific aspect and was enriched by the active participation of a specific group of students. This allowed the LD to be developed step by step after the studies had been evaluated. Between each step, it was possible to optimize the LD accordingly. By incorporating user feedback and iterative refinement, the final design addresses the specific needs and preferences of its target audience, ensuring an optimal UUX. This, in turn, promotes a more productive and immersive learning tool, which can assist students in their online study life, while not overburdening them.

As noted above, this involvement is essential to creating an LD that is accepted and regularly used by students. It has given important perspectives and impulses for the information transfer, the design and the structural and conceptual design of the LD. This illustrates the importance of using the UCD process in the development of a student-centered tool for everyday use in students' learning processes. The design study proved to be very fruitful and provided significant results that are invaluable for further research and effective integration of the LD into the LMS. The strength of the study lies in its structured approach, involving students at every level, providing critical insights into the effective use of dashboard elements and validating design decisions. Findings included the need for a reduced level of information at first access, the ability to add elements as needed, the maintenance of a flat navigation hierarchy and the need to ensure that information is easy to understand for optimal usability. In addition, it is shown at the level of the content elements of the LD that it is crucial that no additional time or cognitive burden is placed on the student in using the LD, such as familiarization or understanding of its functionality. This understanding is important given the potential risk of the dashboard not being used by online students. By incorporating user insights, not just as passive recipients, but as active co-creators of such educational technology to support their learning processes, an accurate reflection of their needs and preferences can be developed. This research and the insights derived from it will serve as a roadmap for the development of the technical prototype plugin for the LMS.

An underlying approach based on the principles of the UCD process underpins this methodology [12]. The development is and will be guided by an iterative and sensitive understanding of the user's needs, preferences, and limitations to ensure that the resulting tool is both functionally effective, appealing to the target audience, and less stressful [11]. Significantly, the process integrates a design study within the broader UCD process for the LD. This combination of design and research approaches facilitates the creation of a tool that is robust and user-centered [14]. The blend of rich narrative insights, systematic validation, and pedagogical considerations has been instrumental in shaping a dynamic, evolving design that has been shown to effectively meet the needs of learners. The synthesis of these components, if thoughtfully designed and implemented, can help bridge the gap between theory and practice and develop those tools that address the needs and perspectives of students [14, 17]. Thus, the focus remains on promoting deeper, more meaningful interactions between learners and educational support systems.

The results of the study suggest that the selection of participants was broadly representative of the majority of the cohort of online students. However, it should be considered that students from other universities could have been included to provide further insight into the study experience of other groups of students. It is noted that the participants selected were considered appropriate, but careful consideration should be given to avoid disadvantaging any group of students. It would be beneficial to rigorously assess the skills and experience of the participants so that they can positively influence the design process. The potential bias or presumption of participants due to previous exposure to information could be a potential drawback that could affect the results of the study.

In terms of the RQs presented earlier, it could be concluded that for RQ1, which assesses how the user interface elements of an online support tool should be designed to effectively support learning, the design study could be summarized in that each of the three phases provided an important building block for answering this question. The first phase, in which the students worked independently over a period of four weeks, allowed them to engage intensively with the material and the research question over this extended period. This first phase offered valuable insights into traditional design principles. After the prototype was developed based on the new findings and tested in a half-day workshop with the students, the group discussions in the conversation session provided insights into 'real' interactions with the LD. Here it was possible to have a direct exchange with the testers and users. Overall, important lessons could be learnt about how such a tool should be designed to effectively support the students' learning process. With regard to RQ2 and how user interfaces and content elements of an online support tool should be designed to promote the UUX, the design study shows how important it is to carry out a UCD process in such a setting in order to gain important insights. For both questions positive and negative feedback was received at each stage.

Overall, the design study supported the implementation of a user-centered LD that supported the students and did not overwhelm them. Through this process, many small details were discovered that might not have been noticed at first glance. For example, familiar elements such as a zoom-in/zoom-out icon to zoom-in/-out on a card were ultimately not so intuitively recognizable that they could be replaced by a labelled interaction element (text + arrow). This became more important in the second phase and was confirmed in the third phase (eye tracking). In summary, a tool has been developed that can be gradually improved in terms of UCD.

5 Outlook

As mentioned earlier, the LD will support SRL with a focus on the use of LA interventions in future versions. In a simulated environment within this study, the integration and use of LA recommendations has already been tested. This was done as a small part of investigating the optimal preparation of content and its elements for an LD that will also be able to apply LA methods. In the follow-up study, with further sub-iterations to follow, the effectiveness of the design as an LAD as a whole will also be examined. In addition, a personalized dashboard as a tool to support SRL will be explored and the need for comparative research to identify the most effective LA interventions and the aspects that can lead to effective support of SRL [30, 31].

Acknowledgements. This work was funded by the German Federal Ministry of Education, grant No. 01PX21001B.

References

1. Baker, R.S., Lindrum, D., Lindrum, M.J., Perkowski, D.: Analyzing Early At-Risk Factors in Higher Education E-Learning Courses. International Educational Data Mining Society. ERIC (2015)
2. Beard, L.A., Harper, C.: Student perceptions of online versus on campus instruction. Educ. Indianapolis Chula Vista **122**(4), 658–663 (2002). Project Innovation
3. Courage, C., Baxter, K.: Understanding Your Users: A Practical Guide to User Requirements Methods, Tools, and Techniques. Gulf Professional Publishing (2005)
4. Cross, N.: Designerly Ways of Knowing. Springer, London (2006). https://doi.org/10.1007/1-84628-301-9
5. Diaz, D.P.: Online drop rates revisited. Technol. Source **3**(3), 35–51 (2002)
6. Din, E.: Ergonomie der Mensch-System-Interaktion–Teil 110: Interaktionsprinzipien (ISO 9241–110: 2020) [Ergonomics of Human-System Interaction-Part 110: Interaction Principles]. Deutsche Fassung EN ISO, pp. 9241–110 (2020)
7. Jivet, I., Scheffel, M., Specht, M., Drachsler, H.: License to evaluate: preparing learning analytics dashboards for educational practice. In: Proceedings of the 8th International Conference on Learning Analytics and Knowledge, pp. 31–40 (2018)
8. Konert, J., Bohr, C., Bellhäuser, H., Rensing, C.:. PeerLA-assistant for individual learning goals and self-regulation competency improvement in online learning scenarios. In: 2016 IEEE 16th International Conference on Advanced Learning Technologies (ICALT), pp. 52–56. IEEE (2016)
9. Krug, S.: Don't Make Me Think, Revisited. A Common Sense Approach to Web and Mobile Usability (2014)
10. Lowdermilk, T.: User-Centered Design: A Developer's Guide to Building User-Friendly Applications. O'Reilly Media, Inc., Sebastopol (2013)
11. Nielsen, J.: Usability Engineering. Morgan Kaufmann, Burlington (1994)
12. Norman, D.: User centered system design. New perspectives on human-computer interaction (1986)
13. Norman, D.: The Design of Everyday Things: Revised and Expanded edn. Basic Books (2013)
14. Schmidt, M., Earnshaw, Y., Tawfik, A.A., Jahnke, I.: Methods of user centered design and evaluation for learning designers. Learn. User Exp. Res. **5**(2), 1–129 (2020)
15. Hasani, L.M., Sensuse, D.I., Suryono, R.R.: User-centered design of e-learning user interfaces: a survey of the practices. In: 2020 3rd International Conference on Computer and Informatics Engineering (IC2IE), pp. 1–7. IEEE, September 2020
16. Schrepp, M., Hinderks, A., Thomaschewski, J.: Design and evaluation of a short version of the user experience questionnaire (UEQ-S). Int. J. Interact. Multimedia Artif. Intell. **4**(6), 103–108. UNIR (2017)
17. Seffah, A., Gulliksen, J., Desmarais, M.C.: An introduction to human-centered software engineering. In: Seffah, A., Gulliksen, J., Desmarais, M.C. (eds.) Human-Centered Software Engineering—Integrating Usability in the Software Development Lifecycle. Human-Computer Interaction Series, vol. 8, pp. 3–14. Springer, Dordrecht (2005). https://doi.org/10.1007/1-4020-4113-6_1
18. Shavelson, R.J., Phillips, D.C., Towne, L., Feuer, M.J.: On the science of educational design research. Educ. Res. **32**(1), 25–28 (2003). https://doi.org/10.3102/0013189X032001025
19. Shneiderman, B.: Designing The User Interface: Strategies for Effective Human-Computer Interaction, 4/e (New edn). Pearson Education India, Noida (1987)
20. Wagemans, J., et al.: A century of Gestalt psychology in visual perception: I. Perceptual grouping and figure--ground organization. Psychol. Bull. **138**(6), 1172 (2012). American Psychological Association

21. Wertheimer, M.: Untersuchungen zur Lehre von der Gestalt. Psychologische forschung **1**(1), 47–58 (1922). Springer

22. Zimmerman, B.J.: Becoming a self-regulated learner: an overview. Theory Pract. **41**(2), 64–70 (2002)

23. Prenkaj, B., Velardi, P., Stilo, G., Distante, D., Faralli, S.: A survey of machine learning approaches for student dropout prediction in online courses. ACM Comput. Surv. (CSUR) **53**(3), 1–34 (2020)

24. Gillett-Swan, J.: The challenges of online learning: supporting and engaging the isolated learner. J. Learn. Des. **10**(1), 20–30 (2017)

25. Croft, N., Dalton, A., Grant, M.: Overcoming isolation in distance learning: building a learning community through time and space. J. Educ. Built Environ. **5**(1), 27–64 (2010)

26. Roy, J.: E-Learning Teaching: Barriers for Isolated Learners. E-Learning-Teaching Strategies and Teachers' Stress in Post Covid-19, pp. 33–38 (2021)

27. Charleer, S., Klerkx, J., Duval, E.: Learning dashboards. J. Learn. Anal. **1**(3), 199–202 (2014)

28. Bennett, L., Folley, S.: Four design principles for learner dashboards that support student agency and empowerment. J. Appl. Res. High. Educ. **12**(1), 15–26 (2019)

29. McKenney, S., Reeves, T.C.: Conducting Educational Design Research. Routledge, London (2018)

30. Molenaar, I., Horvers, A., Dijkstra, S.H.E., Baker, R.S.: Designing dashboards to support learners' self-regulated learning (2019)

31. Heikkinen, S., Saqr, M., Malmberg, J., Tedre, M.: Supporting self-regulated learning with learning analytics interventions–a systematic literature review. Educ. Inf. Technol. **28**(3), 3059–3088 (2023)

32. Poirier, F., Mansouri, K., Safsouf, Y.: Enhanced online academic success and selfregulation through learning analytics dashboards. In: IFIP World Conference on Computers in Education 2022 (WCCE 2022). IFIP's Technical Committee on Education (TC3), August 2022, Hiroshima, Japan. ffhal-04083869f (2022)

33. Goda, Y., Matsuda, T., Yamada, M., Kato, H., Saito, Y., Miyagawa, H.: Design of a learning dashboard in" self-regulator" to support planning for distributed online learning. In: Society for Information Technology and Teacher Education International Conference, pp. 159–161. Association for the Advancement of Computing in Education (AACE), March 2018

34. Shneiderman, B., Plaisant, C., Cohen, M.S., Jacobs, S., Elmqvist, N., Diakopoulos, N.: Designing the User Interface: Strategies for Effective Human-Computer Interaction. Pearson, London (2016)

35. Dave, J.: Enhancing user experience in e-learning: real-time emotional analysis and assessment. Int, J. Eng. Comput. Sci. (IJSECS), **3**(2), 57–64 (2023). https://doi.org/10.35870/ijsecs.v3i2.1206

36. van Eck, M.L., Markslag, E., Sidorova, N., Brosens-Kessels, A., van der Aalst, W.M.P.: Data-driven usability test scenario creation. In: Bogdan, C., Kuusinen, K., Lárusdóttir, M.K., Palanque, P., Winckler, M. (eds.) HCSE 2018. LNCS, vol. 11262, pp. 88–108. Springer, Cham (2019). https://doi.org/10.1007/978-3-030-05909-5_6

37. Larman, C., Basili, V.R.: Iterative and incremental developments. a brief history. Computer **36**(6), 47–56 (2003)

38. Still, B., Crane, K.: Fundamentals of User-Centered Design: A Practical Approach. CRC Press, Boca Raton (2017)

39. Kujala, S.: User involvement: a review of the benefits and challenges. Behav. Inf. Technol. **22**(1), 1–16 (2003)

40. Verbert, K., et al.: Learning dashboards: an overview and future research opportunities. Pers. Ubiquit. Comput.Ubiquit. Comput. **18**, 1499–1514 (2014)

41. Figaredo, D.D., Reich, J., Ruipérez-Valiente, J.A.: Learning analytics and data-driven education: a growing field. Revista Iberoamericana de Educación a Distancia **23**(2), 33–39 (2020)
42. Khalil, M., Ebner, M.: Learning analytics: principles and constraints. In: EdMedia+ Innovate Learning, pp. 1789–1799. Association for the Advancement of Computing in Education (AACE), June 2015
43. De Silva, L.M.H., Chounta, I.A., Rodríguez-Triana, M.J., Roa, E.R., Gramberg, A., Valk, A.: Toward an institutional analytics agenda for addressing student dropout in higher education: an academic stakeholders' perspective. J. Learn. Anal. **9**(2), 179–201 (2022)
44. Sefelin, R., Tscheligi, M., Giller, V.: Paper prototyping-what is it good for? A comparison of paper-and computer-based low-fidelity prototyping. In: CHI'03 Extended Abstracts on Human Factors in Computing Systems, pp. 778–779, April 2003
45. Snyder, C.: Paper Prototyping: The Fast and Easy Way to Design and Refine User Interfaces. Morgan Kaufmann, Burlington (2003)
46. Drzyzga, G., Harder, T., Janneck, M.: Cognitive effort in interaction with software systems for self-regulation - an eye-tracking study. In: Harris, D., Li, WC. (eds.) HCII 2023. LNCS, vol. 14017, pp. 37–52. Springer, Cham (2023). https://doi.org/10.1007/978-3-031-35392-5_3
47. Janneck, M., Merceron, A., Sauer, P.: Workshop on addressing dropout rates in higher education, online – everywhere. In: Companion Proceedings of the 11th Learning Analytics and Knowledge Conference (LAK 2021), pp. 261–269 (2021)
48. Drzyzga, G., Harder, T.: Student-Centered Development of an Online Software Tool to Provide Learning Support Feedback: A Design-study Approach (2022)
49. Holstein, K., McLaren, B.M., Aleven, V.: Intelligent tutors as teachers' aides: exploring teacher needs for real-time analytics in blended classrooms. In: Proceedings of the Seventh International Learning Analytics & Knowledge Conference, pp. 257–266, March 2017
50. Schwendimann, B.A., et al.: Perceiving learning at a glance: a systematic literature review of learning dashboard research. IEEE Trans. Learn. Technol. **10**(1), 30–41 (2016)
51. Christensen, S.S., Spackman, J.S.: Dropout rates, student momentum, and course walls: a new tool for distance education designers. J. Educ. Online **14**(2), n2 (2017)
52. de Oliveira, C.F., Sobral, S.R., Ferreira, M.J., Moreira, F.: How does learning analytics contribute to prevent students' dropout in higher education: a systematic literature review. Big Data Cogn. Comput. **5**(4), 64 (2021)
53. Sáiz-Manzanares, M.C., Marticorena-Sánchez, R., García-Osorio, C.I.: Monitoring students at the university: design and application of a Moodle plugin. Appl. Sci. **10**(10), 3469 (2020)
54. Del Bonifro, F., Gabbrielli, M., Lisanti, G., Zingaro, S.P.: Student dropout prediction. In: Bittencourt, I.I., Cukurova, M., Muldner, K., Luckin, R., Millán, E. (eds.) AIED 2020. LNCS (LNAI), vol. 12163, pp. 129–140. Springer, Cham (2020). https://doi.org/10.1007/978-3-030-52237-7_11

Why are You Blinking at Me? Exploring Users' Understanding of Robotic Status Indicators

E. Liberman-Pincu(⊠) [ID], S. Honig [ID], and T. Oron-Gilad [ID]

Ben-Gurion University of the Negev, 84105 Beer-Sheva, Israel
elapin@post.bgu.ac.il

Abstract. User Confusion leads to misunderstandings about the robot or the situation, and influences customer satisfaction. This study evaluates users' understanding of commercially available robot statuses presented by LED indicators. Images and videos of indicators of nine robots were taken from manufacturers' websites and were manipulated to assess how specific visual qualities of indicators, color, and animation, affect users. One hundred and forty-seven respondents participated in an online study. They were asked to: 1) select the animation that best fits a given status description, 2) rank the compatibility between an indicator and a written status description, and 3) select the status description that best fits a given animation. Results indicated that, in most cases, the manufacturers' intention was not well understood by respondents. Understandability was affected by the indicator's visual qualities and status prevalence. Recommendations and gaps are detailed.

Keywords: Light Signals · Understandability · Human-robot interaction

1 Introduction

Light signals are commonly used by regulatory bodies to convey warnings in different fields, including medical devices, fire alarms, traffic signal lights, emergency vehicles, warning lights in work zones, etc. [1–3]. Light signals' visual appearance is composed of their geometry, color, brightness, and modulation over time, e.g., 'flashing' lights [4].

In the world of robotics, manufacturers and researchers tend to consider using LED indicators as a fast and intuitive way to express a robot's intentions by applying a broad spectrum of animation patterns and colors [5–8]. Light signals are utilized in social robots to relay semantic indications such as facial expressions and gestures. Even simple light expressions can allow people to construct rich and complex interpretations of a robot's behavior [9].

Dynamic light signals, especially blinking lights, trigger social interaction responses and may encourage users' appropriate intervention [10, 11]. Adding flashing lights to a robot may increase users' compliance as it draws better attention [12], but it may also be perceived as more threatening [13, 14]. Yet, these are sporadic studies, and we are not aware of any standards for how to design LED indicators in human-robot interaction (HRI).

© The Author(s), under exclusive license to Springer Nature Switzerland AG 2023
H. P. da Silva and P. Cipresso (Eds.): CHIRA 2023, CCIS 1996, pp. 282–294, 2023.
https://doi.org/10.1007/978-3-031-49425-3_17

Honig et al. [15] looked at customer reviews of small utilitarian domestic robots (e.g., vacuum robots) and extracted the failure types of robots that undergo in domestic settings and how these failures influence customer experience. Using thematic analysis, they grouped reported failures into twelve types and three categories (Technical, Interaction, and Service aiming to gain insight into the problems people described in their reviews. Each ascribed failure was attributed to all possible categories and types that may explain the source of the matter. Most reported failures were related to technical issues (49%), but nearly a third (30%) were related to interaction. Looking at the specific failure types, about 4% of the failures (419) were related to User Confusion, which they defined as "Issues that lead to user misunderstandings of the robot or the situation" (Honig et al. 2022, Table 3), i.e., incompatibility between the robot feedback and its behavior, unclear indicators, difficulty in learning how to operate, or no manual for operating or fixing. Further, the User Confusion category affected customers' satisfaction (as measured by their star rating) by about 17%. User Confusion was not the most dominant category of failures or the most impactful on customer satisfaction, yet we argue that: 1) with the existing knowledge and ISO standards, such confusion can easily be fixed if more attention is given to status indicators in the design process, and 2) that users rely on status indicators to provide them information about their robot's condition and problems, hence, not everything can be understood merely from the context of operation.

In this study, we sought to examine whether robotic manufacturers use LED indicators in a consistent way across robots and contexts of use and whether users understand the meaning behind the LED indicators. As such, we conducted a design deconstruction of LED indicators of nine commercially available robots for domestic and social use cases. We then manipulated the LED designs to explore users' interpretation and understanding of common robotic statuses.

2 Aim and Scope

This study aims to explore and evaluate users' understanding of robots' statuses presented by LED indicators and assess the impact of color and animation on understandability. To achieve this, we followed our methodology for Visual Qualities (VQ) deconstruction

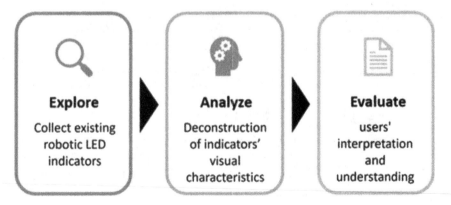

Explore
Collect existing robotic LED indicators

Analyze
Deconstruction of indicators' visual characteristics

Evaluate
users' interpretation and understanding

Fig. 1. Methodology for robotic LED indicators characteristics deconstruction and evaluation.

and evaluation [16, 17]. The methodology consists of three steps, as shown in Fig. 1: Explore existing robotic LED indicators, Analyze their visual characteristics by deconstructing them into color and animation features, and Evaluate users' interpretation and understanding. These steps are detailed in the following sections.

3 Study Design

3.1 Step 1: Explore

The first step is to survey existing robotic design models and their use of LED indicators. For this, we collected images and videos of nine commercial robots with different contexts of use. First, we used the Google search engine to search words such as: "Top Social Robots", "Most popular robots," etc. (the search was conducted in December 2019). Next, we used the robot's manufacturers' manuals, commercial and users' videos, and technical support forums to identify the robot's statuses and the way they were displayed. The LED indicators of nine models [18–26] (Fig. 2) were classified by color, dimensions (proportions), animation, and location on the robot's body.

We excluded dimensions and locations from this evaluation study since these features didn't vary much among the nine robots. We remained with color and animation (e.g., blinking, spinning, etc.).

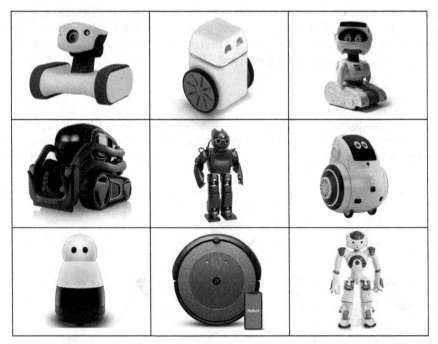

Fig. 2. Selected robots (from top-left): Appbot, Kubo, Misty, Vector, Darwin, Miko, Kury, Roomba, and Nao.

3.2 Step 2: Analyze

We deconstructed the visual characteristics of the LED indicators and compared them by status to seek for a common language among manufacturers. We identified five status types symbolized by LED indicators: In order, Error, Waiting, Processing, and Connected to WIFI. Table 1 details the inner classification of each status type.

For each, we mapped the visual characteristics of the indicators by color: red, green, blue, white, orange, purple, and yellow and animation: static (no animation), blinking, or complex animation (e.g., spinning, sweeping, filling, etc.).

The deconstruction process indicated that manufacturers consistently used red indicators to signify errors. Yet, there was no common pattern of use for other colors and statuses. In addition, most statuses were represented by static (no animation) indicators; the only exception found was the processing status, which was most often communicated using blinking or complex animations. Figure 3 illustrates our findings by color and by animation.

Table 1. List of robots' statuses.

Status type	Examples
In order – the robot is ready to interact with users	In order On Working Charging Fully charged
Processing – the robot is busy processing a command or initializing	Processing order Restarting
Waiting – the robot is waiting for the user to give a particular command or to respond (during the interaction as opposed to in order)	Waiting for response Listening
WiFi connection	WiFi is connected
Error	System error WiFi failure Low battery

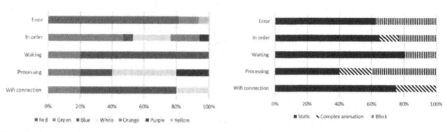

Fig. 3. Left: Led indicators' color mapping by status; Right: LED indicators' animation mapping by statuses.

3.3   Step 3: Evaluate

To evaluate users' understanding of commercially available robots' statuses, we designed
an online questionnaire in Google Forms. The questionnaire consisted of three parts. In
part I, participants were presented with a status description and were asked to select
an animation that best fits it. In part II, participants watched an animation showing a
robot's LED indicator and its meaning as defined by the manufacturer and were asked
to rank their compatibility on a scale of (1–5). In part III, participants were presented
with animation and asked to match it to a written status description that fits it the best.
Each part included one attention check question. Figure 4 illustrates the questionnaire's
structure and presents an example of each part. In addition, participants were asked to
fill out a demographic questionnaire (age, gender, education, and prior experience with
robots).

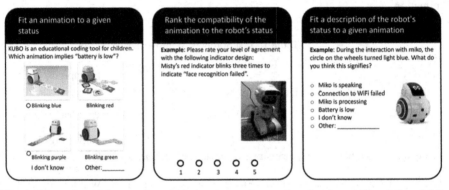

Fig. 4.   Illustration of the questionnaire's structure and examples of each part (from left to right).
In part I, participants were asked to fit an animation to a given status. In part II, participants
watched an animation showing a robot's LED indicator and its meaning by the manufacturer and
were asked to rank their compatibility. In part III, participants were asked to fit a description of
the robot's status to a given animation. Note the images were animated, not static.

The online questionnaire was distributed between February and March 2020 to students (in exchange for course credit) and to the wider public (using social media and
snowball distribution; no compensation was offered).

In total, data from 147 adult respondents were collected (84 females, 63 males).
Most of the respondents were students aged 22–28 years old (M = 29.4 years, SD =
9.85); therefore, we removed age and education from the analysis.

First, we compared the respondents' answers with the manufacturers' intentions, as
they appeared in the manual, to see if users interpreted the LED indicators correctly.
Following, general linear mixed model (GLMM) analyses were conducted to assess the
factors affecting respondents' agreement in part II of the questionnaire and to determine
which respondents' characteristics affect users' understanding of the LED indicators'
meaning in parts I and III.

In addition, based on the data in part III, we conducted a crosstab analysis to assess
the effect of color and animation on status ascription. For this analysis, we were only

looking at the respondents' interpretation with no regard to the correct answer by the manufacturers. Finally, a K-means cluster analysis was conducted to identify repetitive combinations. Results are detailed in the following section.

4 Evaluation Results

4.1 Part I – Fit Animation to a Given Status

This part consisted of 21 questions; in each, respondents were asked to select an animation that, in their opinion, suits a given status best. A total of 2,025 observations were collected. Findings reveal a low success rate; only 44% of the observations matched the manufacturer's intentions, as noted in the operation manual. In most cases, respondents were not able to match the correct animation to the manufacturers' intended meaning. In the following analyses, we delve into the characteristics that affected the indicators' understandability.

4.2 Part II – Rank Agreement with Manufacturer Intentions

This part consisted of 39 questions; in each, respondents were asked to rank their agreement with the design selections of the manufacturers. A total of 3,978 observations were collected. In most cases (58% of the observations), participants had selected either 4-agree (31.5%) or 5-strongly agree (26.5%). Only 20% of the cases were ranked 1-strongly disagree (4%) and 2-disagree (16%). The average rank was 3.6 (SE = 0.2).

We defined *status indicator prevalence* as a binary variable. If a status was communicated through an LED indicator in five or more robots out of the nine, it was defined as 1, else 0. All in all, we found that most manufacturers used LED indicators to symbolize six messages: In order, Error, Low battery, WIFI connection, Charging, and Waiting. LED indicators were less common for the statuses Executing, WIFI failure, Fully charged, Restarting, and Processing, even though these statuses exist in most of the robots and are relevant to the user-robot interaction. Table 2 details the status indicators by prevalence.

Table 2. Status indicators classification by prevalence.

High prevalence indicators *status indicator prevalence = 1**	Low prevalence indicators *status indicator prevalence = 0*
In order	Executing
Error	WiFi failure
Low battery	Fully Charged
WiFi connection	Restarting
Charging	Processing order
Waiting	

* *Status indicator prevalence* was defined as 1 if status was communicated through an LED indicator in five or more robots out of the nine, else 0.

A GLMM analysis was conducted to evaluate the effects of respondents' character-istics (gender and previous experience with robots) and *status indicator prevalence* on respondents' agreement. Indicators' prevalence was found to affect respondents' agree-ment with the manufacturers' choices [$F(1, N = 3467) = 167, p < .001$]. Higher levels of agreement (ranking 4 or 5) correlated with common indicators and lower levels of agreement (ranking 1 or 2) correlated with less common indicators. Respondents' gender or prior experience with robots had no effect. Figure 5 presents two examples.

Please rate your level of agreement with the following indicator design:	
 *Blinking orange	 *Blinking red
Status: WiFi failure	Status: low battery
Low agreement (1,2) 41% Medium agreement (3) 25% High agreement (4,5) 34%	Low agreement (1,2) 5% Medium agreement (3) 13% High agreement (4,5) 82%

Fig. 5. Right: an example of a low prevalence indicator - respondents rated their agreement as lower (more 1–2 rankings); left: an example of a high prevalence indicator - respondents rated their agreement higher (mostly 4–5).

4.3 Part III – Fit a Status to a Given Animation

This part consisted of 15 questions; in each, respondents were asked to select a status that best matched a given animation. A total of 1,530 observations were collected; of those 65% matched the manufacturer's decisions.

Crosstab Analysis. We conducted a crosstab analysis with a Chi-square test of inde-pendence to assess how users interpret the visual features of the indicator (color and animation) and how they affect their status ascription. Six possible status types were examined: In order, Error, Processing, Waiting, Interacting, and Executing, and "I don't know" for visual features that were confusing. Independent effects were the participants' characteristics (gender and prior experience with robots) and the indicator's visual fea-tures (color and animation). The participant's ID was included as a random effect to account for multiple responses of each individual. Table 3 details the factors included in the model.

The indicators' visual features were found to affect the status ascription. A Chi-square test of independence showed a significant association between the indicator color and the status ascription, $X^2 (24, N = 1530) = 1848.3, p < .001$, and a significant association between the indicator's animation and the status ascription, $X^2 (6, N = 1530) = 440, p$

< .01. Participants' gender and prior experience had no significant effect on the status ascription.

The following paragraphs detail the associations by color and animation (see Figs. 6 and 7, respectively).

Table 3. Factors Included In The Analysis Of Part III-Fitting a status to a given animation.

	Factors	Range
Independent		
Participants' characteristics	Gender	Male, Female
	Prior experience	Yes, No
Indicator's visual features*	Color	Red, Green, Blue, White, Orange, Purple, Yellow
	Animation	Static, Blinking
Dependent		
Status type ascription	In order	In order, Fully charged, Set up completed, Face recognition succeeded
	Error	Error, Low battery, Disconnected, Software update failed
	Processing	Processing, Updating program, Charging
	Waiting	Waiting for your commands
	Interacting	Talking, recognizing your voice
	Executing	Executing your commands
	Don't know	

Color. Red indicators were perceived almost unanimously (92.7%, 292 out of 315 observations) as Errors.

Orange indicators mainly were perceived as *Error* (55.2%, 58 out of 105 observations), but also as *Interacting* (17.1%) and *Processing* (16.1%). In addition, 11.5% of the observations were ascribed as "I don't know".

Green indicators mainly were perceived as *In order* (53.5%, 281 out of 525 observations), but also *Executing* (18.3%) and *waiting* (15.2%).

Purple indicators were ascribed by most as *Processing* (66.7%, 40 out of 60 observations) and *Waiting* (16.7%).

Respondents showed the least unanimity regarding blue indicators. These were ascribed mainly as *Waiting* (35.6%, 187 out of 525 observations), *Processing* (21.5%), and *Interacting* (18.9%), but also as *Error, Executing,* and *In order* (less than 7% each). Furthermore, 8% of the observations were ascribed as "I don't know". Figure 6 illustrates the status ascriptions by colors.

Animation. Static light indicators were ascribed as In order (30.7%, 290 out of 945 observations), Error (19.7%), Waiting (18.9%), Interacting (12.6%), and processing

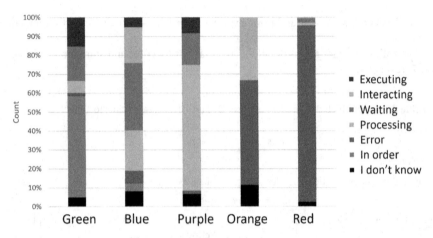

Fig. 6. Statuses ascriptions by colors.

(12%). No one ascribed Executing to a static indicator. In addition, in 6% of the observations, respondents chose "I don't know."

Blinking light indicators were ascribed as Error (35.4%, 297 out of 585 observations), Waiting (20.7%), Executing (19.1%), and processing (16.2%). Only 2.4% of the observations were ascribed as In order. No one ascribed Interacting to a blinking indicator. In addition, in 6.1% of the observations, respondents chose "I don't know."

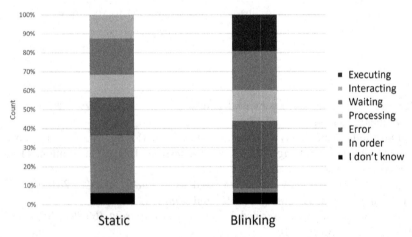

Fig. 7. Status ascriptions by indicators animation.

Cluster Analysis. A K-means cluster analysis was conducted to identify repetitive combinations of color and animation from a bottom-up data-driven approach. First, we determined the number of clusters by looking at the sum of squares and the distribution of respondents among clusters. Once the number of clusters was determined as three, we verified that both color and animation were contributing to the ANOVA model (p < .001).

The 1,530 observations were grouped into three significantly different clusters. Cluster 1 contains 669 observations and represents the *Waiting* status with a static blue indicator. Cluster 2 contains 414 observations and represents the *In order* status with a static green indicator. Cluster 3 contains 447 observations and represents the *Error* status with a blinking red indicator. Table 4 summarizes the cluster analysis outcomes.

Table 4. Repetitive status combinations across color and animation, based on the K-means.

	Cluster 1	Cluster 2	Cluster 3
N	669	414	447
Status	Waiting	In order	Error
Color	Blue	Green	Red
Animation	Static	Static	Blinking

5 Discussion

Communicating the robot status properly is essential to achieving satisfactory, high-quality human-robot interaction. In this exploratory study, we sought to examine whether robot manufacturers use LED indicators to communicate different statuses in a consistent way across different use cases and whether users and manufacturers share a common understanding of the indicators' meanings.

To do so, we surveyed and analyzed the visual features of commercially existing robotic status indicators. We compared manufacturers' expressions of six status types: In order, Error, WIFI connection, Processing, and Waiting. Our findings indicated that manufacturers have no common language except for using the red color to symbolize Error. In addition, users' understanding of the indicators' meaning was low: a success rate of 44% in matching animation to a given status and 65% in interpreting given animations.

Our results are mostly consistent with previous literature. The existing indicator characteristics vary between the different types of robots and are not intuitive in many cases [27]. However, certain characteristics of color or animation can be associated with a specific state relying on previous experience (such as traffic lights) [9]. Still, there are no universal standards (e.g., malfunction was represented by red but also orange, blinking can express malfunction but also processing).

Manufacturers succeeded more in communicating common statuses (e.g., Error, In order, etc.) but were less successful in communicating interaction-related statuses such as executing and processing a command. These findings reveal that the basic language of LED indicators is not satisfactory for the evolving needs of the HRI field. This issue must be addressed because understanding is key for non-expert customers and users to be able to interact with robots easily and comfortably.

Through this investigation, we identified the most common status indicators that are communicated via LED indicators (Table 2). We also present preliminary design guidelines for the color and animation of LED indicators that best suit each status (Table 5). We found meaningful, consistent recommendations only for two statuses: In order and Error. For the other statuses, many gaps and inconsistencies must be further investigated by analyzing other visual features (e.g., dimension, shapes, and location).

Table 5. The most suitable indicator colors and animation for each status.

Status	Color	Animation	Design guidelines
In order	Green	Static	It is better to use a static green LED indicator and avoid red, orange, or purple. A blue indicator may be suitable in some cases
Error	Red	Blinking	It is better to use a blinking red or orange LED indicator to signify Error
Processing	—	Blinking	It is better to use a blinking LED indicator. There is no unanimity regarding the color, except red and green indicators that are less suitable probably because they are more related to Error and In order statuses
Waiting	Blue	Static*	Waiting is best communicated with a static blue LED indicator *Based on the cluster analysis. Note that both static and blinking indicators were ascribed to this status
Interacting	—	Static	There is no unanimity regarding the suitable colors to signify Interacting Although, it is better communicated with static indicators
Executing	—	Blinking	There is no unanimity regarding the suitable colors to signify Executing. Although, it is better communicated with blinking indicators

This work is subject to several limitations. First, looking at existing commercial robots narrowed the possibilities and limited our ability to conduct complete visual feature comparisons. We were also limited to existing pictures of the robots taken from different angles and with varied backgrounds. In addition, using online questionnaires with pictures and animations of the indicators may be less effective than actual **real-world** interactions with robots. Furthermore, we acknowledge that sounds or other behaviors associated with the LED presence may modify users' understanding: e.g., the robot started staring at the user and stopped speaking when the LEDs turned blue. However, in this current study, we deliberately sought to isolate LEDs to achieve a clearer understanding of users' interpretation.

To confirm this study's findings, our next step will be to create and reconstruct new robotic designs (using CAD software to produce 2D and 3D illustrations and animations). These unique designs will allow us to control and isolate different LEDs' visual features (e.g., proportions, locations, shapes, etc.). In addition, we intend to conduct studies involving direct interaction to evaluate the perception of indicators' visual features in real-time settings.

Acknowledgments. This research was supported by the Ministry of Innovation, Science and Technology, Israel (Grant 3-15625), and by the Ben-Gurion University of the Negev through the Helmsley Charitable Trust, the Agricultural, Biological and Cognitive Robotics Initiative, the W. Gunther Plaut Chair in Manufacturing Engineering and by the George Shrut Chair in Human performance management.

References

1. IEC 60601-1-8:2006. Medical electrical equipment. https://www.iso.org/standard/41986.html
2. ISO 7240-23:2013. Fire detection and alarm systems. https://www.iso.org/standard/54400.html
3. Rea, M.S., Bullough, J.D., Radetsky, L.C., Skinner, N.P., Bierman, A.: Toward the development of standards for yellow flashing lights used in work zones. Light. Res. Technol. **50**(4), 552-570 (2018)
4. Ferguson, H.M., Mainwaring, G.: A survey of visual guidance aids for aircraft. Light. Res. Technol. **3**(4), 251–267 (1971)
5. Baraka, K., Paiva, A., Veloso, M.: Expressive lights for revealing mobile service robot state. In: Reis, L., Moreira, A., Lima, P., Montano, L., Muñoz-Martinez, V. (eds.) Robot 2015. AISC, vol. 417, pp. 107–119. Springer, Cham (2016). https://doi.org/10.1007/978-3-319-271 46-0_9
6. Baraka, K., Veloso, M.M.: Mobile service robot state revealing through expressive lights: formalism, design, and evaluation. Int. J. Soc. Robot. **10**(1), 65–92 (2018)
7. Kim, Y., Fong, T.: Signaling robot state with light attributes. : Proceedings of the Companion of the 2017 ACM/IEEE International Conference on Human-Robot Interaction, pp. 163–164, March 2017
8. Song, S., Yamada, S.: Designing LED lights for a robot to communicate gaze. Adv. Robot. **33**(7–8), 360–368 (2019)
9. Song, S., Yamada, S.: Effect of expressive lights on human perception and interpretation of functional robot. In: Extended Abstracts of the 2018 CHI Conference on Human Factors in Computing Systems, pp. 1–6, April 2018
10. Mutlu, B., Forlizzi, J., Nourbakhsh, I., Hodgins, J.: The use of abstraction and motion in the design of social interfaces. In: Proceedings of the 6th Conference on Designing Interactive Systems, pp. 251–260, June 2006
11. Seitinger, S., Taub, D.M., Taylor, A.S.: Light bodies: exploring interactions with responsive lights. In: Proceedings of the Fourth International Conference on Tangible, Embedded, and Embodied Interaction, pp. 113–120, January 2010
12. Crawford, A.: The perception of light signals: the effect of the number of irrelevant lights. Ergonomics **5**(3), 417–428 (1962)
13. Liberman-Pincu, E., David, A., Sarne-Fleischmann, V., Edan, Y., Oron-Gilad, T.: Comply with me: using design manipulations to affect human-robot interaction in a COVID-19 officer robot use case. Multimodal Technol. Interact. **5**(11), 71 (2021)
14. D'Egidio, G., Patel, R., Rashidi, B., Mansour, M., Sabri, E., Milgram, P.: A study of the efficacy of flashing lights to increase the salience of alcohol-gel dispensers for improving hand hygiene compliance. Am. J. Infect. Control **42**(8), 852–855 (2014)

15. Honig, S., Bartal, A., Parmet, Y., Oron-Gilad, T.: Using online customer reviews to classify, predict, and learn about domestic robot failures. Int. J. Soc. Robot. 1–26. (2022)
16. Liberman-Pincu, E., Van Grondelle, E.D., Oron-Gilad, T.: Designing robots with relationships in mind: suggesting two models of human-socially assistive robot (SAR) relationship. In: Companion of the 2021 ACM/IEEE International Conference on Human-Robot Interaction, pp. 555–558, March 2021
17. Liberman-Pincu, E., Oron-Gilad, T.: Impacting the perception of socially assistive robots-evaluating the effect of visual qualities among children. In: 2021 30th IEEE International Conference on Robot & Human Interactive Communication (RO-MAN), pp. 612–618. IEEE, August 2021
18. https://appbot.co/
19. https://kubo.education/
20. https://www.mistyrobotics.com/
21. https://www.digitaldreamlabs.com/
22. https://www.robotlab.com/store/darwin-op2-robot
23. https://miko.ai/
24. https://www.heykuri.com/explore-kuri/
25. https://www.irobot.com/roomba
26. https://www.softbankrobotics.com/emea/en/nao
27. Pörtner, A., Schröder, L., Rasch, R., Sprute, D., Hoffmann, M., König, M.: The power of color: a study on the effective use of colored light in human-robot interaction. In: 2018 IEEE/RSJ International Conference on Intelligent Robots and Systems (IROS), pp. 3395–3402. IEEE, October 2018

Immediate-After Effect of Enhancement Push-Off at a Terminal Stance Phase of Gait Using Heating of Insole Tip for the Development of Smart Insole

Kazushige Oshita(✉)

Department of Human Information Engineering, Okayama Prefectural University, 111 Kuboki, Soja 719-1197, Okayama, Japan
oshita@ss.oka-pu.ac.jp

Abstract. This study investigated the changes in lower limb joint angles and the step length during and immediately-after enhancement of push-off in the gait using heating of insole tip. Twelve healthy males walked on a treadmill under three different conditions; Participants were instructed to 1) walk as usual (CONTROL), 2) widen strides with an enhancement of push-off with normal insole (NORMAL), and 3) widen strides while attempting to enhancement of push-off with the warm area in insole (heated on the insole tip) (HEAT). In the NORMAL- and HEAT-conditions, the hip and ankle range of motions (ROMs) and step length during gait increased during push-off attention. However, ankle ROM and step length in the HEAT-condition increased significantly even immediately-after the use of heated insoles compared to before use. This increase in ROM may have been caused by increased plantar flexion during the terminal stance phase. These results suggest that if the tip of the insole is temporarily heated to enhance push-off when the step length becomes shorter, the step length widen and the effect is maintained even after heating has been removed. Therefore, existing smart insole technology can be used to detect shortened strides, and future insoles may be increased push-off and widened strides by temporarily heating the insole tip.

Keywords: Stride · Step length · Walking · Hip joint · Ankle plantar-flexion

1 Introduction

Many "smart insoles," which measure and visualize walking and/or running via embedded pressure sensors, acceleration/gyro sensors, and GPS sensors, among others in the insole and provide the user with this information, have been developed in recent years [1–4] and have attracted much attention [5]. Users can employ this information to check the state of their locomotion and adjust it accordingly. Thus, current smart insoles allow a user to check their state of gait and running, and adjust their movements based on the information. Some users may only check their condition and may not be able to improve their movements. If the smart insole itself analyses the gait and provides some stimulus to the user via the insole, thereby making the user aware about improving the gait, it would be an "advanced" smart insole.

© The Author(s), under exclusive license to Springer Nature Switzerland AG 2023
H. P. da Silva and P. Cipresso (Eds.): CHIRA 2023, CCIS 1996, pp. 295–306, 2023.
https://doi.org/10.1007/978-3-031-49425-3_18

Although gait consists of cadence and stride (step length), widening strides can be achieved using a variety of strategies, such as landing the swinging leg more forward, enhancing the push-off at the terminal stance phase, swinging the arms more, and increasing trunk rolling. Our previous study investigated how individuals widen their strides when increasing gait speed with wider strides [6]. Eighteen healthy males performed 10-m gait tasks in two conditions: 1) they just walked faster, and 2) they walked faster with wider their strides. Afterwards, participants were asked how they widened their strides. The survey observed that 14 (approximately 80%) of the participants widen their strides in an attempt to extend the swinging leg forward. Two (approximately 10%) of the participants attempted enhancing the push-off at the terminal stance phase, while the remaining 2 participants (approximately 10%) were aware of both of these. Further, the study also examined the effects of widening strides while emphasizing push-off at the terminal stance phase on strides. Fourteen participants who were not aware of push-off at the terminal stance phase when widening their strides performed a 10-m fast walk task with widening the strides while emphasizing the push-off at the terminal stance phase. This experiment observed that the emphasis on push-off resulted in more widened stride than the attempting to extend the swinging leg forward. Therefore, these results suggest that although most of the participants widened their strides while attempting to extend the swinging leg forward, the emphasis on push-off at the terminal stance phase results in more widened strides [6].

Enhancing the push-off at the terminal stance phase of gait may not only widen the strides as previously described, but may also have a variety of advantages. For example, shorter strides have been reported to be associated with lower muscle strength [7]. In particular, one of the hallmarks of age- or disability-related gait is a greater reduction in ankle power output during the terminal stance phase. Age-related impairment in ankle power-generating capacity limits gait speed and step length [8]. In addition, regarding fall prevention, the onset of diminished push-off in the terminal stance phase with aging may independently contribute to lower balance control and precipitate slower gait speeds [9]. These reports suggest that promoting appropriate push-off at the terminal stance phase and improving gait with sufficient strides may be advantageous for the purposes of 1) exercising to increase physical activity, 2) preventing a decrease in gait speed with age, and 3) preventing falls from the perspective of balance control. Actually, although various national guidelines recommend both walking and brisk walking, i.e. walking at a slightly faster speed [10, 11], the summary leaflet of the physical activity guidelines in Japan introduces " + 10 (min) walking with wider strides and faster" [12].

Because of these advantages, attempts have been made to enhance push-off during walking using light tactile stimulation (i.e., a tactile guide) to the plantar surface with an insole [13–15]. A study that heated the insole tip and instructed participants to widen their strides while push-off with the warm area reported that the widening of the step length was greater than if the participants were simply conscious of enhancing their push-off (i.e., without heated insoles) [15]. The heating of insoles is easy because the heat-generating sheet is simply embedded and has already been commercialized as a protective device in cold environments [16, 17]. Therefore, it is expected that the current smart insole technology can detect a shorten in strides, then heat the tip of the insole with a heat-generating sheet, leading to the development of an "advanced smart insole" [15], as described at the beginning of this article. However, previous study has only found a widening of stride when the tip of the insole was heated. Based on the results of this study, insoles should be kept warm to prevent stride shortening [15]. However, prolonged heating may lead to discomfort in the sole (e.g., increased sweating). Furthermore, skin tissue injury will occur once heat applied is 44 °C or above for long time [18], which may lead to low-temperature burns by such a heated insole.

However, the use of such light tactile guides to lead the user to an appropriate movement has been shown to temporarily facilitate movement learning [19, 20]. In the example of gait requiring higher balancing ability (i.e., tandem gait), the presence of a light tactile guide on the leg that provides direction of progression has been reported to not only improve gait performance, but also to improve gait performance even when the guide is removed afterward [20]. If such an immediate-after effect is observed even in the heated insole to prevent shortening of the strides, the aforementioned problem of prolonged heating can be eliminated, and "advanced smart insoles" can be developed. Therefore, this study investigated the immediate-after effect of enhancing push-off of gait using heating of insole tip for the development of "advanced smart insoles."

2   Methods

2.1   Participants

The participants in this study included 12 healthy young males (age: 21–24 years, height; 1.64–1.86 m, weight; 48.7–83.1 kg). Participants were recruited among students of the university. The following inclusion criteria were applied by interview; no current or previous medical history of neural, muscular, or skeletal disorders; having a level of physical fitness that facilitates this study's gait test without any orthopedic aid (supporters, taping, crutches, etc.). Study participation was voluntary, and participants were allowed to drop out at any time. Prior to their inclusion, participants were informed of the study purpose, and informed consent was obtained. This study was approved by the Ethics Committee of Okayama Prefectural University (No. 21–58).

The participants wore tight-fitting shirts and tights for motion capture. In addition, they wore shoes with a thin sole (5 mm thick) covered with an elastic cloth that fitted their feet perfectly (GA-5639, Kinugawa Co. Ltd., Japan). Shoes of various sizes that best fit the participant's foot were selected.

2.2   Gait Task

The experimental protocol and settings for heated insoles were based on a previous study [15]. Participants performed a 2-min walk at 4 km/h on a treadmill (Tempo T82, Johnson Health Tech, Taiwan) three times, with a 3-min break in between (Fig. 1). The first, second, and third gait tasks are referred to as "pre-trial," "mid-trial," and "post-trial," respectively. The trials were performed under three conditions: In the CONTROL condition, the participants walked as usual with a polyurethane insole (normal insole) in the shoe during the three trials. NORMAL condition: Pre- and post-trials were the same as in the CONTROL condition, walking normally; in mid-trials, the participant was instructed to widen the strides with a push-off from the ball of the foot to the toe, using the normal insole. HEAT conditions: Pre- and post-trials were the same as in the CONTROL condition, walking normally; in mid-trials, the insoles were replaced with modified ones during the break. A disposable warmer was attached to tip (the area from the ball of the foot to the toe) of the normal insole (Fig. 1). The temperature of the heated area, measured using a thermometer (FS-300, HuBDIC Co., Ltd., Korea), was confirmed to be above 45 °C. Participants were instructed to widen the strides while attempting to enhancement of push off with the warm area. Every participant performed each condition gait on different days with a random sequence. Participants unfamiliar with treadmill walking were given about 5 min to practice treadmill gait beforehand.

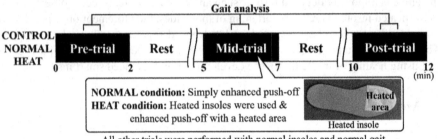

Fig. 1. Experimental protocol.

2.3 Motion Analysis

A 3D motion analysis system consisting of infrared cameras (1,728 × 1,200 pixel) and motion capture software (MApro, ver. 1.0.1, Hu-tech Co., Ltd., Japan) was used to acquire the kinematic data. Reflective markers were placed on the greater trochanter, lateral joint line of the knee, lateral malleolus, calcaneus, and the third metatarsophalangeal joint (Fig. 2). Six infrared cameras were placed around the treadmill to capture all the markers, and data were acquired at 240 fps during the middle 15 s of each gait trial (Fig. 1).

The acquired data were analyzed using 3D motion analysis software (ICpro-Analysis, ver. 2.50, Hu-tech Co., Ltd., Japan) and smoothed using a second-order low-pass Butterworth filter with the cutoff frequency of 5 Hz. The definitions of each joint angle are shown in Fig. 2. The hip joint angle was defined as the angle between the vertical line and thigh (the axis between the greater trochanter and knee). The knee joint angle was defined as the angle between the thigh and lower leg (the axis between the knee and the lateral malleolus). The ankle joint angle was defined as the angle between the knee, lateral malleolus, and third metatarsophalangeal joint. Each of these angles was analysed using the data on the sagittal plane on the right side, and these angular displacements were represented as percentages over the course of the gait cycle (0%–100%). Furthermore, hip joint range of motion (ROM) was evaluated as the difference between the angle at initial contact and the angle at toe-off (i.e., leg swing angle). The knee joint ROM was evaluated from the most flexed position to the most extended position, while the ankle joint ROM was evaluated from the most plantar-flexed position to the most dorsi-flexed position during a single step. The step length during one step was assessed by the horizontal distance travelled by the lateral malleolus markers from heel (the calcaneus marker) ground contact to toe off the ground (the metatarsophalangeal joint marker). These angular variables and step length were evaluated by calculating the average of four consecutive stable steps using the acquired data.

2.4 Statistical Analysis

A two-factor analysis of variance (trials (pre-, mid-, and post-trials) × three conditions (CONTROL, NORMAL, and HEAT)) was performed to compare the means for each angle and step length. If a significant interaction was observed, multiple comparisons were performed for each condition using Holm's method. In addition to the significance tests, an effect size with Cohen's d value was calculated to compare the pre- and post-trial means.

These analyses were performed using js-STAR XR + software (ver. 1.6.0 j, Japan). The level of statistical significance was set at $<5\%$. The effect size was defined as small, moderate, or large depending on whether $d < 0.2$, $0.2 \leq d < 0.8$, or $d \geq 0.8$, respectively.

3   Results

The changes in the hip, knee, and ankle joint ROMs in each condition are presented in Table 1. The hip joint ROM exhibited significant effects between trials and conditions ($P < 0.05$). Their interaction with hip joint ROM was also significant ($P < 0.01$), whereas knee joint ROM did not exhibit a significant interaction between trials and conditions. Although multiple comparisons in the hip joint ROM indicated that was significantly larger in mid-trials compared to pre-trials with a large-sized effect ($d = 1.48$ and 1.10 in NORMAL and HEAT conditions, respectively), there was no significant difference between pre- and post-trials in each NORMAL and HEAT condition. Changes in the hip and knee joint angles during the pre- and post-trials in the HEAT condition are depicted in Fig. 2 A and B. These results indicate that the hip ROM increases when instructing push-off emphasis or attempting to push off with a heated insole, whereas these increases in hip ROM are not observed afterwards when walking normally with a normal insole.

The ankle joint ROM had considerable effects on the trials and conditions ($P < 0.01$), and their interaction was also significant ($P < 0.01$). Multiple comparisons showed a significantly larger ROM in mid-trials than pre-trials with large-sized effects ($d = 1.19$ and 2.26 in the NORMAL and HEAT conditions, respectively) under the NORMAL and HEAT conditions. Although the ankle joint ROM did not differ significantly between pre- and post-trials in the NORMAL condition, a significantly larger ROM was observed in the post-trial compared to the pre-trial in the HEAT condition, with a larger effect ($d = 0.92$). Changes in the ankle joint angles during the pre- and post-trials in the HEAT condition are shown in Fig. 2C. The duration of one full gait cycle was 1.16s pre-trial and 1.17s posttrial, and the effect size was small ($d = 0.12$) (Fig. 2). From this figure, an attempt to enhance the push-off of the warm part appears to increase ankle plantar flexion

Table 1. Means and standard deviations of hip, knee and ankle joint range of motions (ROMs) and step length in each condition.

	Pre-trial	Mid-trial	Post-trial
Hip joint ROM* (°)			
CONTROL	32.2 ± 4.7	31.9 ± 4.8 (d = 0.07)	33.3 ± 5.1 (d = 0.22)
NORMAL	31.7 ± 4.9	40.5 ± 6.8†‡ (d = 1.48)	33.2 ± 5.0 (d = 0.30)
HEAT	32.9 ± 3.2	38.2 ± 6.1†‡ (d = 1.10)	33.2 ± 4.6 (d = 0.08)
Knee joint ROM (°)			
CONTROL	60.4 ± 4.9	62.2 ± 4.1 (d = 0.40)	63.2 ± 4.3 (d = 0.61)
NORMAL	61.2 ± 4.1	61.7 ± 7.1 (d = 0.07)	62.6 ± 3.7 (d = 0.36)
HEAT	62.8 ± 4.4	64.4 ± 7.0 (d = 0.28)	65.2 ± 4.4 (d = 0.55)
Ankle joint ROM* (°)			
CONTROL	28.3 ± 2.3	27.5 ± 2.9 (d = 0.32)	29.2 ± 2.3 (d = 0.41)
NORMAL	29.3 ± 3.9	35.7 ± 6.5†‡ (d = 1.19)	28.3 ± 3.8 (d = 0.26)
HEAT	28.1 ± 2.9	38.7 ± 6.0† (d = 2.26)	31.1 ± 3.6† (d = 0.92)
Step length * (mm)			
CONTROL	585 ± 29	599 ± 42 (d = 0.39)	592 ± 51 (d = 0.17)
NORMAL	583 ± 49	666 ± 76†‡ (d = 1.28)	603 ± 51 (d = 0.40)
HEAT	568 ± 43	698 ± 54†‡ (d = 2.65)	608 ± 37† (d = 0.99)

(*; Significant interaction (trials × conditions), $P < 0.05$. † and ‡; Multiple comparisons, vs. Pre-trial and vs. Post-trial in each condition, $P < 0.05$. Effect sizes (d) were calculated to compare with the pre-trial means in each condition.)

during the terminal stance phase. These results indicate that ankle joint ROM increases by simply instructing push-off emphasis or attempting to push off in a warm area with a heated insole, whereas ankle joint ROM remains larger afterwards when using a heated insole, even when walking normally with a normal insole. This increase in ankle joint ROM may have been caused by increased plantar flexion during the terminal stance phase.

The changes in the step length in each condition are presented in Table 1. The step length had significant effects on the trials and conditions ($P < 0.05$), and their interaction was also significant ($P < 0.01$). Multiple comparisons showed a significantly wider step length in mid-trials than pre-trials with large-sized effects ($d = 1.28$ and 2.65 in the NORMAL and HEAT conditions, respectively) under the NORMAL and HEAT conditions. Although the step length did not differ significantly between pre- and post-trials in the NORMAL condition, a significantly wider step length was observed in the post-trial compared to the pre-trial in the HEAT condition, with a large-sized effect ($d = 0.99$). These results indicate that step length widened by attempting to push off in a warm area with a heated insole or simply instructing push-off emphasis, whereas it

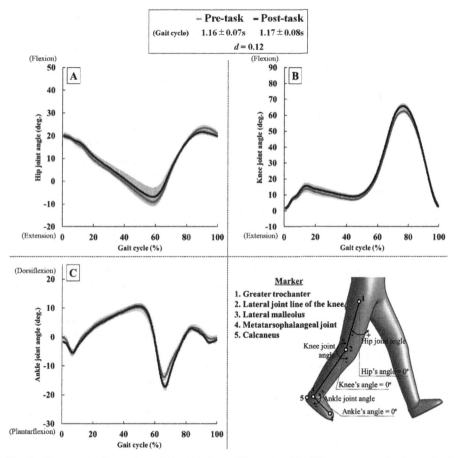

Fig. 2. Changes in the angles of hip (A), knee (B), and ankle (C) movements in the sagittal plane during the gait cycle for the HEAT condition in pre- and post-trials. Values are means ± standard errors of mean. The definitions of each joint angle: Positive values indicate flexion of hip and knee and ankle dorsiflexion. Negative values indicate extension of hip and knee and ankle plantarflexion.

remains wider afterwards of using a heated insole, even when walking normally with a normal insole.

4 Discussion

This study investigated the effect of changes in lower limb joint angles and step length immediately-after enhancement of push-off in the gait using heating of insole tip. The results indicated that the hip and ankle joint ROM and the step length during gait increased significantly either with instructions only (NORMAL condition) or with the use of heated insoles (HEAT condition). There was no increase in hip ROM immediately after the instructions were removed in the NORMAL condition or after the heated insoles were removed in the HEAT condition. Similarly, the ankle joint ROM did not increase after the instructions were removed in the NORMAL condition. However, ankle joint ROM and the step length immediately-after removing the heated insoles were significantly increased compared to that before using the heated insole under HEAT conditions. This increase in ankle joint ROM may be due to the increased ankle plantar flexion during the terminal stance phase.

In the present study, ankle joint ROM and the step length during gait increased in both push-off emphasis instructions and push-off emphasis with heated insoles. This was similar to the results of a previous study on heated insoles [15]. However, the ankle joint ROM and step length immediately after removing the instructions or heated insoles was unclear. The results of this study showed that, although there were no significant immediate after-effects on the increase in ankle joint ROM and step length with instructions alone, there were significant immediate after-effects with heated insoles. More specifically, the ankle joint ROM was significantly larger and step length was significantly widened immediately after removing the heated insole than before using it. These results indicate that the effect of temporarily augmenting push-off in the terminal stance phase with a heated insole remains immediately-after its removal. Previous studies have reported that when appropriate movements are temporarily learned by tactile guide during gait and posture maintenance, such movements are maintained even immediately after the guide is removed [19, 20]. Therefore, it is believed that motor learning is promoted by actively moving one's body parts appropriately based on light tactile guidance [20]. In the HEAT condition in the present study, the specific push-off position could be perceived by the heated insole, which may have facilitated the learning of the specific movement of the ankle joint. The joint angle change (Fig. 2C) also showed that the maximum plantar flexion of the ankle joint (i.e., push-off) increased after the use of the heated insole. Therefore, providing a specific guide for push-off using light tactile sensation (heating insoles in this study) to the plantar surface can facilitate the temporary learning of push-off enhancement.

The step length affects not only movement of the ankle joint but also the hip joint [21]. An increase in hip joint ROM using a heated insole was also observed in this study and a previous study [15]. However, the immediate-after effect of removing the heated insole was not observed in the hip joint. The hip joint angle changes before and after the use of the heated insole shown in Fig. 2A were almost similar. The instructions given to the participants in this study were to enhancement of the push-off and not to provide any instructions regarding hip joint movement. Therefore, this increase in hip joint ROM was assumed to have been caused as a result of the increased push-off. In addition, although there is a specific guide (i.e., a heated insole) for ankle joint movement to increase push-off, there is no specific guide for hip joint movement. Therefore, a temporary learning effect on the hip joint may not have been observed because there were no instructions or specific guides for the movement of the hip joint.

A concern in previous study on "advanced smart insoles" using heated insoles was that keeping the insoles warm for a long time would cause discomfort and low-temperature burns on the sole [15]. The results of this study suggest that by temporarily heating the tip of the insole to emphasize push-off to the user, the enhancement of push-off is sustained even if heating is stopped. The results can be applied (Fig. 3) to1) detect a shortening of strides using currently available smart insole technology (i.e., using sensors for foot pressure distribution, acceleration, gyro, etc.); 2) temporarily heat the insole with a heated sheet attached to the tip of the insole upon detection of a shortening of strides; and 3) the user can be aware of how to push-off by the heated area and the strides are widened, and the widening of strides can be maintained even after the insole heating is deactivated. It would be possible to develop "advanced' smart insoles" in this process.

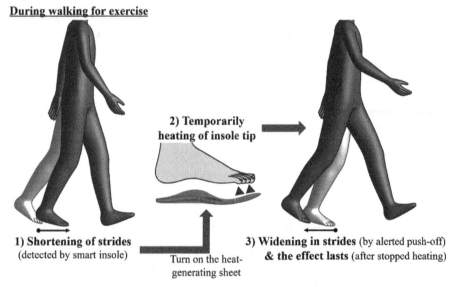

During walking for exercise

2) Temporarily heating of insole tip

1) **Shortening of strides** (detected by smart insole)

Turn on the heat-generating sheet

3) **Widening in strides** (by alerted push-off) **& the effect lasts** (after stopped heating)

Fig. 3. Concept of "advanced" smart insole. During walking for exercise, 1) detect a shortening of strides using currently smart insole technology; 2) temporarily heat the insole with a heated sheet attached to the tip of the insole; and 3) the user can be aware of how to push-off by the heated area and the stride is widened, and the widening of stride can be maintained after the heating is deactivated.

However, there is still a need to provide evidence for several issues in the development of such "advanced' smart insoles". The main focus of this study was walking as an exercise in a young population. A "brisk walk" is recommended for such an exercise purpose [10–12, 22]. Therefore, results similar to those of the present study show that walking at normal speed needs to be verified at faster walking speeds. Further, the duration of the immediate-after effects of ankle joint ROM and widening stride observed in the present study should also be investigated. In addition, although only male and small number of participants were included in the present study, there are sex differences in age-related decline in walking ability [23, 24]. Future studies should include female participants and large sample size. Furthermore, actually the data are specific for treadmill walking it should be interesting to replicate the experiment on over-ground walking. Therefore, it is still unclear whether the strides will be widened in actual walking. These issues need to be clarified in order to develop an "advanced" smart insole.

5 Conclusion

This study investigated the effect of changes in gait motion during and immediately after enhancing push-off by wearing an in-shoe insole with a heated tip. The results show that the hip joint ROM increased during the use of the heated insoles, but there was no difference immediately after use compared to that before use. In contrast, ankle joint ROM and the step length increased significantly during and immediately after the use of the heated insole compared to before use. This change may have been caused by increased plantar flexion during the terminal stance phase. The prolonged use of heated insoles during walking may lead to plantar discomfort and low-temperature burns. However, the results of the present study suggest that if the tip of the insole is temporarily heated to enhance push-off when the strides become shorter, the strides widen and the effect is maintained even after heating has been removed.

Acknowledgment. This research was supported by The Okayama Foundation for Science and Technology and JSPS KAKENHI Grant Number JP21K06364.

References

1. A Tan, A.M., Fuss, F.K., Weizman, Y., Troynikov, O.: Development of a smart insole for medical and sports purposes. Procedia. Eng. **112**, 152–156 (2015). https://doi.org/10.1016/j.proeng.2015.07.191
2. Lin, F., Wang, A., Zhuang, Y., Tomita, M.R.: Xu, W: Smart Insole: a Wearable sensor device for unobtrusive gait monitoring in daily life. IEEE Trans. Ind. Inform. **12**, 2281–2291 (2016). https://doi.org/10.1109/TII.2016.2585643
3. Drăgulinescu, A., Drăgulinescu, A.M., Zincă, G., Bucur, D., Feieş, V., Neagu, D.M.: Smart socks and in-shoe systems: state-of-the-art for two popular technologies for foot motion analysis, sports, and medical applications. Sensors **20**, 4316 (2020). https://doi.org/10.3390/s20154316
4. Subramaniam, S., Majumder, S., Faisal, A.I., Deen, M.J.: Insole-based systems for health monitoring: current solutions and research challenges. Sensors **22**, 438 (2022). https://doi.org/10.3390/s22020438
5. Ziagkas, E., Loukovitis, A., Zekakos, D.X., Chau, T.D., Petrelis, A., Grouiosm, G.: A novel tool for gait analysis: validation study of the smart insole PODOSmart®. Sensors **21**, 5972 (2021). https://doi.org/10.3390/s21175972

6. Takebe, M., Oshita, K.: Influence of emphasizing push-off at the terminal stance phase on stride length and gait speed during fast walking. Walking Res. **26**, 111–117 (2022). (In Japanese with English abstract)

7. Ostrosky, K.M., VanSwearingen, J.M., Burdett, R.G., Gee, Z.: A comparison of gait characteristics in young and old subjects. Phys. Ther.Ther. **74**, 637–644 (1994). https://doi.org/10.1093/ptj/74.7.637

8. McGibbon, C.A.: Toward a better understanding of gait changes with age and disablement: neuromuscular adaptation. Exerc. Sport Sci. Rev.. Sport Sci. Rev. **31**, 102–108 (2003). https://doi.org/10.1097/00003677-200304000-00009

9. Browne, M.G., Franz, J.R.: Does dynamic stability govern propulsive force generation in human walking? R. Soc. Open Sci. **29**, 171673 (2017). https://doi.org/10.1098/rsos.171673

10. U.S. department of health and human services. Physical activity guidelines for Americans, 2nd edn. https://health.gov/paguidelines/second-edition/pdf/Physical_Activity_Guidelines_2nd_edition.pdf

11. National Health Service UK. Walking for health. https://www.nhs.uk/live-well/exercise/running-and-aerobic-exercises/walking-for-health/

12. National Institute of Health and Nutrition Japan. Active Guide 2013 (summary leaflet). https://www.nibiohn.go.jp/eiken/english/research/pdf/active_guide2013.pdf

13. Okoba, R., Hasegawa, M., Yoshizuka, H., Honda, Y., Ichiba, M., Asami, T.: Particular protrusion perception arising from plantar sensory input and task guidance enhances lower limb joint dynamics during gait. J. Phys. Ther. Sci.Ther. Sci. **31**, 261–266 (2019). https://doi.org/10.1589/jpts.31.261

14. Takebe, M., Oshita, K.: Effect of push-off facilitation by protrusions attached to the insole tip on lower limb joint range of motion and step length during brisk gait. Jpn. J. Ergon. In press. (In Japanese with English abstract)

15. Oshita, K.: Gait improvement by alerted push-off via heating of insole tip. Healthcare **10**, 2461 (2022). https://doi.org/10.3390/healthcare10122461

16. Chen, Z., Li, J., Song, W., Lu, Y., Cao, B.: Smart wireless charging heating insoles: Improving body thermal comfort of young males in an extremely cold environment. Cloth. Text. Res. J. **40**, 220–234 (2022). https://doi.org/10.1177/0887302X20973960

17. Hurford, R.: Chapter 2: Types of smart clothes and wearable technology. In: McCann, J., Bryson, D. (eds.) Smart clothes and wearable technology, pp. 25–44. Woodhead Publishing, UK (2009). https://doi.org/10.1533/9781845695668.1.25

18. Ong B.B.: Injury, fatal and nonfatal -Burns and scalds-. In: Payne-James, J., Byard, R.W., Corey, T.S., Henderson, C. (eds.) Encyclopedia of forensic and legal medicine, vol. 3, pp. 90–98. Elsevier, Oxford, UK (2005). https://doi.org/10.1016/B0-12-369399-3/00209-3

19. Oshita, K., Yano, S.: Effect and immediate after-effect of lightly gripping the cane on postural sway. J. Physiol. Anthropol.Anthropol. **35**, 14 (2016). https://doi.org/10.1186/s40101-016-0096-4

20. Oshita, K.: Immediate after-effects of shapes of clothing worn on tandem gait performance. Acta Bioeng. Biomech.Bioeng. Biomech. **23**, 79–85 (2021). https://doi.org/10.37190/ABB-01847-2021-02

21. Judge, J.O., Davis, R.B., 3rd., Ounpuu, S.: Step length reductions in advanced age: the role of ankle and hip kinetics. J. Gerontol. A Biol. Sci. Med. Sci.Gerontol. A Biol. Sci. Med. Sci. **51**, 303–312 (1996). https://doi.org/10.1093/gerona/51a.6.m303

22. Stamatakis, E., Kelly, P., Strain, T., Murtagh, E.M., Ding, D., Murphy, M.H.: Self-rated walking pace and all-cause, cardiovascular disease and cancer mortality: individual participant pooled analysis of 50 225 walkers from 11 population British cohorts. Br. J. Sports Med. **52**, 761–768 (2018). https://doi.org/10.1136/bjsports-2017-098677

23. Callisaya, M.L., Blizzard, L., Schmidt, M.D., McGinley, J.L., Srikanth, V.K.: Sex modifies the relationship between age and gait: a population-based study of older adults. J. Gerontol. A Biol. Sci. Med. Sci. **63**, 165–170 (2008). https://doi.org/10.1093/gerona/63.2.165

24. Doyo, W., Kozakai, R., Kim, H.Y., Ando, F., Shimokata, H.: Spatiotemporal components of the 3-D gait analysis of community-dwelling middle-aged and elderly Japanese: age- and sex-related differences. Geriatr. Gerontol. Int.. Gerontol. Int. **11**, 39–49 (2011). https://doi.org/10.1111/j.1447-0594.2010.00632.x

An Intuitive Interface for Technical Documentation Based on Semantic Knowledge Graphs

Frieder Loch[(✉)] and Markus Stolze

Department of Computer Science, Ostschweizer Fachhochschule, Rapperswil, Switzerland
`frieder.loch@ost.ch`

Abstract. Maintaining technical documentation is a challenge. Products are becoming more complex, product lifecycles are getting shorter, and the number of product variants is increasing. Manuals that guide personnel in the use and maintenance of products are critical to their efficient and safe operation. Authoring system for technical documentation therefore increasingly apply semantic models to control the cost of maintaining technical documentation. Working with formal semantic structures is challenging for technical writers who usually work with plain, written text. This paper presents an intuitive interface for a semantic knowledge graph to facilitate the adoption and use of semantic models in technical documentation. The interface allows working with unstructured text and to postpone its semantification. Users can add semantic annotations in an iterative and incremental way. The interface was developed using a user-centered design process and subjected to an evaluation with technical writers. The results indicate that technical writers could use the prototype successfully and enjoyed the underlying concepts. Further iterations will extend the system and, for example, use artificial intelligence to suggest semantic links to improve the quality of the knowledge graph.

Keywords: Human computer interaction · Semantic knowledge graph · Technical documentation · User-centered design

1 Challenges in Technical Documentation

Every product needs comprehensive documentation to describe its operation and maintenance. Creating and maintaining technical documentation for complex technical systems, such as mining equipment or industrial machinery, is challenging because these systems are complex and come in many product variants that require specific documentation depending on their features.

In the past, technical documentation was created using text editors. This approach makes technical documentation hard to update and maintain, since the reuse of plain text documentation fragments or the updating of such information is hard. Software for technical documentation has changed to address these challenges. There has been a trend towards.

H. P. da Silva and P. Cipresso (Eds.): CHIRA 2023, CCIS 1996, pp. 307–317, 2023.
https://doi.org/10.1007/978-3-031-49425-3_19

- *increasing semantics* of the data models and increasing granularity of those models and
- *increasing integration* of data from diverse sources (e.g., engineering, logistics).

The German Standardization Roadmap Industry 4.0 [5] emphasizes the need for semantic unambiguity and interoperability. To meet these requirements, information about technical products must be provided in a semantic and machine-readable structure. Frequently used data structures for semantically annotated data are knowledge graphs and knowledge graph-based ontologies [12].

Over the past twenty years, STAR AG has developed a comprehensive knowledge graph-based meta model and associated tools to capture, manage and distribute semantic information, to support after-sales processes such as maintenance and troubleshooting. This model and the tools are successfully used by companies such as Daimler, Ferrari, Hilti, Liebherr, Vaillant, and Volvo Trucks.

With current tools, capturing product knowledge in knowledge graphs requires significant training. This is an obstacle to scalability to all product information and wider market adoption. The research project Smart Knowledge Capture addresses these challenges and aims to make tools for interacting with knowledge graphs more accessible by developing intuitive interfaces and AI-based assistance. Another goal is to give technical writers a shortcut to information owned by other stakeholders through an intelligent knowledge capturing tool.

This paper contributes a user interface that simplifies capturing instructions in a semantic knowledge graph. The interface allows working with unstructured text and hides the underlying semantic data model. The instructions are incrementally enriched with semantic information. In addition to providing intuitive interaction, this interface should make more transparent how the information in the knowledge graph will be displayed later, for instance in a manual. The interface was developed in an iterative, user-centered process based on contextual inquiry and evaluated with technical writers.

2 Editing of Knowledge Representations

Semantic data models are being applied in many domains. However, ontology authoring tools did not gain traction apart from experts. Ontology engineering tools typically lack a user-centered perspective [15]. These tools have improved, but still have usability issues. The literature proposes an emphasis on the needs of "normal users" instead of "power users" when designing such tools since people with no formal training in knowledge representation are increasingly working with ontologies and other knowledge representations [6, 7]. The study of Dzobor et al. [7] highlights shortcomings of current editing tools such as unclear error messages or a tendency to display too much information at once.

Successful interaction with ontology editing tools depends on knowledge of the low-level languages and frameworks [7]. The Protégé editor is a popular editor for the modelling of ontologies [10]. Semantic Wikis use semantic information to express relations between information to facilitate reuse and semantic queries [3]. Evaluations indicated that the usability of such applications for different stakeholders, especially the ones without expertise in knowledge representation, is an issue [1].

The design of editing interfaces for people without expertise in semantic data models is critical. This is especially true for user-facing applications such as in technical documentation software. However, subject-matter experts or technical writers without training in knowledge representation struggle with existing editing tools.

Several approaches introduce a user-centered approach in the design of ontology authoring tools. Usage patterns in ontology authoring tools such as Protégé are analyzed to derive different user types and, for instance, make the tool adaptive to the user type [14]. Other approaches use ontology visualization. Their aim is to visualize ontologies to facilitate their understanding and editing by users [8]. However, these approaches focus on users with knowledge in ontology engineering and not on the integration into user-facing applications.

The gap between concrete objects and the abstract knowledge representation needs to be bridged. Oberhauser et al. [11] and Stobbe et al. [13] propose an approach that creates description of interactions with software using automated video analysis and the analysis of interactions with a focus on legacy systems. Thereby, semantic information can be created without having to interact with the knowledge graph directly.

According to the previous discussions, a user-centered interface for semantic technical documentation should meet the following requirements:

- **R1: User-Centered Design.** The interface will be developed using a user-centered approach. This ensures the usability of the tool for different skill levels.
- **R2: Interface for non-experts.** The interface should be usable by technical writers without knowledge engineering expertise. Evaluations will be conducted with such users to validate this requirement.
- **R3: Simple and Application-Oriented Interface.** The primary means of interaction is unstructured text. This should make working with the software less abstract.

This paper contributes an interface that facilitates the creation of a semantic knowledge graph for technical documentation. The interface is developed in a user-centered process and evaluated with technical editors.

3   Challenges with Existing Tools

As discussed in the previous section, interacting with a semantic knowledge representation is a challenge. Technical writers must follow the constraints of the data model and decide which components and tools they need before starting to create documentation. For example, to create the instruction "Loosen the battery using a screwdriver" the objects *battery* and *screwdriver* need to be created in the knowledge graph. These parts are transformed to text when they are being published for different media. This forces writers to follow the structure of the semantic data model and requires a steep learning curve. Furthermore, the effects of the edits on the data model are not visible immediately. Our interface reverses this approach. The instruction can be entered first as unstructured text and the tools can be annotated later.

Reusing information through semantic linking is critical to realizing the benefits of the semantic knowledge graph. For example, tasks may require the preparatory action of removing a cover before accessing an engine. If these tasks reference this preparatory action, they can be easily adapted. A new model may have a modified cover that is removed differently. If these tasks replicate the information, the technical writer must adapt the information multiple times. This approach (*Copy, paste, and modify*) can introduce errors. Therefore, it is critical for an interface for technical documentation to facilitate annotating and reusing information.

4   Contextual Inquiry and Interface Design

The user-centered design process started with a contextual inquiry study. The goal of this study was to understand the tasks of technical writers and their characteristics and motivations. From this study, personas were synthesized to guide the development of the prototypes. The prototypes were evaluated in usability walkthroughs and refined accordingly. The final interface was implemented, backed by the semantic knowledge graph, and evaluated with technical writers.

4.1   Contextual Inquiry Study

Contextual design considers data from prospective users as the main criterion for deciding on the structure of the system [9]. The goal is to make sense of real-life working situations to understand the characteristics and motivations of potential users to better empathize with them. This includes the tasks that they perform and the tools they currently use. Various research methods are used, such as interviews, low-fidelity prototypes, and scenarios [2]. We also wanted to collect problems with existing tools. Considering both, their characteristics and problems with existing tools should inform a user-centered design process.

These methods aim to understand the context-of-use. This comprises the human, physical, organizational, historical and social environment in which a technology is used to tailor the application to this context [2].

Contextual inquiry usually depends on being present where the work is done. However, the studies were conducted during the measures to contain the COVID-19 pandemic. Therefore, the contextual inquiry had to be conducted remotely and some methods were not applicable. Instead of a participating observation, we asked participants to provide us with video recordings of common tasks. Based on the results of the video analysis, we designed semi-structured interviews with the same persons to inquire on the tasks in the videos.

Video Analysis. We asked the participants to record videos of regular work tasks. The goal of the video analysis was to understand the tasks of technical writers. We asked the participants to provide additional explanations of the tasks. If possible, the participants provided thinking-aloud information on any issues that they were facing. This approach combined the contextual interview with elements of a diary study [2].

Personal interviews were conducted based on the results of the video analysis. This was done to establish a successful partnership with the people who actually do the work, in order to understand their tasks properly [9].

Four technical writers with various levels of experience and educational backgrounds (e.g., academic training in technical writing or career changers) participated in the study. The participants maintain technical documentation in various domains, such as software or industrial machinery. Each participant recorded about one hour of videos. The results of the video analysis were synthesized as an affinity diagram that clusters recurrent issues under emerging themes.

Results of the Video Analysis. A frequent task in technical writing at our project partner is the migration of technical documentation into the semantic knowledge graph. This is often done when new customers are onboarded. The main challenge is to map the existing documentation to the objects in the semantic knowledge graph. This is challenging due to the variety of objects in the knowledge graph that, for instance, can be used to model different tasks.

We observed that technical writers often relied on the layout preview to verify that their changes to the knowledge graph had the intended effect. Even experienced technical writers were unsure whether they chose the correct semantic structures. Step types tended to be chosen based on the desired appearance in the final manual and not whether they are semantically correct. Later interviews confirmed this observation and suggested that working directly on the abstract structures of the semantic knowledge graph is not intuitive. This observation motivated the idea to allow editing the knowledge graph in a way that resembles the visual layout of the resulting documentation, thereby removing the abstraction of working on the knowledge graph.

Individual Interviews. The video analysis revealed frequent tasks and issues of technical writers. Personal interviews were carried out to ensure the correct interpretation of the incidents in the videos and to clarify possible misconceptions. The interview addressed recurrent themes that were identified in the video analysis. The interview consisted of three parts.

1. **Motivation and Background.** The first part addressed the motivations of the participants with regards to their work as technical writers. It was, for instance, discussed why they decided to work in this domain, what they find satisfying about their job, and what makes good technical documentation.
2. **Processes in Technical Writing.** Participants explained how they organize their work and how they collaborate with colleagues. This should help understanding common work processes.
3. **Working with the Existing Software.** The aim of these questions was to understand how the existing software is used and how it could be improved. This should lead to concrete ideas for features of the interface. Incidents that were observed in the video analysis were discussed as well.

Creation of Personas. Personas represent individual users with distinct motivations and characteristics and should be created based on user research [4]. The process for deriving personas based on research data was based on Cooper et al. [4]. The main part is to create dimensions that describe the characteristics of users. These dimensions were created based on the insights gathered by user research. This process was done in a more qualitative manner than the quantitative approach suggested by Cooper. Below are three example dimensions that characterize our personas.

- One dimension was whether the participants take pride in well-written and well-set text. This aspect varied between technical writers with a background in a technical profession and technical writers with specific academic training in technical writing.
- Another dimension was the extent to which the technical writers were interested in the semantic information model and its quality. This aspect was critical since a high quality of the information model allows, for instance, to reuse information and work more efficiently.
- Another dimension concerned whether the participants enjoy working with innovative technology. This is independent of the concrete technology, but concerns liking a technology for the sake of being a new technology.

The characteristics of the interview participants were located on these dimensions. Clusters of characteristics were identified to create three personas. We developed the following personas.

- **Pragmatic.** Someone who is interested in getting the job done and has no strong preferences with regards to the applied tools, if good text can be produced.
- **Semantic Expert.** Someone who is interested in working out the semantic structures and filling them in perfectly. Information must be structured properly while avoiding redundancies as much as possible.
- **Career Changer.** Someone who started working in a technical profession and switched to technical writing as a second career. This person is not too interested in semantic models and has significant technical knowledge about the tasks.

4.2   Design of the Interface

The interface was created based on the results of the contextual inquiry studies that were described in the previous section. The design process was iterative and started with low-fidelity prototypes that were refined later.

The main design idea was to allow for incremental semantification. The user should be able to work with unstructured text and delay the semantification. This should allow use cases such as entering unstructured notes that an editor receives from technicians without having to store them in a note-taking application first. This should hide the complexity of the underlying semantic model until the user decides to use it, and help inexperienced users in getting gradually acquainted with the semantic model.

Description of the Interface. The interface (see Fig. 1) consists of three panels. The left column locates the task in the information model (e.g., by identifying the product, the product variant, and the task) and gives an overview of the steps of the task. The middle column allows the creation and maintenance of the steps of the task. The right column allows editing details for the step that the user has selected in the middle column, such as linking materials that are needed in the selected step. This is a common structure of application interfaces (overview & detail).

The middle column provides functions to create and edit steps. Most steps instruct the user to perform an action, often using a tool. Other steps require checking a value and provide information on how to react to different results. Each task consists of a pre-task a main task and a post-task. The pre-task describes preparatory work before

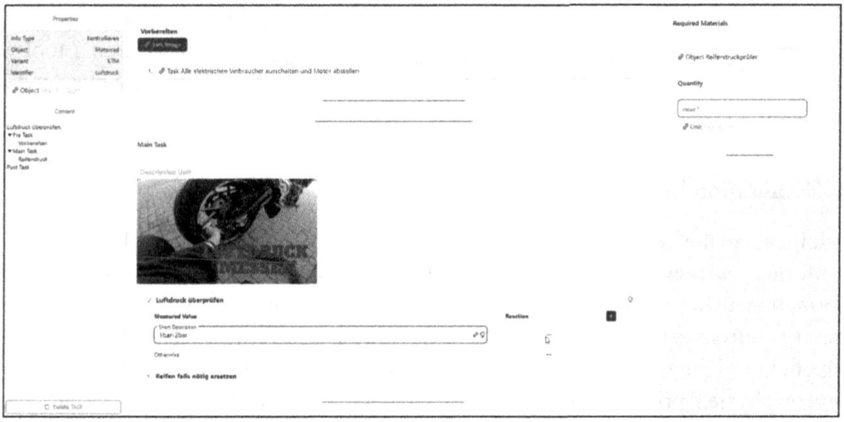

Fig. 1. Interface of the text-based interface for technical documentation.

starting the main task. In our case, it is necessary to turn off the engine before checking the air pressure. The post-task concerns work after the main task, such as cleaning up. Different main tasks often share pre- and post-tasks. The information model includes more complex types that were omitted in the prototype.

Horizontal lines indicate where the user can add steps. Hovering over the lines displays a plus-sign that allows adding distinct types of instructions. Instructions can be simple instructions, tasks that structure related instructions, or tasks that describe a check step and what to do in case of different results. A new instruction can also be added by pressing Enter in the previous step. The user can delete, modify, and reorganize the steps using drag and drop.

An important task is linking instructions with materials, such as required tools. This is handled in the right column. Linking materials is desirable since this allows reuse and increases the quality of the knowledge graph. The interface aids the user when creating links. It suggests objects that may be linked to the task. A flashing bulb next to the label of the step indicates that a suggestion for a link is available. The system provides the suggestions using a full text search through the existing data model.

Technical Implementation. The system consists of a frontend and a backend. Both components communicate using REST-interfaces and web sockets. The frontend is implemented using state-of-the-art web technologies. React serves as the frontend framework and MobX for state management. For the design of interface, Ant Design and Tailwind CSS were used. The backend communicates with the semantic data storage using a REST-interface.

5   Evaluation

A qualitative evaluation of the final interface addressed whether technical writers would accept such an interface and whether the interface was suitable for interacting with a semantic knowledge graph. Therefore, we were interested in suggestions for improving the prototype, as well as a comparison of the prototype with the existing tool for technical documentation. A quantitative comparison of the prototype with the existing tool was not performed due to the significant difference in the supported functionality and the complexity of the existing tool.

5.1 Evaluation Procedure

Participants in the evaluation performed a realistic documentation task. They were given an informal, written description of a maintenance task and instructed to formalize this information using our interface. This process is often required when a new product variant is introduced or when a manual is reviewed. Such reviews are often conducted in the field or in the workshop with technicians. The results of these reviews are usually noted on physical printouts of the manuals and later validated and entered into the system by dedicated editors.

Setup and Metrics. The participants received a video introducing the interface prior to the evaluation. This was done to familiarize the participants with the prototype and to reduce the effects of novelty. The evaluation began with a sample task that the facilitator performed to provide an overview of the prototype and introduce its functions. After this introduction, the participants performed the task. Participants completed the evaluation tasks independently. However, the facilitator was available to assist and asked clarifying questions when encountering potential issues.

The facilitator asked the participants to think-aloud during the evaluation. In addition, we used the System Usability Scale (SUS) to evaluate the usability of the interface and compare it to the usability of the tool that they use regularly. The participants completed the SUS after the evaluation.

The evaluations were conducted remotely via a web conference. Since a VPN connection was required to use the prototype, which was not available to the participants, they controlled the prototype using screen sharing software (MS Teams/TeamViewer).

Participants. Nine people participated in the study. All participants worked as technical editors and used the same tool. They worked in different domains, mostly focusing on the documentation of technical equipment.

The evaluation sessions were intended to be individual sessions. Two sessions were conducted in groups due to time constraints. In this case, one participant controlled the system while the other participants observed the interactions and provided comments. Five sessions were conducted in total.

5.2 Results and Discussion

Participants were able to successfully interact with the prototype in the evaluation after only a short training period. All participants could complete the tasks and enjoyed the simple interface and the use of modern interaction techniques (e.g. drag and drop).

Participants mentioned that the interface would be particularly useful for simple tasks and tasks performed by infrequent users, such as subject matter experts. Such an interface could be provided on a mobile device to support the use of the application in the field, for example, when reviewing or updating documentation. In such cases, using the desktop software may be too complex and result in users creating paper notes that must be manually transferred.

Results of the System Usability Scale. The results of the SUS questionnaire supported the positive results of the evaluation. The participants found the application to be not unnecessarily complex (med $= 3$)[1] and to be easy to use (med $= 3.5$). They agreed that the operation of the application can be learned easily (med $= 4$). Most participants would like to use the application on a regular basis (med $= 3$). The resulting SUS score of 65 indicates the good usability of the interface.

The scores for the prototype were superior to those for the current software. The most visible differences concerned that participants perceived the existing software to be harder to learn (med $= 1$ vs. med $= 4$) and that much expertise is required to being able to use the software (med $= 4$ vs. med $= 1.5$). However, the comparison of a full-fledged software to a prototype should be interpreted with caution. Nevertheless, these results indicate that the design ideas were well received.

Suggested Improvements. The evaluations provided ideas for improving the prototype. An important feature is keyboard navigation. It should be possible to create new steps and navigate between steps using keyboard shortcuts. Keyboard navigation not only improves accessibility, but also helps experienced users working more quickly. Keyboard navigation should use conventions and shortcuts that other applications use. Another consideration was to allow users to store tools and tasks that they use frequently. This should allow to create meaningful shortcuts and customize the application for different tasks.

Further suggestions concerned the visual presentation. For instance, splitting the interface into three panels (see Fig. 1) was difficult in some cases. Actions in the right panel that are triggered in the middle panel tend to be overlooked by the participants.

Remote Testing. The remote setup for the usability tests worked well. The use of web conferencing facilitated the recording of the sessions for later analysis and increased the flexibility in scheduling. Participants used the prototype via screen sharing without significant problems. Only the facilitator's ability to interact with the prototype to assist the participants was limited. A thorough briefing of the participants and an opportunity to practice at the beginning is crucial to explain the limitations of the remote testing setup to the participants, such as the latency when using the mouse in a screen sharing session or possible issues with different keyboard layouts.

6 Conclusion and Outlook

This paper described the development of an intuitive interface for the creation and maintenance of technical documentation using an iterative, user-centered process. The interface was intended to replace or complement directly working with the knowledge graph. The

---

[1] Scores range from 0 (fully disagree) to 4 (fully agree). We report median values due to the low number of participants.

interface should facilitate working with semantic structures for users with little or no experience. An evaluation validated the design ideas. The evaluation indicate that the interface can facilitate editing tasks while maintaining the benefits of the underlying semantic model.

The evaluation had a qualitative focus. Future evaluations should include a quantitative comparison with existing applications and be conducted over a longer period. Performance on longer editing tasks should be evaluated as well. This will provide an estimate of the return on investment (ROI) of implementing the interface and introducing it to the existing software.

Work is ongoing to extend the existing interface to other technical editing tasks, such as the creation of new product variants, for example when introducing a new generation of a product. This is a complex operation. It is necessary to decide which information can be reused from the existing variant and which information needs to be adapted to match the characteristics of the new variant. A wizard that guides technical writers can speed up this process and eliminate potential errors. It should also be evaluated whether the concept of the interface can be transferred to other editing tasks (e.g., the creation of product descriptions) without losing its benefits.

Another line of work concerns the introduction of AI-based assistance in the authoring process. This assistance can suggest tools or tasks that can be linked in a particular context of an instruction. The goal is to ease the process of finding and linking resources. By increasing the amount of linked information, the quality of the knowledge graph and the documentation improves. The integration of this assistance into the prototype and the evaluation of the suggestions of the assistance is ongoing. This includes how the user interface should present the suggestions to the user (i.e., confidence score of the suggestion, display of alternatives or explanation of the applied model) and whether the suggestions are useful.

References

1. Barok, D., Boschat Thorez, J., Dekker, A., et al.: Archiving complex digital artworks. J. Inst. Conserv.Conserv. **42**, 94–113 (2019). https://doi.org/10.1080/19455224.2019.1604398
2. Benyon, D.: Designing User Experience: A Guide to HCI, UX and Interaction Design. Pearson (2013)
3. Boulos, M.N.K.: Semantic wikis: a comprehensible introduction with examples from the health sciences. JETWI 1 (2009). doi: https://doi.org/10.4304/jetwi.1.1.94-96
4. Cooper, A., Reimann, R., Cronin, D.: About face. Wiley, The essentials of user interface design (2007)
5. DIN/DKE: German Standardization Roadmap on Industry 4.0. (2020). https://www.din.de/en/innovation-and-research/industry-4-0/german-standardization-roadmap-on-industry-4-0-77392. Accessed 02 Feb 2023
6. Dzbor, M., Motta, E.: Engineering and customizing ontologies. In: Hepp, M., Leenheer, P., Moor, A., et al. (eds.) Ontology Management. Springer, vol. 7, pp. 25–57. US, Boston, MA (2008)
7. Dzbor, M., Motta, E., Aranda, C., et al.: Developing ontologies in OWL: an observational study. In: OWL: Experiences and Directions Workshop (2006)
8. Fu, B., Steichen, B.: Supporting user-centred ontology visualisation: predictive analytics using eye gaze to enhance human-ontology interaction. IJIIDS **15**, 28 (2022). https://doi.org/10.1504/IJIIDS.2022.120143

9. Holzblatt, K., Beyer, H.: Contextual Design. Morgan Kaufmann, Design for Life (2016)
10. Horridge, M., Gonçalves, R.S., Nyulas, C.I., et al.: WebProtégé: a cloud-based ontology editor. In: Liu, L., White, R. (eds.) Companion Proceedings of the 2019 World Wide Web Conference, pp. 686–689. ACM, New York (2019)
11. Oberhauser, J., Gieschke, R., Rechert, K.: Automation is documentation: functional documentation of human-machine interaction for future software reuse. IJDC **17**, 11 (2022). https://doi.org/10.2218/ijdc.v17i1.836
12. Rosen, R., Fischer, J., Boschert, S.: Next generation digital twin: an ecosystem for mechatronic systems? IFAC-PapersOnLine **52**, 265–270 (2019). https://doi.org/10.1016/j.ifacol.2019.11.685
13. Stobbe, O., Rechert, K., von Suchodoletz, D.: Demonstration of an integrated system for platform-independent description of human-machine interactions. In: Coates, S., Pearson, D., O'Meara, E., et al. (eds.) Proceedings of the 11th International Conference on Digital Preservation, pp. 377–378 (2014)
14. Vigo, M., Jay, C., Stevens, R.: Protégé4US: harvesting ontology authoring data with protégé. In: Presutti, V., Blomqvist, E., Troncy, R., et al. (eds.) The Semantic Web: ESWC 2014 Satellite Events, vol. 8798, pp. 86–99. Springer International Publishing, Cham (2014)
15. Vigo, M., Matentzoglu, N., Jay, C., et al.: Comparing ontology authoring workflows with Protégé: in the laboratory, in the tutorial and in the 'wild.' J. Web Semant. **57**, 100473 (2019). https://doi.org/10.1016/j.websem.2018.09.004

Augmenting the Human in Industry 4.0 to Add Value: A Taxonomy of Human Augmentation Approach

Jacqueline Humphries[1,2,3](✉) ⓘ, Pepijn Van de Ven[2,3] ⓘ, and Alan Ryan[2] ⓘ

[1] Technological University of the Shannon, Limerick, Ireland
jacqueline.humphries@tus.ie
[2] University of Limerick, Limerick, Ireland
[3] Confirm Manufacturing Research Centre, Limerick, Ireland

Abstract. There is a lack of clarity about how to augment the human in manufacturing. For practitioners, this creates challenges in understanding which technologies to invest in for specific automation goals, and where the value-add exists.

A narrative review of the literature is conducted through which the relationship between augmentation and automation is clarified. Definitions for Augmentation, and the Augmented Human, and a new Taxonomy of Human Augmentation are proposed.

Five classes of augmentation are identified: Physical, Collaborative Physical, Sensory, Embedded Intelligence, and Collaborative Social Intelligence. How the Taxonomy is applied to each goal of automation is illustrated. Finally the value-add of the classes is explored through industrial use cases, and the potential impact on manufacturing key performance indicators is summarised.

This novel Taxonomy of Human Augmentation unifies the existing research, and provides a common description of each class of augmentation, which can assist practitioners in seeking and exploring augmentation solutions.

Keywords: Augmentation · Automation · Industry 4.0

1 Introduction

Technology has enabled radical and rapid change to the factory floor and the role of the human. The human is being substituted by automation on repetitive manual work. This automation is not new, and dates back to early work on man-machine symbiosis, Fitts' function allocation, and human-automata research [1–3]. However, due to the technological advances under Industry 4.0, the level and nature of automation is increasing. Now, the human's cognitive processes, such as decision making, are also being automated. Yet it is not always practicable or effective to substitute humans by automation [4, 5]. This is because the human brings unique attributes to the production floor that enable it to run smoothly and prevent error from occurring, and thus ensure their place in the Factories of the Future [6–13]. As such, the design of Industry 4.0 systems must be human-centric,

H. P. da Silva and P. Cipresso (Eds.): CHIRA 2023, CCIS 1996, pp. 318–335, 2023.
https://doi.org/10.1007/978-3-031-49425-3_20

with the human augmented by technology to perform their work as and when needed [14, 15]. This type of approach requires a change in humans' work, and requires new types of technology innovation [16]. The risk is that in choosing the wrong technology the expected impacts will not be realised, and indeed may lead to disillusionment with the approach.

2 Objectives

The objective of this paper is explore how the human can be augmented by technology in production. Following a literature review, the research proposes a Taxonomy of Human Augmentation Solutions, applicable for Operator 4.0, who is described as a smart and skilled operator where the routine is removed allowing them space to perform cooperative work with machines [15, 17]. In doing so, it addresses the research gap identified in Mirco Moencks et al. [4] that "an industrial practitioner would need information on the value-add of augmentation technologies". The work then expands on Mattsson et al. [17] Cognitive Automation Strategy for Operator 4.0 by showing how automation could be implemented, using our Taxonomy of Human Augmentation. In doing so, it fulfils the advice of Dolgui, Sgarbossa, and Simonetto [18] who suggest that guidance or frameworks are needed when introducing Industry 4.0 technologies so as to enable an understanding of how strategy can be implemented.

The impact of this research is that it is the first such paper that draws together disparate works on augmentation, and provides guidance to industry practitioners on what type of augmentation would suit particular automation goals, and have an impact of their key performance indicators (KPI).

The rest of this paper is structured as follows: In the next section the research method is described. Thereafter in the Results and Discussion section, the relationship between automation and augmentation is explored, and definitions provided. Next a new Taxonomy of Human Augmentation is set out. Each class of augmentation is outlined, and examples provided to illustrate the value-add. The value-add is linked to potential KPIs. How the classes of Human Augmentation can be applied to the Levels of Automation is presented. Finally in our conclusions, future research opportunities are identified.

3 Research Method

Research on augmentation has heretofore been disparate works, that consider augmentation from a conceptual or theoretical basis, or works that outline a particular augmentation solution. A narrative review is conducted to draw together the findings and recommendations of these works into a cohesive Taxonomy of Human Augmentation suitable for industrial applications. A search is conducted on the Web of Science and ScienceDirect databases. The search string is limited to Articles, and included the terms (('augmented human' OR 'augmented workforce' OR 'smart operator') AND ('industry 4' OR 'cyber'). The number of papers retrieved are 1,014. An initial screening reveals a large number of articles dealing with specific applications not relevant to the research question, and so the terms NOT ('Reality' OR 'Virtual' OR 'Education' OR 'Attack' OR 'Hygiene' OR 'Radio' OR 'maturity' OR 'grid' OR 'anomaly' OR 'lean') are added, reducing the number of returned papers to be screened (n = 373). A review of the article titles and abstracts is conducted and papers excluded. The exclusion criteria used are (i) the work is not related to industrial application that uses humans in the process, (ii) the search terms are mentioned as background or as context, and do not form a substantial part of the text (iii) there is no access to full text, (iv) it is similar, or a duplicate of, another article. Three hundred and thirty eight papers are excluded (n = 338). The articles included in the review (n = 35) are assessed by reading the full paper. Further papers are discovered by following the references of important articles.

The literature review does not list all the possible technologies that are available, as this list would become outdated quickly. Indeed a recent literature review by Dornelles et al. [19] lists the Industry 4.0 technologies currently available, and links technologies to operator roles. Instead the literature review identifies the classes of augmentation, with examples of technology within those classes so that the value-add is captured.

4 Results and Discussion

4.1 Defining and Distinguishing Augmentation and Automation

There is a lack of a common language in the research, with the terms automation and augmentation being used interchangeably. First, the blurred relationship between automation and augmentation is explored, and then the terms are defined.

The essence of human *augmentation* research, according to Engelbart [20] and Raisamo et al. [21] is that systems can support rather than displace the human. This is the same as Romero's description of *automation*. Romero et al. [22] describe the shift required to build systems for Operator 4.0 as a new design and engineering philosophy based in the application of *automation* in new ways to *further enhance* the human in their physical, sensorial and cognitive capabilities.

Fässberg, Fasth and Stahre [6] describe cognitive *automation* as the amount of information, and the technique in which it is provided to the human, in order to know what, how and when to do a specific task in the most efficient way. Whereas automation normally reduces the human input by substitution, this description implies enhancing the human input. Engelbart [20] uses a similar analogy in discussing *augmentation*, and suggests that composite processes are decomposed into human and artefact processes, so that the human can focus on their specific task. Engelbart [20] explains that whilst humans can solve complex problems, it is augmentation that breaks down a complex problem for them so that they can approach it in small steps. It is clear though that augmentation is interdisciplinary, enabled largely through information technologies, but one that also considers the socio and psychosocial perspective.

The blurring of the boundary between the terms augmentation and automation though is understandable. An example is where the system determines that a part does not meet a quality threshold, and signals the same to the human. In doing so the system has automated the quality function by performing the quality check and therefore reduced the human input, and has augmented the human by providing them with additional insight into the execution. Thus whilst the improper use of the terms leads to confusion, automation and augmentation are complementary, and should not be viewed as discrete but overlapping research areas [23]. How augmentation supports each automation goal needs to be considered in any human-technology solution.

For the purpose of this work, and based on this research, the terms are defined as follows: Automation is the application of technology, programs and processes to reduce human input so the system takes on the role heretofore executed by the human. Augmentation is an interdisciplinary field that enhances or amplifies the human abilities for desirable effects [15, 20, 21, 24].

There is also a disparity in the definition of an Augmented Human. Pirmagomedov & Koucheryavy [25] and De Boeck & Vaes [26] describe the Augmented Human having their human abilities enhanced to 'super-human' powers. Lee et al. [27] define the augmented human as one 'whose physical, intellectual, and social ability are enhanced by the augmented/virtual reality and the smart ICT technology'. Longo et al. [28] in their perspectives for the Smart Operator, refer to the Augmented Operator as one who can receive and send data and information from and to a cyber-twin context through a direct connection. So the implication is that the human is augmented only when using digital twin technologies. Romero, Stahre, et al. [15, 22] use the following formula: Operator + Augmented Reality = Augmented Operator. The implication here is that the operator is augmented only when using augmented reality devices. Based on the literature review, and the definitions herein, the Augmented Human is defined as follows: The Augmented Human is a human whose human abilities are enhanced or amplified for desirable effects.

4.2 A Proposed Taxonomy of Human Augmentation

In this section a synthesis of the literature is outlined. The common themes are drawn together into a proposed Taxonomy of Human Augmentation.

Cimini et al. [29] tabulate technologies by whether they provide physical or cognitive support. Similarly Moencks et al. [4] propose the human can be augmented physically or cognitively. In an earlier work, Wandke [30] on assistance for human-machine integration also views augmentation from a cognitive and physical perspective. The need for assistance for cognitive functions is presented. As is the need for physical assistance such as the use of signals to provide situation awareness, and the use of force or levers to augment action execution.

Other works identify three types of augmentation: physical, cognitive and sensory. For instance, Romero et al. [15] use the term automation aiding, and refer to aids for enhanced physical capabilities, enhanced sensing capabilities, and enhanced cognitive capabilities. They call for interfaces such as augmented reality or human-machine interfaces as cognitive aids. They state that these aids support Operator 4.0's new or increased cognitive workload in diagnosis, situational awareness, decision making and planning. Raisamo et al. [21] use categories almost identical to that of Romero et al. [15]. They divide augmentation into three categories – augmented sensing, augmented action and augmented cognition. Similarly, Zolotová et al. [5] and Pirmagomedov & Koucheryavy [25] refer to the need to augment the humans' physical, sensing, and cognitive capabilities.

The above suggest one type of cognitive augmentation, but Zheng et al. [12] suggest that this can be subdivided further into two. The first is intelligence augmentation where there is human-system collaboration; and the second is intelligence augmentation based on cognitive models embedded within a computer system. Their first model is termed 'human-in-the-loop augmented intelligence with human-computer collaboration'. Their second model is termed 'cognitive computing based augmented intelligence, in which a cognitive model is embedded in the machine learning system'. This model could be based on artificial intelligence, machine learning, or analytics on big data that provides smart intelligence. With respect to their former model, collaborative intelligence, they explain that the human and the system "adapt to and collaborate with each other, forming a two-way information exchange and control". They speak to the need for cross-task, cross-domain contextual relations, and the need for breaking through the human-computer interaction barrier, so that the collaboration is natural.

Wandke [30] explores the cognitive functions in which humans can be assisted, as (1) motivation, activation and goal setting; (2) perception; (3) information integration, generating situation awareness; (4) decision-making, action selection; (5) action execution; and (6) processing feedback of action results. Some of these cognitive functions are collaborative with the system, such as information integration of the human and systems information, similar to the collaborative intelligence of Zheng et al. [12].

Thorvald et al. [31] discuss augmentation as supporting the operator through technology. They describe the Cognitive Operator 4.0 as a collaboration between humans and systems symbiotically performing a task. Augmentation types proposed are sensing augmentation for perception and awareness, and cognitive augmentation to aid understanding. The cognitive augmentation achieved through deep learning is similar to the embedded intelligence of Zheng et al. [12] achieved by big data insights.

Romero et al. [15] describe augmentation when referring to the changing role of the operator. The operator will be one or more types, being super-strength (e.g. through the use of Exoskeletons), augmented (e.g. using augmented reality tools), virtual operator (e.g. in a virtual environment), healthy (e.g. using wearable devices to track well-being), smarter (e.g. using agent or artificial intelligence for planning activities), collaborative (e.g. interacting with CoBots), social (e.g. sharing knowledge using a social network) and analytical (e.g. using Big Data analytics). These are a mix of physical (super-strength, augmented, virtual and healthy), collaborative physical (collaborative), and cognitive (smarter, analytical). Romero et al. [15] do not mention sensory augmentation, but are one of the first to highlight social augmentation.

Jiao et al. [33] also refer to the need for augmented collaborative cognition, which they describe in similar terms to the work of Zheng et al. [12]. Jiao et al. state that human-automata integration requires collaboration from multiple agents, human and/or machines, in a social machine. In their work, the social machine enables collaboration which will be of the form cooperation, competition, or coordination. There are some similarities with the 'social operator' outlined in Romero, Bernus, et al. [15] and Casla et al. [32] who 'shares knowledge using a social network'. The sharing of knowledge being a form of collaboration. De Boeck & Vaes [26] though expand on social augmentation as enhancing 'social ability by supporting empathy, interaction (both human-to-human and human-to-computer interaction), means of communication, and collaboration'. The themes emerging from the research are captured in Table 1.

Having explored the descriptions of each of these, we propose that all of this work could be drawn together to create a new Taxonomy of Human Augmentation. Five classes

Table 1. Human Augmentation Themes arising from the Literature.

	Physical	Collaborative Physical	Sensory	Embedded Intelligence	Collaborative Social Intelligence
Casla et al. (2019)		✓			
Cimini et al. (2020)	✓				
De Boeck & Vaes (2021)	✓		✓	✓	✓
Engelbart (1962)					✓
Huber et al. (2018)			✓		
Jiao et al. (2020)					✓
Lee et al. (2018)	✓		✓	✓	
Maier, Ebrahimzadeh and Chowdhury, (2018)			✓		
Moencks et al., (2022)	✓			✓	
Pirmagomedov & Koucheryavy (2021)	✓		✓	✓	
Raisamo et al. (2019)	✓		✓	✓	
Romero, Bernus, et al., (2016)	✓		✓		✓
Thorvald et al. (2021)		✓	✓	✓	
Wandke, (2005)	✓				✓
Zheng et al. (2017)					✓
Zolotová et al. (2020)	✓		✓	✓	

are identified in the Taxonomy, and are represented graphically in Fig. 1. No hierarchy is proposed.

Each of the classes of augmentation are now described, with examples of industrial applications provided to illustrate the value-add.

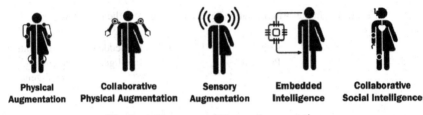

| Physical Augmentation | Collaborative Physical Augmentation | Sensory Augmentation | Embedded Intelligence | Collaborative Social Intelligence |

Fig. 1. A Taxonomy of Human Augmentation.

Physical Augmentation

Physical augmentation includes devices such as moveable robotic arms, wearables, augmented and virtual realities, or exoskeletons where focus is on flexibility of manual operations [29]. The system understands the human's actions and maps to corresponding actions in local or remote environments. Subclasses include motor augmentation, amplified force, speech input, gaze-based controls, teleoperation, and remote presence.

One example of physical augmentation is the work of Garcia et al. [36]. The human's hand movements are translated into movements for the robotic system. Physical augmentation can also be seen in the work of Longo, Nicoletti and Padovano [37]. They design and develop a framework for augmented humans in Industry 4.0. Their Sophos-MS project uses AR to provide humans with real time assistance. They report that the augmented humans outperform traditionally trained humans.

In the European Factories of the Future Research Association (EFFRA) project Human Manufacturing (HuMan), exoskeleton prototypes enhance the physical and operational capabilities of the workers. The first exoskeleton provides lower back assistance when picking boxes. The second supports the human worker when they have to maintain the arms in an elevated position for long times on repetitive tasks such as drilling, clamping, and riveting a high number of screws in the assembly of an aircraft [38].

Physical augmentation through the use of sensor based wearables features in the work of Al-Amin et al. [39]. Assembly workers have a wearable on their left and right hands. Simple sensors capture the movement of each hand, and when taken together produce an action recognition result. This system provides real time measurement of the human's location and activity, and can be used in detecting error, for training, or to identify continuous improvement initiatives.

The value-add of Physical Augmentation is the ability to control and manipulate objects from a distance. The value-add of wearables such as exoskeletons assist in physical demands, reduce human physical fatigue, can detect health and well-being, and increase their safety and productivity [19, 32]. The value-add of AR is the digital provision of additional intelligence onto the production line. Another value-add of alternative realities is that it augments the human in terms of the scalability, humans can work on multiple projects from different geographical locations.

The next category is Collaborative Physical Augmentation. This is distinquished from Physical Augmentation in that there is collaboration between the physical system and the human, missing from Physical Augmentation.

Collaborative Physical Augmentation

Collaborative Physical Augmentation is where the human co-operates with physical technology in the performance of a joint collaborative task. The system senses the human's actions and responds with collaborative actions in local or remote environments. The level of collaboration between the two agents, human and collaborative technology, can range from co-existence in a shared physical space through to full collaboration on a shared task [31]. Examples of Collaborative Physical Augmentation include Collaborative Robots (CoBots) and Industrial Robots [5].

In the Adaptive Automation in Assembly for BLUE collar workers project (A4BLUE), the collaborative assembly of a latch value, named IK4-TEKNIKER, is outlined. The human communicates with the industrial robotic system on the actions to execute through voice control, gesture commands and through selection of options on a mobile application [40].

A simulation model on collaborative physical augmentation is outlined in Winkelhaus et al. [41]. Order picking is the subject in this simulation. Baseline costs are determined for picking by humans, and picking by fully automated robotic systems. These are compared to the costs for a hybrid model in which the human and the robot perform the tasks collaboratively. The advantages of the collaboration are that the robots are able to pick all items without additional costs and without making mistakes, but there are additional costs for standardized packaging. The flexibility of the human means that they can pick anything without having to be pre-programmed, yet may make error. The hybrid collaborative model has benefits in terms of throughput, and lower total costs per pick than the baseline models.

The value-add of collaborative physical augmentation is that physically demanding or unsafe tasks can be executed by the robot, protecting the safety and wellbeing of the human [19, 22], and the synergy achieved by using both humans and robotic systems may lead to lower costs whilst also achieving better flexibility and reducing error [41].

Sensory Augmentation

The next class is Sensory Augmentation. In this class, the system reads multisensory information, which is interpreted and presented to the human. Subclasses include augmented vision, hearing, tactile, smell and taste. An example is the measurement of odours beyond the capacity of normal human olfactory system.

Computer vision is performed by machine learning algorithms and can be applied to various use-cases such as object detection, motion tracking, facial recognition, action recognition, human pose estimation, behaviour analysis, and change detection. In production for example, vision systems are employed to perform a visual check of a final product, such as whether the label is applied correctly to packaging, or whether the wafer is the correct colour and shape. For instance, Burresi et al. [42] investigate the use of computer vision systems for quality checking, in this instance verifying the presence or absence of parts.

Alternatively, sensory augmentation may perceive, process the sensory data *and* make decisions about what data to present to the human [42]. For example, in Knoch et al. [43] computer vision compares the humans' actions to the process model for assembly workflow to determine error. Multiple distance sensors, infrared cameras, convolutional neural networks and Haar wavelets are used. The system can 'see' and analyse the human posture, so as to determine the human's actions. The human's actions and the materials picked are then correlated with a process model and assembly workflow, which determines the production time as 'time per state' and quality as 'frequency of error'. A test accuracy of 99.25% on thirty-eight possible assembly states is achieved. Material picking is evaluated on participants performing sixteen picks on which an accuracy of 99.48% is found.

The value-add is an enhanced sensory function, which Romero et al. [15] call "providing humans with bionic ears and eyes".

Embedded Intelligence Augmentation
The next class refers to Embedded Intelligence Augmentation. This seeks to support the human with routine and non-routine cognitive capabilities, such as perception, problem solving and applying creativity. The system thinks, reasons and problem-solves for the human. This may occur independently, or the system may have a closed-loop to the human and detect and adapt to their situational needs. So, the system uses analytical tools to interpret a scenario, and responds by providing the human with some information.

An example of Embedded Intelligence Augmentation is seen in Kristiansen et al. [44]. In their work the assembly process is monitored. On finding an error, a database of errors is mined to return the error type, which is presented to the human.

The value-add of Embedded Intelligence Augmentation is access to the vast stores of information, which can be quickly searched and retrieved. If necessary statistical and machine learning algorithms can be applied to make predictions on the data.

Collaborative Social Intelligence Augmentation
The fifth and final class is Collaborative Social Intelligence Augmentation where the agents collaborate to achieve a mutual goal with elements of cooperation, competition, or coordination. In this class the objective is human-system intimacy or symbiosis [45]. The agents are human and system. The system breaks down complex problems, and locates and provides context, temporal, sensitive and adequate information to the human with respect to the task. Where there is collaboration between humans, or between humans and a system, there is a social element and communication between the agents. The system must be able to infer the goal, detect error and take predictive action, as would occur in the natural collaboration between humans. The environment must be safe for the human and the system to work together in the shared physical space.

In Bicho, E. et al. [46] the system and the human collaborate on the assembly process. There is clean handover in the collaboration process between the agents. The human's actions are observed, then the appropriate complementary action by the system determined. So for instance if the human does not tighten a screw on the part, the system will then tighten it. If the human does tighten the screw correctly, the system recognises this and does not intervene. The collaboration then allows both agents to respond to each other's actions.

The value-add in Collaborative Social Intelliegence Augmentation is the synergy that is realised. This value-add is very much the core of Industry 5.0, where systems will be human-centric, with the human working collaboratively with systems in a symbiotic relationship, working together to the same production goals.

4.3 Appropriate Augmentation for Different Levels of Automation

Having identified and classified the various augmentation classes, it is now possible to recommend applicable augmentation classes to solve automation goals. One description of automation, Frohm et al.'s 'Levels of Automation' [47], features regularly in the literature. It ranges from 1 (totally manual) to 7 (totally automated), as shown in the left-most column of Table 2, and is typical of other descriptions of automation in the literature [48–51]. The proposed augmentation solutions for each level are set out in the right-most column of Table 2.

Table 2. Frohm et al. [47] Levels of Automation with suitable augmentation classes from the proposed Taxonomy of Augmentation.

AUTOMATION LEVEL	ENABLING AUGMENTATION
1. Totally manual	No augmentation
2. Decision giving	Physical Augmentation and/or Collaborative Physical Augmentation and/or Collaborative Social Intelligence Augmentation and/or Embedded Intelligence Augmentation
3. Teaching	Physical Augmentation and/or Collaborative Physical Augmentation and/or Collaborative Social Intelligence Augmentation
4. Questioning	Collaborative Social Intelligence Augmentation and/or Embedded Intelligence Augmentation
5. Supervision	Sensory Augmentation and/or Collaborative Social Intelligence Augmentation and/or Embedded Intelligence Augmentation
6. Intervening	Sensory Augmentation and/or Embedded Intelligence Augmentation
7. Totally automatic	Substitution. No augmentation

The applicable augmentation will be dependent upon the context in which it is being applied. For instance, the delivery of new Standard Operating Procedure instructions would fit with the goal of *Level 3: Teaching* for which Physical Augmentation, Collaborative Physical Augmentation and Collaborative Social Intelligence Augmentation are proposed. A decision would have to be made if Physical Augmentation, such as teaching through AR, is suitable for the particular environment to which it is being deployed, for example it may not be appropriate in a clean production room. Collaborative Social Intelligence Augmentation could work step-by-step with the human, advising the human if an error occurs, and/or working alongside the human eventually giving way to less support as the human becomes more familiar with the process.

In *Level 5: Supervision*, Sensory Augmentation is the most commonly used augmentation with computer vision performing the quality check on the product, or performing human action analysis to identify whether the necessary actions are conducted. Collaborative Social Intelligence Augmentation could be used to either flag or step-in if there is a mistake in the work. Embedded Intelligence Augmentation might be appropriate where statistical analysis on the work is required to be done. For example, if part of the production process used additive manufacturing, sub-volumetric measurement of the part could be conducted by the embedded intelligence which would then signal to the human if the part passes the quality control check [52].

4.4 Value-Add of Augmentation

The Director of Global Quality and Regulatory Affairs for a multinational manufacturing organization, with a base in Ireland, explains that KPIs provide the common and easily understood language and tool to monitor progress and value-add. They use thirty-seven KPIs for the Quality Function alone, in addition to numerous KPIs across Operations and other functional areas. The value-add of augmentation identified in this research, is represented as potential impact on KPIs, and is presented in Table 3. Given the vast range of KPIs, this list is not exhaustive but serves as a guide only.

Table 3. Value-Add of Each Augmentation Class.

Augmentation Class	Potential Value-Add	Possible Key Performance Indicators impacted
Physical Augmentation	Enhance the physical and operational capabilities of the worker, reduce physical fatigue, and increase their safety and productivity Wearables can detect the health and well-being of workers Provides real time measurement of the human's location and activity, and can be used in detecting error, for training, or for continuous improvement initiatives Improved Scalability through the ability to control and manipulate objects from a distance, connecting teams virtually in the Company. With alternative realities, humans can work on multiple projects from different geographical locations. The value-add is better utilisation of expert knowledge and skills across locations	Reduction in 'Absenteeism Rate' Reduction in 'Health & Safety Incidents' Reduction in 'Employee Turnover' Improvement in 'Productivity', Reduction in 'Error Rate', and 'Failed Products' Labour and overheads savings by a reduction in travel and better utilisation of resources will impact KPIs such as Reduced 'Production Costs'

(continued)

Table 3. (*continued*)

Augmentation Class	Potential Value-Add	Possible Key Performance Indicators impacted
Collaborative Physical Augmentation	Increased throughput on standardised high-volume lines, which do not suit Total Automation, i.e. some human involvement or flexibility is required Synergy achieved by using both humans and robotic systems may lead to lower costs and reduce error Dirty, monotonous or repetitive tasks can be performed by technology so that humans can concentrate on other tasks Physically demanding or unsafe tasks can be executed by the robot, protecting the safety and wellbeing of the human Teaching workers on unfamiliar lines	Increased 'Throughput' Improved KPIs with respect to Quality Improvements in Staff Morale, reflected in KPIs such as Reduction in 'Employee Turnover', and Improvements to 'Employee Engagement', and 'Employee Satisfaction' Reduction in 'Health & Safety Incident Rate' Reduced 'Onboarding Costs' and 'Training Cost per Employee', and Reduced 'Time to Productivity'
Sensory Augmentation	The value-add is an enhanced sensory function beyond the capacity and speed of normal human abilities, leading to improved performance Ability to monitor employees and business productivity by performing object detection, motion tracking, facial recognition, action recognition, human pose estimation, behaviour analysis, and change detection. These can be used to identify error, perform quality control checks, tag failed quality products, or identify where the human is not performing an assembly process correctly, identify parts in a process more prone to error. This leads to a reduction in the effort of human supervision hours Knowledge can be used to intervene and stop error from propagating through the system	Improved 'Overall Operations Effectiveness', 'Production Volume', and Reduced 'Production Costs' Reduction in 'Error Rate' Reduction in Effort for Quality Function Reduced 'Customer Returns (Rejects)' Increased Impact from Continuous Improvement initiatives Improved 'Production Schedule Attainment', Increased 'Throughput', Improved 'Yield', Reduced 'Work-in-Process', Reduced 'Scrap', Improved 'First Pass Yield Rate', Reduction in 'Non-Compliance Events'

(*continued*)

Table 3. (*continued*)

Augmentation Class	Potential Value-Add	Possible Key Performance Indicators impacted
Embedded Intelligence Augmentation	The digitalisation of the production floor, and the fast access by the worker to the vast stores of information, improves decision making, can question production quality and flag the same to the human, supervises work, and can intervene or predict likely future causes of concern, say such as machine failures. These all have a major impact on performance	Significant impact on a wide range of Production KPIs, such as Improvements to 'Total Cycle Time', 'Production Schedule Attainment', 'Throughput', 'Production Volume', and Reductions to 'Production Costs', 'Downtime', 'Error Rate' and so on
Collaborative Social Intelligence Augmentation	The value-add is a human-centric workplace, with the human working collaboratively with systems in a symbiotic relationship It positively impacts culture, shifting from a culture where human performance is evaluated with respect to productivity targets, but towards an appreciation of the rounded and skilled human There is value-add in the synergy between human and machine	Impact on HR KPIs such as Reduction in 'Employee Turnover', and Improvements to 'Employee Engagement', 'Employee Satisfaction', Reduced 'Onboarding Costs'. 'Training Cost per Employee', and Reduced 'Time to Productivity' Synergy should impact production and quality KPIs such as Improved 'First Pass Yield Rate', Reduction in 'Non-Compliance Events' and so on

This paper presents a new Taxonomy of Human Augmentation and proposes likely value-add opportunities. It is not, and does not purport to be a cost-benefit analysis. However, we note that the value-add of each of the augmentation classes is the benefit to the organisation over the costs to implement the technology. Benefits and costs may be real or perceived. To generate the value-add, there will be additional costs in technology development, implementation and commissioning, which may impact KPIs such as 'Manufacturing Cost as a Percentage of Revenue', 'Energy Cost Per Unit', and so on. It is up to the practitioner to calculate the 'Return on Investment' and make their own judgement call as to the value for their particular unique circumstances.

Further it should be noted that impact will not be realised solely by the implementation of some new technology under one of the classes. Technology, in of itself, is not the panacea for all manufacturing problems. A successful Technology Implementation Process is required to be followed to ensure that there is buy-in from all stakeholders. In addition, there may be a myriad of issues around change implementation, Technology

Readiness Levels, Capability Maturity, Smart Manufacturing and Industry 4.0 maturity models [53], that need to be considered to realise potential impacts.

5 Conclusion

In this paper, we draw together disparate works on augmentation. A definition for Augmentation, and the Augmented Human are presented following a review of the literature. Augmentation is shown to support automation, but should be treated as a separate but complementary area of research.

Following a literature review, a Taxonomy of Human Augmentation suitable for the Factories of the Future is presented. We identify five different classes of Augmentation: Physical, Collaborative Physical, Embedded Intelligence, Collaborative Social Intelligence and Sensory. There may be some overlaps between the classes, such as the possibility for Embedded Intelligence being integrated into Physical Augmentation. For instance, Augmented Reality, a Physical Augmentation technology, may not only be able to perceive and overlay images onto a scene, but may also be able to access embedded data stores to identify what is happening within the scene. The degree of overlapping between the classes cannot yet be quantified, until such time as there is a maturity of the technology for each class.

Each of these classes is explored, and examples of where they are being used in Industry are provided so that the value-add can be understood. The types of augmentation which are appropriate for automation goals is provided. This taxonomy therefore extends the Mattsson et al. [17] Strategy for Cognitive Automation for Operator 4.0, as it recommends appropriate augmentation solutions for automation problems.

Knowledge of the value-add, and identifying the potential KPIs impacted by each class in the taxonomy provide practitioners with further information to decide on solutions to solve their own particular automation needs. In doing so, the research gap identified in Mirco Moencks et al. [4] that industrial practitioners need information on the value-add of augmentation is addressed. However, it is warned that in order to realise the potential impact on KPIs a successful Implementation Plan should be followed.

In exploring the role of augmentation within automation, and suggesting augmentation classes for each level of automation, this paper contributes to the theories of human-centred automation systems. The use of a standard Taxonomy, and definitions allow for like-for-like comparisons and will aid better decision making.

5.1 Limitations

There is a lack of use of a standard nomenclature in discussing human augmentation, with relevant research using terms such as cognitive automation, human-technology integration, Operator Assistance Systems, human-cyber-physical-systems, machine augmented intelligence, intelligence amplification, Holistic Quantified Self and Human 2.0. Given the lack of standardised terms, it is possible that not all relevant research has been uncovered in this literature review process. Furthermore, the descriptions of the various use cases of augmentation have been abstracted from the texts based on our understanding of augmentation. Despite this limitation, this novel Taxonomy of Human Augmentation does unify the existing research, and provides a common description of each augmentation type which can assist practitioners in seeking and exploring augmentation solutions.

5.2 Further Research

Mirco Moencks et al. [4] identified a research gap as being a need to analyse industrial use cases and prototypes for impact, which we have addressed. We have shown a number of examples of augmentation in practice. However, there is a need for empirical evidence, with larger case studies, often missing in Industry 4.0 research [9, 54, 55]. This lack of experimental data in realistic industrial settings has an impact on generalizability [54]. Further research should provide empirical evidence of the value-add of augmentation solutions of the types listed in the Taxonomy, so that practitioners can better understand the value-add, and contribution to their KPIs.

Further, with respect to the Collaborative Social Intelligence Augmentation class, there are currently technical and theoretical limitations which need addressing, in particular, how can context-specific information be provided at the right time, in the right place, to the right human. The problem is that the human is unpredictable and unique, their knowledge is constantly changing, and they can make mistakes. From a human-machine symbiosis perspective this causes challenges as how to switch control from one agent to another. Liu and Wang [56], and Zhang et al. [57] suggest that this is due to the lack of theoretical and computational models in human-automata research which characterize human knowledge and behaviours, and the interactions between humans and machines. At present the potential of this class is limited to confined activities with an *a priori* determination of likely human behaviours, where we reduce the human to a solipsistic representation of knowledge replicable within the machine [58]. This is not in keeping with the true nature of a symbiotic relationship.

Finally, there are socio-technical considerations of augmenting the workforce, which should be investigated further, such as the impact of augmentation on human factors, and how to ensure safety of the human whilst being augmented.

Acknowledgment. This research is co-funded by the Enterprise Ireland and European Regional Development Fund (ERDF) under Ireland's European Structural and Investment Funds (ESI) Programmes 2014–2020.

References

1. Fitts, P.: Human Engineering for an Effective Air-navigation and Traffic-control. National Research, London (1951)
2. de Winter, J.C.F., Dodou, D.: Why the fitts list has persisted throughout the history of function allocation. Cogn. Technol. Work **16**, 1–11 (2014). https://doi.org/10.1007/s10111-011-0188-1
3. Licklider JCR: Man-Computer Symbiosis. IRE Trans Hum Factors Electron HFE-1, 4–11 (1960). https://doi.org/10.1109/THFE2.1960.4503259

4. Moencks, M., Roth, E., Bohné, T., et al.: Augmented Workforce Canvas: a management tool for guiding human-centric, value-driven human-technology integration in industry. Comput. Ind. Eng. **163**, 107803 (2022). https://doi.org/10.1016/j.cie.2021.107803

5. Zolotová, I., Papcun, P., Kajáti, E., et al.: Smart and cognitive solutions for Operator 4.0: Laboratory H-CPPS case studies. Comput Ind Eng **139**, 105471 (2020). https://doi.org/10. 1016/j.cie.2018.10.032

6. Fässberg, T., Fasth, Å., Stahre, J.: A classification of carrier and content of information. Proc 4th CIRP Conf Assem Technol Syst 1–4 (2012)

7. Krugh, M., Mears, L.: A complementary cyber-human systems framework for industry 4.0 cyber-physical systems. Manuf. Lett. **15**, 89–92 (2018). https://doi.org/10.1016/j.mfglet.2018. 01.003

8. Maettig, B., Foot, H.: Approach to improving training of human workers in industrial applications through the use of Intelligence Augmentation and Human-in-the-Loop. In: 2020 15th International Conference on Computer Science & Educ. (ICCSE). IEEE, pp. 283–288 (2020)

9. Kadir, B.A., Broberg, O., Conceição, C.S. da: Current research and future perspectives on human factors and ergonomics in Industry 4.0. Comput Ind Eng 137, 106004 (2019). https:// doi.org/10.1016/j.cie.2019.106004

10. Pfeiffer, S (2016) Robots, Industry 4.0 and Humans, or Why Assembly Work Is More than Routine Work. Societies 6:16. https://doi.org/10.3390/soc6020016

11. Su, Q., Liu, L., Whitney, D.E.: A systematic study of the prediction model for operator-induced assembly defects based on assembly complexity factors. IEEE Trans. Syst. Man, Cybern. - Part A Syst. Hum. **40**, 107–120 (2010). https://doi.org/10.1109/TSMCA.2009.203 3030

12. Zheng, N., Liu, Z., Ren, P., et al.: Hybrid-augmented intelligence: collaboration and cognition. Front. Inf. Technol. Electron. Eng. **18**, 153–179 (2017). https://doi.org/10.1631/FITEE.170 0053

13. Neumann, W.P., Winkelhaus, S., Grosse, E.H., Glock, C.H.: Industry 4.0 and the human factor – a systems framework and analysis methodology for successful development. Int. J. Prod. Econ. **233**, 107992 (2021). https://doi.org/10.1016/j.ijpe.2020.107992

14. Fantini, P., Pinzone, M., Taisch, M.: Placing the operator at the centre of Industry 4.0 design: modelling and assessing human activities within cyber-physical systems. Comput. Ind. Eng. **139**, 105058 (2020). https://doi.org/10.1016/j.cie.2018.01.025

15. Romero, D., Bernus, P., Noran, O., et al.: The operator 4.0: human cyber-physical systems, adaptive automation towards human-automation symbiosis work systems. In: Advances in Production Man. Systems. Initiatives for a Sustainable World, pp. 677–686 (2016)

16. Davenport, T.H., Kirby, J.: Only humans need apply: winners and losers in the age of smart machines. Harper Business (2016)

17. Mattsson, S., Fast-Berglund, Å., Li, D., Thorvald, P.: Forming a cognitive automation strategy for operator 4.0 in complex assembly. Comput. Ind. Eng. **139** (2020). https://doi.org/10.1016/ j.cie.2018.08.011

18. Dolgui, A., Sgarbossa, F., Simonetto, M.: Design and management of assembly systems 4.0: systematic literature review and research agenda. Int. J. Prod. Res. **60**, 184–210 (2022). https:// doi.org/10.1080/00207543.2021.1990433

19. Dornelles, J.de A., Ayala, N.F., Frank, A.G.: Smart working in industry 4.0: how digital technologies enhance manufacturing workers' activities. Comput. Ind. Eng. **163**, 107804 (2022). https://doi.org/10.1016/j.cie.2021.107804

20. Engelbart, D.C.: Augmenting human intellect: a conceptual framework (1962)

21. Raisamo, R., Rakkolainen, I., Majaranta, P., et al.: Human augmentation: past, present and future. Int. J. Hum. Comput. Stud. **131**, 131–143 (2019). https://doi.org/10.1016/j.ijhcs.2019. 05.008

22. Romero, D., Stahre, J., Wuest, T., et al.: Towards an operator 4.0 typology: a human-centric perspective on the fourth industrial revolution technologies. In: Proceedings of the International Conference on Computers and Industrial Engineering, pp 1–11 (2016)
23. Raisch, S., Krakowski, S.: Artificial intelligence and management: the automation–augmentation paradox. Acad. Manag. Rev. **46**, 192–210 (2021). https://doi.org/10.5465/amr.2018.0072
24. Davenport, T.H., Kirby, J.: Beyond Automation. Harv. Bus. Rev (2015)
25. Pirmagomedov, R., Koucheryavy, Y.: IoT technologies for augmented human: a survey. Internet of Things **14**, 100120 (2021). https://doi.org/10.1016/j.iot.2019.100120
26. De Boeck, M., Vaes, K.: Structuring human augmentation within product design. Proc. Des. Soc. **1**, 2731–2740 (2021). https://doi.org/10.1017/pds.2021.534
27. Lee, J., Kim, E., Yu, J., et al.: Holistic quantified self framework for augmented human, pp 188–201 (2018)
28. Longo, F., Nicoletti, L., Padovano, A.: New perspectives and results for smart operators in industry 4.0: a human-centered approach. Comput. Ind. Eng. **163**, 107824 (2022). https://doi.org/10.1016/j.cie.2021.107824
29. Cimini, C., Pirola, F., Pinto, R., Cavalieri, S.: A human-in-the-loop manufacturing control architecture for the next generation of production systems. J. Manuf. Syst. **54**, 258–271 (2020). https://doi.org/10.1016/j.jmsy.2020.01.002
30. Wandke, H.: Assistance in human–machine interaction: a conceptual framework and a proposal for a taxonomy. Theor. Issues Ergon. Sci. **6**, 129–155 (2005). https://doi.org/10.1080/1463922042000295669
31. Thorvald, P., Fast Berglund, Å., Romero, D.: The Cognitive Operator 4.0 (2021)
32. Casla, P., Larreina, J., Fletcher, S., et al.: Human-centered factories from theory to industrial practice. Lessons learned and recommendations (2019)
33. Jiao, J., Zhou, F., Gebraeel, N.Z., Duffy, V.: Towards augmenting cyber-physical-human collaborative cognition for human-automation interaction in complex manufacturing and operational environments. Int. J. Prod. Res. **58**, 5089–5111 (2020). https://doi.org/10.1080/00207543.2020.1722324
34. Huber, J., Shilkrot, R., Maes, P., Nanayakkara, S.: Assistive augmentation (Cognitive Science and Technology), 1st ed. Springer, Singapore (2018). https://doi.org/10.1007/978-981-10-6404-3
35. Maier, M., Ebrahimzadeh, A., Chowdhury, M.: The tactile internet: automation or augmentation of the human? IEEE Access **6**, 41607–41618 (2018). https://doi.org/10.1109/ACCESS.2018.2861768
36. Garcia, M.A.R., Rojas, R., Gualtieri, L., et al.: A human-in-the-loop cyber-physical system for collaborative assembly in smart manufacturing. Procedia CIRP **81**, 600–605 (2019). https://doi.org/10.1016/j.procir.2019.03.162
37. Longo, F., Nicoletti, L., Padovano, A.: Smart operators in industry 4.0: a human-centered approach to enhance operators' capabilities and competencies within the new smart factory context. Comput. Ind. Eng. **113**, 144–159 (2017). https://doi.org/10.1016/j.cie.2017.09.016
38. European Factories of the Future Research Association: HuMan Project Tests Exoskeletons (2017). https://www.effra.eu/project-news/human-project-tests-exoskeletons. Accessed 1 Nov 2022
39. Al-Amin, M., Qin, R., Tao, W., et al.: Fusing and refining convolutional neural network models for assembly action recognition in smart manufacturing. Proc. Inst. Mech. Eng. Part C J. Mech. Eng. Sci. **236**, 2046–2059 (2022). https://doi.org/10.1177/0954406220931547
40. A4blue (2016). https://a4blue.eu/. Accessed 1 Nov 2022
41. Winkelhaus, S., Zhang, M., Grosse, E.H., Glock, C.H.: Hybrid order picking: a simulation model of a joint manual and autonomous order picking system. Comput. Ind. Eng. **167**, 107981 (2022). https://doi.org/10.1016/j.cie.2022.107981

42. Burresi, G., Lorusso, M., Graziani, L., et al.: Image-based defect detection in assembly line with machine learning. In: 2021 10th Mediterranean Conference on Embedded Computing (MECO), pp 1–5. IEEE (2021)
43. Knoch, S., Herbig, N., Ponpathirkoottam, S., et al.: Sensor-based human-process interaction in discrete manufacturing. J. Data Semant. **9**, 21–37 (2020). https://doi.org/10.1007/s13740-019-00109-z
44. Kristiansen, E., Nielsen, E.K., Hansen, L., Bourne, D.: A novel strategy for automatic error classification and error recovery for robotic assembly in flexible production. J. Intell. Robot. Syst. **100**, 863–877 (2020). https://doi.org/10.1007/s10846-020-01248-3
45. Hancock, P.A., Jagacinski, R.J., Parasuraman, R., et al.: Human-automation interaction research. Ergon. Des. Q. Hum. Fact. Appl. **21**, 9–14 (2013). https://doi.org/10.1177/106480 4613477099
46. Bicho, E., Erlhagen, W., Louro, L., et al.: A dynamic field approach to goal inference, error detection and anticipatory action selection in human-robot collaboration. New Front. Hum.-Robot Interact., 135–164 (2011)
47. Frohm, J., Lindström, V., Stahre, J., Winroth, M.: Levels of automation in manufacturing. Ergon. Int. J. Ergon. Hum. factors **30**(3) (2008)
48. Draper, J.V.: Teleoperators for advanced manufacturing: applications and human factors challenges. Int. J. Hum. Fact. Manuf. **5**, 53–85 (1995). https://doi.org/10.1002/hfm.453005 0105
49. Fereidunian, A., Lehtonen, M., Lesani, H., et al.: Adaptive autonomy: smart cooperative cybernetic systems for more humane automation solutions. In: 2007 IEEE International Conference on Systems, Man and Cybernetics. IEEE, pp 202–207 (2007)
50. Vagia, M., Transeth, A.A., Fjerdingen, S.A.: A literature review on the levels of automation during the years. What are the different taxonomies that have been proposed? Appl. Ergon. **53**, 190–202 (2016). https://doi.org/10.1016/j.apergo.2015.09.013
51. Parasuraman, R., Sheridan, T., Wickens, C.: A model for types and levels of human interaction with automation. IEEE Trans. Syst. Man Cybern., 286–297 (2000)
52. Afroz, A.S., Inglese, F., Stefanini, C., Milazzo, M.: STL_Process: A .STL-based preprocessor for robot path planning in manufacturing and quality control processes. SoftwareX 15, 100725 (2021). https://doi.org/10.1016/j.softx.2021.100725
53. Mittal, S., Khan, M.A., Romero, D., Wuest, T.: A critical review of smart manufacturing and Industry 4.0 maturity models: implications for small and medium-sized enterprises (SMEs). J. Manuf. Syst. **49**, 194–214 (2018). https://doi.org/10.1016/j.jmsy.2018.10.005
54. Gürerk, Ö., Bohné, T.M., Alvarez Alonso, G.: Productivity and learning effects of head-mounted AR displays on human-centered work. SSRN Electron. J. (2018). https://doi.org/10.2139/ssrn.3264118
55. Kamble, S.S., Gunasekaran, A., Gawankar, S.A.: Sustainable industry 4.0 framework: a systematic literature review identifying the current trends and future perspectives. Process. Saf. Environ. Prot. **117**, 408–425 (2018). https://doi.org/10.1016/j.psep.2018.05.009
56. Liu, Z., Wang, J.: Human-cyber-physical systems: concepts, challenges, and research opportunities. Front. Inf. Technol. Electron. Eng. **21**, 1535–1553 (2020). https://doi.org/10.1631/FITEE.2000537
57. Zhang, M., Liu, W., Tang, X., et al.: Human-cyber-physical automata and their synthesis, pp. 36–41 (2022)
58. Cunningham, J.: Human and not too human. In: Dharamsi, K., Clemis, D. (eds.) Liberal Education: Analog Dreams in a Digital Age, pp. 61–84. Vernon Press, Delaware, United States (2023). https://doi.org/10.1007/s41245-023-00169-x

Gesture Me: A Machine Learning Tool for Designers to Train Gesture Classifiers

Marcus Winter[✉] , Phil Jackson , and Sanaz Fallahkhair

School of Architecture, Technology and Engineering, University of Brighton, Brighton, UK
{marcus.winter,prj11,s.fallahkhair}@brighton.ac.uk

Abstract. This paper contributes to the body of work examining how designers can be supported in integrating machine learning (ML) capabilities into their designs for novel applications and services. It presents an online tool enabling designers and other non-specialist audiences to define body gestures, interactively and iteratively train and test a classifier to recognise these gestures, and integrate the trained classifier into a template web application. An empirical evaluation with MSc User Experience Design students and practitioners, all of whom had previous experience in web development but not in ML, found that the tool enables them to define, train and test a gesture recognition classifier with little or no help, and that engagement with the tool advances their understanding of the capabilities, limitations and operational aspects of ML. The evaluation confirmed the value of visualising the ML perspective and encouraging designers to experiment with ML to support their experiential learning. The study led to design recommendations that can inform the development of tools supporting designers to ideate and prototype ML-enhanced applications.

Keyword: UX design · Machine learning · Gesture recognition

1 Introduction

Machine Learning (ML), once the exclusive domain of ML experts capable of designing, implementing, training and deploying ML models, is becoming increasingly commoditised with the emergence of model repositories offering a wide range of open-source, often pre-trained, ML models for a range of general use cases. Many of these models are optimised for inferencing on consumer-level hardware, and they are increasingly being integrated into end-user products and services. Amershi and colleagues describe this emerging class of "AI-infused systems" as "harnessing AI capabilities that are directly exposed to the end user" [5:1], and offer a comprehensive set of guidelines informing the interface and interaction design of such ML-enhanced products. These guidelines are helpful in particular during the latter stages of the design process, represented as the second diamond in the Design Council's double diamond design framework [10], which is concerned with "designing things right". However, they offer little support during the earlier stages of the design process, represented by the first diamond in that framework, which is concerned with "designing the right thing" (ibid). These stages

H. P. da Silva and P. Cipresso (Eds.): CHIRA 2023, CCIS 1996, pp. 336–352, 2023.
https://doi.org/10.1007/978-3-031-49425-3_21

involve exploring a problem space and defining specific challenges to address, requiring a good understanding by designers of the capabilities, properties and limitations of ML when formulating possible solutions. Yang [48] points out that designers need to be ML literate in order to ideate and conceptualise ML-enhanced products, yet several studies found that designers currently lack appropriate ML knowledge. Both [11] and [49] report that designers have a poor understanding of the capabilities and limitations of ML, while [46] found that many designers have a skewed view of which tasks are easier or more difficult for ML to tackle, for example assuming that ML performs better at generic object recognition than at specific object recognition. The same study (ibid) also found that most designers have little knowledge or even awareness of conceptual and operational aspects of ML such as assessing the quality of training data, understanding possible sources of bias, or interpreting uncertainty in model predictions. Regarding the ideation of novel ML-enhanced products, [49] report that designers often have difficulties in identifying ways how ML can help to improve products, while [46] found that designers' ideas for ML applications are often very abstract, referring more to an application area than an application, or very complex, requiring a whole range of ML capabilities and wider sensing technologies.

Efforts to make ML more accessible to designers and improve their ML literacy range from traditional learning approaches, involving books (e.g. [19]) and online articles (e.g. [13]) about ML concepts and technologies, to experiential learning approaches, where designers experiment with ML in workshops (e.g. [14]) and taught courses (e.g. [32]) to gain a better understanding of how they can integrate it with their designs and their design practice. A survey of 102 design professionals and students [46] found that designers have a strong preference for the latter and consider experiential ways of learning as most useful in advancing their ML literacy.

Gesture Me is an online environment where designers (and others non-experts lacking ML expertise) can interactively and iteratively, define, train, test and deploy a classifier, and then use the results of their engagement in a practical context. The purpose of *Gesture Me* is twofold: on the one hand, it aims to make ML more accessible to designers, enabling them to experiment with the technology and quickly prototype applications; on the other hand, it supports designers' experiential learning about ML through guided interactive engagement. The first iteration of *Gesture Me*, presented here, focuses on developing suitable processes, language and design patterns that enable non-expert users to train a classifier for human body gestures. Future versions will then extend this concept to other ML capabilities.

The main contributions of this paper are (i) an interactive environment for designers to define, train, test and deploy a classifier for human body gestures; (ii) an analysis of challenges in the interaction design of the iterative training process based on a formative empirical evaluation; and (iii) an assessment how experiential learning from engagement with the tool advances designers' ML literacy.

The following sections contextualise the developed online environment by briefly discussing related efforts in commercial and academic settings; describe the functionality, interaction design and technical implementation of *Gesture Me*; report on the methodology and findings of a formative evaluation of the developed tool; and set out future work as part of the conclusions.

2 Background

The need to make ML more accessible to designers has been expressed both in popular and academic literature [11, 18, 19, 25, 48]. Focusing in particular on ML as a "design material" [11, 20, 51] to enhance products and services with new capabilities, rather than as a tool to support the design process, Gillies et al. [18] point out that designers' firm rooting and rich methodology in user-centred design puts them in a prime position to develop novel ML-enhanced applications that address users' needs by prioritising the user experience over technical and commercial aspects. Continuing this thread, Dove et al. [11] call for design-led, rather than technology-led, development of ML applications and services as a way to explore new uses of the technology and address persistent issues around fairness, accountability and transparency in many current ML applications.

A major obstacle towards design-led ML application development is that designers often lack the required ML knowledge to successfully integrate it into their designs and their design process. Several studies [4, 11, 12, 46, 49, 50] found that most designers have little knowledge of the conceptual, technical and operational aspects of ML required to understand its capabilities and limitations, and to design, train, test and deploy models as part of their design products.

Yang et al. [49] categorise efforts to improve designers' understanding of ML into didactic and experiential approaches: while the former are based on the assumption that a better conceptual and technical understanding of ML helps designers to make better use of it in their products, the latter are based on the assumption that sensitizing designers to ML capabilities and design possibilities through hands-on engagement is more fruitful. This view is not only supported by learning theory, which contends that experiential learning through experience from active engagement is particularly effective in adult education [8, 21], but also by recent survey results showing that designers find experiential ways of learning most useful in advancing their ML literacy [46]. To address this problem, Yang et al. call for "research on new tools and techniques that make it easier for designers to ideate, sketch and prototype what new forms ML might take, and new contexts in which ML might be appropriate" [49:279].

Gesture Me enables designers to quickly and easily train a gesture classifier without requiring any technical ML knowledge, while mitigating their lack of conceptual and operational knowledge about ML through a light-weight approach to guided interaction, which structures the process into sequential steps while also allowing for iteration and model updating. As an interactive environment enabling people to train and optimise a ML model, it takes inspiration from, and extends, a research into interactive ML [3, 4, 7, 12, 16, 17], while also drawing on research into Machine Teaching [4, 37, 50], which offers paradigm shift towards a human-centred perspective on training ML models, aiming to improve the efficacy of the "teachers" rather than the accuracy of the "learners" [4].

Several existing systems can be related to *Gesture Me* in purpose and/or approach. This includes closed commercial tools, such as Apple Create ML [6], Obviously AI [31] or Runway ML [33], educational tools, such as Machine Learning for Kids [26], or tools to generally broaden access and uptake of ML by hobbyists and developers, such as Teachable Machine [41]. In addition, there are several research projects and related prototypes described in the literature that aim to make ML more accessible to designers and/or non-experts in general. A comprehensive overview of low- and no-code platforms for ML application development is provided in [23]. The following paragraphs briefly discuss some examples illustrating different approaches and capabilities, ranging from the least to the most technical.

Malsattar and colleagues [27] address the difficulty for designers to quickly prototype ML-enabled applications, which is complicated by the need to train and integrate a related ML model with the required capabilities. They present ObjectResponder, a mobile prototyping tool based on Google Cloud Vision's object recognition framework. The tool recognises objects in the live camera feed and enables designers to create written responses to objects, which are then uttered by the mobile device using text-to-speech functionality. An empirical evaluation of the tool involved designers to prototype concepts for intelligent context-aware interactions in the wild. It found that engagement with the tool helped designers to think more broadly about application ideas and gain a better understanding of the limitations of the technology, as it enabled them to look at the context from the perspective of an ML model. The authors propose that the "non-human perspective" in the design context complements the human perspective and leads to a richer and more nuanced understanding than the one designers could develop on their own.

Targeting novice-users, Mishra and Rzeszotarski [29] focus in particular on transfer learning [42] as a way to shorten and simplify ML model creation and training by adapting expert curated models to new problems. They describe an interactive training tool for handwritten character recognition enabling users to create, modify, train and test models, and offering functionality to probe a model with specific inputs, inspect model components and investigate model output. An empirical evaluation of their system found that non-experts' progress in creating, training and testing models was frequently impeded by inaccurate perceptions of the ML process.

Sanchez and colleagues [34] describe research to identify novice users' teaching strategies and develop guidelines for designing IML systems for the general public. Their web-based sketch recognition system uses a deep neural network that can be trained incrementally by novice users, defined as people who are not literate in ML or computer science. An empirical evaluation of their system found that novice users employed heterogeneous teaching strategies in terms of training size, variability and sequencing, and that engagement with the system helped them to develop their understanding of relevant training data features and the system's inner workings.

Focusing on industrial designers, Sun et al. [40] developed a workflow and related environment that takes into account designers' limited knowledge about ML and lack of advanced programming skills. The authors point out the trade-off between ease-of-use and flexibility in existing systems, arguing that current systems are either easy-to-use toolkits for beginners, with limited functionality to access diverse ML capabilities or influence the ML process, or flexible toolkits for experts, which provide access to a range of ML capabilities but require expert knowledge of ML and advanced programming skills. Bridging this gap, the authors present ML Rapid, an IDE enabling users to write and execute code covering all steps in the ML process (data collection; data annotation; model construction; model training; model inference; model updating). An empirical evaluation involving 30 junior students of industrial design, who had advanced knowledge of open-source hardware and related development tools, but only limited understanding of ML, showed that most participants appreciated the ease of development using ML-Rapid, and found that it provided the necessary functionality and flexibility for prototyping ML-empowered products.

Gesture Me adds to this field a ML tool for designers and other non-expert users to interactively train a gesture classifier. It covers the whole process from exploring how the system understands body poses, to defining gestures, iteratively collecting training data, training and testing the classifier, and finally integrating the trained classifier in an application prototype. A discussion of the system's functionality, interaction design, and technical implementation is provided in the following section.

3 Prototype Application

Gesture Me enables users to train their own classifier to recognise body gestures such as crossing your arms, pointing to the left or right, etc. It was developed primarily for web designers and developers who might want to integrate embodied interaction into their applications, however, given that web technologies are increasingly being used for cross-platform application development, the potential target audience is much wider and includes designers and developers of interactive experiences more generally. For instance, one of the original use cases guiding an earlier version of the tool was based on development teams in museums seeking to turn touch-based information screens (typically built with web technologies) into gesture-based systems in a post-COVID environment where shared touch surfaces become problematic.

An important secondary purpose of the developed tool is to support designers in learning about the capabilities, limitations and operational aspects of ML by making the process transparent and accessible. This includes showing users 'what the computer sees' to better understand how the machine interprets their embodied interaction, visualising training data to assess its quality, and enabling users to interactively test their classifier and amend training data in an iterative process, until they are satisfied with its performance.

3.1 Functionality

The tool guides users through a series of steps covering the whole process from exploring and defining gestures, training and testing the classifier, to finally downloading the trained classifier and a related web application template. Each step in the process aims to address aspects of ML that designers and ML novices are known to struggle with:

- **Welcome.** Besides briefly explaining the purpose and functionality of the tool, this screen also clarifies security and privacy aspects, which designers must consider when developing applications, and have been shown to be concerned about [46], but might find difficult to assess due to their lack of technical and operational knowledge of ML [11, 46, 50].
- **Explore Gestures.** This screen allows users to experiment with the underlying ML model for human pose estimation in a live preview. It addresses designers' lack of

understanding of the capabilities and limitations of ML models [11, 46, 50] and adds a "non-human perspective" [27] to the process by enabling users to see what the ML model sees.

- **Define Gestures.** After exploring how the system understands their poses, this screen enables users to define the body gestures they would like the model to recognise. Besides defining gesture labels, users can also identify which body parts the classifier should consider when classifying gestures (Fig. 2) in order to optimise performance. Separating the definition of gestures from training aims to scaffold users' conceptual understanding of ML [11, 46, 50] and addresses criticism of low- and no-coding environments as lacking flexibility and tuning options [40].
- **Train Recognition.** In this step, users can collect training data for each defined gesture. Samples are collected interactively, with a live preview of users' body poses and relevant screen prompts indicating which gesture to perform and how many sample were collected (Fig. 1). The process is iterative, with the live preview exiting after collecting 10 samples; the user reviewing collected samples and deleting ones that do not reflect the gesture; then collecting more samples as required. Visualising samples as pose previews (Fig. 2) enables users to better understand their training data [3, 16, 46], while enabling users to iteratively collect, inspect and delete the training data samples meets the need to modify past teaching actions [34].
- **Test Recognition.** Following the collection of training data, the underlying classifier is updated on the fly and users can test its performance in a live preview by performing gestures in front of the camera. The live preview displays recognised gestures and confidence levels, enabling users to assess its performance. They can then return to the training screen to collect more training data or delete samples, if they want to improve the classifier performance, or proceed to the download screen if they are happy with the classifier performance. The immediacy of the train/test steps based on

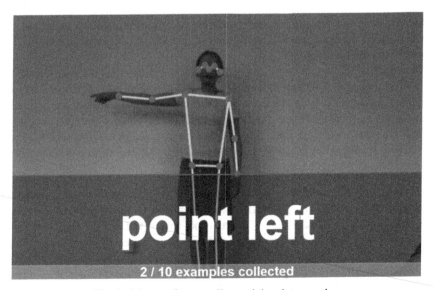

Fig. 1. Live preview to collect training data samples.

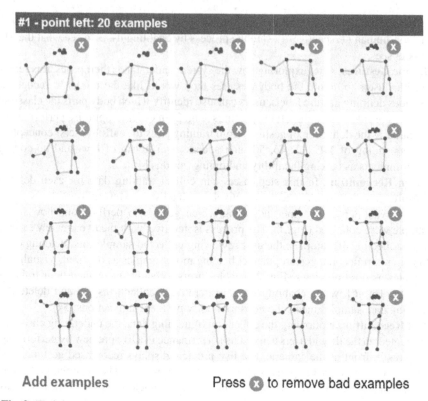

Fig. 2. Training data visualisation with options to delete individual samples and collect more training samples.

live previews enables users to empirically assess the performance of their classifier, which they otherwise would find difficult to do [46], and to explore the effects of modifying their training data [34].

- **Download.** Following training and testing, users can download the classifier and an application template that provides the required technical infrastructure for the classifier to load the underlying ML model for human pose estimation, access the webcam, and generate standard Document Object Model [44] events for recognised gestures. This supports users with limited technical expertise and operational knowledge of ML [11, 46, 50], while accounting for the particular skills set of web designers as the immediate target audience.

User are able to save/restore training sessions by downloading/uploading saved sessions to/from their local computer. This mechanism was preferred over storing session data online, to signal to users that their data is not shared and that they have ownership and control over both their training data and trained classifier. Being able to save and restore training sessions adds flexibility and also allows for classifiers to be modified and improved over time, for example by collecting additional training data in the context in which the classifier will be deployed, to account for specific lighting conditions or other factors impacting its performance.

3.2 Technical Implementation

The prototype is implemented as a web application running in standards-compliant browsers on all major platforms. It is based on Tensorflow.js [38], a JavaScript implementation of the Tensorflow open-source software library for ML [1], using either WASM or WebGL for hardware acceleration. For gesture recognition, the system uses a pre-trained instance of MoveNet [43] as a feature extractor, yielding body pose data in the 17 point COCO format [24] from a live video stream. The pose data is normalised before relevant key points (defined by the user) are extracted for gesture recognition via a k-nearest neighbours (k-NN) algorithm.

4 Methodology

A formative evaluation was carried out with a view to inform future development by empirically identifying usability problems in current prototype, getting qualitative feedback on the current user interface and interaction design, and assessing whether, and to what extent, interaction with the system advances designers' ML literacy.

4.1 Sample

The study involved 16 participants, consisting of 14 MSc User Experience Design (UXD) students at the University of Brighton, and two members of staff with a professional background in UXD and web design.

The sample covers a range of ages (Fig. 3a) and skills, with most participants self-rating their design skills significantly higher than their programming skills (Fig. 3b). None of the participants had any previous experience in training a ML model or using ML in their designs. The sample size has been shown to be sufficient for formative evaluation studies and reflects industry practice. For example, [35] surveyed 21 usability studies with an average sample size of 10, while [30] found that 5–8 participants in heuristic evaluations can find 85% of problems in user interfaces.

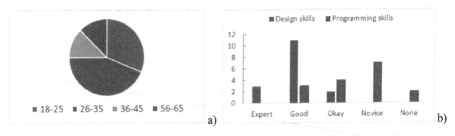

Fig. 3. Participants' age profile (a) and self-rated design and programming skills (b).

4.2 Procedure and Data Collection

The study design was scrutinized by the University of Brighton's Research Ethics Committee and received a favourable opinion. It involved individual sessions with participants at the university's usability lab, structured into three parts:

User Testing (15–20 min). At the start of each session, participants found the prototype readily loaded in a browser tab. They were asked to train a classifier for body gestures and verbalise their thoughts following the think-aloud protocol [15] while completing a series of tasks:

1. Define two body gestures
2. Train the classifier to recognise the gestures
3. Test the trained classifier
4. Repeat steps 2–3 until satisfied that the classifier accurately recognises the gestures
5. Download a template application with the trained classifier and test if it works

A researcher in the room took observation notes of participants' interactions and utterances. The researcher only intervened when participants got stuck and could not proceed with the task at hand.

Post Interview (3–10 min). Following the user testing, participants took part in a short interview, where the researcher followed up on observed issues arising during the interaction and took notes of participants' answers.

Post Questionnaire (10–15 min). Following the interview, participants completed a questionnaire consisting of the Post-Study System Usability Questionnaire (PSSUQ) [22], the Student Assessment of Learning Gains (SALG) questionnaire [36], and demographic information.

4.3 Data Analysis

Qualitative observation notes and interview notes were transcribed and analysed independently by two authors using an emergent coding process described in [28]. This involved first a data reduction step and then a data visualisation step to identify common themes. Themes identified in the two separate analyses were then discussed and synthesised by both researchers together, using affinity diagrams as described in [9]. This resulted in a set of consolidated themes from these two datasets and allowed for triangulation between observed interaction (observation notes) and self-reported views about the experience (interview notes) to inform findings.

Quantitative PSSUQ data was analysed as described in [22], while quantitative SALG data and demographic data were simply aggregated. Open answers to the SALG questionnaire were analysed in the same way as qualitative data from observations and interview, but treated as a separate data set reflecting its focus on learning from the experience.

5 Discussion of Findings

5.1 Supporting Designers to Train a Classifier

The analysis of qualitative observation and interview notes revealed several themes around supporting designers in training a gesture classifier:

Learnability. Many participants (8/16) asked for more detailed information about what the tool does and how it works, including its capabilities and limitations (e.g., P13: *"I think the tool was useful and I would understand how to use it quickly but felt there could have been clearer instruction as to the type of gestures that were possible before attempting to use it"*), and instructions for each step in the process what they should do to achieve the best results. While some participants read all the information provided for various steps, others remarked that written information might not be effective (e.g., P8: *"people won't read the screen"*) and suggested instead an on-boarding video demonstrating how the tool is used in a typical scenario might be more effective.

Experimentation. Most participants (10/16) appreciated the opportunity to experiment with the system and see a preview of their estimated body pose overlaid on the live camera video stream in the Explore screen. This included trying out different body poses, including various edge cases (e.g., standing sideways; back to camera; etc.); noting and commenting on the system's limitations (e.g., unable to recognise fingers); and contemplating the feasibility of gestures to be recognised by the system. While one participant was unclear about the purpose of the Explore step, asking for more information, the engagement and experimentation by most participants confirms the value of this step, which helps designers to better understand the problem by providing a "non-human perspective" [27].

Scope and Functionality. Related to users' exploration of limitations, several participants (6/16) commented on the system not being able to recognise the gestures they had in mind. This included, for instance, clap or wave gestures based on movements rather than still poses (P11), or a 'wink' gesture after noticing that the system recognises people's eyes (P2). While these misconceptions are in large part due to a lack of clarity in the terminology and the provided information, they chime with literature reporting that designers often have unrealistic expectations of what ML can and cannot do [11, 46]. The findings confirm that hands-on experimentation is an effective way for designers to calibrate their expectations of ML capabilities and limitations.

Conceptual Understanding. Many participants (8/16) were unclear about the purpose of the default "no gesture" visible in the Define step, presumably conceptualising gesture recognition as positive detection rather than a classification problem. Instructions explaining to participants that they would need to collect training data for "no gesture" in the Train step were ignored by several participants (6/16), resulting in an information message that they need to collect samples for all gestures (including "no gesture") before they can proceed to test their classifier. Some participants (4/16) got stuck at this point and needed a hint from the researcher to continue with the task. While these difficulties can be attributed to a lack of sufficient guidance and information in the prototype, they also betray many designers' weak conceptual understanding of ML [11, 46]. How this problem should be addressed depends on the context and purpose of the training environment. From a user experience perspective, it might be preferable to hide the default "no gesture" and collect samples for it in the background without the user noticing, while from a didactic perspective it might be preferable to keep "no gesture" visible in order to support designer' conceptual understanding of the classifier they train.

Optimisation. Functionality to optimise the classifier's accuracy was used only by some participants, while many others did only what was required to complete the task. Only 3/16 participants explored the option to specify which body parts the system should take into account when classifying gestures; only 9/16 returned to the Train step to collected more training samples after testing their classifier; and only 5/16 made use of the option to delete selected samples from their training data. As improving model performance is undoubtedly useful in application development [40], participants' sporadic use of this functionality might at least in part be due to the study context (a set task in a lab environment) and not be reflective of potential situated action [39]. This interpretation is supported by anecdotal evidence from a related research project [47], where users of the same tool engaged in extended train/test iterations to improve the accuracy of their gesture classifier.

Integration Support. Several participants (5/16) pointed out that they did not understand the provided example code. While this might be less of a problem in a more realistic environment, where UX designers work in teams together with developers, it should be addressed in future iterations with more information, tutorials and examples on how to integrate the trained classifier into an application.

5.2 Usability

Several of the themes discussed above are also reflected in the PSSUQ results, shown in Table 1 and compared against the industry standard reported in [35] (see Fig. 4).

Table 1. Mean scores (n = 16) in the Post-Study System Usability Questionnaire [22].

#	Question	Score
1	Overall, I am satisfied with how easy it is to use this system	2.63
2	It was simple to use this system	2.44
3	I was able to complete the tasks and scenarios quickly using this system	2.69
4	I felt comfortable using this system	1.88
5	It was easy to learn to use this system	2.56
6	I believe I could become productive quickly using this system	2.31
7	The system gave error messages that clearly told me how to fix problems	4.00
8	Whenever I made a mistake using the system, I could recover easily and quickly	2.94
9	The information (introduction, on-screen messages) provided was clear	3.19
10	It was easy to find the information I needed	2.50
11	The information was effective in helping me complete the tasks and scenarios	3.25
12	The organization of information on the system screens was clear	2.31
13	The interface of this system was pleasant	1.81
14	I liked using the interface of this system	1.75
15	This system has all the functions and capabilities I expect it to have	3.00
16	Overall, I am satisfied with this system	2.50

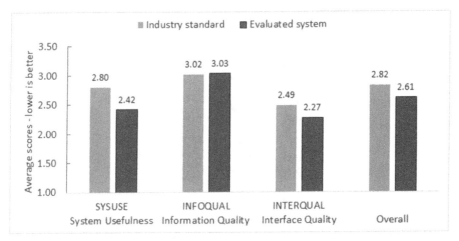

Fig. 4. Average scores for System Usefulness (Q1–6), Information Quality (Q7–12), and Interface Quality (Q13–16) in the Post-Study System Usability Questionnaire [22], shown against the industry standard based on 21 studies with a total of 210 participants [35].

Unfavourable scores for Q7 (4.00), Q9 (3.19) and Q11 (3.25) contributed to a total score of 3.03 for Information Quality, which is slightly worse than the industry standard of 3.02 and strongly indicates a need to improve the information design of the prototype. By contrast, favourable scores for Q4 (1.88), Q13 (1.81) and Q14 (1.75) contributed to total scores of 2.42 for System Usefulness and 2.27 for Interface quality, which are better than the respective industry standards of 2.80 and 2.49. They reflect the perceived usefulness of the tool and participants' appreciation of visualisations enabling them to understand the problem from a ML perspective.

5.3 Learning Gains

A detailed analysis of participants' answers to the SALG questionnaire [36] is beyond the scope of this paper, however, average scores for learning gains (Fig. 5) show that engagement with the tool, which for many participants was their first experience in training a ML model, considerably advanced their understanding of a range of ML aspects (importance of good quality training data; uncertainty in ML inference; limitations of ML). It also increased their interest and confidence in using gesture recognition, and ML more generally, in their designs. Finally, it increased participants' critical awareness of ML issues, including capabilities and limitations, and potential privacy implications.

Answers to open questions relate learning gains to specific aspects in the prototype and further support some of the findings discussed above. When asked which aspect of the tool helped them most in learning about ML, most participants answered that the visualisation of how the ML model predicts their body poses was the most useful feature (e.g., P13: "*Showing me how the computer understands my body, movement and poses with overlayed [sic] graphics*"). Overlaying detected body poses over the live camera image helped their understanding of the level of detail recognised by the system, and consequently what kind of gesture they could define with a realistic expectation that it

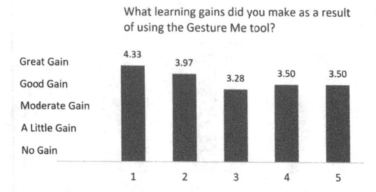

What learning gains did you make as a result of using the Gesture Me tool?

1 - Understanding of ML aspects (training data, uncertainty, limitations)
2 - Interest in using using gesture recognition and ML in my designs
3 - Confidence in using gesture recognition and ML in my designs
4 - Critical awareness of ML issues (capabilities, limitations, privacy)
5 - Integrating ML in my design practice

Fig. 5. Participants' self-reported learning gains from engagement with the tool, based on average scores (n = 16) for responses to the SALG questionnaire [36], with response options ranging from 1 - No Gain to 5 - Great Gain.

would be recognised (e.g., P16: "*sensing exact body posture, which helped me realise that i could add more details in my gesture if i wanted*").

Closely related, many participants pointed out that visualising training samples as miniature previews of body poses helped them to better understand their training data (e.g., P12: "*recognise human body parts and translate them into referencing pictures*"; P15: "*The body graph of trained data*").

Finally, several interaction design aspects were highlighted by participants as helping their understanding of ML. This included in particular being able to define their own gestures after exploring how the system estimates their body poses (e.g., P11: "*Being able to define different gestures*"), collection and reviewing training data in batches of 10 samples (e.g., P5: "*I also thought the 10 chances to try the movements and then tick them off afterwards was good*") and showing live confidence scores for detected gestures during testing (e.g., P9: "*the confidence score also helped me know if I needed to train the model again*").

5.4 Significance and Implications

The findings are significant both in the context of developing tools that support designers in ideating and prototyping ML-enhanced applications [49], and in the wider context of helping designers to gain a better understanding ML as a design material [46]. Regarding the development of tools supporting designers' active experimentation with ML, the evaluation leads to four recommendations:

1. **Provide Guidance:** Reflecting designers' lack of conceptual, technical and operational understanding of ML [11, 46, 50], a consistent theme in the evaluation was the need for more information explaining the purpose, scope and limitations of the tool, and to provide guidance throughout the process on how to get the best results in each step. Given that many users don't read written information [45], developers should consider alternative media such as videos, interactive tutorials and practical examples to convey information.

2. **Manage Expectations:** Vague terminology in the user interface, misunderstood capabilities of ML [11, 46, 50], and a mismatch between the training process and how users would like to train a model [4], can all lead to unrealistic expectations of the scope, purpose and functionality of a system. Managing these with clear terminology and well presented information, while undertaking every effort to meet users' needs, can help to avoid disappointment and lead to more productive usage.

3. **Present the ML Perspective:** Some of the strongest aspects in the evaluated tool relate to visualising the ML perspective. This goes beyond providing a "non-human perspective" [27] in the design context, and generally includes situations where users' understanding of the ML perspective is critical, such as for instance visualising how an ML model understands training samples to support users' efforts in curating and optimising training datasets.

4. **Encourage Experimentation:** Novice users' first efforts to train a classifier are unlikely to take full advantage of a system's functionality and lead to optimal results. The evaluation shows that users appreciate the opportunity to explore the ML perspective before starting to train their classifier, but also that they need encouragement and motivation to optimise their classifier. Systems should meet this need with suitable interaction designs that promote iterative training/testing and follow suggestions in [2] to guide users in selecting training samples that improve the classifier performance.

Regarding the wider need for designers to learn about conceptual, technical and operational aspects of ML in order to better understand the technology as a design material, the study has shown that designers can derive strong learning gains from just a single session of engagement with the tool, confirming literature [46] that experiential learning through hands-on engagement is a suitable way for them to learn about ML.

6 Conclusions

This paper presents an online tool enabling designers to experiment with ML as a design material by defining, training and testing a gesture classifier, and then integrating it in a prototype application. An empirical evaluation with designers, including MSc User Experience Design students and staff with a professional design background, confirmed the value of encouraging experimentation and visualising the ML perspective, but also identified aspects that can be improved, leading to design recommendations that can inform the development of similar tools. The study also showed that designers' engagement with the tool leads to significant learning gains, confirming its underlying rationale and warranting further research and development.

Our future work will focus on encouraging users to optimise their classifiers, supporting them in improving the quality of their training data, and exploring how our findings can be transferred to other ML capabilities besides gesture recognition.

Acknowledgments. We would like to thank MSc User Experience Design students and staff at the University of Brighton for taking part in the evaluation study and sharing their views. We also would like to thank the reviewers of this paper for their time and valuable comments.

References

1. Abadi, M., Barham, P., Chen, J., Chen, Z., Davis, A., Dean, J., et al.: Tensorflow: a system for large-scale machine learning. In: Proceedings of the 12th USENIX Symposium on Operating Systems Design and Implementation (OSDI 2016). arXiv:1605.08695 (2016)
2. Amershi, S., Fogarty, J., Kapoor, A., Tan, D.: Overview based examples selection in mixed-initiative interactive concept learning. In: Proceedings of the UIST 2009, pp. 247–256. ACM (2009)
3. Amershi, S., Fogarty, J., Kapoor, A., Tan, D.: Effective end-user interaction with machine learning. In: Proceedings of the 25th AAAI Conference on Artificial Intelligence, pp. 1529–1532. AAAI Press (2011)
4. Amershi, S., Cakmak, M., Knox, W.B., Kulesza, T.: Power to the people: the role of humans in interactive machine learning. AI Mag. 35(4), 105–120 (2014)
5. Amershi, S., Weld, D., Vorvoreanu, M., Fourney, A., Nushi, B., Collisson, P., et al.: Guidelines for human-AI interaction. In: Proceedings of the 2019 CHI Conference on Human Factors in Computing Systems, pp. 1–13. ACM (2019)
6. Apple Create ML. https://developer.apple.com/machine-learning/create-ml/. Accessed 05 July 2023
7. Bernardo, F., Zbyszynski, M., Fiebrink, R., Grierson, M.: Interactive machine learning for end-user innovation. In: Proceedings of the AAAI 2017 Spring Symposium on Designing the User Experience of Machine Learning Systems. Technical Report SS-17-04. Association for the Advancement of Artificial Intelligence (AAAI) (2017)
8. Brookfield, S.: Adult learning: an overview. Int. Encyclopedia of Education, **10**, 375–380 (2012)
9. Courage, C., Baxter, K.: Understanding your users: a practical guide to user requirements methods, tools, and techniques. Gulf Professional Publishing (2005)
10. Design Council: The Double Diamond, https://www.designcouncil.org.uk/our-resources/the-double-diamond/. Accessed 05 July 2023
11. Dove, G., Halskov. K., Forlizzi, J., Zimmerman, J.: UX design innovation: challenges for working with machine learning as a design material. In: Proceedings of the 2017 CHI Conference on Human Factors in Computing Systems, pp. 278–288. ACM (2017)
12. Dudley, J.J., Kristensson, P.O.:. A review of user interface design for interactive machine learning. ACM Trans. Interact. Intell. Syst. 1(1), 1 (2018). ACM (2018)
13. Drozdov, S.: An intro to machine learning for designers. https://uxdesign.cc/anintro-to-machine-learning-for-designers-5c74ba100257. Accessed 05 July 2023
14. Elliott, L., Dieleman, S., Roberts, A., White, T., Grimm, H., Tesfaldet, M., et al.: Machine learning for creativity and design. NeurIPS 2020 Workshop. https://neurips2020creativity.github.io/. Accessed 05 July 2023
15. Ericsson, K.A., Simon, H.A.: Protocol Analysis: Verbal Reports as Data. MIT Press, Cambridge, MA (1993)

16. Fails, J.A., Olsen Jr., D.R.: Interactive machine learning. In: Proceedings of the IUI 2003, pp. 39–45. ACM (2003)
17. Fogarty, J., Tan. D., Kapoor, A., Winder, S.: CueFlik: interactive concept learning in image search. In: Proceedings of the CHI 2008, pp. 29–38. ACM (2008)
18. Gillies, M., Fiebrink, R., Tanaka, A., Garcia, J., Bevilacqua, F., Heloir, A., et al.: Human-centred machine learning. In: Proceedings of the 2016 CHI Conference Extended Abstracts on Human Factors in Computing Systems, pp. 3558 - 3565. ACM (2016)
19. Hebron, P.: Machine learning for designers. O'Reilly Media (2016)
20. Holmquist, L.E.: Intelligence on tap: artificial intelligence as a new design material. Interactions **24**(4), 28–33 (2017)
21. Kolb, D. A.: Experiential learning: experience as the source of learning and development. FT Press (2014)
22. Lewis, J.R.: Psychometric evaluation of the post-study system usability questionnaire: the PSSUQ. Proceed. Human Factors Soc. Annual Meeting **36**(16), 1259–1260 (1992)
23. Li, L., Wu, Z.: How can No/Low code platforms help end-users develop ml applications? - a systematic review. In: Chen, J.Y.C., Fragomeni, G., Degen, H., Ntoa, S. (eds.) HCI International 2022 – Late Breaking Papers: Interacting with eXtended Reality and Artificial Intelligence. HCII 2022. LNCS, vol. 13518. Springer, Cham (2022). https://doi.org/10.1007/978-3-031-21707-4_25
24. Lin, T.Y., et al.: Microsoft COCO: common objects in context. In: Fleet, D., Pajdla, T., Schiele, B., Tuytelaars, T. (eds.) Computer Vision – ECCV 2014. ECCV 2014. LNCS, vol. 8693. Springer, Cham (2014). https://doi.org/10.1007/978-3-319-10602-1_48
25. Lovejoy, J.: The UX of AI. Google Design. https://design.google/library/ux-ai/. Accessed 17 Jan 2020
26. Machine Learning for Kids. Teach a computer to play a game. https://machinelearningfor kids.co.uk/. Accessed 05 July 2023
27. Malsattar, N., Kihara, T., Giaccardi, E.: Designing and prototyping from the perspective of AI in the Wild. In: Proceedings of the Designing Interactive Systems Conference (DIS 2019), pp. 1083–1088. ACM (2019)
28. Miles, M.B., Huberman, A.M.: Qualitative data analysis. Sage Publishing (1984)
29. Mishra, S., Rzeszotarski, J.M.: Designing interactive transfer learning tools for ML non-experts. In: Proceedings of the 2021 CHI Conference on Human Factors in Computing Systems, pp. 1–15. ACM (2021)
30. Nielsen, J., Molich, R.: Heuristic evaluation of user interfaces. In: Proceedings of the SIGCHI Conference on Human Factors in Computing Systems, pp. 249–256. ACM (1990)
31. Obviously AI. The fastest, most precise no-code AI tool ever. https://www.obviously.ai/. Accessed 05 July 2023
32. Osmany, S.: Introduction to machine learning for designers. harvard university graduate school of design, https://www.gsd.harvard.edu/course/introduction-to-machine-learning-for-design ers-spring-2022/. Accessed 05 July 2023
33. Runway ML. Advancing creativity with artificial intelligence. https://runwayml.com/. Accessed 05 July 2023
34. Sanchez, T., Caramiaux, B., Françoise, J., Bevilacqua, F., Mackay, W.: How do people train a machine? Strategies and (Mis) Understandings. In: Proceedings of the ACM Conference on Human-Computer Interaction (CSCW1), pp. 1–26. ACM (2021)
35. Sauro, J., Lewis, J. R.: Quantifying the user experience: practical statistics for user research. Morgan Kaufmann (2016)
36. Seymour, E., Wiese, D., Hunter, A.B.: Student Assessment of Learning Gains (SALG). University of Colorado at Boulder, Bureau of Sociological Research (2016)

37. Simard, P.Y., Amershi, S., Chickering, D.M., Pelton, A.E., Ghorashi, S., Meek, C., et al.: Machine teaching: a new paradigm for building machine learning systems. Technical Report. arXiv:1707.06742. Microsoft Research (2017)

38. Smilkov, D., Thorat, N., Assogba, Y., Nicholson, C., Kreeger, N., Yu, P., et al.: Tensorflow. js: Machine learning for the web and beyond. In: Proceedings of the Machine Learning and Systems, vol. 1, pp. 309–321. MLSys (2019)

39. Suchman, L. A.: Plans and situated actions: The problem of human-machine communication. Cambridge University Press (1987)

40. Sun, L., Zhou, Z., Wu, W., Zhang, Y., Zhang, R., Xiang, W.: Developing a toolkit for prototyping machine learning-empowered products: the design and evaluation of ML-rapid. Int. J. Des. **14**(2), 35 (2020)

41. Teachable Machine. Train a computer to recognize your own images, sounds, and poses. https://teachablemachine.withgoogle.com/. Accessed 05 July 2023

42. Torrey, L., Shavlik, J.: Transfer learning. Handbook of research on machine learning applications and trends: algorithms, methods, and techniques, vol. 1, pp. 242–264 (2009). ACM (2009)

43. Voter, R., Li, N.: Next-Generation Pose Detection with MoveNet and TensorFlow.js. https://blog.tensorflow.org/2021/05/next-generation-pose-detection-with-movenet-and-tensorflowjs.html. Accessed 05 July 2023

44. W3C (1998). Level 1 Document Object Model Specification, Version 1.0, W3C Working Draft. https://www.w3.org/TR/WD-DOM/. Accessed 05 July 2023

45. Weinreich, H., Obendorf, H., Herder, E., Mayer, M.: Not quite the average: An empirical study of Web use. ACM Trans. Web (TWEB), **2**(1), 1–31 (2008). ACM (2008)

46. Winter, M., Jackson, P.: Flatpack ML: How to support designers in creating a new generation of customizable machine learning applications. In: Marcus, A., Rosenzweig, E. (eds.) Design, User Experience, and Usability. Design for Contemporary Interactive Environments. HCII 2020. LNCS, vol. 12201. Springer, Cham (2020). https://doi.org/10.1007/978-3-030-49760-6_12

47. Winter, M., Sweeney, L., Mason, K., Blume, P.: Low-power machine learning for visitor engagement in museums. In: Proceedings of the 6th International Conference on Computer-Human Interaction Research and Applications (CHIRA 2022), pp. 236–243. INSTICC ScitePress (2022)

48. Yang, Q.: The role of design in creating machine-learning-enhanced user experience. In 2017 AAAI Spring Symposium Series. AAAI Press (2017)

49. Yang, Q., Scuito, A., Zimmerman, J., Forlizzi, J., Steinfeld, A.: Investigating how experienced UX designers effectively work with machine learning. In: Proceedings of the 2018 Designing Interactive Systems, pp. 585–596. ACM (2018)

50. Yang, Q., Suh, J., Chen, N.C., Ramos, G.: Grounding interactive machine learning tool design in how non-experts actually build models. In: Proceedings of the 2018 Designing Interactive Systems, pp. 573–584. ACM (2018)

51. Yang, Q.: Machine learning as a UX design material: how can we imagine beyond automation, recommenders, and reminders? In AAAI Spring Symposia, vol. 1, no. 2.1, pp. 2–6. AAAI Press (2018)

A Case Study on Netychords: Crafting Accessible Digital Musical Instrument Interaction for a Special Needs Scenario

Nicola Davanzo[1]([✉]) [iD], Federico Avanzini[1] [iD], Luca A. Ludovico[1] [iD],
Davys Moreno[2] [iD], António Moreira[2] [iD], Oksana Tymoshchuk[2] [iD],
Júlia Azevedo[3] [iD], and Carlos Marques[3] [iD]

[1] Laboratory of Music Informatics (LIM), Department of Computer Science "Giovanni Degli Antoni", University of Milan, Via Celoria 18, 27133 Milan, Italy
{nicola.davanzo,federico.avanzini,luca.ludovico}@unimi.it
[2] Research Centre on Didactics and Technology in the Education of Trainers, 3810-193 Aveiro, Portugal
davys.moreno@ua.pt
[3] Artistic School Conservatory of Music Calouste Gulbenkian, Av. Artur Ravara, 3810-096 Aveiro, Portugal

Abstract. Musical expression significantly impacts individual development, enriching cognitive, emotional, and social capacities. This influence is particularly profound in young individuals with cognitive or physical impairments. To address this, we devised an ecosystem of software tools, paired with specially designed hardware devices, such as an eye tracker. Our approach empowers even severely impaired users, with no prior music education, to achieve musical performance. In this paper, we detail a case study involving a child with cerebral palsy, providing an examination of the strengths and shortcomings of our approach. By utilizing a specialized instrument, called *Netychords*, the child achieved a significant milestone, namely the enrollment in Portugal's Arts Education Program, which fostered musical interaction with his peers and educators. This paper focuses on the technical aspects of the user's experience with the instrument, which catalyzed numerous redesign phases, adapting it to the child's unique needs and motor abilities. Our analysis of this adaptive design process strives to offer valuable insights to extend our approach to cater to various special needs scenarios.

Keywords: Accessibility · Digital musical instruments · Cerebral palsy · Music education · Special needs · Eye tracking

1 Introduction

Music education can have a significant impact on the cognitive, emotional, and social development of individuals. Research has shown that active engagement with music can lead to the development of emotional skills, particularly in the field of music education [5]. A systematic review focused on the effects of music on children's emotional development revealed that short-term music training can improve cognitive abilities, such as verbal intelligence and executive function [35]. Music training has also been found to enhance emotion comprehension in children [43]. Longitudinal studies have highlighted the benefits of music programs for at-risk children, such as improved neural encoding of speech sounds [25]. Musical experiences in childhood have been shown to accelerate brain development, particularly in language acquisition and reading skills [18]. Moreover, advantages are not limited to the early stage of life: music-making opportunities can also contribute to the well-being of older individuals [19].

The term "Special Needs" (SN), is commonly used to describe individuals who require support for a range of disabilities that may be medical, mental, or psychological. This broad category includes those with learning disabilities, speech or language disorders, physical disabilities, emotional and behavioral conditions, as well as various developmental or intellectual disabilities [31,47]. Despite the well-documented benefits of music education, its accessibility remains a challenge for individuals with the context of SN. Lubet's book and the "Reshape Music" report by Youth Music highlight how opportunities to participate in musical activities are frequently obstructed for such individuals [27,53]. The complexity of disability, a "multidimensional experience" with significant measurement and classification challenges [51,52], further compounds this issue. Individuals with SN often encounter barriers to accessing music education and reaping its developmental benefits. Such barriers to music education for individuals with SN vary, encompassing physical, social, and financial dimensions. Furthermore, traditional musical instruments, barring a few exceptions, often rely on the use of hands, fingers, breath, mouth/lips, and feet, leading to considerable barriers for individuals with motor disabilities.

Digital technologies, in particular *Digital Musical Instruments* (DMIs), have the potential to support people with SN in their musical learning and development, providing sensory stimulation, facilitating communication and interactions, and enhancing learning experiences through gamification and interactive multimedia. Recent research has highlighted the potential of ad-hoc software products and interactive devices as support tools in music education for children with SN. For example, digital technologies can provide sensory stimulation [7], facilitate communication and interactions [8,26,46], and enhance learning experiences through gamification and interactive multimedia [2,3,50].

From 2018 to 2022, the *Department of Education and Psychology at the University of Aveiro* (DEP-UA) led a project exploring the use of *Accessible Digital Musical Instruments* (ADMIs) for facilitating music education for children with special needs (SN). This project, with a focus on revising classroom practices in Portuguese primary schools' Arts Education Programmes of Music (AEPM), aimed to promote inclusion in musical activities [33,34], enhancing our understanding of inclusive arts education, and the role of digital technologies and ADMIs in facilitating access for students with impairments. As part of a pilot study approved by the University's Ethics and Deontology Committee, DEP-UA researchers conducted targeted experimental activities with a 7-year-old child affected by cerebral palsy, seeking to generalize the learnings from this specific scenario to benefit primary school music education broadly.

Since 2018, the Laboratory of Music Informatics at the University of Milan (LIM-UM), Italy, has centered its research on their ecosystem of ADMIs design and development, particularly for motor disabilities such as quadriplegia. Seeing potential applicability to the child, DEP-UA researchers sought collaboration. This venture involved preliminary studies for identifying suitable technologies and interaction modes for the child and led to adaptations for his specific motor skills. Involving the child, his family, and educators, this collaboration facilitated the child's participation in Portugal's Arts Education Program, necessitating further technological adjustments over his educational journey.

This paper focuses on the technical aspects of the experimentation. It details the customization of *Netychords*, an Accessible Digital Musical Instrument designed for musicians with motor disabilities, supported by software tools, libraries, and hardware. The paper documents the evolution of the instrument since its initial publication in 2021 [14], based on insights gained from the case study. It reviews the challenges faced and progress made in tailoring the instrument's interaction strategies to meet the child's unique needs. Additionally, it highlights the child's subsequent participation in the Arts Education Programme, showing the potential impact of our ADMI development ecosystem in a real-world educational setting.

The remainder of this paper is structured as follows: Sect. 2 provides essential literature background information and a comprehensive analysis of the tools within our development ecosystem; Sect. 3 reviews the main characteristics of *Netychords*; In Sect. 4, we delve into the case study involving the child participant. We proceed by detailing their user profile, the bespoke instrument modifications implemented to suit their needs, and the adaptations needed for their participation in formal music education; Sect. 5 contains reflections on our experiences and attempts to extrapolate our findings to the broader context of customizing ADMIs for individuals with Special Needs. This work aims to promote further discussion and exploration in our research field by detailing the practical challenges and successes encountered in our journey to include a child with SN in music making.

2   Background

2.1   Context

At the beginning of their project DEP-UA researchers looked for possible music learning solutions developed in other institutions and/or countries, to provide for the needs of the child. To this end, they conducted, analyzed, and published a series of documented searches, by means of various literature reviews [33,34]. In these reviews, research works were found that explored both the capacity that students with disabilities possess to acquire musical knowledge using digital technologies and the development of music technologies dedicated to this population.

Examples of the latter can be found in a multimedia tool called PLAIME (PLAtform for the Integration of handicapped children in Music Education) [6], and some technological solutions which can be used to enhance music learning in primary education using Mobile Virtual Reality [24]. Other examples are provided by the development of ADMIs such as Arcana Instruments [1] and Sound-Beam.[2] Some studies analyze the use of eye-tracking technologies in Immersive Virtual Reality (IVR) learning environments created by using head-mounted displays [45]. For the development of their research work, the DEP-UA researchers focused on searching for information on the design and/or adaptation of Digital Musical Instruments for the accessibility context, so that the child could have access to music education programs in Portugal [33,34].

DMIs are generally defined as instruments in which sound generation is based on digital means and is achieved by the performer through physical actions detected by sensing devices [30,32]. Thus, these musical instruments have the potential to add to the accessibility of music, relative to traditional instruments, because they allow for different, unconventional, modes of interaction [16]. The term Digital Musical Instrument is not sharply defined in the literature and often overlaps with other forms of musical interfaces. The project undertaken by the LIM-UM researchers primarily focuses on the development of *performance instruments*, following a more stringent definition supplied by Malloch et al.'s conceptual framework [29]. According to this framework, musical interfaces involve interaction behaviors that can be categorized as skill-, rule-, or model-based. Skill-based musical instruments mirror their traditional counterparts in performance and context, demanding internalized movements, muscle memory, and a deep engagement with the instrument's feedback. These instruments also present stringent time constraints for interaction.

Accessible Digital Musical Instruments are specially designed to be used by individuals with disabilities and SN. The literature on accessible interfaces has highlighted the importance of ADMIs and related works in this field. Frid [16] offers a comprehensive review of ADMIs and their use contexts, categorizing them based on interaction channels and modalities. As Frid notes, there have been several recent initiatives and charity organizations focused on developing ADMIs, as well as companies producing ADMIs with inclusive music practices at the core of their mission. Harrison and McPherson [20] identify two types of ADMIs:"therapeutic devices" that provide low-barrier expressive instruments for music-making in group workshops or therapy sessions, and "performance-focused instruments" that enable performers to achieve virtuosity comparable to traditional instruments. LIM-UM's research focuses on the latter category, which requires more practice and is suitable for contexts such as accessible orchestras. ADMIs are engineered to accommodate various disability types, as categorized into *physical, sensory,* and *cognitive* groups according to the framework proposed by Davanzo & Avanzini [9], taking inspiration from the classification systems provided by Sears et al. [44] and The Washington Group on Disability

---

[1] Arcana Instruments website: https://arcanainstruments.com/.

[2] SoundBeam website: https://www.soundbeam.co.uk/.

Statistics [52, p.26]. Physical disabilities impact motor skills and proprioception, sensory ones affect senses like sight, touch, and hearing, while cognitive disabilities impede learning and brain-related skills. ADMIs targeted at musicians with physical impairments are designed to leverage the users' residual motor abilities. Davanzo & Avanzini's framework categorizes the extent of catered motor disability from 'quadriplegic Paralysis', with only neck-upward control, to 'Lock-In', with only eye control. It implies that, in some cases, ADMIs for quadriplegic users could be extended to those with less restrictive motor impairments, provided the interaction channels above the neck remain functional.

Since the main focus of researchers at LIM-UM are instruments for quadriplegic users, they coined the term *HeaDMIs* [11] to redefine the concept of ADMI as one shaped entirely around the residual motor abilities of the musician, adapting its interaction modalities to the remaining viable physical interaction channels. In the aforementioned work, interaction channels suitable for HeaDMIs are summarized into four principal groups [11]: *eyes* (e.g. gaze pointing), *mouth* (e.g. voice and breathing), *head* (e.g. rotation and neck tension), and *brain* (e.g. mental state and motor imagery). An essential aspect of the development of HeaDMIs and Digital Musical Instruments, in general, is the challenge of mapping the physical interaction channels of a performer to musical events or outcomes. The term *mapping* usually refers to the strategy employed to establish this link between the performer's action and the musical result [11,30].

A 2020 study by Davanzo & Avanzini [11] examines 15 HeaDMIs, most of which use gaze pointing as their primary interaction channel for note selection. Gaze pointing refers to the selection of visual elements on a screen through one's gaze, detected through eye trackers. Gaze-based instruments include examples such as *Lumiselo* [1], which uses gaze and breath aided by head-mounted goggles with an eye tracker and a breath sensor for pitch control and note manipulation; *EyeHarp* [49], a gaze-controlled instrument with a dual-layer interface for performing melodies and looping accompaniments; *Eye Conductor*[3], which incorporates gaze pointing, eyebrow movements, and mouth-lip movements for varied control levels; and *EyeJam* [36], which enables melody playing through a unique "context-switching" interaction paradigm using two identical on-screen keyboards. Notably, only EyeHarp allows a certain degree of chord playing control, while other chord-playing Accessbile Digital Musical Instruments rely on other interaction channels, such as tongue-activated PET boards, mouth-moved cursors, or electroencephalogram-based interfaces, as in *Tongue-Controlled Electro-Musical Instrument* [39], *Jamboxx*[4], and *P300 Harmonies* [48].

2.2   The LIM-UMDevelopment Ecosystem

Building on this theoretical framework, in the past years, the LIM-UM staff crafted an ecosystem of software and hardware tools that explicitly caters to

---

[3] Eye Conductor, from A. Refsgaard's website: https://andreasrefsgaard.dk/projects/eyeconductor/.

[4] Jamboxx official website, on Web Archive: https://andreasrefsgaard.dk/projects/eyeconductor/.

quadriplegic musicians or aspirants. Specifically, this ecosystem addresses quadriplegic disabilities, not incorporating intersectional scenarios involving other types of disabilities such as sensory or cognitive impairments.

The ecosystem encompasses a suite of software Digital Musical instruments, each acting as a comprehensive interaction-solution package including action-to-sound mapping strategies, keyboard layouts, and more. These instruments provide *reference items*, serving as self-contained, fully operational starting points for customization operations tailored to individual needs. Notably, these instruments are "mute", meaning they are MIDI controllers with no sound generation unit, delegating this role to external synthesizers, which ensures extensive customization options and a broad array of sound choices. The chronology of developed instruments includes *Netytar*[5] [15], which utilizes gaze pointing and breath pressure detection for note selection and intensity control, and features an automated scrolling virtual keyboard. *Netychords*[6] [14] is a polyphonic Accessible Digital Musical Instrument that combines gaze pointing and head movement for chord selection and strumming. *Resin*[7] [12] is a monophonic ADMI that manipulates MIDI note selection and sound intensity through mouth shape and head rotation. *DJeye*[8] [4] is an eye-controlled DJ tool for fundamental mixing operations and incorporates unique eye interactions like winking. *Kiroll*,[9] similar to *Netytar*, uses eye gaze and breath for sound control with a scrolling keyboard layout.

Those instruments are all released under GNU GPL-v3 Free Open Source license. Except for DJEye (which relies on the *JUCE*[10] library), all of them were developed using the C# language within *NithDMIs*, an open-source software library part of the LIM-UM ADMIs ecosystem. This library facilitates the swift development and customization of HeaDMIs by offering a modular architecture and straightforward programming metaphors. It addresses various facets of an ADMI structure, including sensor interfacing, MIDI protocol communication, and audio analysis assistance. The library supports cost-effective or easily assembled sensors and peripherals via DIY methods.

The NithDMIs library supports the *NithSensors*[11] collection of open-source hardware peripherals, including a breath pressure sensor, a head tracker, and a speaker plus microphone system used in Resin. Additional peripherals such as a tooth pressure sensor are being developed to broaden the range of tools suitable for individuals with quadriplegia. These peripherals prioritize ease of construction, open-source microprocessors, easily procurable materials, and hardware reproducibility through the publication of construction projects and schemes

---

[5] *Netytar GitHub* repository: https://github.com/LIMUNIMI/Netytar; Web version link: https://annafusari.github.io/netytarweb/.

[6] *Netychords GitHub* repository: https://github.com/LIMUNIMI/Netychords.

[7] *Resin GitHub* repository: https://github.com/LIMUNIMI/Resin.

[8] *DJeye GitHub* repository: https://github.com/LIMUNIMI/DJeye.

[9] *Kiroll GitHub* repository: https://github.com/LIMUNIMI/Kiroll.

[10] *JUCE* official website: https://juce.com/.

[11] *NithSensors GitHub* repository: https://github.com/Neeqstock/NITHSensors.

under Creative Commons licenses. A standard and simple communication protocol ensures interchangeability, abstraction and easy mappings implementation.

3   Characterization of Netychords

Among the instruments available in the ecosystem, the child protagonist of our experimental activities showed a preference for *Netychords*, primarily driven by the possibility to make ensemble music and the subsequent prompt gratification. Here we review its main characteristics.

First published in 2021 [14], *Netychords* is a polyphonic HeaDMI that addresses the lack of Accessible Digital Musical Instruments able to play chords. It allows chord performance through a dual-control mechanism involving gaze pointing for note selection, and head movements for chord strumming. Head and eye tracking are known as effective interaction methods for accessible applications, demonstrating varying performance in selection tasks as per Fitts' Law tests [10]. Gaze pointing exhibits rapidity and stability, especially after data filtration, whereas head movement is slower yet highly stable. Nevertheless, the potential speed limitation of saccadic eye movements [21] may impact the efficiency of rapid sequences, especially in melodic lines, while could be adequate for chord changes. *Netychords* can be operated through low-cost sensors. It employs a *Tobii*[12] eye tracker for note selection and an ad-hoc head tracker (*NithHT*), part of the aforementioned *NithSensors* collection, built using an *MPU-6050/GY521* accelerometer/gyroscope and an *Arduino Uno* microcontroller for head rotation detection. A demonstration video of the instrument being played is available on YouTube.[13]

The interface, as it appears on screen, along with a complete depiction of the software and the related devices necessary for its operation, is depicted in Fig. 1. As in the image, the instrument's virtual keyboard presents color-coded keys denoting different chords: each root note corresponds to a unique color, while rows of color codes denote their chord family. Each key possesses a round-shaped gaze-sensitive area, or *occluder*, whose size may differ from the key's size, being balanced against the eye tracker's inherent signal noise to optimize selection accuracy versus movement length. *Netychords* uses an auto-scrolling feature to present unlimited keys on a limited screen, centering the key under the user's gaze, exploiting the eyes' natural smooth pursuit capabilities [42]. The scrolling speed is proportional to the square of the distance from the observed point to the screen center, creating an infinite playing region.

Eye gaze typically moves through short saccades [41]: the instrument features a key layout designed to minimize large and unwieldy saccadic eye movements. Its key arrangement is based on the *Stradella* bass system[14], commonly

---

[12] *Netychords* is compatible with both Tobii gaming series eye trackers and those designed for accessibility.

[13] *Netychords* demo video on YouTube: https://youtu.be/D18603o46ho.

[14] Balestrieri, D. (1979): Registers of the Standard Stradella Keyboard. http://www. accordions.com/articles/stradella.aspx.

Fig. 1. A laptop running *Netychords*, with a *Tobii* eye tracker and *NeeqHT* head tracker. *Netychords'* full interface is shown, in its default configuration.

found in Italian accordions, which organizes chords according to the circle of fifths. In this layout, each column represents a root note, while each row symbolizes a different voicing or chord family, as illustrated in [14, Fig. 3]. Unlike the *Stradella* system, which usually comprises four chord families, Netychords includes eleven of them: major, minor, dominant 7th, diminished 7th, major 7th, minor 7th, dominant 9th, dominant 11th, suspended 2nd, suspended 4th, and half-diminished 7th. To adapt to the specifics of gaze interaction, the original *Stradella* layout has been modified in a new layout, dubbed *Simplified Stradella*. All chords families have been grouped into five groups (major, minor, dominant, diminished, and half-diminished). Differently from *Stradella*, the starting chord for each row varies according to the chord family, with the harmonized diatonic scale chords clustered together to minimize eye movement for musical pieces in a single key. Figure 2 depicts a section of the layout which clusters in a small square all the chords necessary to play the harmonization of the C-major diatonic scale. The specific chord names are inscribed within the keys, while scale degrees are indicated beneath. Rows are characterized by chords of identical types. The direction of the circle-of-fifths, in horizontal movements, is demonstrated by an arrow. Additionally, genre-specific presets have been created by selectively omitting rows, facilitating music styles such as pop, rock, and jazz.

The current version of *Netychords* incorporates a straightforward system for customizing presets through the editing, addition, or removal of chord rows. This feature enables musicians and educators to craft user-tailored presets suitable for a specific music genre or piece.

In its initial design, *Netychords* employed head rotation, specifically yaw, to trigger chord strumming, converted into MIDI note on/off events and velocities. The sound intensity, or MIDI velocity, was originally proportional to the deviation from a calibrated central position. A subsequent revision tied sound

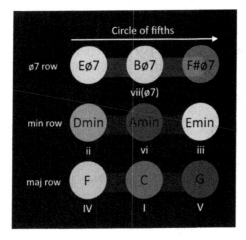

Fig. 2. Detail of the *Simplified Stradella* layout. The 9 keys are associated with the harmonization of the C-Major scale.

intensity to the average rotational speed before rotation reversal, eliminating the need for a central zone and precise absolute head position tracking. This allowed the use of simpler accelerometer sensors, forgoing a magnetometer. The strumming interface provided visual feedback on the fixated key, with a white handle indicating the relative head rotation [14, Fig. 6].

4   Case Study

In this section, we will present the case study involving a Portuguese child with cerebral palsy, as mentioned in Sect. 1. The experimentation aimed at the inclusion of the young user in classroom music activities thanks to the adoption and customization of *Netychords*. The process involved the child, his family, his caregivers, and the two research groups defined in Sect. 1, namely DEP-UA and LIM-UM researchers.

4.1   User's Profile

A preliminary study involving interviews with the child and his family was conducted by the DEP-UA researchers with the aim of characterizing the user. Utilizing structured interview scripts the Portuguese researchers gathered insights from the family and the child's professional care team [33, 34]. At the start of the period under study, the child was 7 years old and was attending primary school. The child is diagnosed with cerebral palsy, manifesting a severe dyskinetic form in his upper limbs, resulting in involuntary movements and bilateral restrictions. Further, the child displays signs of hypotonia, particularly noticeable in his lower limbs. Alongside these conditions, the child is also diagnosed with epilepsy. He can move with a wheelchair and walker, needing support from people to perform his daily activities. He cannot speak or write in a conventional manner, but he is able to interact with his peers. The family, together with professional caregivers, have been working hard to develop his communication and learning capabilities. Communication occurs through gestures, facial expressions, and the use of assistive devices, namely a laptop, *Grid 3*,[15] and the *Tobii PC Eye Mini*[16] [33,34].

The child never had the opportunity to engage in musical performance experiences before. Our project introduced him to the realm of musical performance and expression for the first time. Therefore, the child also needed a basic introduction to both music theory and performance through the Accessible Digital Musical Instrument under exam.

The child and his family spent a period in Italy in July 2021. During this time, a number of interactions occurred with LIM-UM staff in order to choose the best-fitting tool, tailor the experience, and adapt the control interface.

4.2 Instrument Tailoring

During the first interaction with LIM-UM researchers, a key challenge we encountered was the child's difficulty in utilizing *Netychords* or the other instruments as intended. A significant issue arose due to the child's spastic movements and mild difficulty in controlling residual body movements. Despite these challenges, gaze pointing did not present any notable problems. In fact, eye trackers employing Near Infrared technology can tolerate minor head movements without losing signal and with minimal inaccuracy. These devices comprise illuminators and cameras that track the pupil's position and the Purkinje corneal reflections within the eye, allowing for the triangulation of the gaze point [37].

Conversely, following head movement with the *NithHT* head tracker proved to be difficult due to the child's small spastic movements. In fact, such an instrument demands precise control of head movement, as the detection resolution for the strumming action is exceptionally high. Additionally, the full range of head rotation cannot be exploited, as excessive rotation would cause issues in gaze-pointing detection and hinder the ability to simultaneously view the screen. This added to the concern that the proposed interaction method may not be initially intuitive or natural for him, requiring time to master, and potentially leading to the child's discouragement.

During the first encounter, we attempted a solution that considered the child's residual movement capabilities in his left or right arm. In the field of accessibility, large keys are frequently employed to compensate for limited mobility.

---

[15] *Grid 3* is a software tool for users with cognitive or speech neuromotor limitations. Its use needs to be complemented with adapted accessories, in this case, an eye tracker.

[16] *PC Eye Mini* by *Tobii Dynavox* is an eye tracker peripheral that allows users with neuromotor limitations to access the computer through eye movement and gaze tracking. It allows the user to work with potentially any application that can be controlled with the mouse, through its emulation.

As a preliminary step, we created a mock-up of a large key by attaching a sizable plastic plate (e.g., a CD case) to the computer keyboard's spacebar, thus simulating an accessible key. This way, the keypad would have replaced the strumming mechanism by substituting head rotation, renouncing temporarily the ability to control sound intensity dynamics. Gaze pointing would have maintained its role in chord selection. This approach was then assessed for viability, with plans to refine it in future iterations. This solution however proved not functional, as the child's arm movement induced even stronger spastic head movements, resulting in difficulties in gaze pointing detection and a sudden lack of eye tracking signal. The outcome of the initial meeting was primarily marked by a sense of frustration, discouragement, and resignation for both the child and his relatives, who were present during the tests.

Subsequently, we implemented on-the-fly solutions to provide instrument customizations tailored to the child's needs that emerged during the meeting. The first solution, called *auto-strumming*, introduced a straightforward mechanism enabling the automatic strumming of chords. The user gazes at the key corresponding to the desired chord, which is then played at full velocity. The user is only required to select the preferred tempo (in BPM) and the strumming follows a basic 4/4 time pattern, with a chord played every beat. The second solution, called *blink strumming*, allows a strum to be executed at full velocity when both eyes blink simultaneously. Such a strategy is generally robust and easy to implement. For instance, in *Tobii* eye trackers, it is sufficient to detect if the eye signal is lost for a specific number of samples to trigger an event of type "eyes not present". The ability to voluntarily blink is typically retained by most individuals, barring severe diseases or conditions (e.g., facial paralysis conditions such as Bell's Palsy [17]). Nonetheless, implementing this paradigm presents several challenges. Firstly, the frequent occurrence of involuntary eye blinks requires distinguishing them from voluntary ones to prevent inadvertent note performance. Voluntary blinks are typically rapid, making their duration a possible discriminator. However, prompting users for prolonged eye closure might cause unwanted delayed audio feedback, potentially hindering high-tempo interactions [40]. Secondly, sustained eyelid muscle activity could result in fatigue due to an unaccustomed frequency of movement. Additionally, eye closure during *blink strumming* results in temporary gaze point absence, which could prove problematic at high tempos with abrupt eye closures. This absence not only obscures the selected chord during the blink but also causes brief eye-tracking inaccuracies, as the signal does not necessarily persist on the last observed point with open eyes. Finally, to our knowledge, no existing research explores human blinking capacity in terms of rhythm, such as maximum frequency and speed constraints.

During the second meeting, the implemented changes were explained to the child, who was given the opportunity to try them out. The blink-based solution did not prove immediately effective: The young user found it somewhat challenging and frustrating to navigate through blinking, despite the solution technically working. Conversely, the automatic strumming solution proved immediately sat-

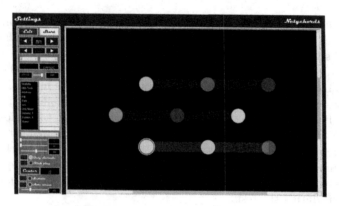

Fig. 3. The old version of *Netychords'* interface, with settings located on a left sidebar.

isfying, allowing him to play independently and enjoy the process of music creation. This method required less cognitive and physical effort and this likely played a key role in his appreciation. He explored the keyboard layout and various chords available for several dozen minutes before being asked to limit the chords played to a few specific ones, in order to let one of his tutors improvise a melody with a violin. The latter collaborative activity provided a sense of "playing together", which was a totally new experience for the child. The two continued to play for several minutes, and both the child and his family were visibly satisfied at the end of the experience. At the end of the session, the family requested guidance on how to use the software at home in Portugal.

After the period in Italy, the child enrolled in the *Arts Education Programme* in Portugal, overseen by an expert in Special Educational Needs. As a consequence, several changes and enhancements were implemented in *Netychords*, as documented in Sect. 4.3. Additionally, the instrument interface was completely reworked to achieve the following objectives: **(a)** Obtain more screen space – The settings column, previously located on the left side of the screen, was converted into a pop-up accessible through a button/switch; **(b)** Create a system for saving customizations – A system was introduced to develop new presets for layouts, save them, and select them upon subsequent launches. This allows both the user and the teacher to create specific layouts for each song or exercise; **(c)** Provide autonomous control over the software with no external support – A straightforward system was implemented to provide users with SN with full control over the interface. Firstly, buttons were enlarged to compensate for eye tracker signal noise (eg. approximately 1° on the visual angle for the *Tobii Eye Tracker 5* [22]). Additionally, to address potential size insufficiency, the last gazed button will be highlighted in a special color (yellow) and remain selected even if the gaze moves out of its area. A hybrid interaction selection strategy (as defined in [13]) is employed, wherein the gaze is used to select targets, and either double blinking or head strumming confirms the selection and activates the visual element (Figs. 3 and 4).

Fig. 4. An updated *Netychords'* interface featuring a retractable settings panel and accessibility solutions such as and gaze-based settings navigation solutions.

Future enhancements for Netychords based on our observations will include enriching the auto-strumming feature: while the current version was found effective, its simplicity leaves room for refinement. For instance, instead of the constant quarter beat strumming pattern, we could introduce a variety of advanced patterns and a basic beat sequencer for customization. An automatic arpeggiator to sequence notes within a chord could enrich the customizability. Moreover, the present version does not offer control of sound intensity dynamics with auto-strumming or blink strumming. A feasible solution might be integrating breath-based control. This system would utilize gaze pointing for chord selection, blinking for chord selection/change, and breath for controlling dynamics.

4.3   Adaptations in Arts Education Program

The effectiveness of the customized version of the instrument, in terms of music education and practice, was evaluated thanks to the enrollment of the young user in Portugal's Arts Education Program. An early phase was dedicated to establishing the prerequisites necessary for the child to participate. In fact, after adapting the instrument interface and features to take into account the user's characteristics, also curricular activities and goals had to be readjusted.

A constant dialogue was established between the researchers who designed the instrument (from LIM-UM) and the teachers along with the child's tutors (including DEP-UA researchers). The aim was to foster an environment of continuous improvement for the instrument and its setup, accommodating various requests as they arose. The majority of the instrument's modifications were primarily centered around the need for pedagogical supports, such as simplification tools, visualization systems, and customization of layouts. Gradually, various features were introduced. For example, in accordance with the educators' requests, the instrument was provided with some simplified views, to highlight smaller sections of the keyboard: *diatonic 3* shows only the diatonic harmonization of a major (akin to Fig. 2), while simplified single-row presets like *only major* or *only minor* show respectively only the major chords of such harmonization (which are the I, IV and V degrees of the scale) or the minor chords (ii, iii and vi degrees).

In particular, significant adaptations were implemented by the Piano teacher and the Music Training teacher. For the former course, these included: (**i**) Composing and arranging accompaniments for performance in *Netychords*; (**ii**) Suggesting modifications for the layout, interaction, and mapping strategies to meet the instrument programme requirements (**iii**) Adapting scores for simultaneous reading and playing.

The teacher dedicated significant effort to exploring the technical possibilities provided by the *Netychords* instrument and structured a music education program around its unique capabilities. One of the initial modifications required was the re-adjustment of the repertoire of songs taught to the child. Some compositions were also adapted to accommodate the constraint imposed by the constant auto-strumming pattern. Given the specific characteristics of *Netychords* as a harmonic instrument, the teaching was centered on the harmonic elements usually delegated to the left hand in traditional piano instruction. Out of the classical repertoire typically provided in piano teaching, few selected pieces were maintained. The remaining repertoire was composed explicitly for *Netychords* by the piano teacher, reflecting the instrument's unique characteristics. A significant aspect of standard music instruction involves mastering the control of sound dynamics or intensity. However, the tailored strumming solutions (auto-strumming/blink-strumming) implemented for the child did not provide a way to control dynamics. Consequently, this aspect of instruction was temporarily deferred until an accessible method for the child to manage dynamics is identified.

Concerning the Music Theory course, adaptations comprised: (**i**) Establishing codes for various rhythmic cells which the student could quickly write using *Grid3* and an eye tracker; (**ii**) Facilitating auditory chord identification through distinct facial expressions for major and minor chords. Specific emphasis was placed on teaching structured theory based on the unique key layout of *Netychords* (described in Sect. 3). For instance, the child was taught the sequence corresponding to the various degrees of diatonic harmonization of a scale, enabling him to identify the different degrees. Similarly, considerable attention was also dedicated to mastering the circle of fifths.

Within his music education period, the child was able to engage in multiple public music presentations and small concerts, including two piano performances. The first performance included a solo piece and a duet with the teacher, with the child playing harmony and the teacher handling the melody. In the second performance, the child performed his own harmonically composed piece, accompanied by a teacher's melody, demonstrating collaborative performance.

As a result of these efforts, the child's involvement in musical activities proved engaging. It was enabled through agreed curricular adaptations, consistent with the School Leaving Certificate Profile Policies. Those cater to varied learning styles, adjust objectives without compromising the curriculum, and introduce alternative learning respectively.

With regard to this, and to provide an example, throughout the musical activities it was found that the child presented a degree of voluntary control over his foot movement, albeit limited. This observation was made by their piano teacher who noticed the child tapping his foot rhythmically on a flat part of his wheelchair. Upon informal testing, it was confirmed that this movement was indeed voluntary and controllable. Given this discovery, further studies are planned to explore potential instrument adaptations that could capitalize on this newfound motor ability. For instance, a dynamic-sensitive stomp pedal could be implemented to perform temporally controlled strumming. The pedal would detect the intensity of the beat and map it onto the strumming intensity. This device could be built using dynamic resistors or piezoelectric sensors, aligning with the Open Source Hardware standards set for the *NithSensors* collection.

5   Generalization and Reflections

A key understanding, arising from the necessity for personalization in interaction design for musicians with motor disabilities, is the distinctiveness of each individual's condition, thus the need for interaction customization. Disabilities are often classified into specific patterns such as quadriplegia or hemiplegic paralysis, with the assumption that affected individuals will display a specific set of movement capabilities and be able to rely on certain interaction channels. Although generalizations may be made during the initial instrument design phases to cater to the needs of a particular population (e.g. quadriplegics), those generalizations are not always effective. Common factors, such as the interplay between interaction channels, as exemplified in the child's case, further complicate the situation. We argue that, in interaction design, it is crucial to account for those complex interplays between channels. As a result, we highlight the importance of enabling swift customization of instruments in the last design phases to create an interaction style specifically tailored to the individual concerned.

As a *first solution* to achieve this, a set of easily accessible mappings directly within the software interface could be provided, eliminating the need for specialized computer-science expertise from the users. Potential systems could also be investigated and developed to automatically generate mappings based on different connected sensor peripherals. As a *second solution*, a software developer with expertise in accessible interaction could intervene to rapidly develop specific mappings. This requires instruments to be designed using modular and efficient code, employing frameworks that facilitate effortless customization, alteration, and implementation of new interaction techniques and support for novel sensors. While the former solution could address the most common scenarios, the latter solution's drawback is the requirement for intervention from skilled personnel. In both scenarios, we suggest the open-source philosophy which characterizes our framework, so that specific solutions devised by an IT expert for a given user could be shared with the community. Those can successively be included in the software interface and converted into automatic mappings, thus falling under the first option. This underlines the significance of a modular framework, remarking on the value of flexibility and adaptability in designing accessible instruments.

While customization is essential, it is important to note the significance of a shared repertoire developed collectively on a musical instrument, as emphasized by Magnusson and Hurtado [28]. This notion somewhat pushes toward the idea of a community-shared experience, which may seem contradictory to the need for adaptation and individual customization. Nevertheless, as an instrument's expressive potential and playing style are influenced by its mapping strategies [23], those could be designed in a way that the instrument's characteristics are similar for everyone, providing at least a partial common structure (e.g., keys layout). In our opinion eye tracking related interaction channels, encompassing gaze pointing and blinking, could serve well this purpose. Except for extreme conditions such as *completely locked-in syndrome* [38], the ability to move one's eyes is often preserved even in the presence of complex disabilities. While not free from limitations (as analyzed in [11] and [13]) gaze pointing and blinking could serve as a robust common ground shared across various instruments, while other channels could be dedicated to different aspects of musical interaction.

As a final remark, since musical instruments (and HeaDMIs in particular) are usually skill-intensive and challenging to master, it can be difficult to discern whether a user is merely disheartened, the musical experience is not engaging, or the required movements are genuinely uncomfortable, awkward, or even impossible to perform given a specific disability. In our case study, language barriers with the child, who struggled with clear articulation, undoubtedly exacerbated the situation, as he was unable to thoroughly and effortlessly convey his impressions.

6   Conclusions

This paper's case study revealed several limitations and constraints encountered during the design, implementation, and adaptation process. These included technical issues regarding the usability of some interface controls and problems in communicating with users. Despite years of experience in developing a software tool ecosystem and careful intervention planning, field experimentation was necessary to identify problematic aspects. The experimentation also raised unanswered questions, such as which functionalities developed or revised for the child could be beneficial to other users with similar disabilities.

A forthcoming publication will present a qualitative analysis from an educator's point of view, based on the researcher/observer's notes from the experience, which is the emphasis of the DEP-UA researchers work. The evaluation will concentrate on the connections formed among diverse stakeholders, including the child, educators, researchers, fellow music students, and family members. Furthermore, it will investigate interactions within varying environments, the reciprocal influences between these environments and their respective contexts, and their intersection with larger encompassing contexts.

It is important to note that the specific scenario may have influenced the scope and generalizability of the findings, potentially introducing biases that could have affected the results. Nevertheless, the authors hope that the results can contribute to a broader understanding of the subject matter and promote wider adoption of digital technologies in music education and expressiveness. The authors believe that some aspects of their approach are transferable, particularly the methodologies, experimental designs, and techniques that have demonstrated effectiveness. Thus, the insights gained from the single case study can serve as a foundation for broader investigations involving larger sample sizes, diverse populations, or different contexts.

This research could signify a societal impact, particularly in the educational realm for children with cerebral palsy, by illuminating their learning challenges and proposing music as a potential developmental strategy, thus laying the groundwork for further research and novel implementations.

Acknowledgements. This work is financed by FCT – Foundation for Science and Technology via the PhD scholarship 2020.07331.BD and the UIDB/00194/2020 project, referring to CIDTFF – Research Center in Didactics and Technology in the Training of Trainers and it was made possible with the collaboration of various partners. We appreciate FUNDATION ALTICE and CRTIC (ICT Resource Centres, Portugal) for providing technology and support products, the Camara Municipal de Estarreja, and Biogerm, S.A (Portugal) for logistical support.

References

1. Bailey, S., Scott, A., Wright, H., Symonds, I.M., Ng, K.: Eye. breathe. music: creating music through minimal movement. In: Proceedings Conference Electronic Visualisation and the Arts (EVA 2010), pp. 254–258. London, UK (Jul 2010)
2. Baratè, A., Ludovico, L.A., Oriolo, E.: Investigating embodied music expression through the leap motion: experimentations in educational and clinical contexts. In: McLaren, B.M., Reilly, R., Zvacek, S., Uhomoibhi, J. (eds.) CSEDU 2018. CCIS, vol. 1022, pp. 532–548. Springer, Cham (2019). https://doi.org/10.1007/978-3-030-21151-6_25
3. Beveridge, S., Cano, E., Agres, K.: Rhythmic entrainment for hand rehabilitation using the leap motion controller. In: 19th International Society for Music Information Retrieval Conference, Paris, France (2018)
4. Bottarelli, F., Davanzo, N., Presti, G., Avanzini, F.: DJeye: towards an accessible gaze-based musical interface for quadriplegic DJs. In: Proceedings of the 2023 Sound and Music Computing Conference. Stockholm, Sweden (Jun 2023)
5. Campayo-Muñoz, E., Cabedo-Mas, A.: The role of emotional skills in music education. Br. J. Music Educ. **34**(3), 243–258 (2017). https://doi.org/10.1017/S0265051717000067
6. Cano, M.D., Sanchez-Iborra, R.: On the use of a multimedia platform for music education with handicapped children: a case study. Comput. Educ. **87**, 254–276 (2015). https://doi.org/10.1016/j.compedu.2015.07.010
7. Cibrian, F.L., Tentori, M., Weibel, N.: A musical interactive surface to support the multi-sensory stimulation of children. In: Proceedings of the 10th EAI International Conference on Pervasive Computing Technologies for Healthcare, pp. 241–244 (2016)
8. Clements-Cortès, A.: High-tech therapy: music technology in music therapy. Can. Music. Educ. **54**(4), 37–39 (2013)

9. Davanzo, N., Avanzini, F.: A dimension space for the evaluation of accessible digital musical instruments. In: Proceedings of the 20th International Conference on New Interfaces for Musical Expression (NIME '20). NIME '20 (Jul 2020)

10. Davanzo, N., Avanzini, F.: Experimental evaluation of three interaction channels for accessible digital musical instruments. In: Miesenberger, K., Manduchi, R., Covarrubias Rodriguez, M., Peňáz, P. (eds.) ICCHP 2020. LNCS, vol. 12377, pp. 437–445. Springer, Cham (2020). https://doi.org/10.1007/978-3-030-58805-2_52

11. Davanzo, N., Avanzini, F.: Hands-free accessible digital musical instruments: conceptual framework, challenges, and perspectives. IEEE Access 8, 163975–163995 (2020). https://doi.org/10.1109/ACCESS.2020.3019978

12. Davanzo, N., Avanzini, F.: Resin: a vocal tract resonances and head based accessible digital musical instrument. In: Proceedings of the 2021 AudioMostly Conference Trento, Italy (online conf.) (Sep 2021)

13. Davanzo, N., Avanzini, F.: Design concepts for gaze-based digital musical instruments. In: Proceedings of the 2022 Sound and Music Computing Conference, pp. 477–483. Saint-Etiénne, France (Jun 2022)

14. Davanzo, N., De Filippis, M., Avanzini, F.: Netychords: an accessible digital musical instrument for playing chords using gaze and head movements. In: Proceedings of the '21 International Conference on Computer- Human Interaction Research and Applications (CHIRA '21). Online conf. (2021)

15. Davanzo, N., Dondi, P., Mosconi, M., Porta, M.: Playing music with the eyes through an isomorphic interface. In: Proc. of the Workshop on Communication by Gaze Interaction, pp. 1–5. ACM Press, Warsaw, Poland (2018). https://doi.org/10.1145/3206343.3206350

16. Frid, E.: Accessible digital musical instruments—a review of musical interfaces in inclusive music practice. Multimodal Technol. Interact. 3(3), 57 (2019). https://doi.org/10.3390/mti3030057

17. Gilden, D.H.: Bell's Palsy. N. Engl. J. Med. 351(13), 1323–1331 (2004). https://doi.org/10.1056/NEJMcp041120

18. Habibi, A., Cahn, B.R., Damasio, A., Damasio, H.: Neural correlates of accelerated auditory processing in children engaged in music training. Dev. Cogn. Neurosci. 21, 1–14 (2016). https://doi.org/10.1016/j.dcn.2016.04.003

19. Hallam, S., Creech, A., McQueen, H., Varvarigou, M., Gaunt, H.: The facilitator of community music-making with older learners: characteristics, motivations and challenges. Int. J. Music. Educ. 34(1), 19–31 (2016)

20. Harrison, J., McPherson, A.P.: Adapting the bass guitar for one-handed playing. J. New Music Res. 46(3), 270–285 (2017)

21. Hornof, A.J.: The prospects for eye-controlled musical performance. In: Proceedings of 14th International Conference on New Interfaces for Musical Expression (NIME'14). NIME 2014, Goldsmiths, University of London, UK (Jul 2014)

22. Housholder, A., Reaban, J., Peregrino, A., Votta, G., Mohd, T.K.: Evaluating accuracy of the Tobii eye tracker 5. In: Kim, J.-H., Singh, M., Khan, J., Tiwary, U.S., Sur, M., Singh, D. (eds.) IHCI 2021. LNCS, vol. 13184, pp. 379–390. Springer, Cham (2022). https://doi.org/10.1007/978-3-030-98404-5_36

23. Hunt, A., Wanderley, M.M., Paradis, M.: The importance of parameter mapping in electronic instrument design. J. New Music Res. 32(4), 429–440 (2003). https://doi.org/10.1076/jnmr.32.4.429.18853

24. Innocenti, E.D., et al.: Mobile virtual reality for musical genre learning in primary education. Comput. Educ. 139, 102–117 (2019). https://doi.org/10.1016/j.compedu.2019.04.010

25. Kraus, N., et al.: Music enrichment programs improve the neural encoding of speech in at-risk children. J. Neurosci. **34**(36), 11913–11918 (2014)
26. Lee, L., Chang, H.Y.: Music technology as a means for fostering young children's social interactions in an inclusive class. Appl. Syst. Innov. **4**(4), 93 (2021)
27. Lubet, A.: Music, Disability, and Society. Temple University Press (2011)
28. Magnusson, T., Hurtado, E.: 2007: the acoustic, the digital and the body: a survey on musical instruments. In: Jensenius, A.R., Lyons, M.J. (eds.) A NIME Reader. CRSM, vol. 3, pp. 317–333. Springer, Cham (2017). https://doi.org/10.1007/978-3-319-47214-0_21
29. Malloch, J., Birnbaum, D., Sinyor, E., Wanderley, M.M.: Towards a new conceptual framework for digital musical instruments. In: Proceedings 9th International Conference on Digital Audio Effects. pp. 49–52. Montreal, Canada, September 18–20, 2006 (2006)
30. McGlynn, P.: Interaction Design for Digital Musical Instruments. Ph.D. thesis, National University of Ireland, Maynooth (2014)
31. McLeskey, J., Rosenberg, M.S., Westling, D.L.: Inclusion: Effective Practices for All Students. Loose-Leaf Version, Pearson Education (Mar (2017)
32. Miranda, E.R., Wanderley, M.: New Digital Musical Instruments: Control And Interaction Beyond the Keyboard. A-R Editions Inc, Middleton, Wis, 1st edition edn. (Jul 2006)
33. Moreno, D., Moreira, A., Tymoshchuk, O., Marques, C.: A child with cerebral palsy in arts education programmes: building scaffoldings for inclusion. In: Costa, A.P., Reis, L.P., Moreira, A., Longo, L., Bryda, G. (eds.) WCQR 2021. AISC, vol. 1345, pp. 172–190. Springer, Cham (2021). https://doi.org/10.1007/978-3-030-70187-1_13
34. Moreno, D., Moreira, A., Tymoshchuk, O., Marques, C.: Análise de conteúdo utilizando o webqda: Opção metodológica para caracterizar uma criança com paralisia cerebral. New Trends in Qualitative Research 2, 687–702 (Jul 2020). https://doi.org/10.36367/ntqr.2.2020.687-702, https://publi.ludomedia.org/index.php/ntqr/article/view/127
35. Moreno, S., Bialystok, E., Barac, R., Schellenberg, E.G., Cepeda, N.J., Chau, T.: Short-term music training enhances verbal intelligence and executive function. Psychol. Sci. **22**(11), 1425–1433 (2011)
36. Morimoto, C.H., Diaz-Tula, A., Leyva, J.A.T., Elmadjian, C.E.L.: Eyejam: a gaze-controlled musical interface. In: Proceedings of the 14th Brazilian Symposium on Human Factors in Computing Systems, pp. 37:1–37:9. IHC '15, ACM, Salvador, Brazil (2015). https://doi.org/10.1145/3148456.3148493
37. Morimoto, C.H., Mimica, M.R.M.: Eye gaze tracking techniques for interactive applications. Comput. Vis. Image Underst. **98**(1), 4–24 (2005). https://doi.org/10.1016/j.cviu.2004.07.010
38. Murguilday, A.R., et al.: Transition from the locked in to the completely locked-in state: a physiological analysis. Clin. Neurophysiol. **122**(5), 925–933 (2011). https://doi.org/10.1016/j.clinph.2010.08.019
39. Niikawa, T.: Tongue-controlled electro-musical instrument. In: Proceedings of the 18th International Congrerss on Acoustics. vol. 3, pp. 1905–1908. Acoustical Society, International Conference Hall, Kyoto, Japan (Apr 2004)
40. Pfordresher, P., Palmer, C.: Effects of delayed auditory feedback on timing of music performance. Psychol. Res. **66**(1), 71–79 (2002). https://doi.org/10.1007/s004260100075
41. Purves, D., et al.: Types of eye movements and their functions. Neuroscience. 2nd edition, pp. 361–390 (2001)

42. Robinson, D.A., Gordon, J.L., Gordon, S.E.: A model of the smooth pursuit eye movement system. Biol. Cybern. **55**(1), 43–57 (1986). https://doi.org/10.1007/BF00363977

43. Schellenberg, E.G., Mankarious, M.: Music training and emotion comprehension in childhood. Emotion **12**(5), 887–891 (2012)

44. Sears, A., Young, M., Feng, J.: Physical disabilities and computing technologies: an analysis of impairments. In: Sears, A., Jacko, J.A. (eds.) The Human-Computer Interaction Handbook, chap. 42, pp. 829–852. Lawrence Erlbaum Associates, second edn. (2008)

45. Shadiev, R., Li, D.: A review study on eye-tracking technology usage in immersive virtual reality learning environments. Comput. Educ. **196** 104681 (2022). https://doi.org/10.1016/j.compedu.2022.104681

46. Swingler, T., Brockhouse, J.: Getting better all the time: using music technology for learners with special needs. Aust. J. Music. Educ. **2**, 49–57 (2009)

47. Turnbull, A., Turnbull, R., Wehmeyer, M.L., Shogren, K.A.: Exceptional Lives: Special Education in Today's Schools. Pearson, Upper Saddle River, N.J., 7th edition edn. (Jan 2012)

48. Vamvakousis, Z., Ramirez, R.: P300 harmonies: a brain-computer musical interface. In: Proceedings of the 2014 International Computer Music Conference/Sound and Music Computing Conference, pp. 725–729. Michigan Publishing, Athens, Greece (Sep 2014)

49. Vamvakousis, Z., Ramirez, R.: The EyeHarp: a gaze-controlled digital musical instrument. Front. Psychol. **7**, 906 (2016). https://doi.org/10.3389/fpsyg.2016.00906

50. Wong, M.W.y.: Fostering musical creativity of students with intellectual disabilities: strategies, gamification and re-framing creativity. Music Educ. Res. **23**(1), 1–13 (2021)

51. World Health Organization: International classification of functioning, disability and health (2001)

52. World Health Organization: World report on disability (2011)

53. Music, Y.: Reshape Music. Tech. rep, Youth Music (Oct (2020)

Author Index

A

Agius, May   I-53
Aguirre, Maia   I-89
AlBayaa, Mohammad   I-40
Althekair, Abdulaziz   I-40
Avanzini, Federico   I-353
Azevedo, Júlia   I-353

B

Baja, Caroline   II-160
Bernhauer, David   II-231
Blanc, Charly   I-21
Boccignone, Giuseppe   I-163
Boden, Alexander   II-160
Böhm, Lukas   II-160
Borghese, N. Alberto   I-163
Borghesi, Francesca   II-258
Bossauer, Paul   II-160
Boudry, Lionel   I-21
Boulc'h, Dorian Le   II-13
Bouma, Debby   I-121
Brambilla, Susanna   I-163
Brandenburger, Jessica   I-201
Bruni, Attila   II-299
Bulgaro, A.   II-3

C

Charleer, Sven   II-349
Chauhan, Praveen   II-121
Chirico, Alice   II-258
Chitti, Eleonora   I-163

D

D'Attanasio, Simona   II-13
da Silveira, Aleph Campos   II-24
Dalléas, Tanguy   II-13
Davanzo, Nicola   I-353
De Paoli, Irene   II-43
Dégallier-Rochat, Sarah   I-21
Deka, Chinmoy   II-121
del Pozo, Arantza   I-89

del Valle, Alexandro   I-244
Di Campi, Alessia M.   II-43
Dini, Silvia   II-244
Doush, Iyad Abu   I-40
Drzyzga, Gilbert   I-262, II-176

E

Esau, Margarita   II-84

F

Fallahkhair, Sanaz   I-336
franzó, alessandro   II-299

C

Ghinea, Gheorghita   II-24
Graichen, Lisa   I-232
Graichen, Matthias   I-232

H

Harder, Thorleif   I-262, II-176
Herrewijn, Laura   II-349
Hinderks, Andreas   I-143
Hoksza, David   II-231
Honig, S.   I-282
Humphries, Jacqueline   I-318

I

İnce, Gökhan   II-66
Ishii, Hirotake   I-216
Ito, Shingo   I-187

J

Jackson, Phil   I-336
Janneck, Monique   I-201, II-176

K

Kopp, Stefan   I-110
Kriglstein, Simone   II-326, II-338
Kroth, Kalvin   II-160

L

Langlois, Danielle K. II-338
Lawo, Dennis II-84, II-160
Levashova, Tatiana I-69
Li, Yue II-192
Li, Yuwen II-192
Liang, Hai-Ning II-192
Liang, Jiachen II-192
Liang, Zilu I-244
Liberman-Pincu, E. I-282, II-3
Loch, Frieder I-307
Lombardi, Riccardo I-163
Luccio, Flaminia L. II-43
Ludovico, Luca A. I-353, II-244

M

Mackay, Wendy E. I-3, II-212
Mancuso, Valentina II-258
Marot, Antoine II-212
Marques, Carlos I-353
Maury-Castañeda, Natalia II-104
Meiners, Anna-Lena I-143
Méndez, Ariane I-89
Mohana, M. II-24
Moreira, António I-353
Moreno, Davys I-353
Murtas, Vittorio II-258

N

Nautiyal, Saurabh II-121, II-137
Neifer, Thomas II-84, II-160
Nembrini, Julien I-21
Noda, Ayumi I-216

O

Odeh, Mohanned I-40
Omata, Masaki I-187
Oron-Gilad, T. I-282, II-3
Oshita, Kazushige I-295

P

Pagáč, Tomáš II-326
Peska, Ladislav II-231
Piumarta, Ian I-244
Pocock, Christine I-53
Ponomarev, Andrew I-69

Porter, Chris I-53
Potur, Caner II-66

R

Ripamonti, Laura A. I-163
Rizzi, Alessandro II-244
Ryan, Alan I-318

S

Sahel, Wissal II-212
Santos, Celso Alberto Saibel II-24
Sarti, Beatrice II-244
Sharawi, Marwa I-40
Shimoda, Hiroshi I-216
Shrivastava, Abhishek II-121, II-137
Sixtova, Ivana II-231
Skopal, Tomas II-231
Smirnov, Alexander I-69
Sonderegger, Andreas I-21
Stevens, Gunnar II-84
Stöbitsch, Ariane II-160
Stolze, Markus I-307
Subashini, P. II-24

T

Thomaschewski, Jörg I-143
Torralbo, Manuel I-89
Treur, Jan I-121
Tymoshchuk, Oksana I-353

U

Ueda, Kimi I-216
Ugarte, Willy II-104

V

Valero Gisbert, María Joaquina II-244
Van de Ven, Pepijn I-318
Verel, Marie II-13
Verkijika, Silas Formunyuy II-277
Villarruel-Vasquez, Sergio II-104

W

Wang, Minglei II-315
Wendemuth, Andreas I-110
Winter, Marcus I-336

Printed in the United States
by Baker & Taylor Publisher Services